SANKAREA

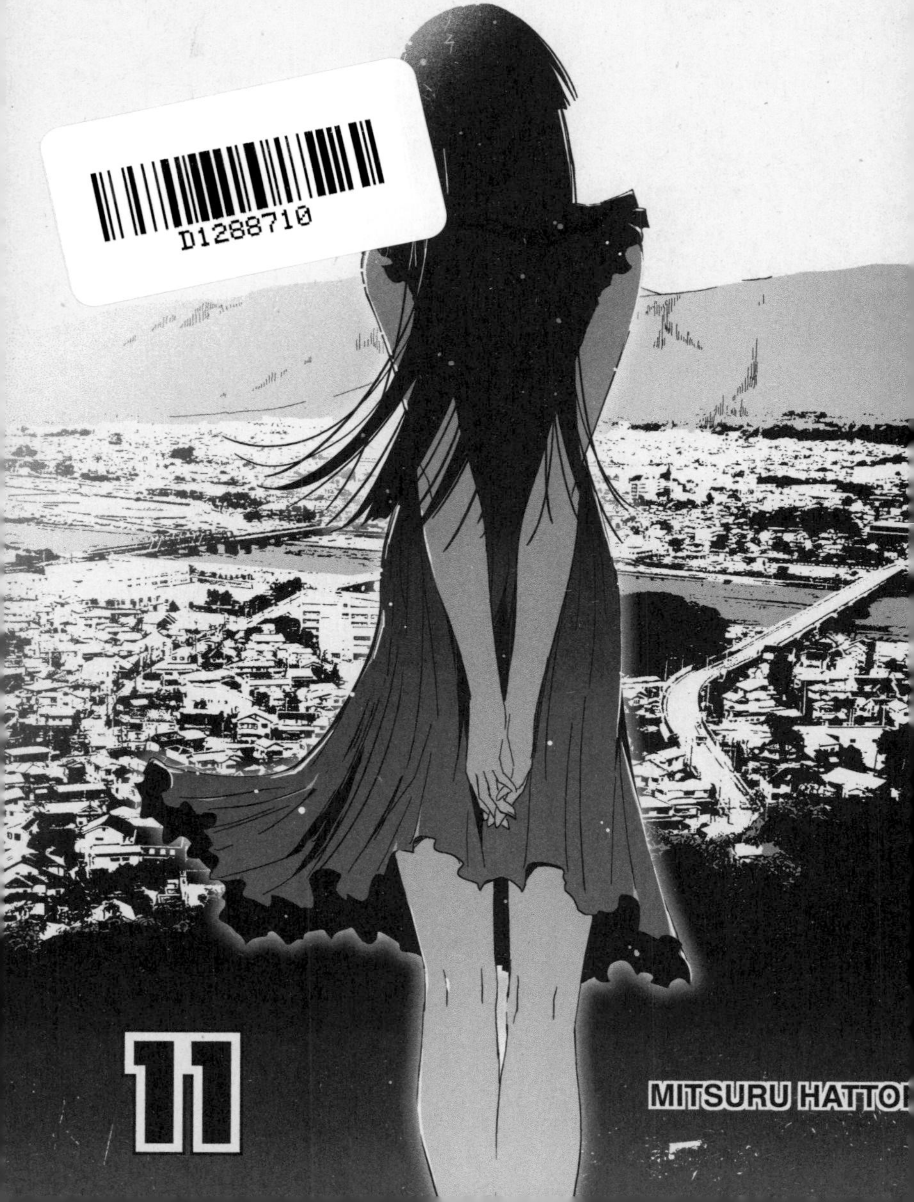

11

MITSURU HATTO

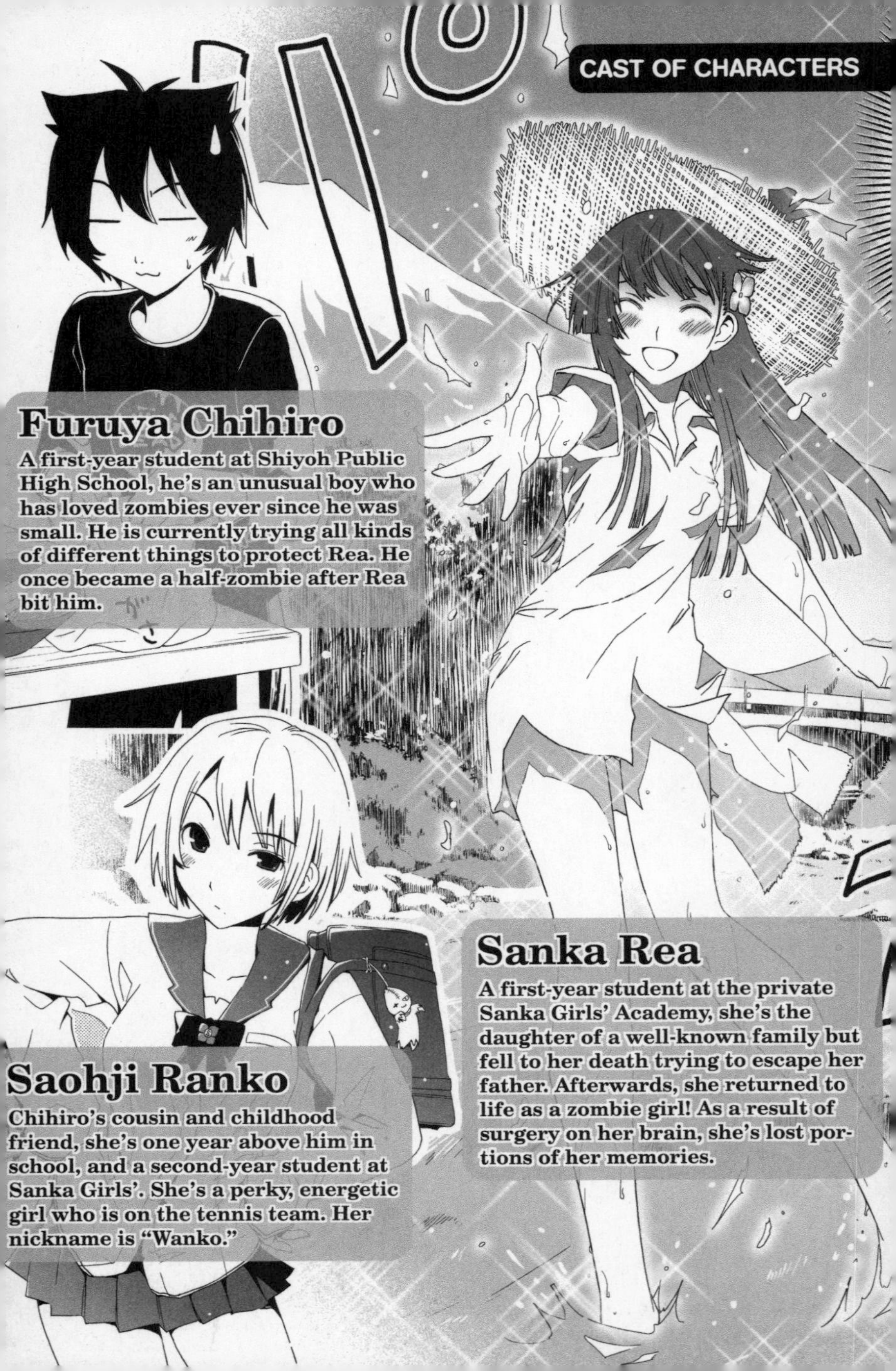

Furuya Chihiro

A first-year student at Shiyoh Public High School, he's an unusual boy who has loved zombies ever since he was small. He is currently trying all kinds of different things to protect Rea. He once became a half-zombie after Rea bit him.

Sanka Rea

A first-year student at the private Sanka Girls' Academy, she's the daughter of a well-known family but fell to her death trying to escape her father. Afterwards, she returned to life as a zombie girl! As a result of surgery on her brain, she's lost portions of her memories.

Saohji Ranko

Chihiro's cousin and childhood friend, she's one year above him in school, and a second-year student at Sanka Girls'. She's a perky, energetic girl who is on the tennis team. Her nickname is "Wanko."

Kurumiya Darin Arciento

An expert in zombie research who came to Japan from the southern islands to visit Professor Boyle (Grandpa). She has a strange passion for her research. Despite her looks, she's younger than Rea.

18

Darin's faithful pet. It's been zombified and half-mechanized.

THE FURUYA FAMILY

Dad

His real name is Furuya Dohn. He's the head priest at Shiryohji Temple. He agreed to Rea and Darin living in their home, saying only, "Should be fine, right?"

Grandpa

The very person who first created the reanimation elixir. His name is Jogoroh, but at ZoMA he was called Professor Boyle.

Bub

He was hit by a car and died, but came back to life thanks to the elixir Chihiro and Rea made.

Furuya Mero

A reliable first-year middle school student, she manages all the housework for the Furuya family. She loves to read the Heart Sutra.

STORY

Otoki, a zombie who had been frozen in an ice cave, divulged the truth to Chihiro. Otoki revealed the untold story behind the birth of the elixir and the tragic history that fell upon Jogoroh. When this shocking story touched upon the accident that claimed the life of Chihiro's mother, Yuzuna, Chihiro's memories of his final moments with his mother returned. Chihiro's mother had become a zombie to keep her promise to her children and the gruesome fate that befell her has allowed Chihiro to understand the destiny that awaits all zombies... Following this, Otoki shed this mortal coil in unison with Jogoroh and after parting from Otoki, Chihiro returned home to learn of Rea's sudden turn for the worse. Now, Chihiro readies himself before Rea, who has already begun to attack people...

MITSURU HATTORI presents

I LOVED YOU...

CONTENTS

SERIALIZED IN BESSATSU SHONEN MAGAZINE, JULY 2014 - OCTOBER 2014, DECEMBER 2014.

SANKAREA 11

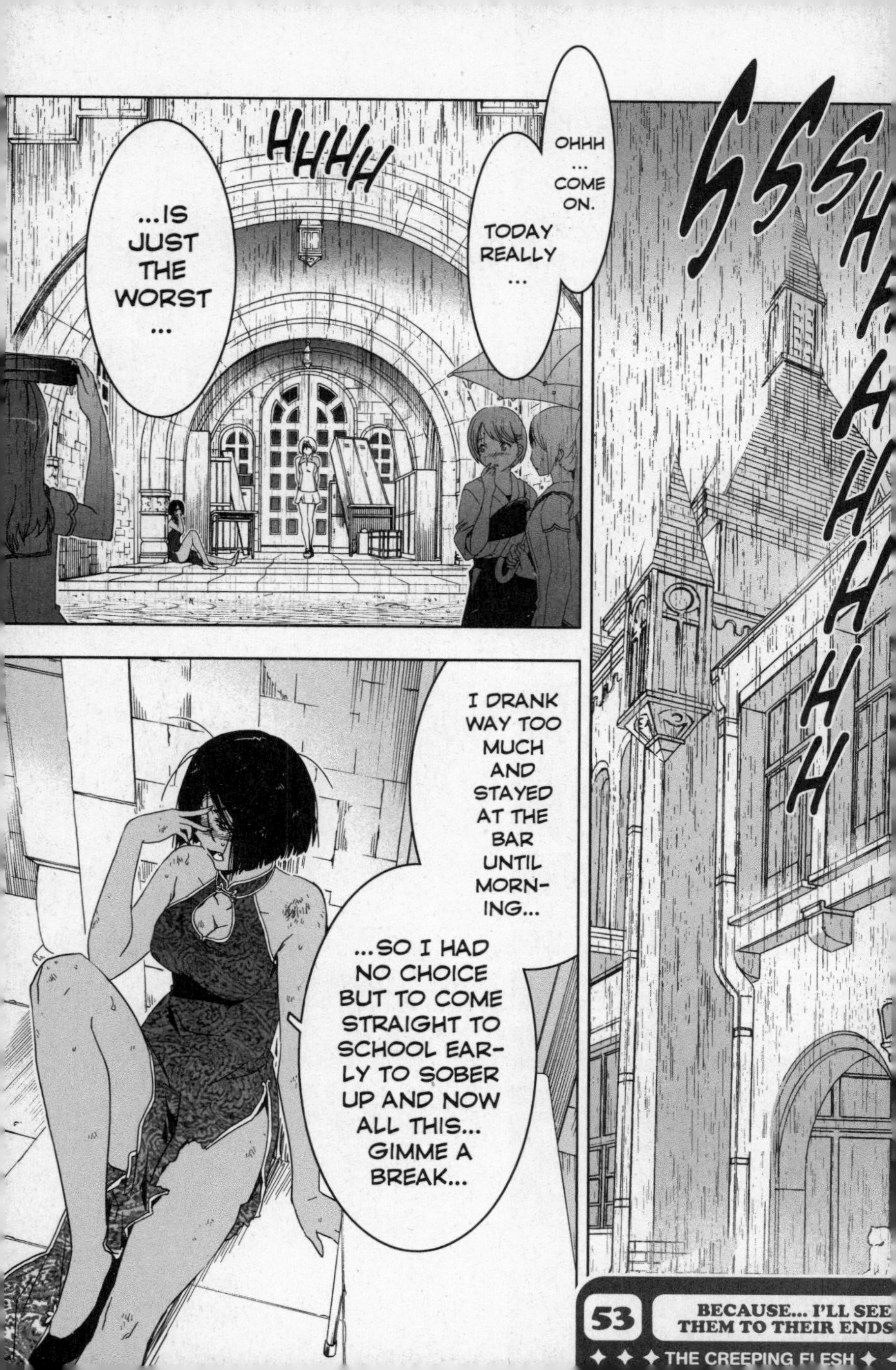
SSSHHHHHHHH
53
BECAUSE... I'LL SEE THEM TO THEIR ENDS
✦ ✦ ✦ THE CREEPING FLESH ✦
OHHH ... COME ON.
TODAY REALLY ...
HHHH
...IS JUST THE WORST ...
I DRANK WAY TOO MUCH AND STAYED AT THE BAR UNTIL MORNING...
...SO I HAD NO CHOICE BUT TO COME STRAIGHT TO SCHOOL EARLY TO SOBER UP AND NOW ALL THIS... GIMME A BREAK...

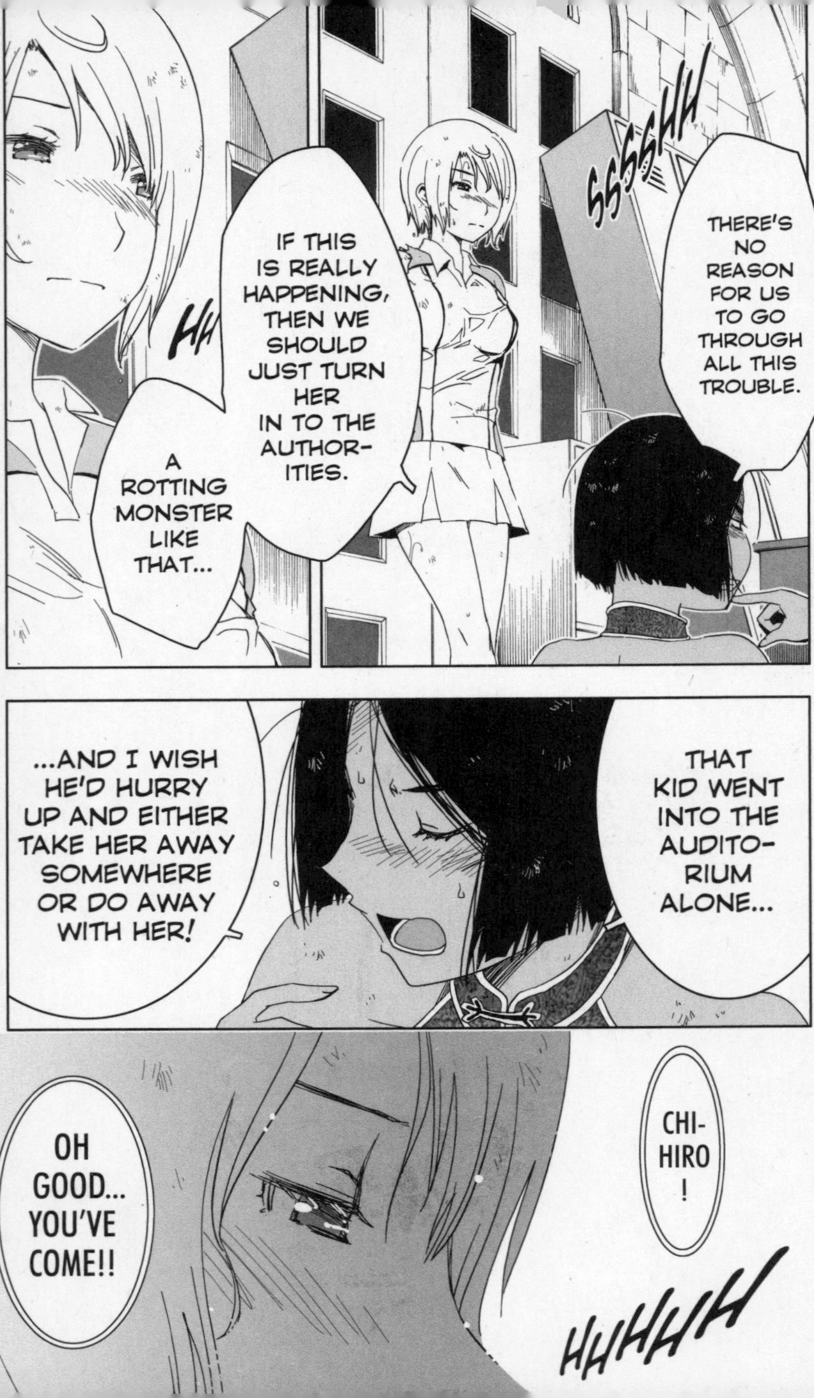
SSSSHH
THERE'S NO REASON FOR US TO GO THROUGH ALL THIS TROUBLE.
IF THIS IS REALLY HAPPENING, THEN WE SHOULD JUST TURN HER IN TO THE AUTHORITIES.
HH
A ROTTING MONSTER LIKE THAT...
THAT KID WENT INTO THE AUDITORIUM ALONE...
...AND I WISH HE'D HURRY UP AND EITHER TAKE HER AWAY SOMEWHERE OR DO AWAY WITH HER!
CHIHIRO!
OH GOOD... YOU'VE COME!!
HHHHHH

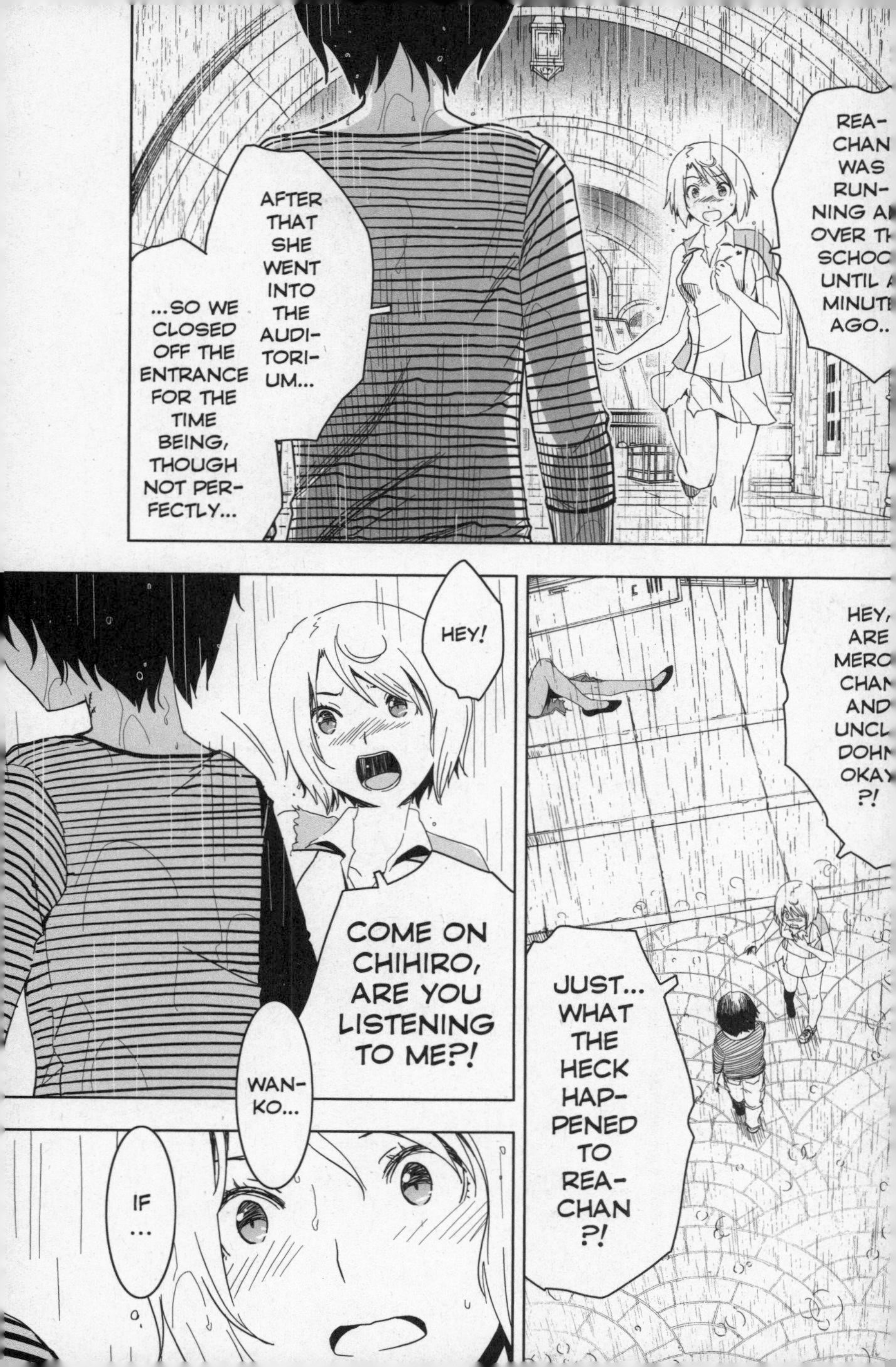
REA-CHAN WAS RUN-NING A OVER TH SCHOO UNTIL A MINUT AGO..
AFTER THAT SHE WENT INTO THE AUDITORIUM...
...SO WE CLOSED OFF THE ENTRANCE FOR THE TIME BEING, THOUGH NOT PERFECTLY...
HEY, ARE MERO CHAN AND UNCL DOHN OKAY ?!
JUST... WHAT THE HECK HAPPENED TO REA-CHAN?!
HEY!
COME ON CHIHIRO, ARE YOU LISTENING TO ME?!
WAN-KO...
IF ...

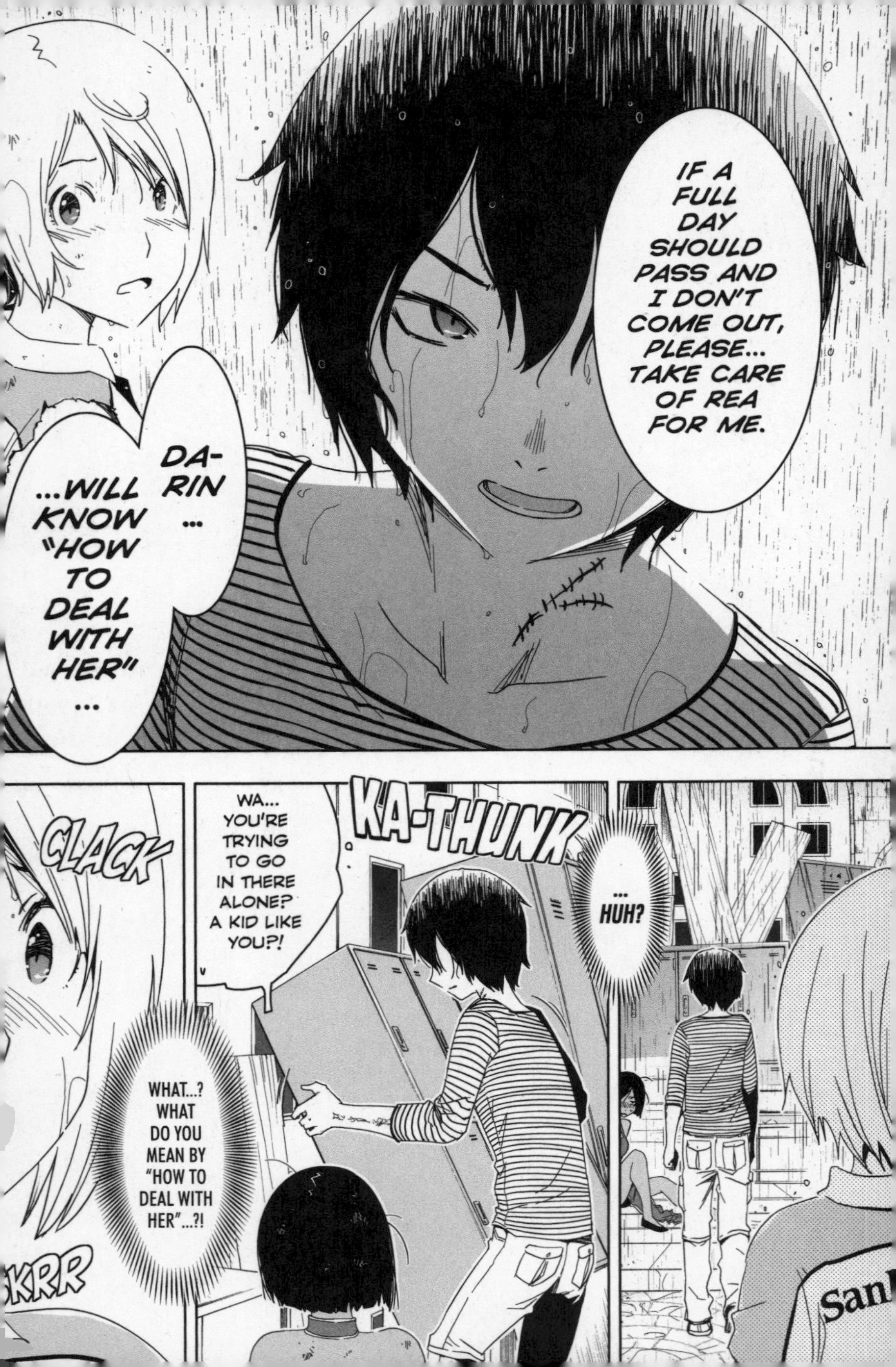
IF A FULL DAY SHOULD PASS AND I DON'T COME OUT, PLEASE... TAKE CARE OF REA FOR ME.
DA-RIN... ...WILL KNOW "HOW TO DEAL WITH HER"...
...HUH?
KA-THUNK
WA... YOU'RE TRYING TO GO IN THERE ALONE? A KID LIKE YOU?!
CLACK
WHAT...? WHAT DO YOU MEAN BY "HOW TO DEAL WITH HER"...?!
SKRR

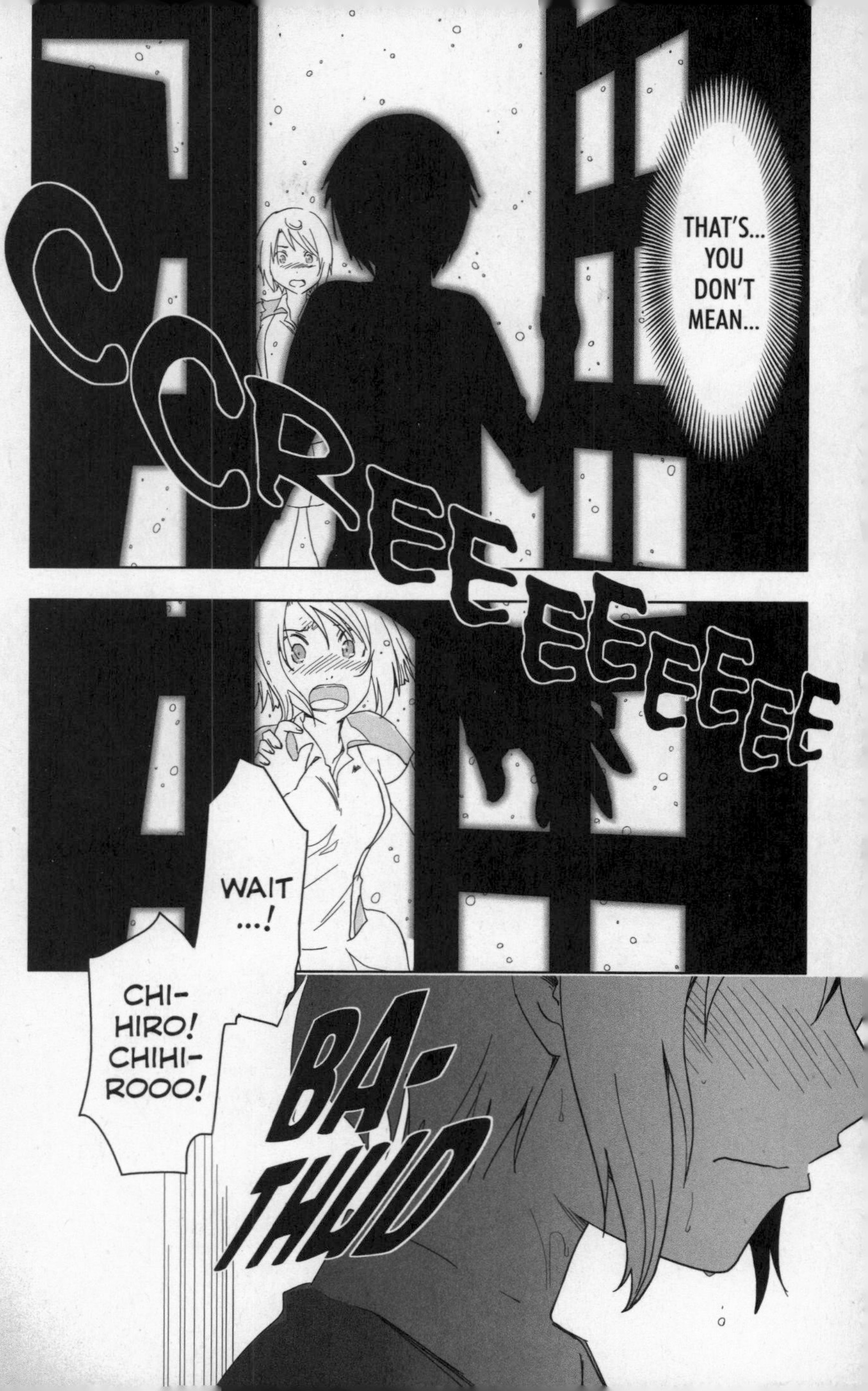

THAT'S... YOU DON'T MEAN...
CCREEEEEEEEE
WAIT ...!
CHI-HIRO! CHIHI-ROOO!
BA-THUD

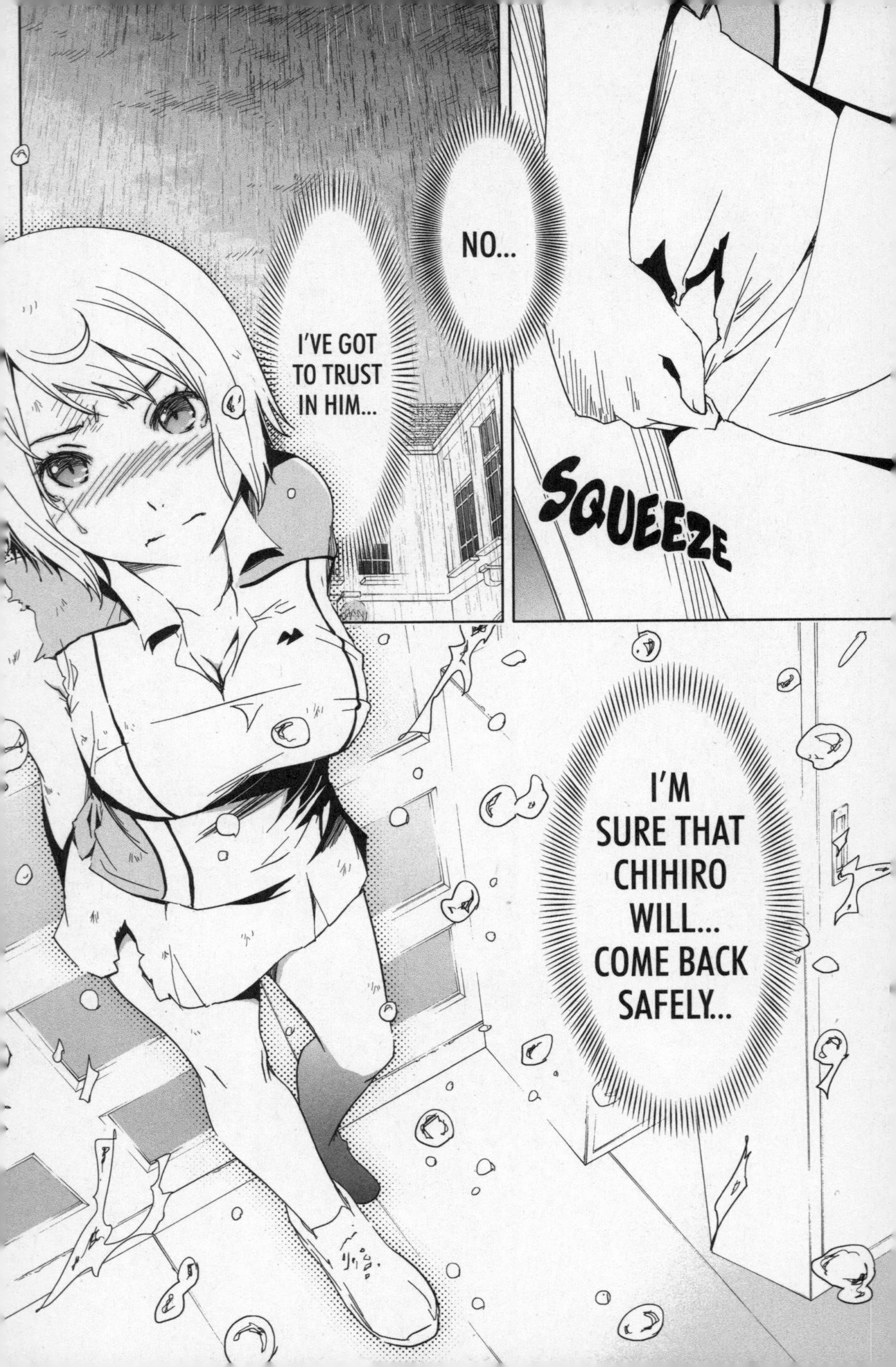
SQUEEZE
NO...
I'VE GOT TO TRUST IN HIM...
I'M SURE THAT CHIHIRO WILL... COME BACK SAFELY...

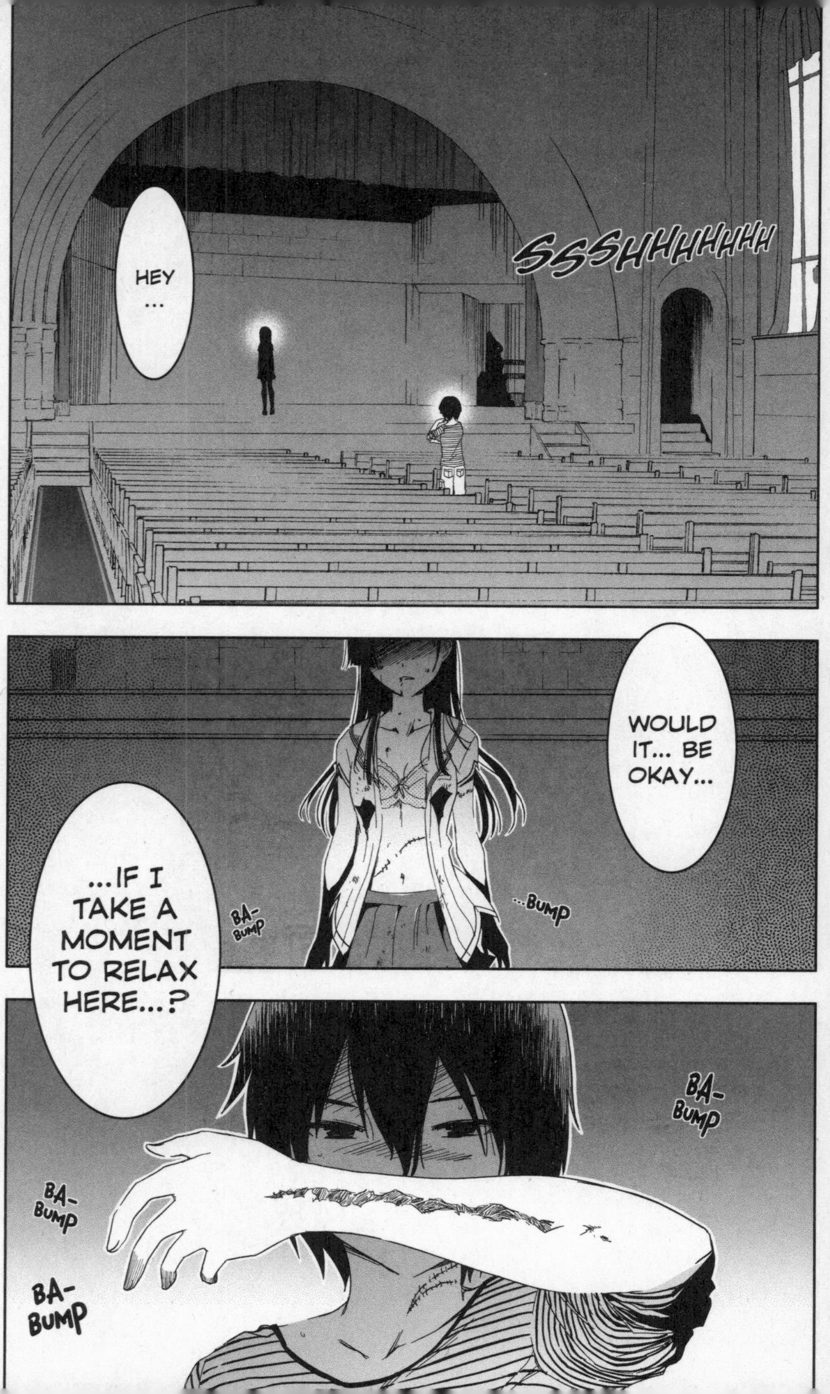
SSSHHHHHHH
HEY ...
WOULD IT... BE OKAY...
...BUMP
BA-BUMP
...IF I TAKE A MOMENT TO RELAX HERE...?
BA-BUMP
BA-BUMP
BA-BUMP

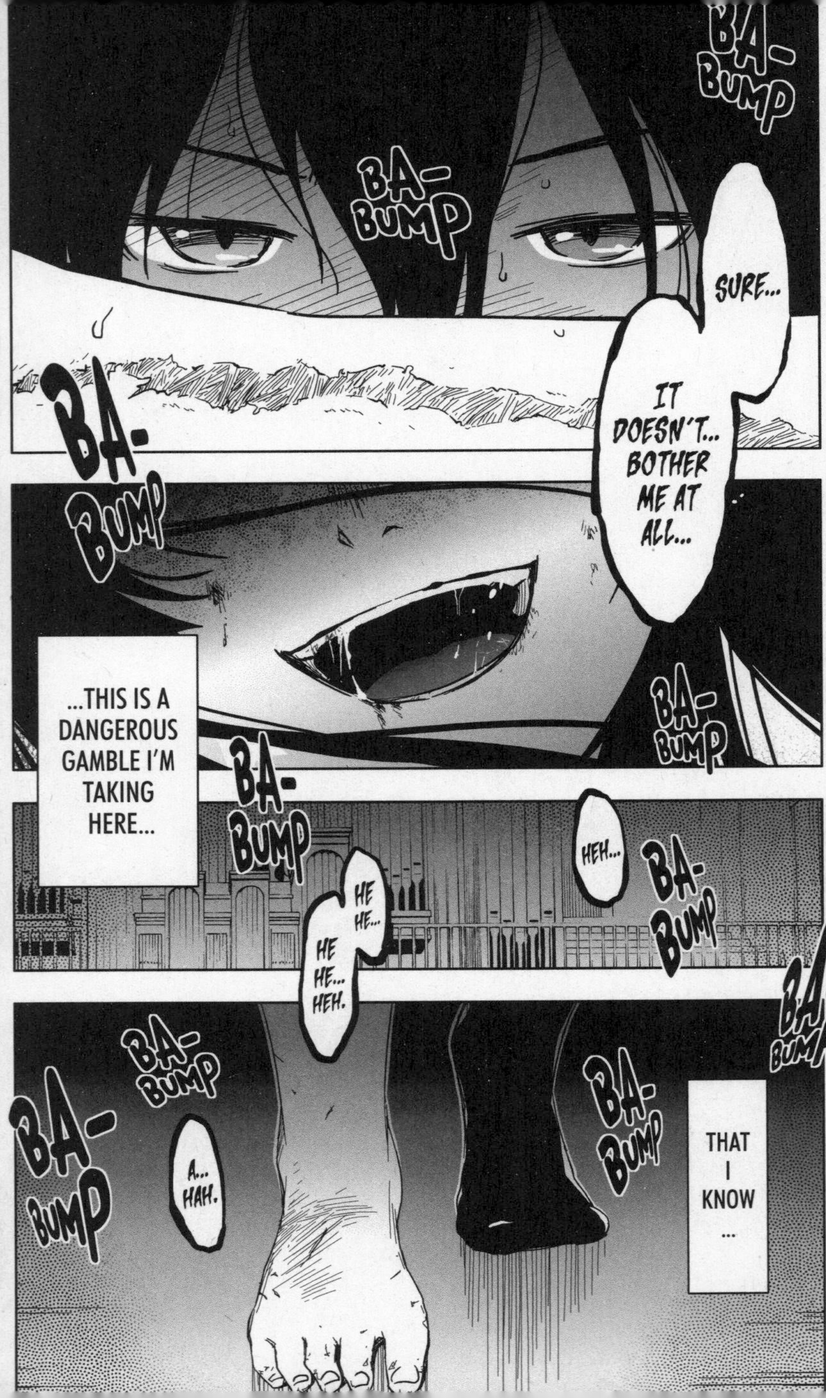
BA-BUMP
SURE...
BA-BUMP
IT DOESN'T... BOTHER ME AT ALL...
BA-BUMP
BA-BUMP
...THIS IS A DANGEROUS GAMBLE I'M TAKING HERE...
BA-BUMP
HEH...
BA-BUMP
HE HE...
HE HE... HEH.
BA-BUMP
BA-BUMP
THAT I KNOW ...
A... HAH.
BA-BUMP
BA-BUMP

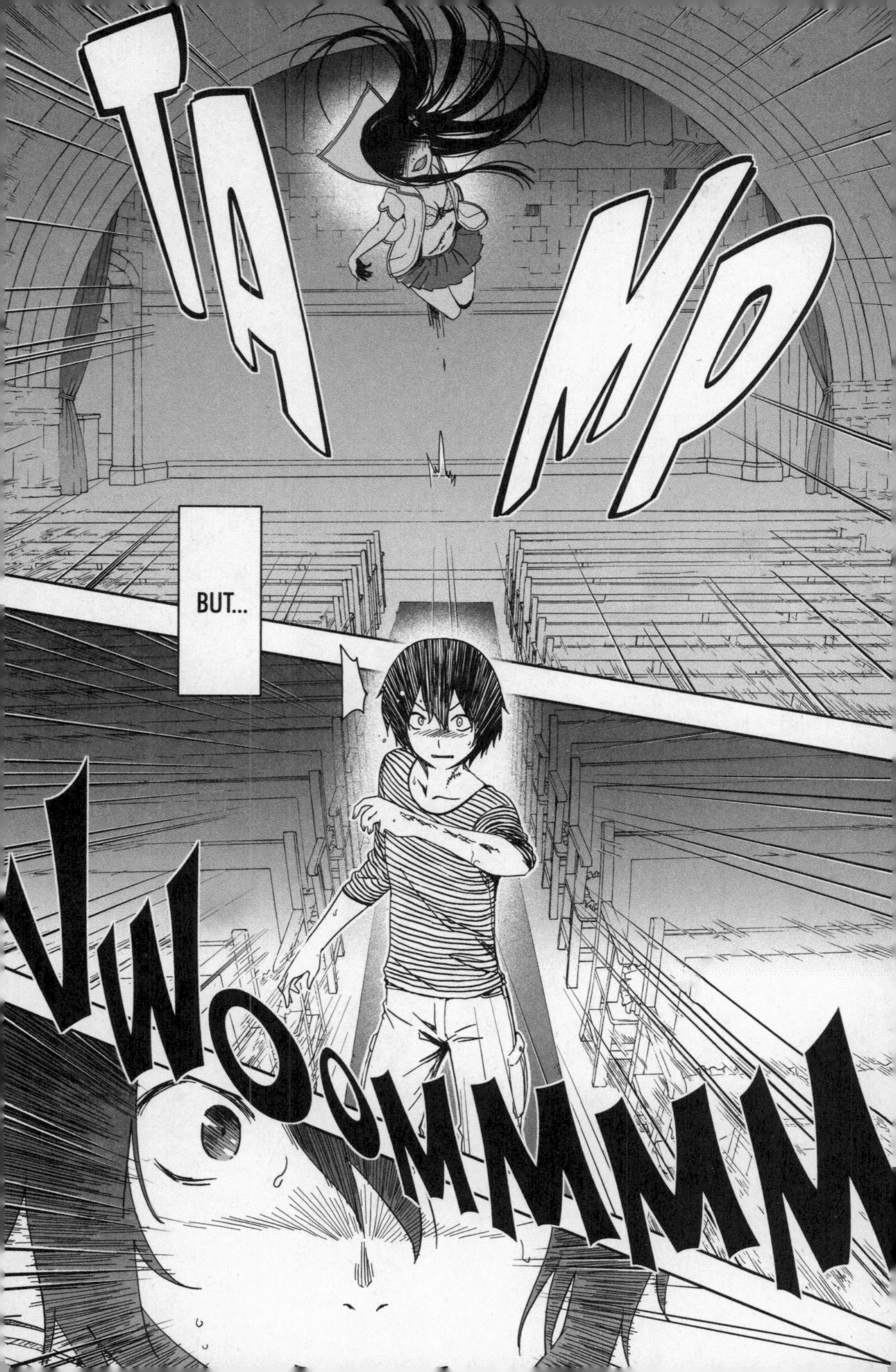
TIAMP
BUT...
VWOOOMMMMM

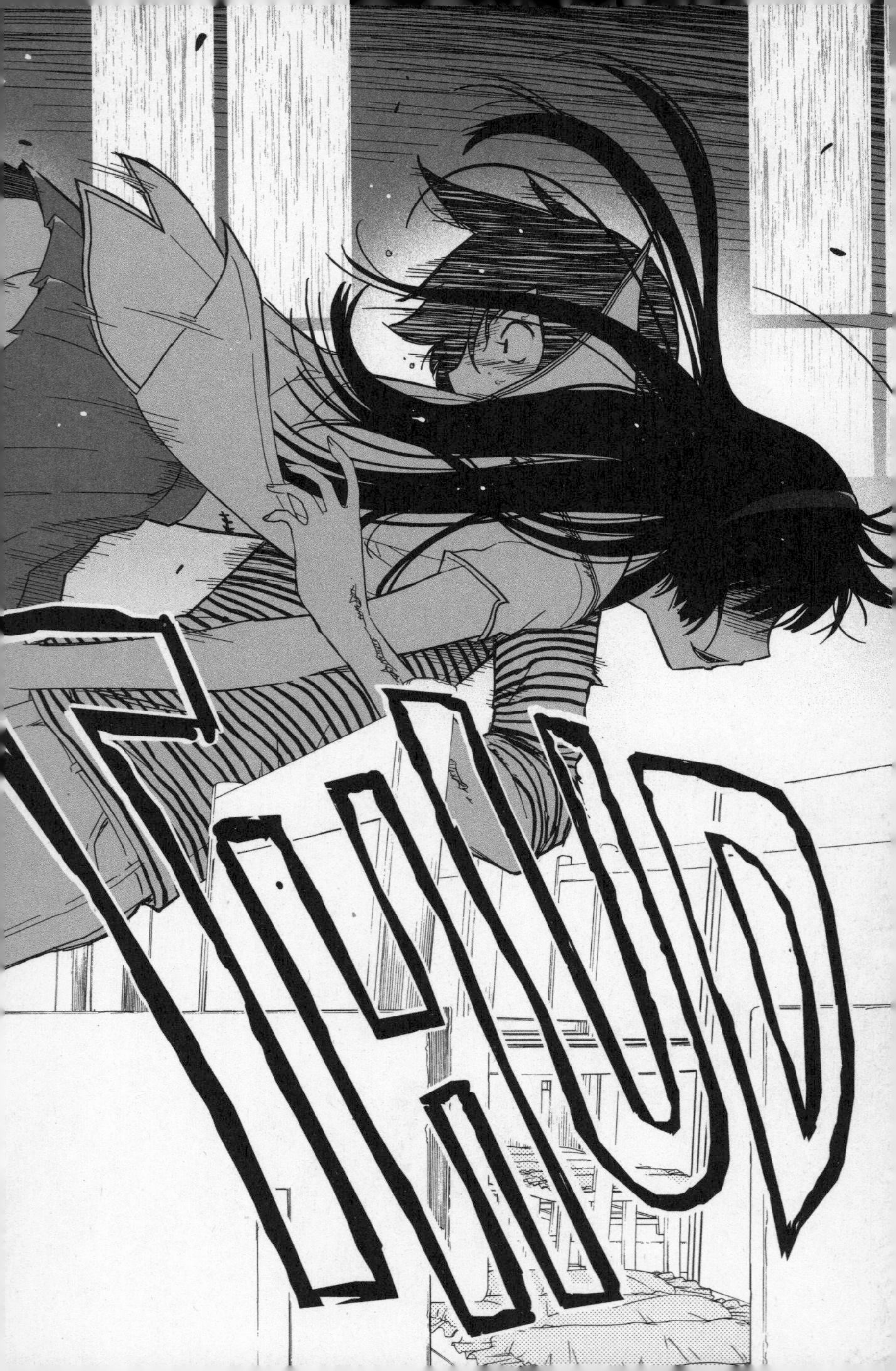
THUD

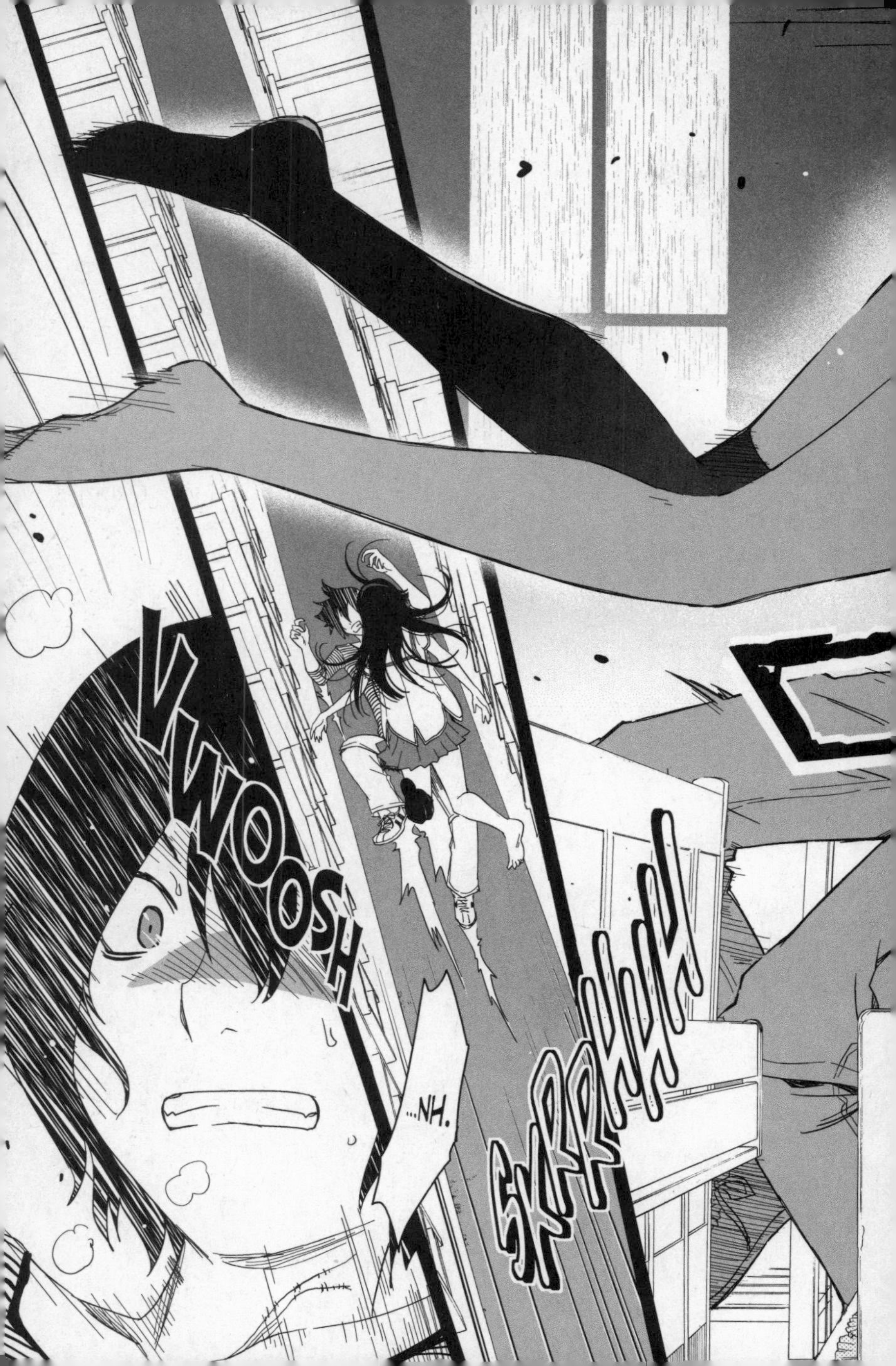

WOOSH
...NH.

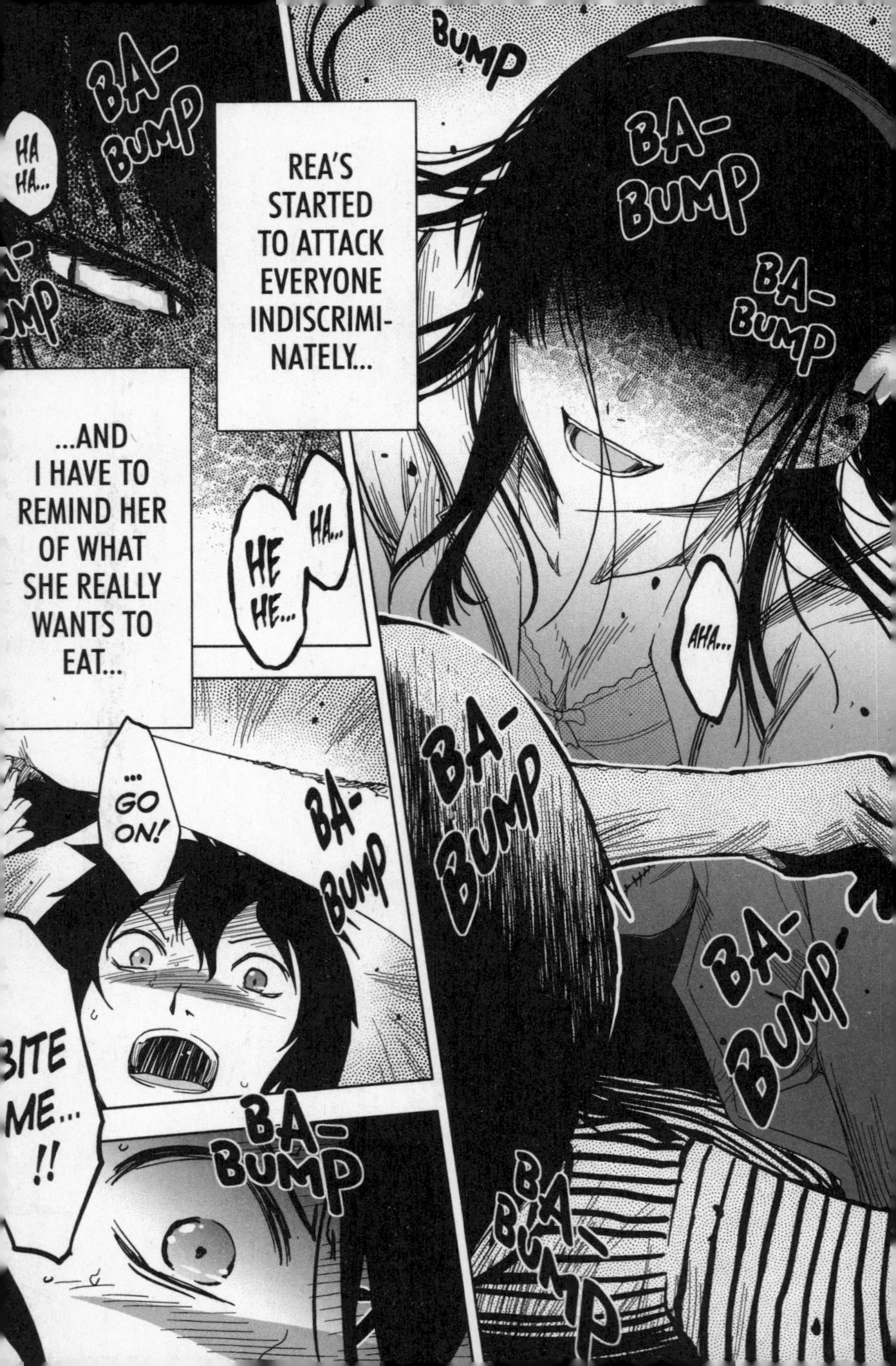
BUMP
BA-BUMP
BA-BUMP
AHA...
BA-BUMP
BA-BUMP
BA-BUMP
BA-BUMP
HA HA...
REA'S STARTED TO ATTACK EVERYONE INDISCRIMI-NATELY...
...AND I HAVE TO REMIND HER OF WHAT SHE REALLY WANTS TO EAT...
HA...
HE HE...
... GO ON!
BA-BUMP
BITE ME... !!
BA-BUMP

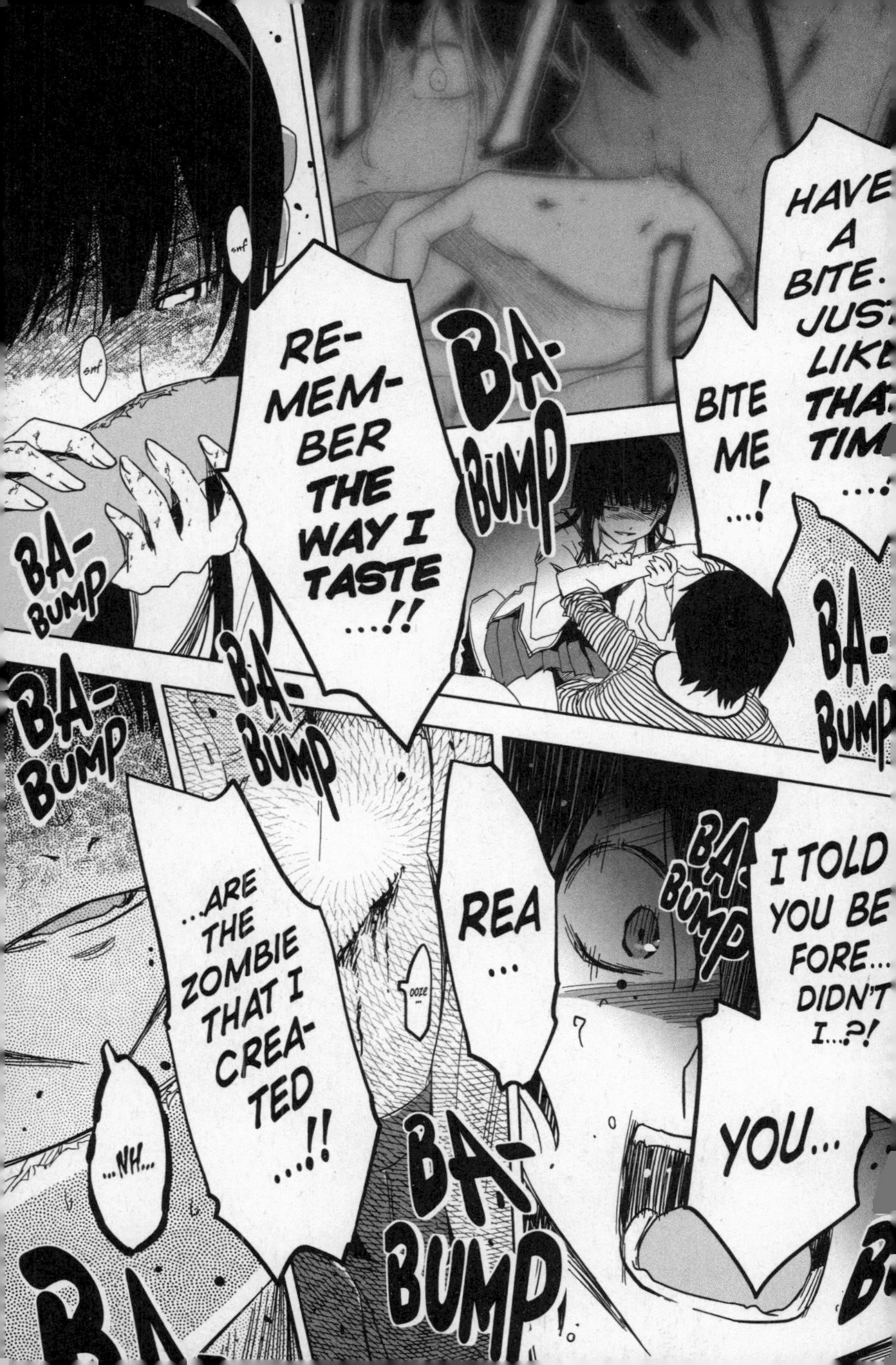
HAVE A BITE. JUS LIKE THA TIM...
BITE ME...!
BA-BUMP
BA-BUMP
snf
snf
RE-MEMBER THE WAY I TASTE...!!
BA-BUMP
BA-BUMP
I TOLD YOU BE FORE... DIDN'T I...?!
YOU...
BA-BUMP
REA...
BA-BUMP
ooze...
...ARE THE ZOMBIE THAT I CREA-TED...!!
BA-BUMP
...NH...

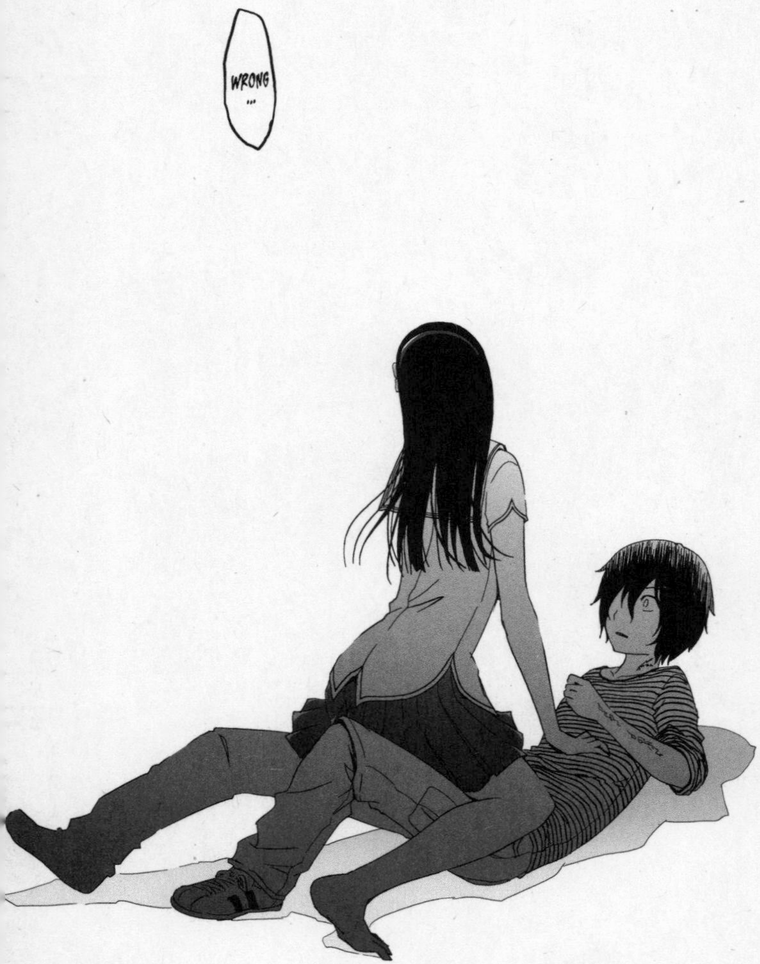
WRONG
...

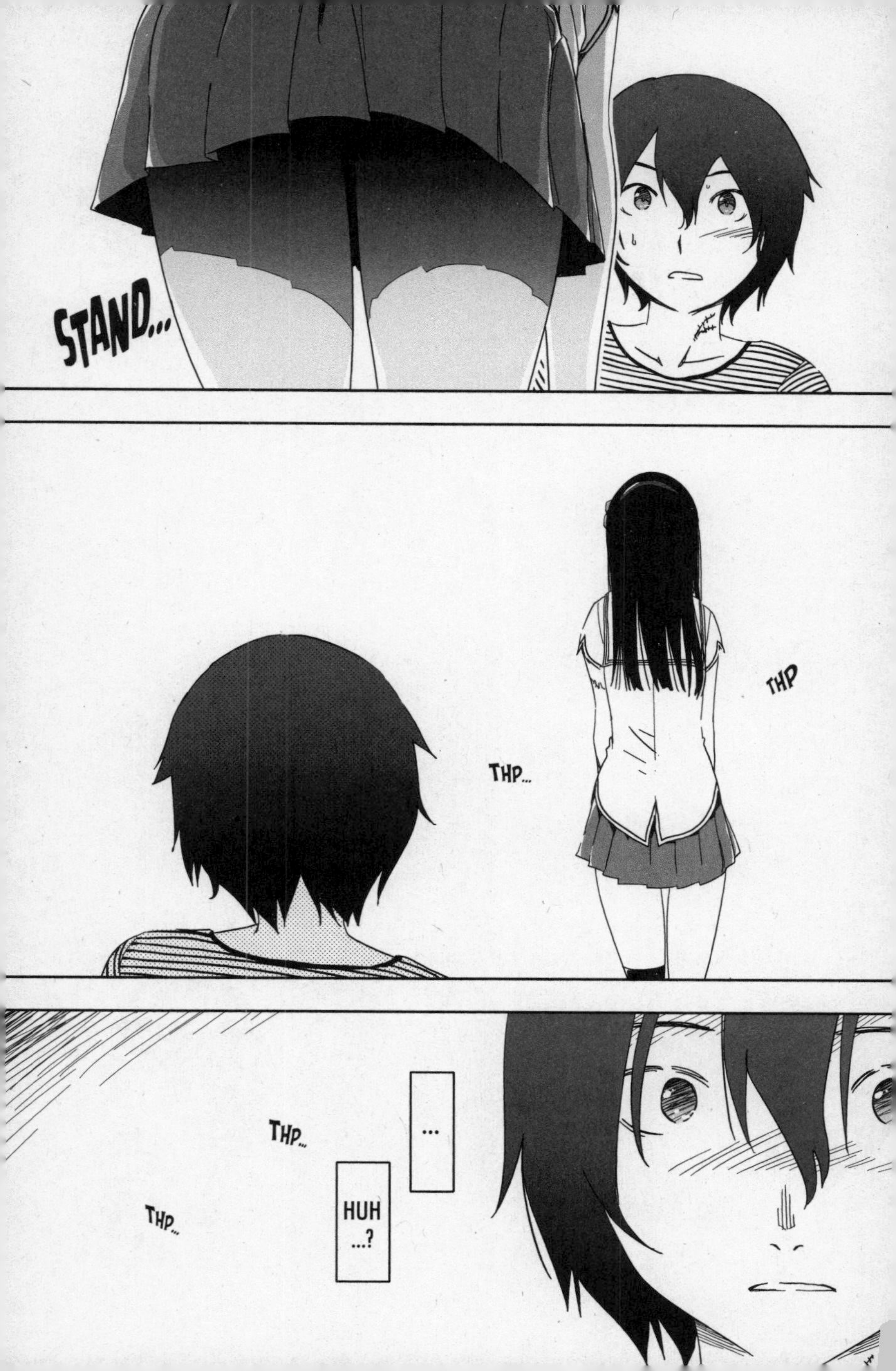
STAND...
THP
THP...
...
HUH ...?
THP...
THP...

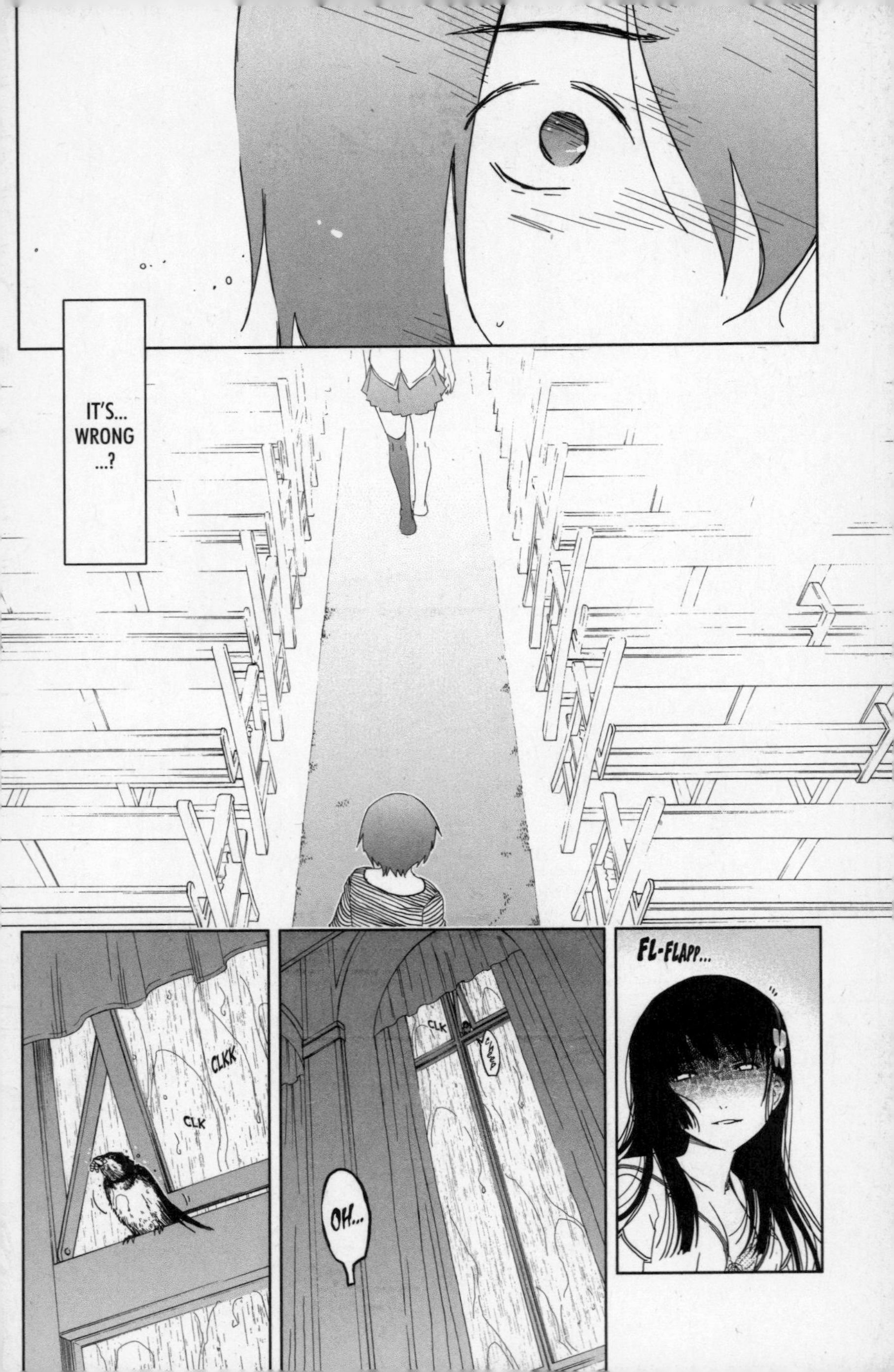

...
IT'S... WRONG ...?
FL-FLAPP...
CLK
CHEEP
OH...
CLKK
CLK

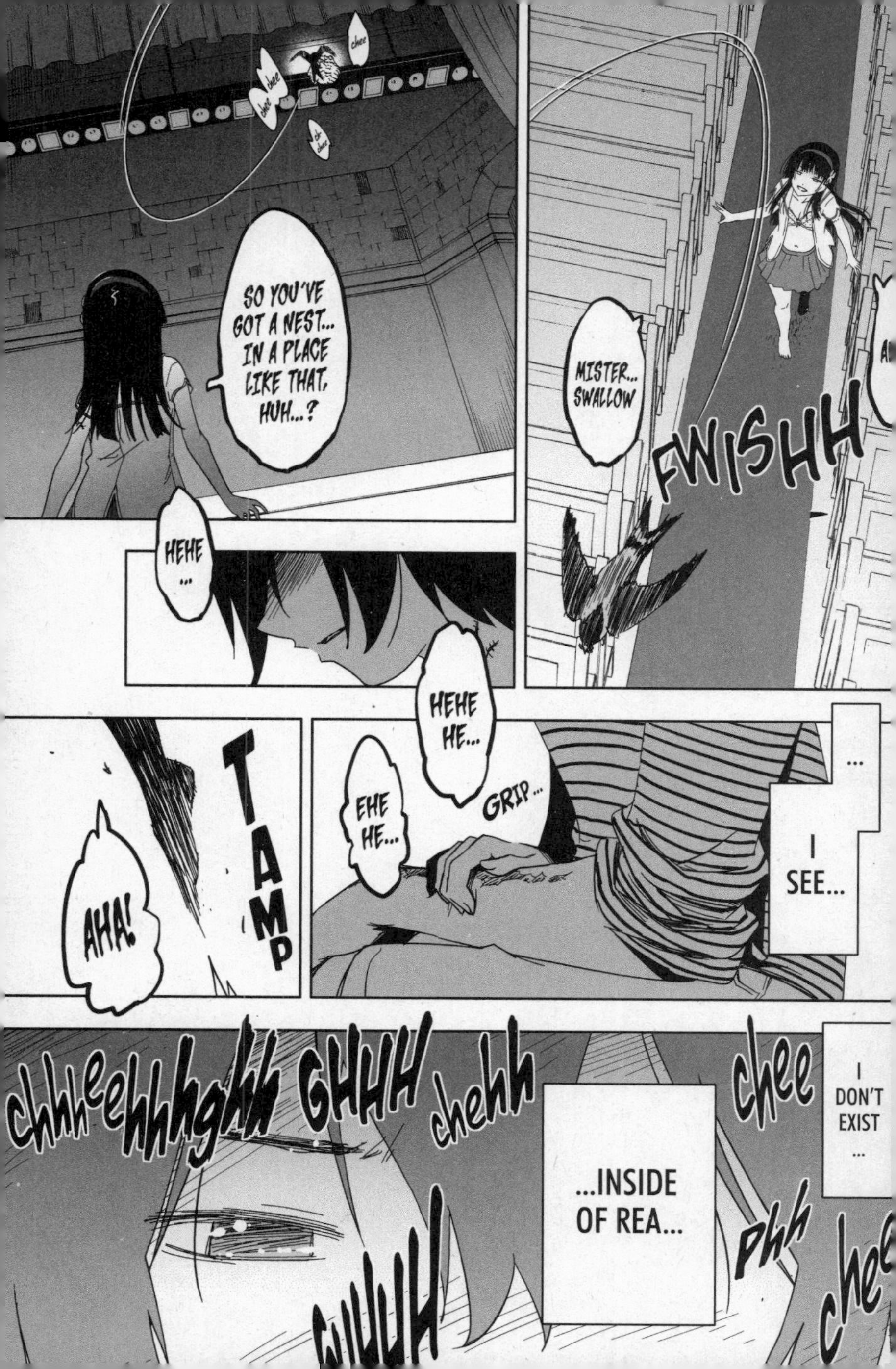
MISTER... SWALLOW
FWISHH
chee
chee chee
ch chee
SO YOU'VE GOT A NEST... IN A PLACE LIKE THAT, HUH...?
HEHE ...
... I SEE...
HEHE HE...
GRIP...
EHE HE...
TAMP
AHA!
I DON'T EXIST ...
chee
...INSIDE OF REA...
chee
Phh
chehh
WHUH
GHHH
chhheehhhghh

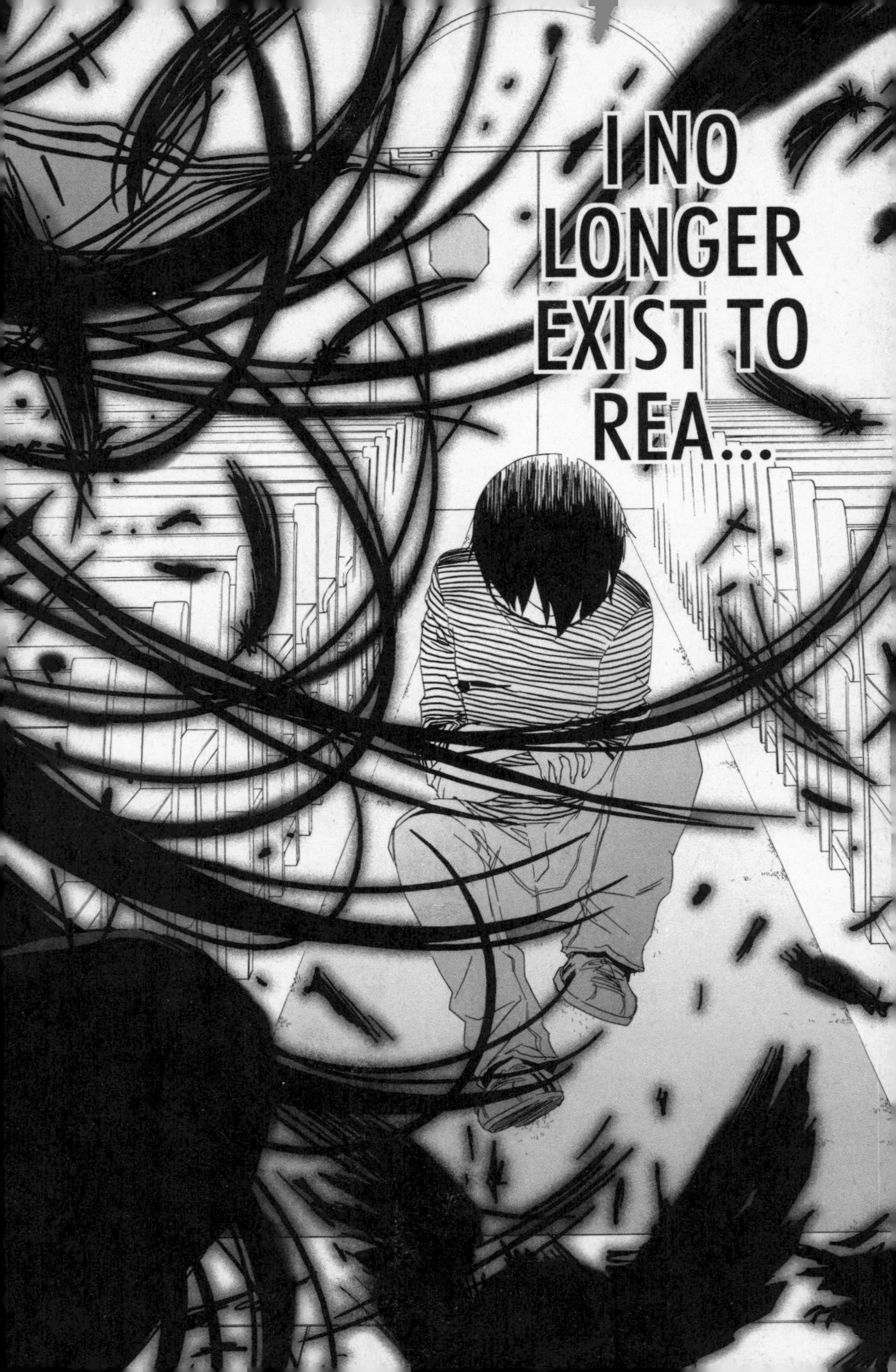
I NO LONGER EXIST TO REA...

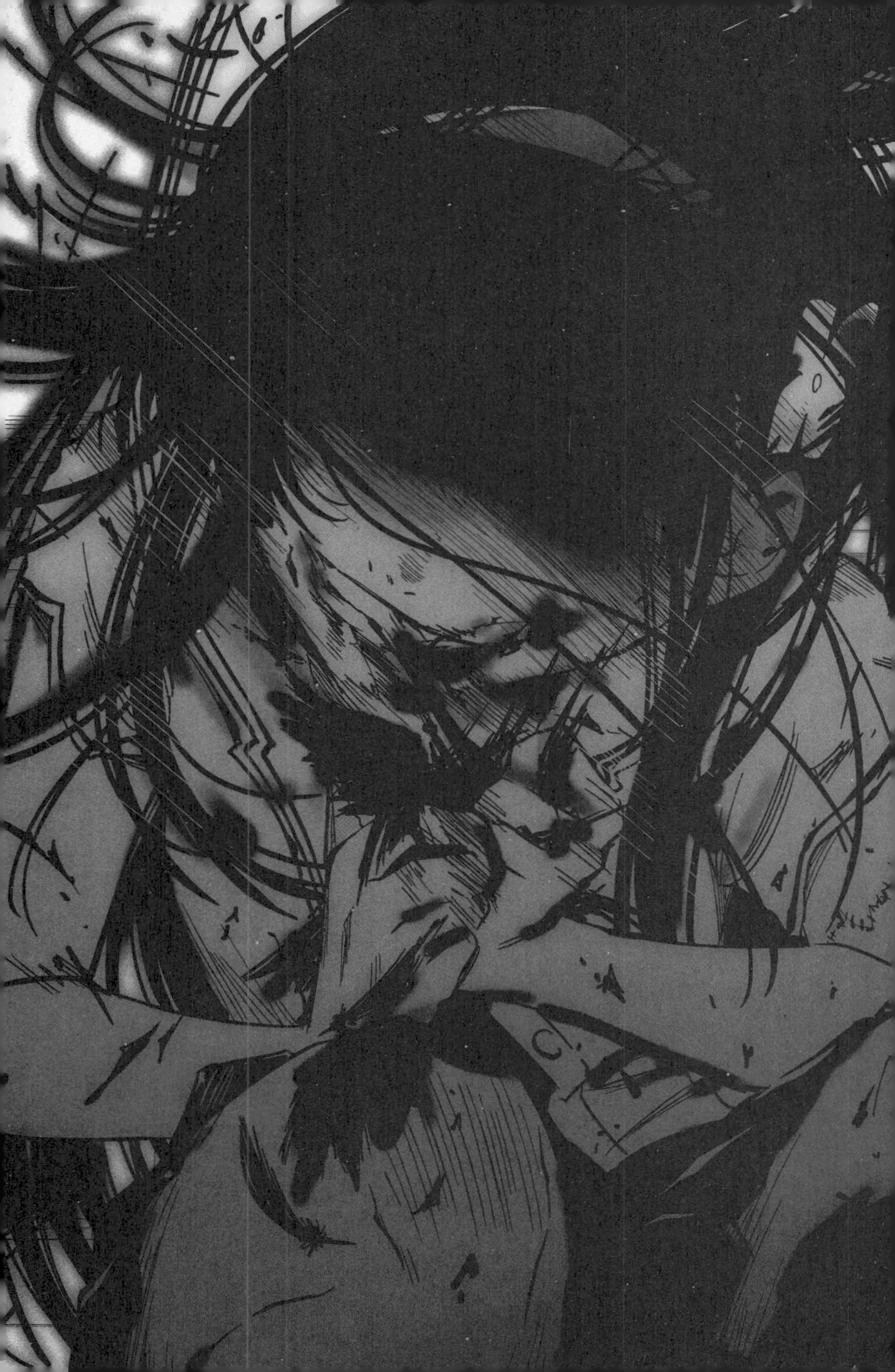

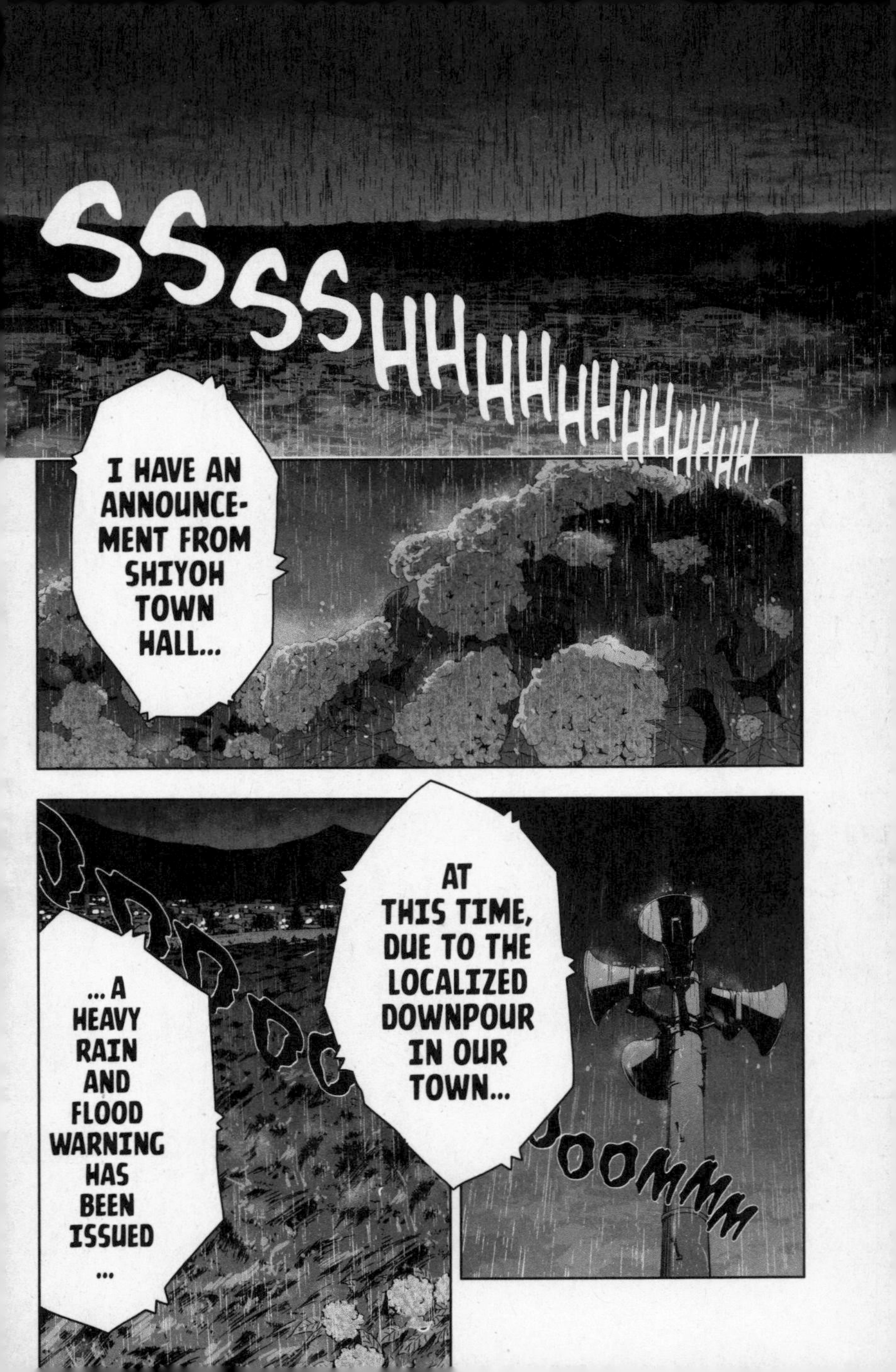
SSSSHHHHHHHHHHHHH
I HAVE AN ANNOUNCEMENT FROM SHIYOH TOWN HALL...
AT THIS TIME, DUE TO THE LOCALIZED DOWNPOUR IN OUR TOWN...
OOMMMM
... A HEAVY RAIN AND FLOOD WARNING HAS BEEN ISSUED ...

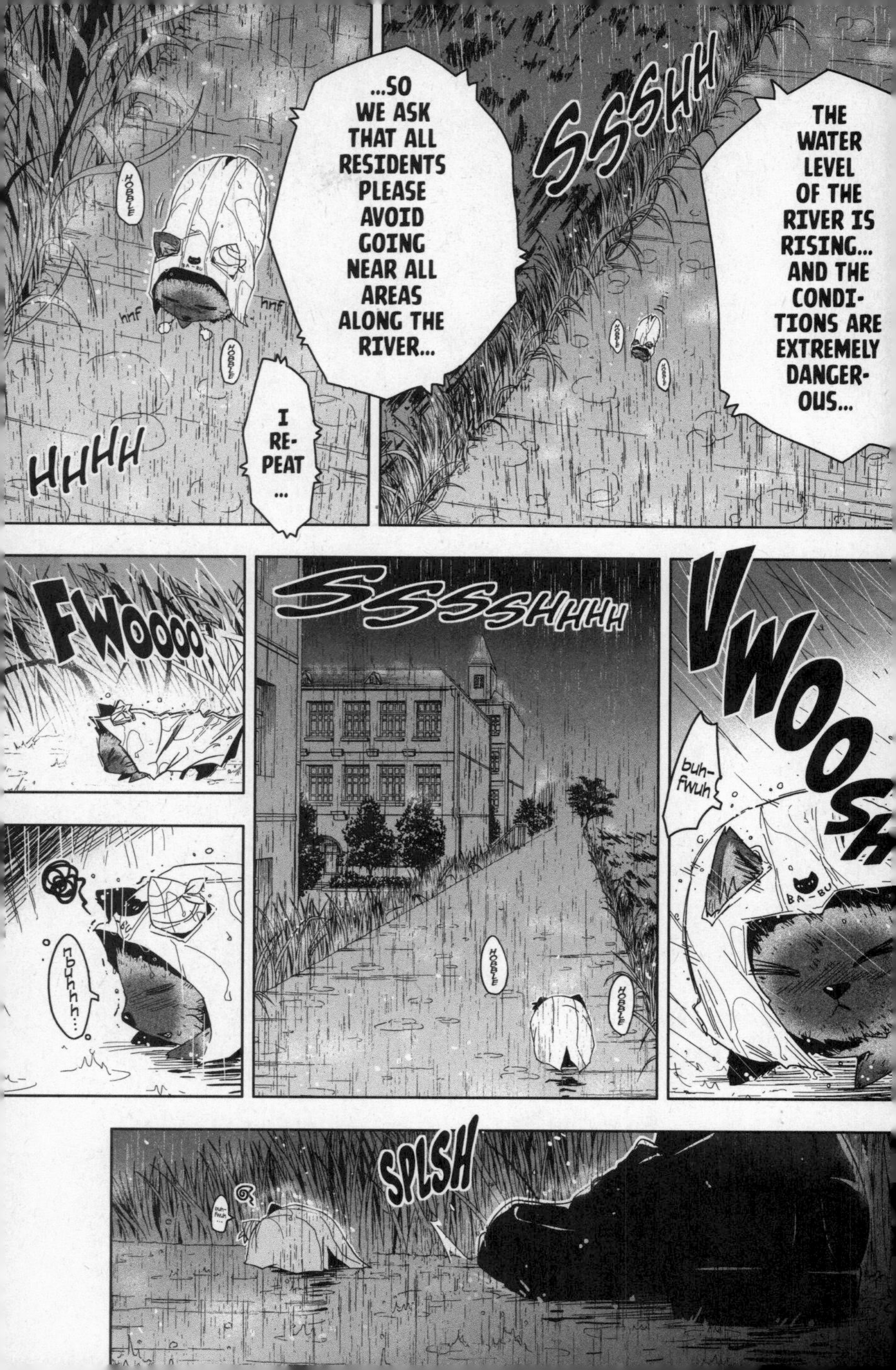
SSSHH
THE WATER LEVEL OF THE RIVER IS RISING... AND THE CONDITIONS ARE EXTREMELY DANGEROUS...
HOBBLE
HOBBLE
...SO WE ASK THAT ALL RESIDENTS PLEASE AVOID GOING NEAR ALL AREAS ALONG THE RIVER...
I RE-PEAT...
HOBBLE
hnf
hnf
HOBBLE
HHHH
VWOOOSH
buh-fwuh
BA-BU
SSSSHHHH
HOBBLE
HOBBLE
FWOOOO
nbuhhh...
SPLSH

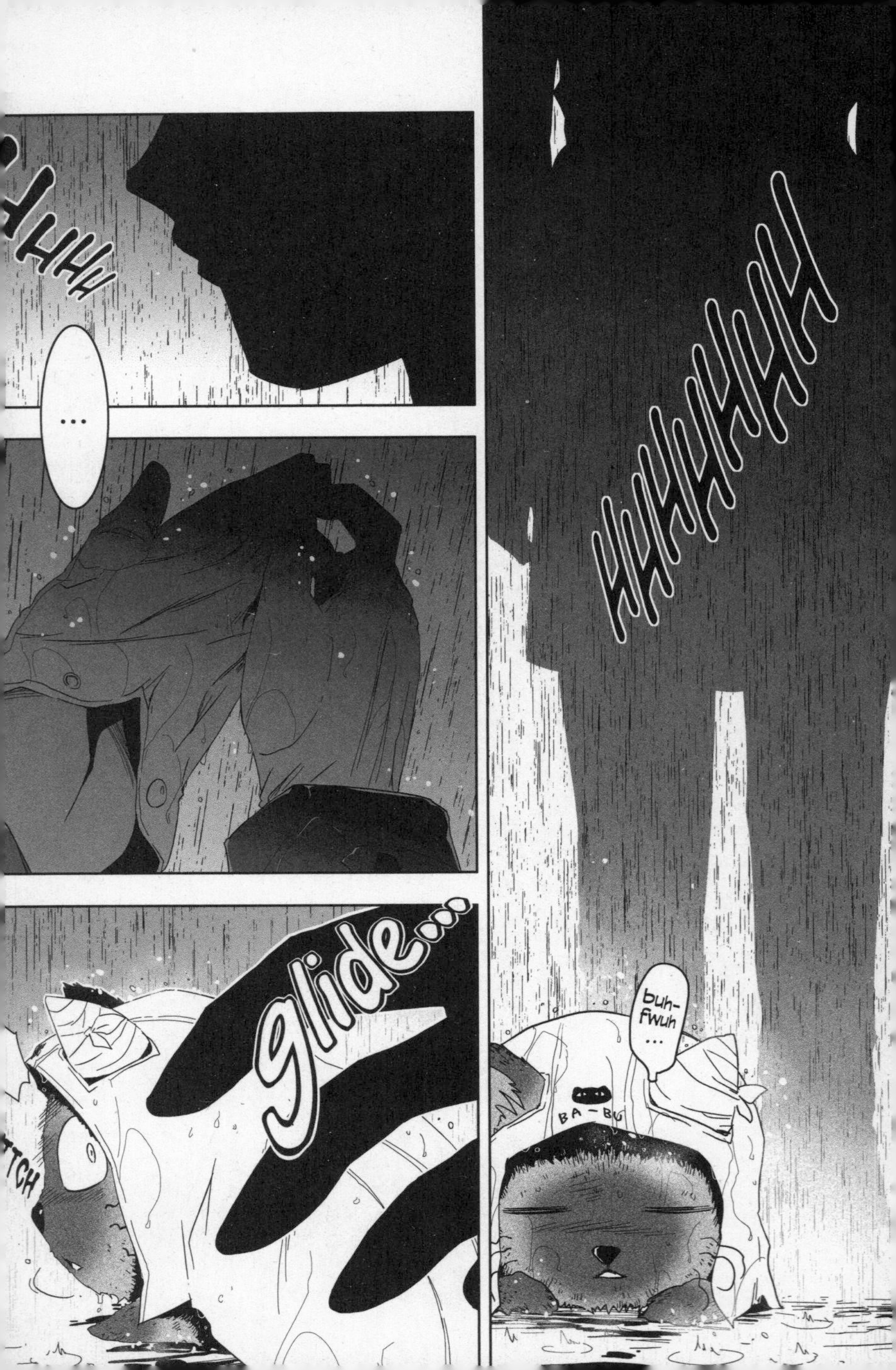
HHHHHHHHHH
buh-fwuh ...
BA-BU
HHHH
...
glide...

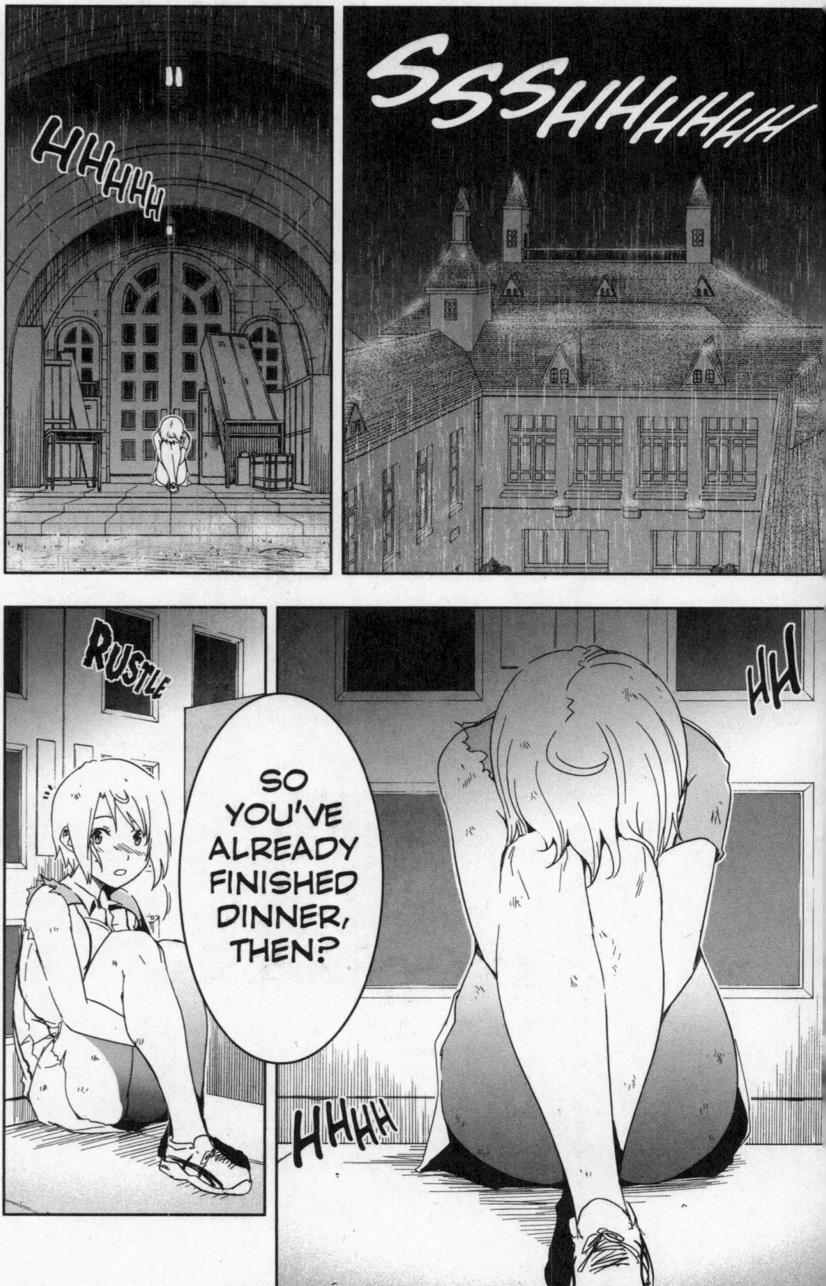
SSSHHHHHHH
HHHHH
HH
HHHH
RUSTLE
SO YOU'VE ALREADY FINISHED DINNER, THEN?

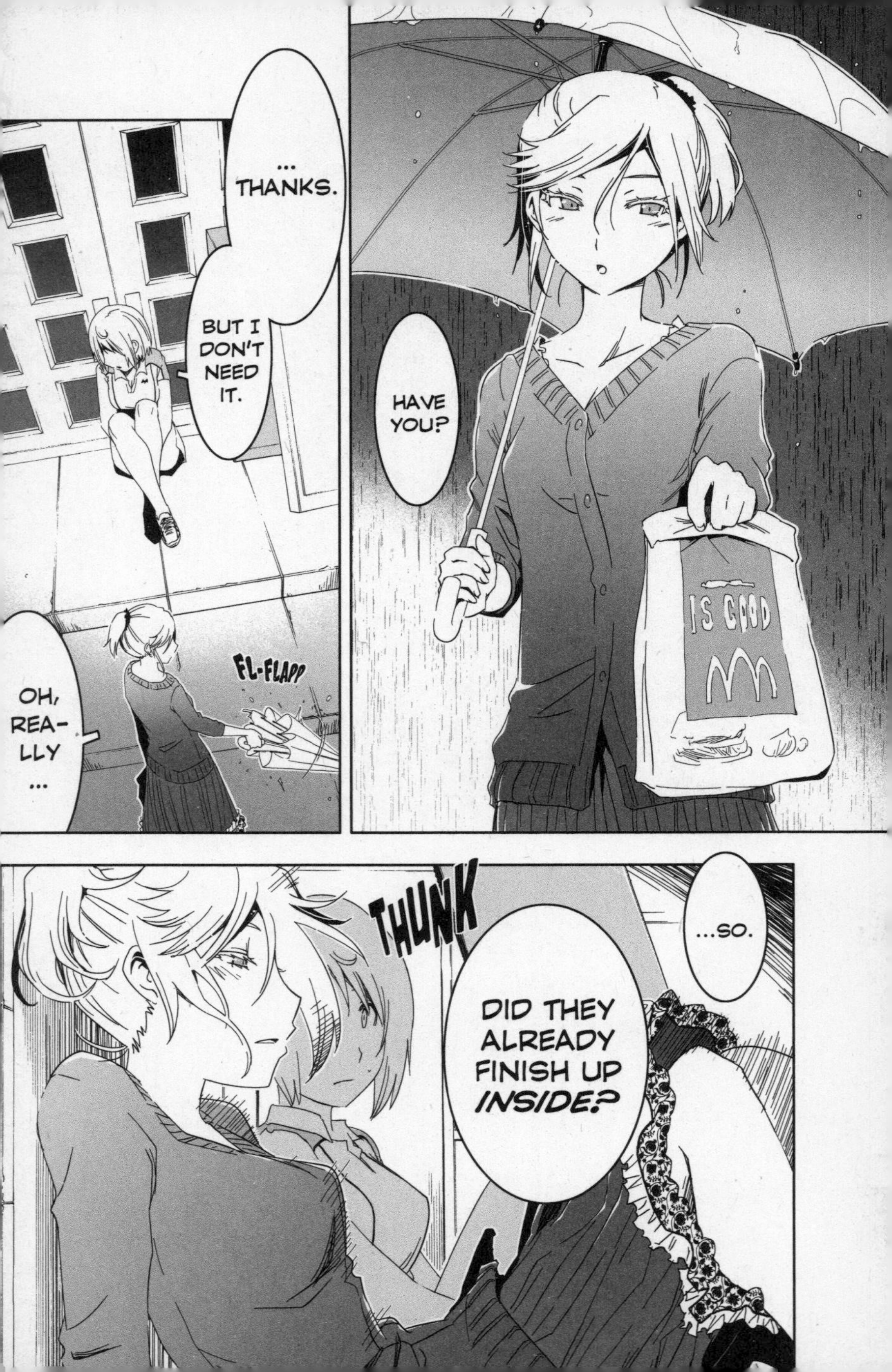
HAVE YOU?
IS GOOD
...THANKS.
BUT I DON'T NEED IT.
FL-FLAPP
OH, REALLY...
THUNK
...SO.
DID THEY ALREADY FINISH UP *INSIDE?*

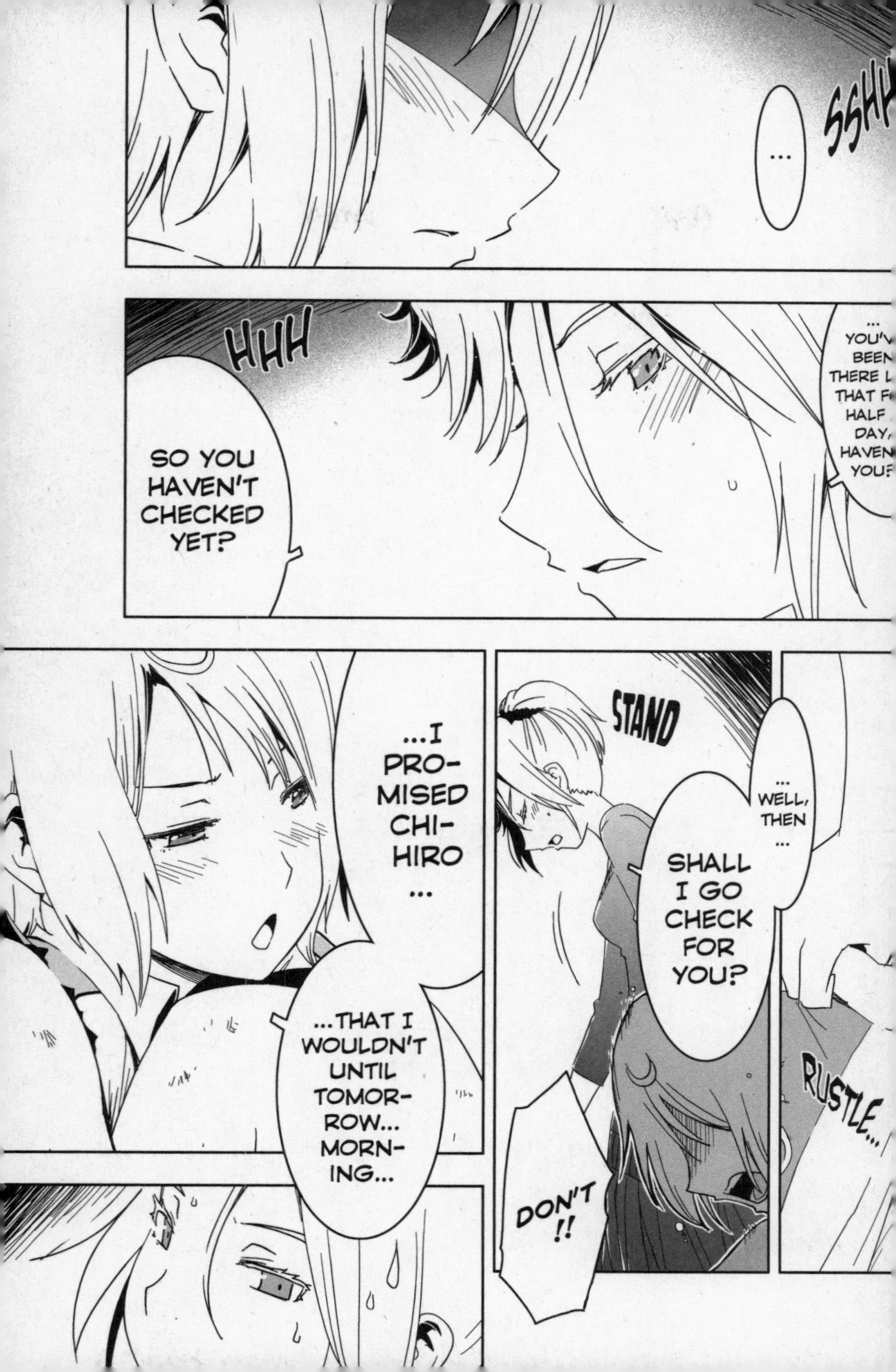
SSHH
...
... YOU'V BEEN THERE L THAT F HALF DAY, HAVEN YOU?
HHH
SO YOU HAVEN'T CHECKED YET?
RUSTLE...
... WELL, THEN ...
STAND
SHALL I GO CHECK FOR YOU?
DON'T !!
...I PROMISED CHIHIRO ...
...THAT I WOULDN'T UNTIL TOMORROW... MORNING...

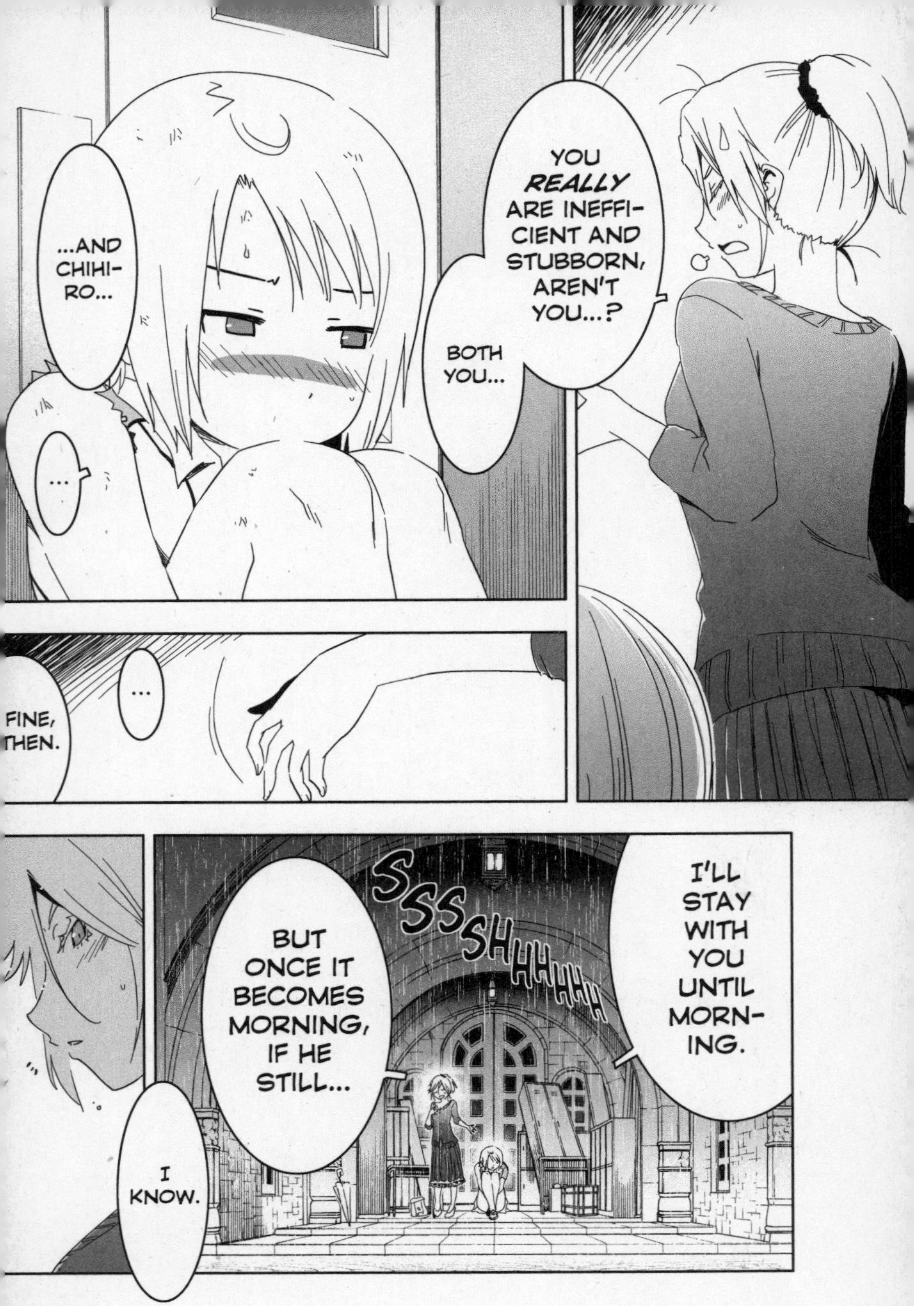
YOU *REALLY* ARE INEFFICIENT AND STUBBORN, AREN'T YOU...?
BOTH YOU...
...AND CHIHIRO...
...
...
FINE, THEN.
I'LL STAY WITH YOU UNTIL MORNING.
SSSHHHHHHH
BUT ONCE IT BECOMES MORNING, IF HE STILL...
I KNOW.

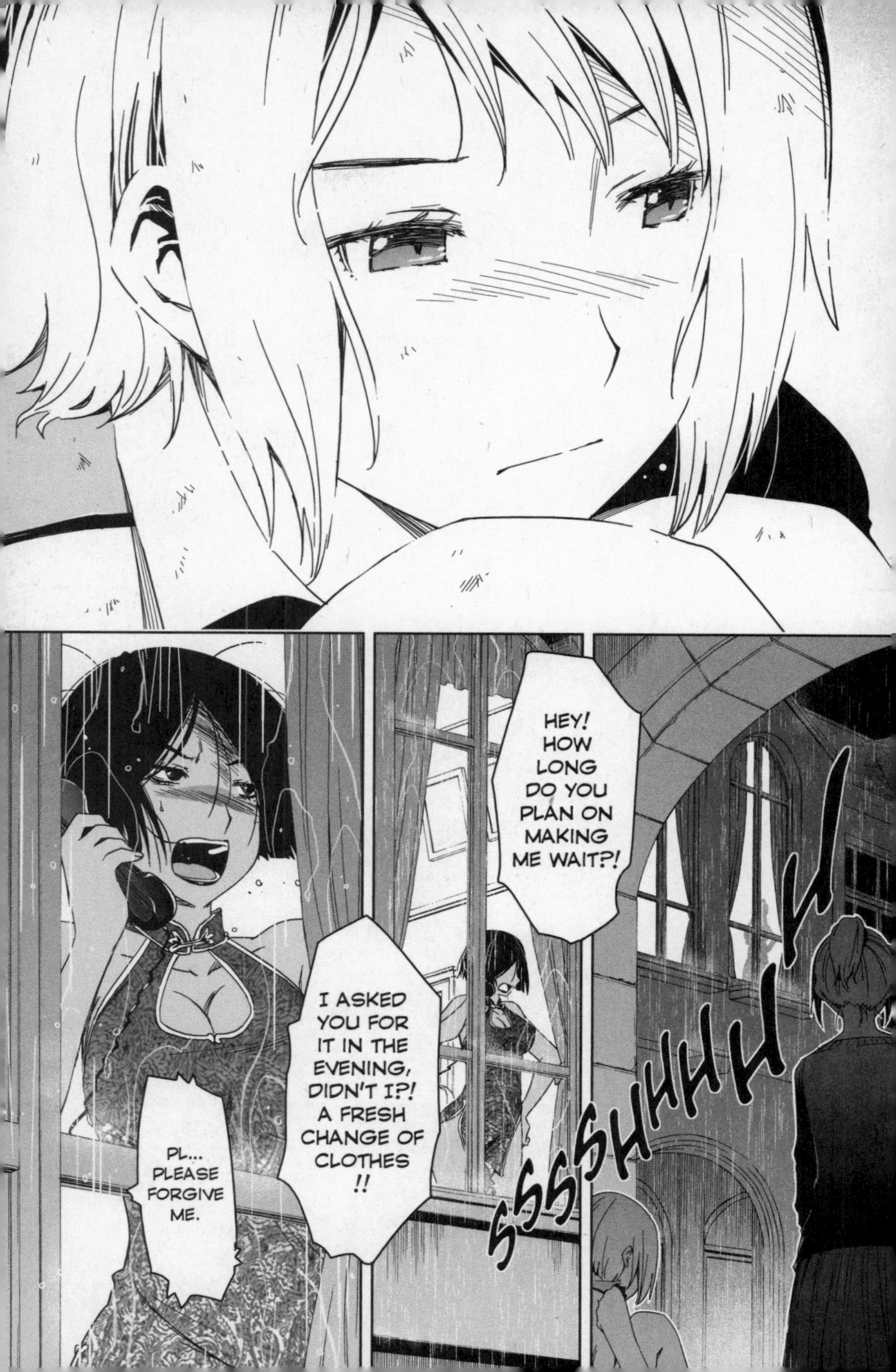
SSSSHHHHH
HEY! HOW LONG DO YOU PLAN ON MAKING ME WAIT?!
I ASKED YOU FOR IT IN THE EVENING, DIDN'T I?! A FRESH CHANGE OF CLOTHES!!
PL... PLEASE FORGIVE ME.

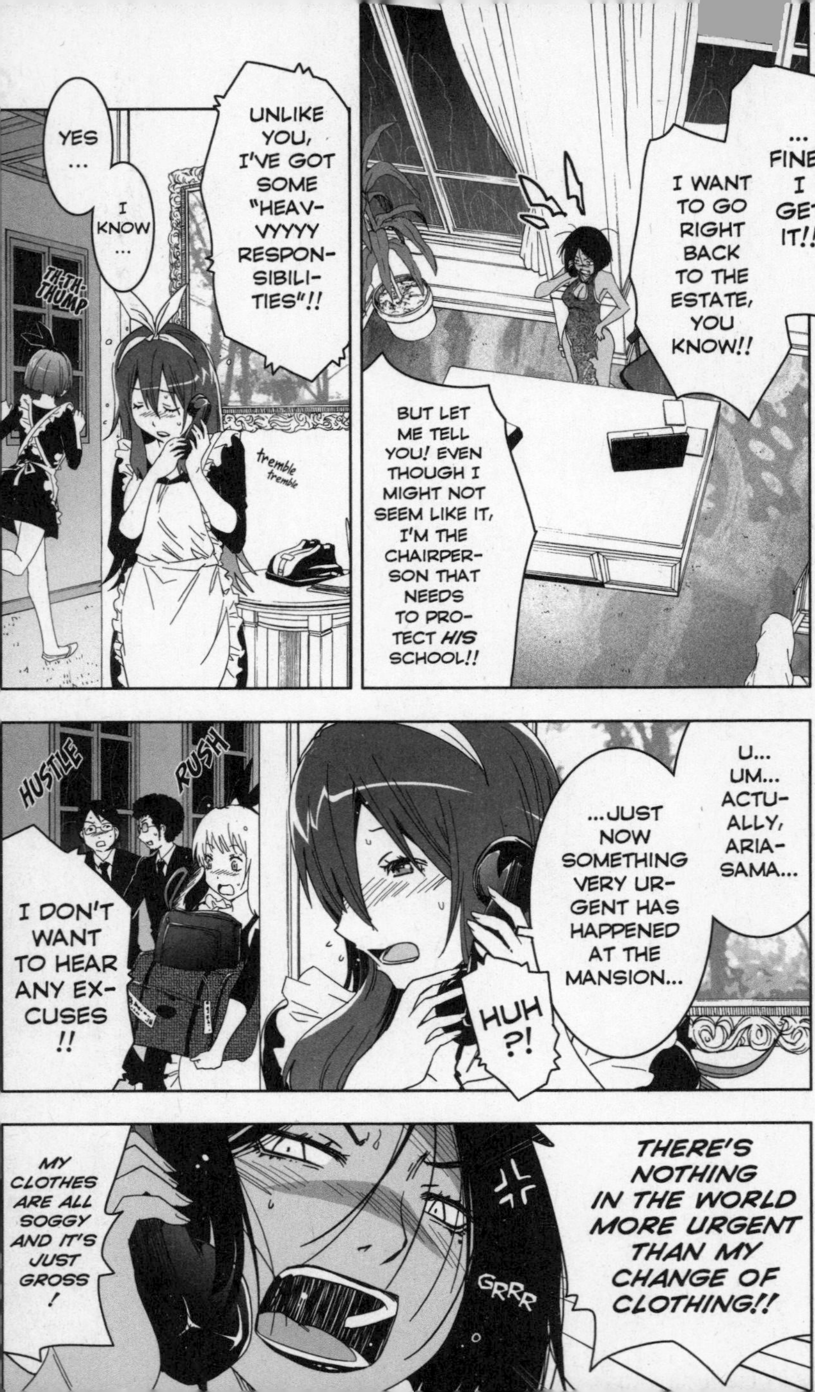
... FINE! I GET IT!!
I WANT TO GO RIGHT BACK TO THE ESTATE, YOU KNOW!!
BUT LET ME TELL YOU! EVEN THOUGH I MIGHT NOT SEEM LIKE IT, I'M THE CHAIRPERSON THAT NEEDS TO PROTECT *HIS* SCHOOL!!
UNLIKE YOU, I'VE GOT SOME "HEAVVYYYY RESPONSIBILITIES"!!
YES ...
I KNOW ...
TH-TH-THUMP
tremble tremble
U... UM... ACTUALLY, ARIA-SAMA...
...JUST NOW SOMETHING VERY URGENT HAS HAPPENED AT THE MANSION...
HUH ?!
RUSH
HUSTLE
I DON'T WANT TO HEAR ANY EXCUSES !!
THERE'S NOTHING IN THE WORLD MORE URGENT THAN MY CHANGE OF CLOTHING!!
GRRR
MY CLOTHES ARE ALL SOGGY AND IT'S JUST GROSS !

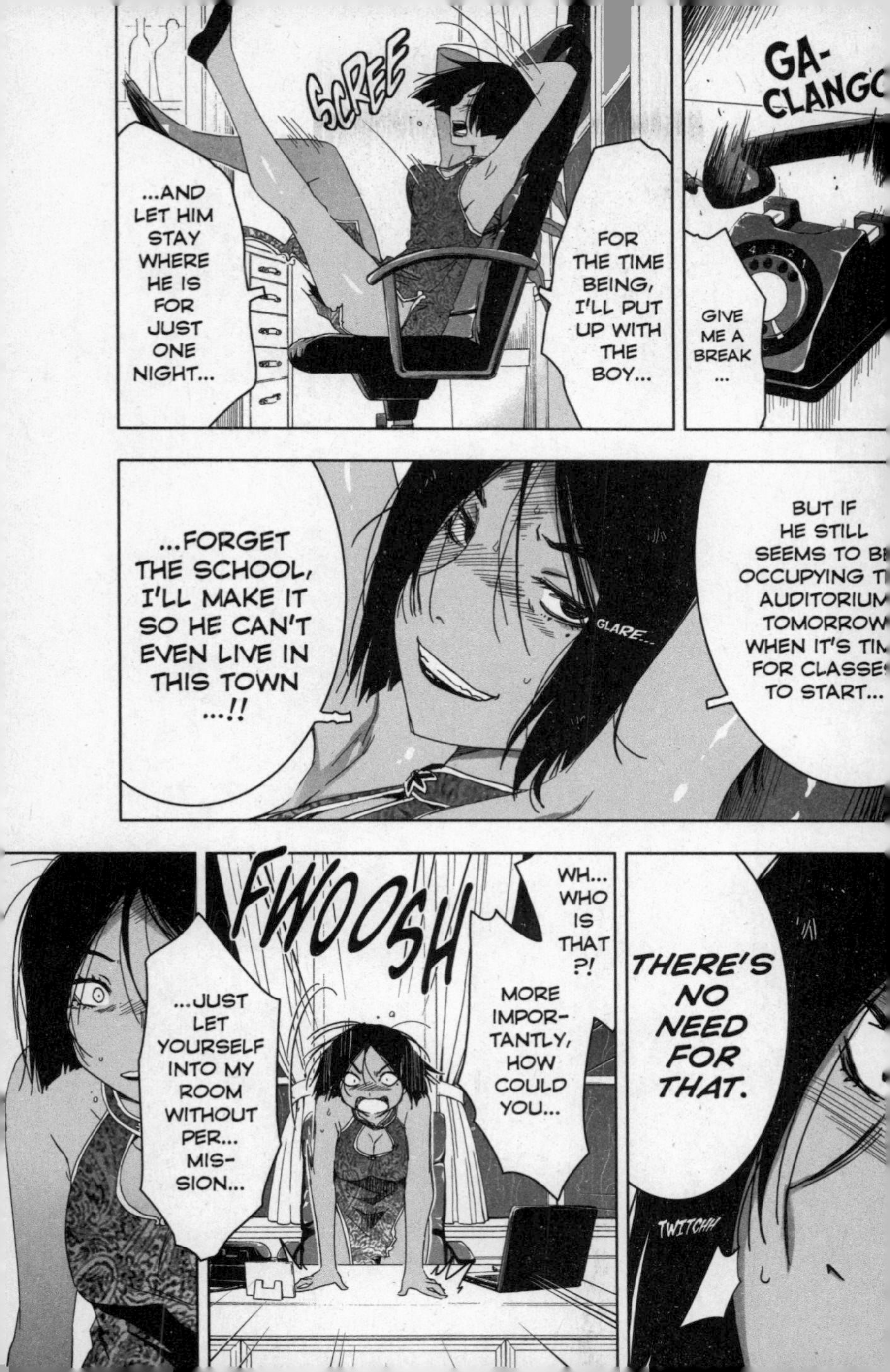
GA-CLANGO
GIVE ME A BREAK ...
SCREE
FOR THE TIME BEING, I'LL PUT UP WITH THE BOY...
...AND LET HIM STAY WHERE HE IS FOR JUST ONE NIGHT...
BUT IF HE STILL SEEMS TO B OCCUPYING T AUDITORIUM TOMORROW WHEN IT'S TIM FOR CLASSES TO START...
GLARE...
...FORGET THE SCHOOL, I'LL MAKE IT SO HE CAN'T EVEN LIVE IN THIS TOWN ...!!
THERE'S NO NEED FOR THAT.
TWITCH!!
FWOOSH
WH... WHO IS THAT?!
MORE IMPORTANTLY, HOW COULD YOU...
...JUST LET YOURSELF INTO MY ROOM WITHOUT PER... MISSION...

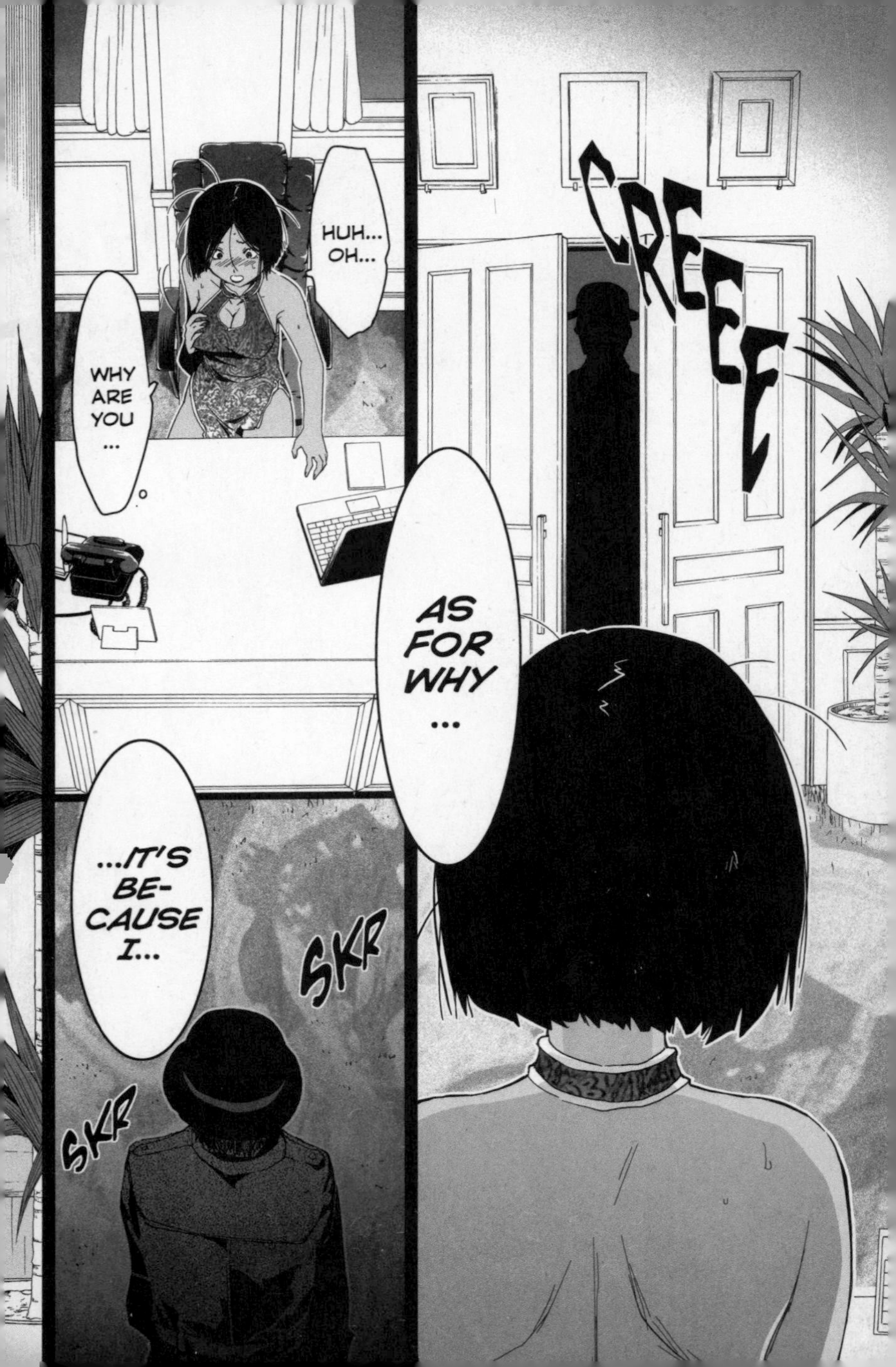
HUH... OH...
WHY ARE YOU ...?
CREEE
AS FOR WHY ...
...IT'S BE-CAUSE I...
SKR
SKR

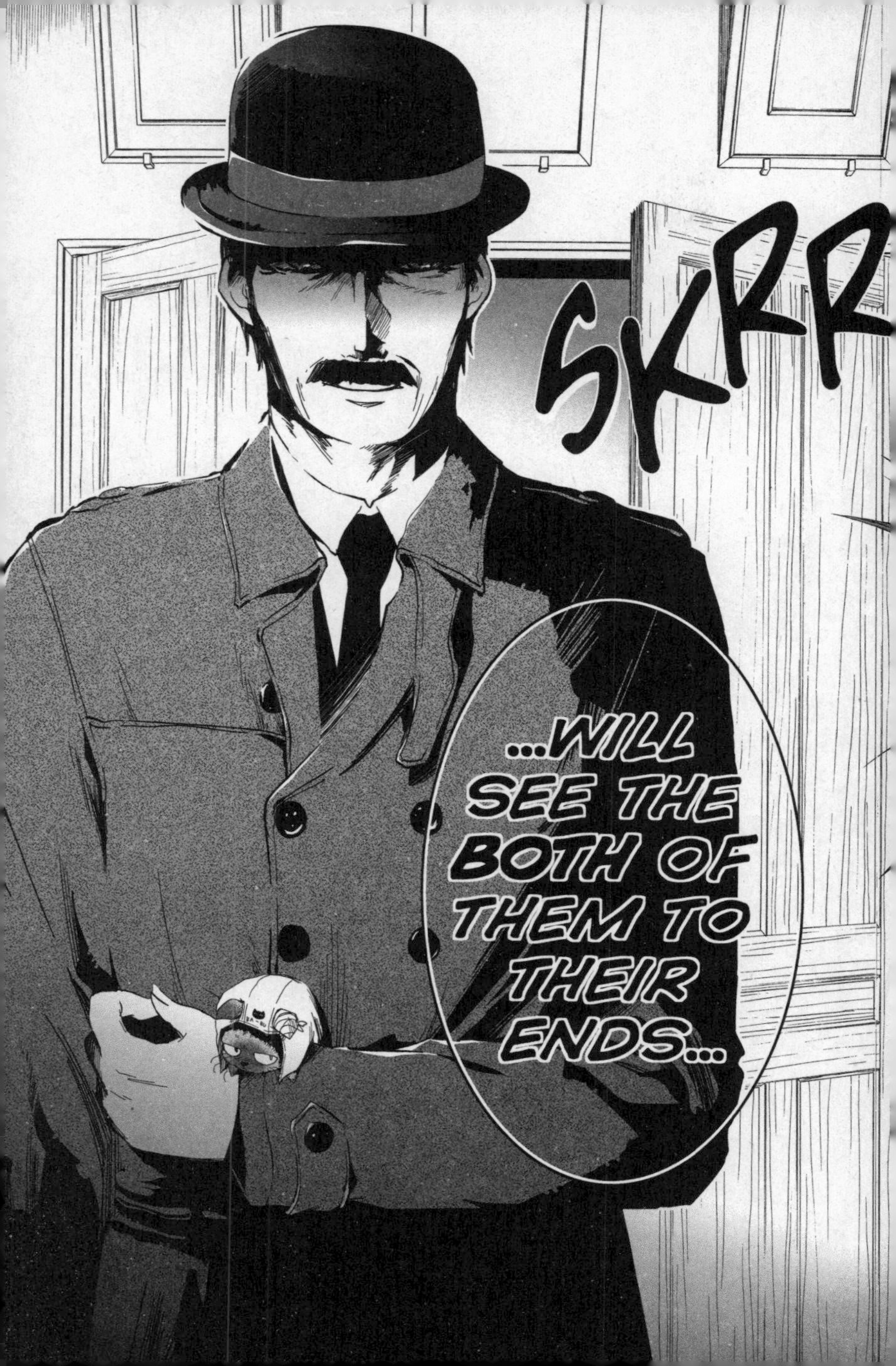
SKRR
...WILL SEE THE BOTH OF THEM TO THEIR ENDS...

SANKAREA

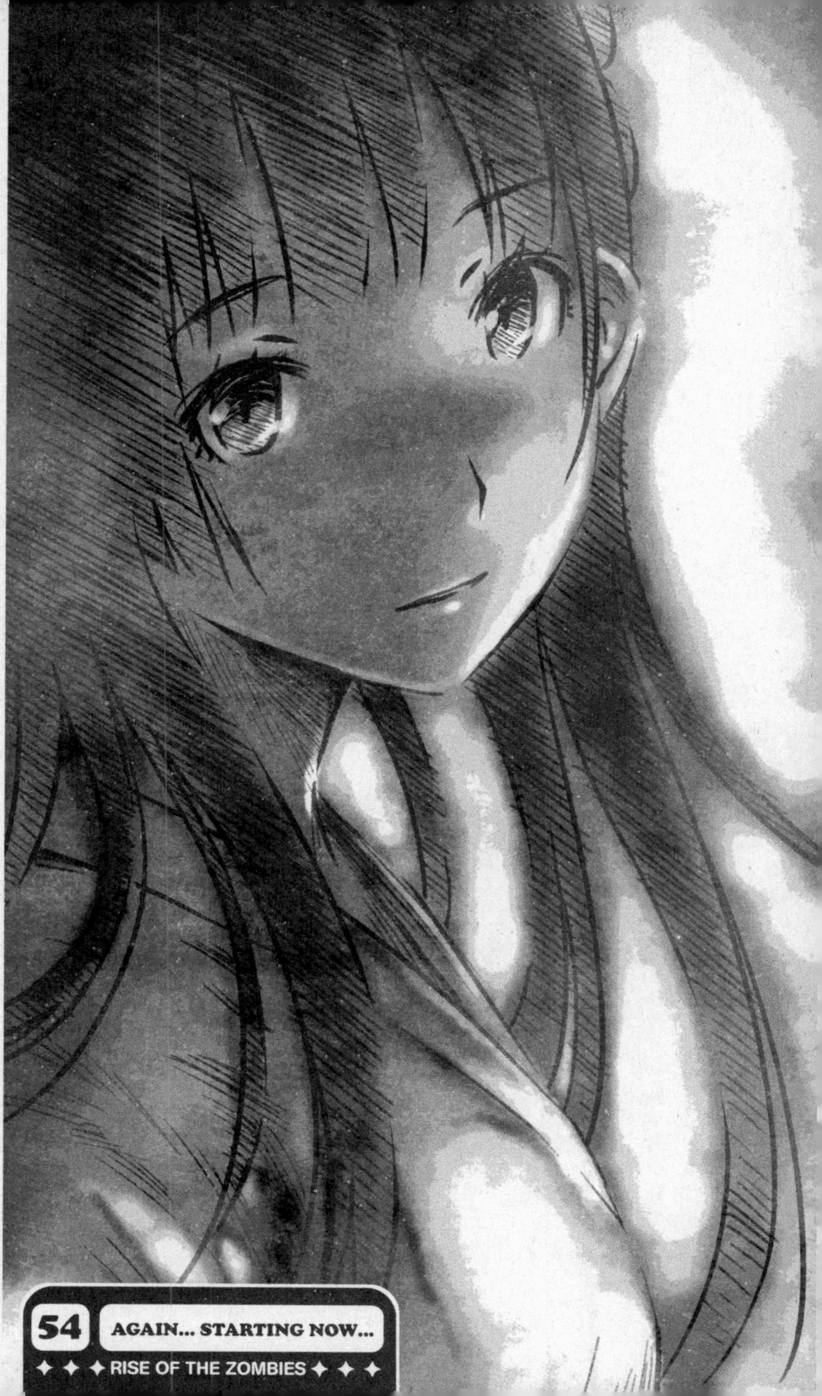
54
AGAIN... STARTING NOW...
✦ ✦ ✦ RISE OF THE ZOMBIES ✦ ✦ ✦

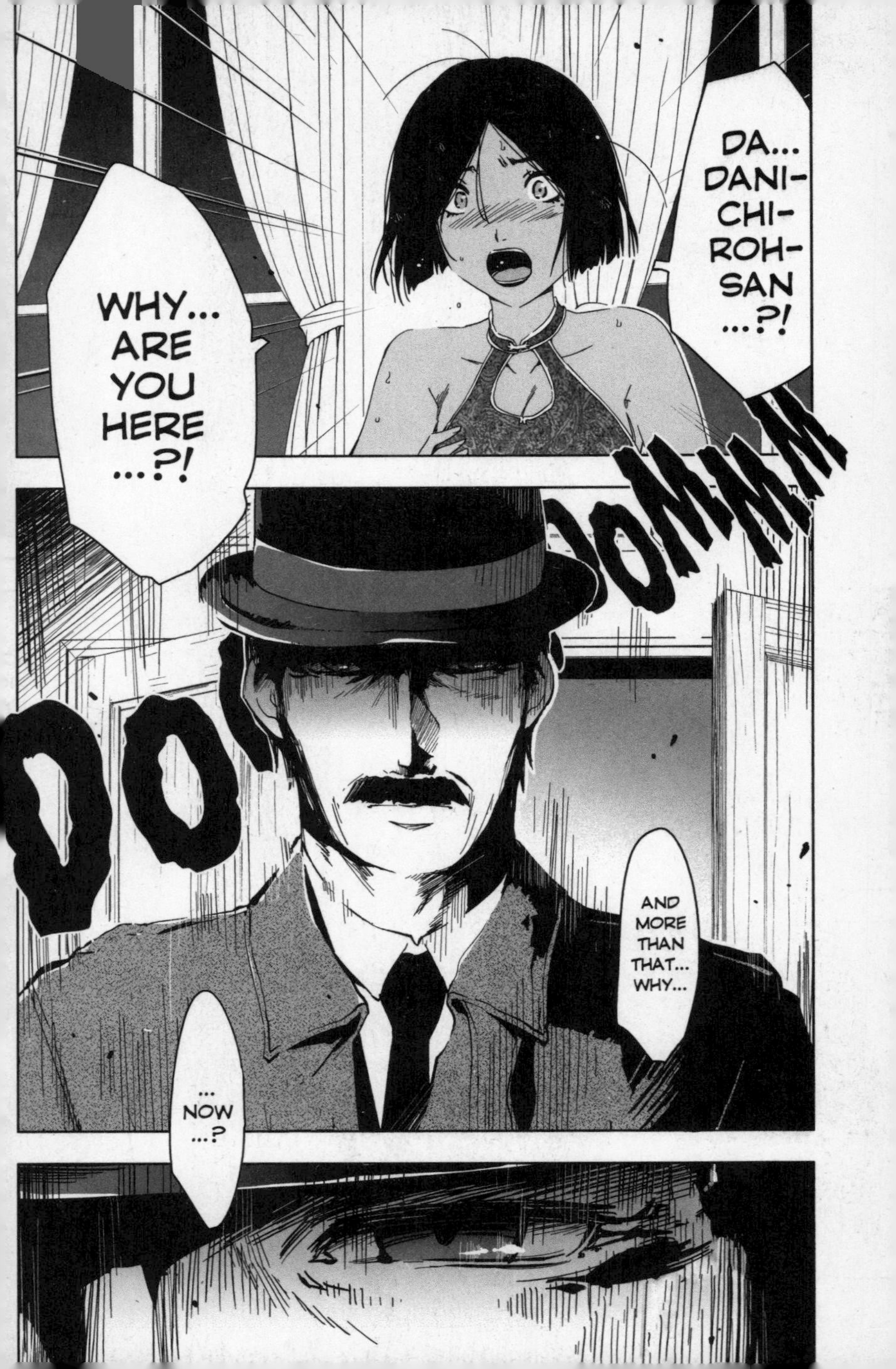
DA... DANI-CHI-ROH-SAN ...?!
WHY... ARE YOU HERE ...?!
DOMMM
DO
AND MORE THAN THAT... WHY...
... NOW ...?

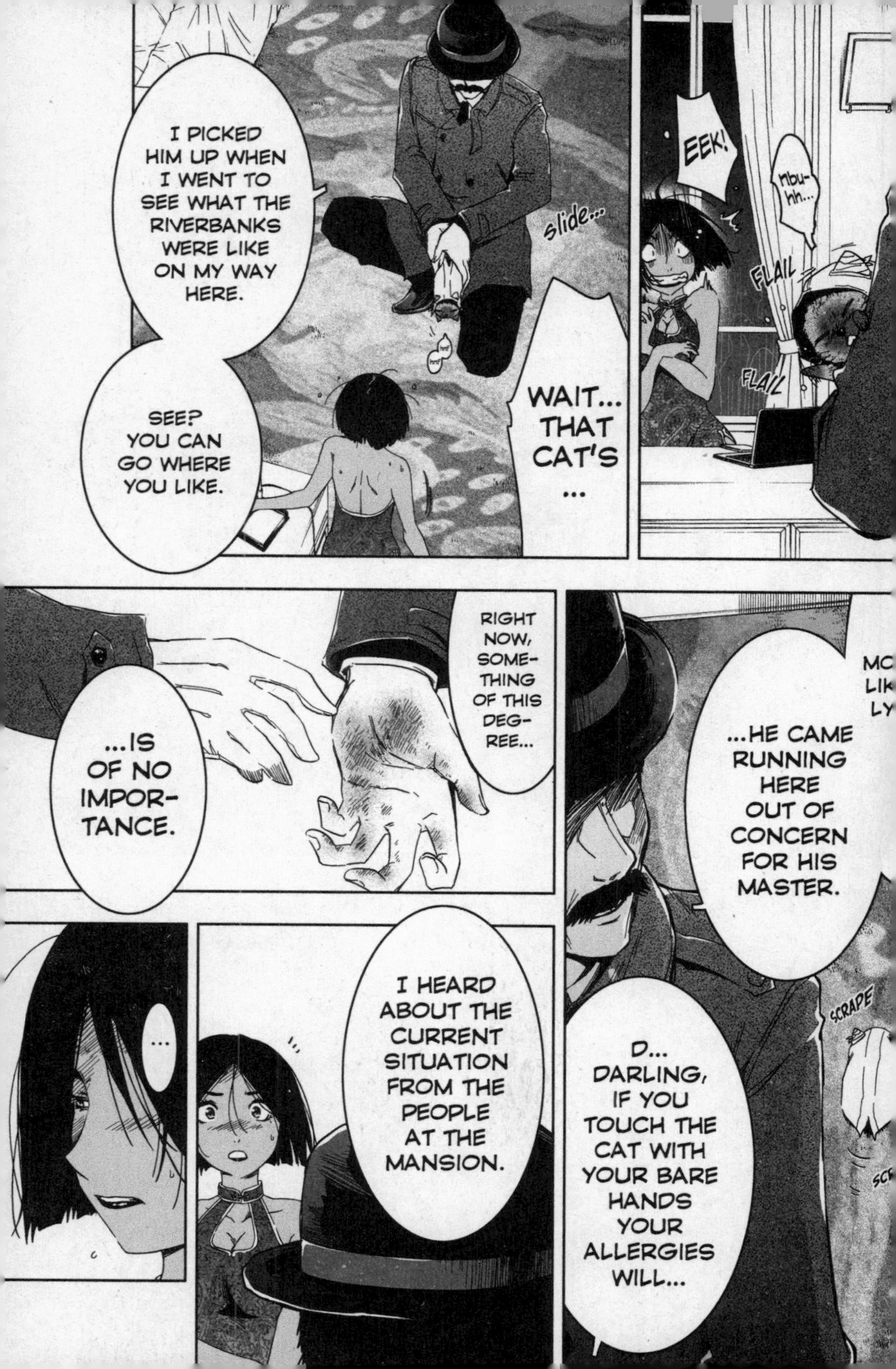
EEK!
nbu-hh...
FLAIL
FLAIL
I PICKED HIM UP WHEN I WENT TO SEE WHAT THE RIVERBANKS WERE LIKE ON MY WAY HERE.
slide...
WAIT... THAT CAT'S ...
SEE? YOU CAN GO WHERE YOU LIKE.
MC LIK LY
...HE CAME RUNNING HERE OUT OF CONCERN FOR HIS MASTER.
SCRAPE
D... DARLING, IF YOU TOUCH THE CAT WITH YOUR BARE HANDS YOUR ALLERGIES WILL...
SC
RIGHT NOW, SOME-THING OF THIS DEG-REE...
...IS OF NO IMPOR-TANCE.
I HEARD ABOUT THE CURRENT SITUATION FROM THE PEOPLE AT THE MANSION.
...

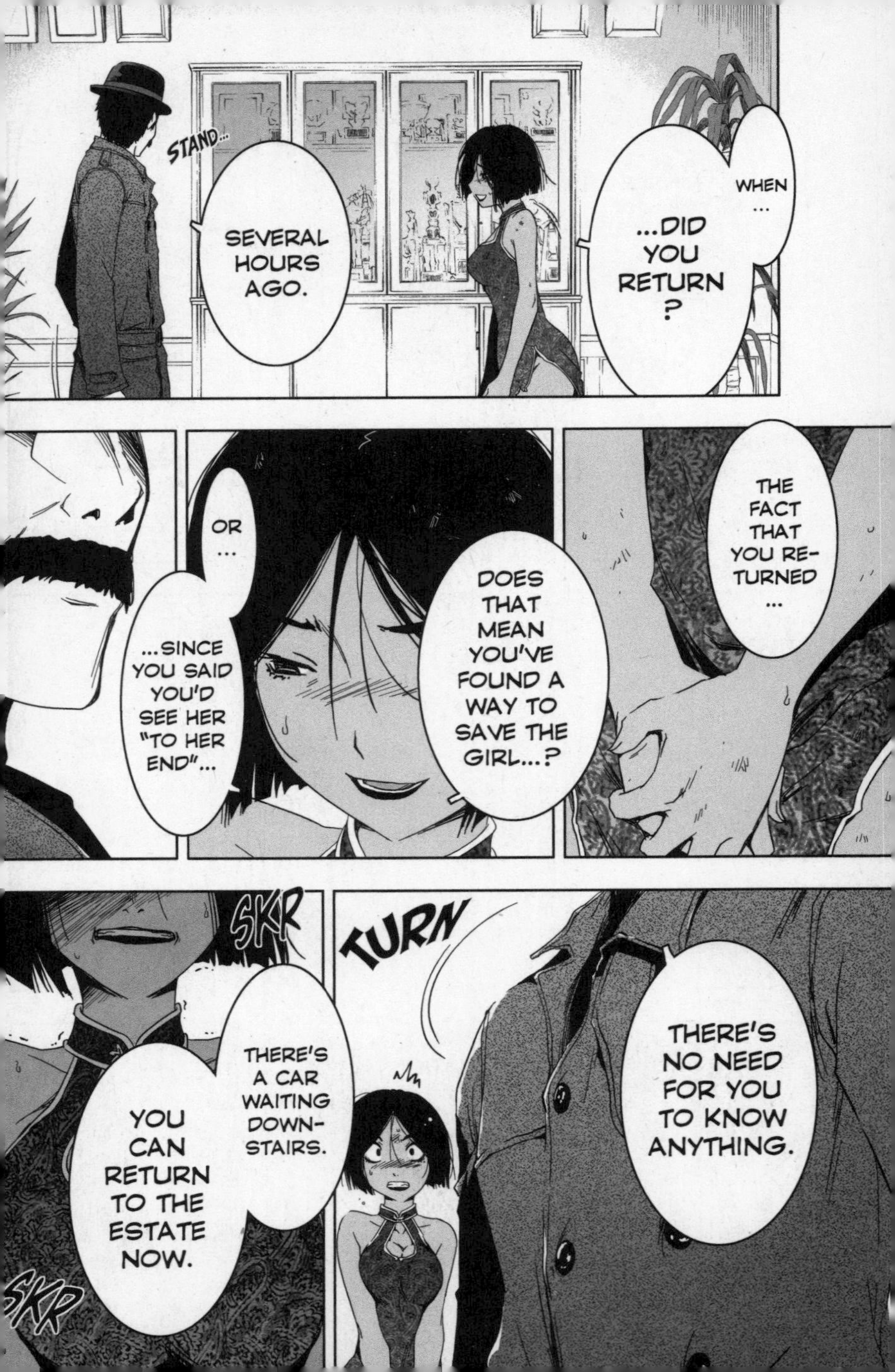

WHEN ...
...DID YOU RETURN?
SEVERAL HOURS AGO.
STAND...
THE FACT THAT YOU RE-TURNED ...
DOES THAT MEAN YOU'VE FOUND A WAY TO SAVE THE GIRL...?
OR ...
...SINCE YOU SAID YOU'D SEE HER "TO HER END"...
THERE'S NO NEED FOR YOU TO KNOW ANYTHING.
TURN
SKR
THERE'S A CAR WAITING DOWN-STAIRS.
YOU CAN RETURN TO THE ESTATE NOW.
SKR

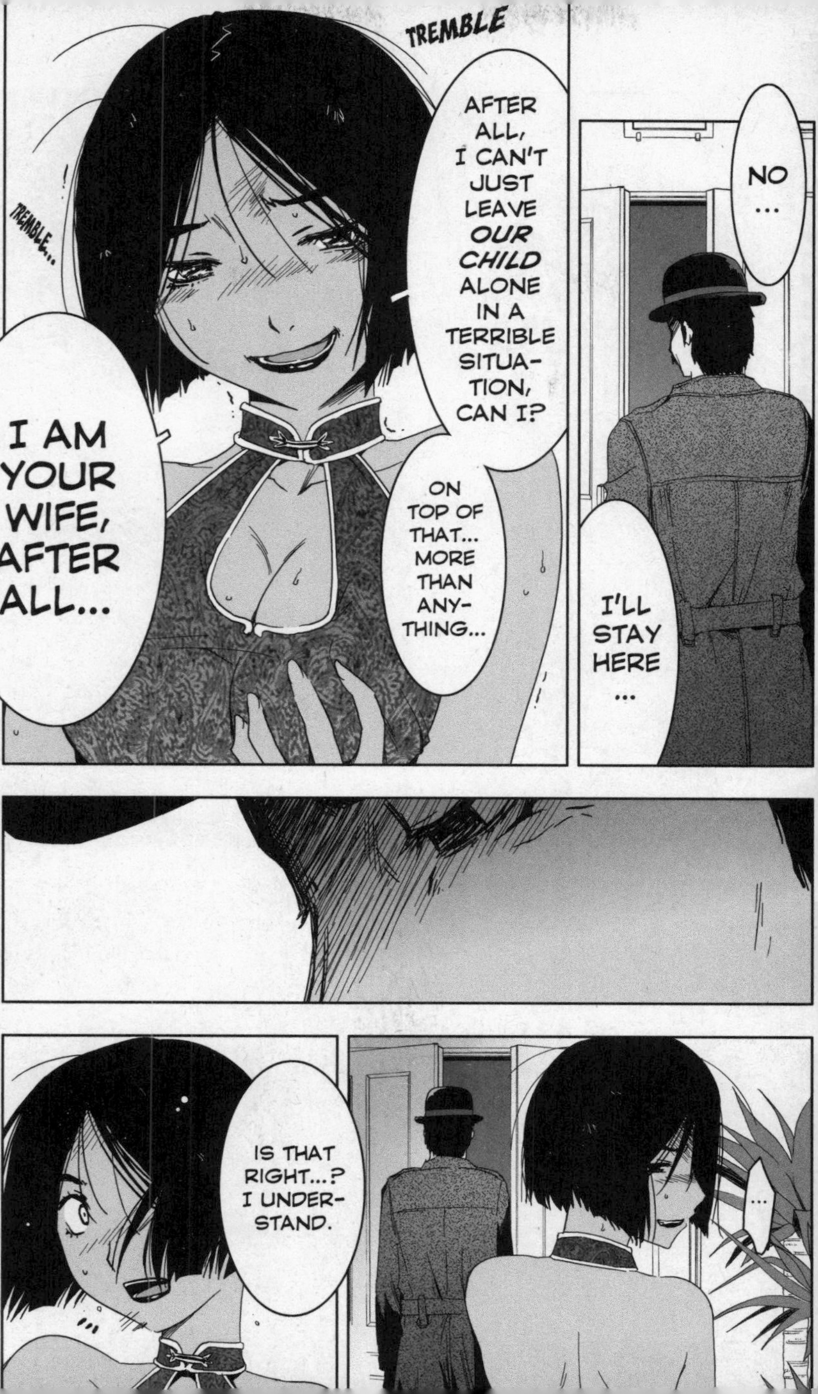
NO ...
I'LL STAY HERE ...
TREMBLE
AFTER ALL, I CAN'T JUST LEAVE OUR CHILD ALONE IN A TERRIBLE SITUATION, CAN I?
TREMBLE...
ON TOP OF THAT... MORE THAN ANYTHING...
I AM YOUR WIFE, AFTER ALL...
...
IS THAT RIGHT...? I UNDERSTAND.
...

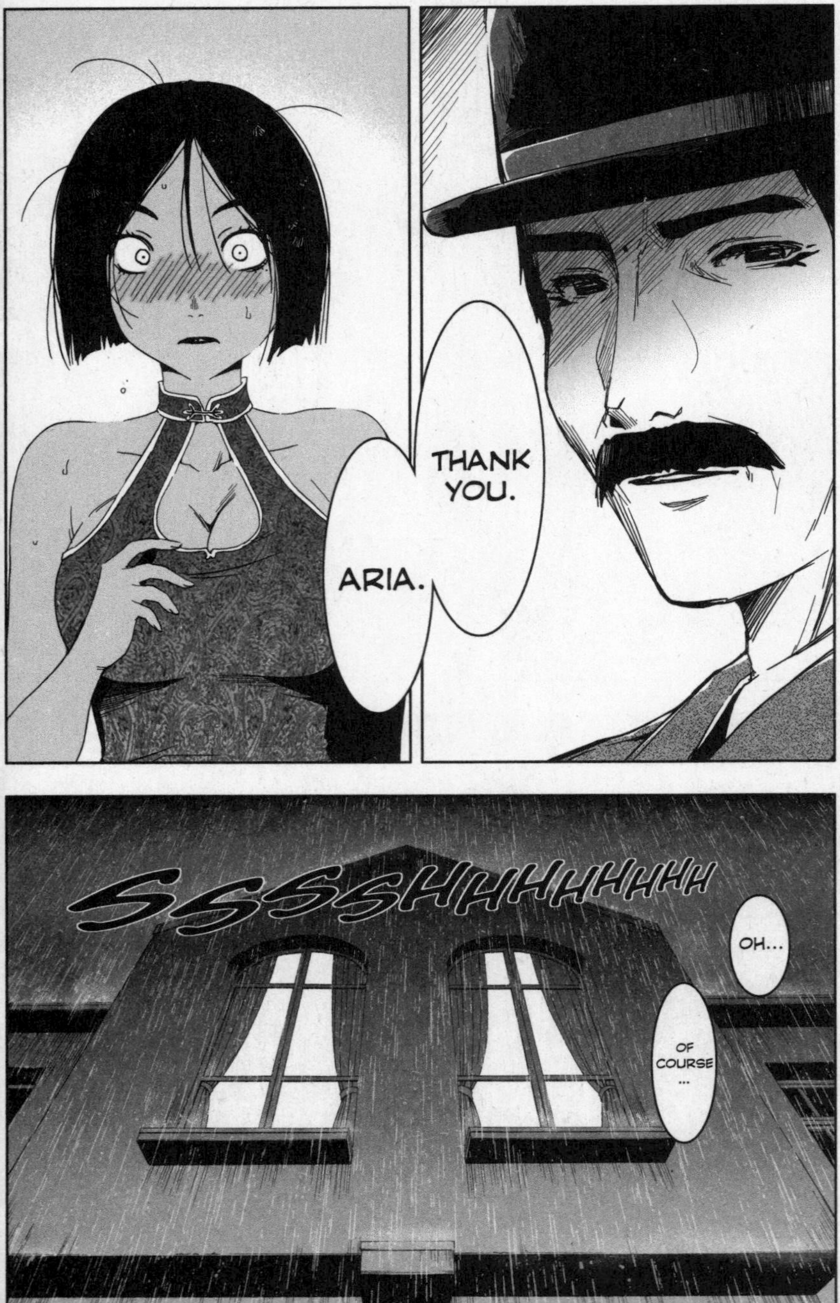
THANK YOU.
ARIA.
SSSSHHHHHHHH
OH...
OF COURSE ...

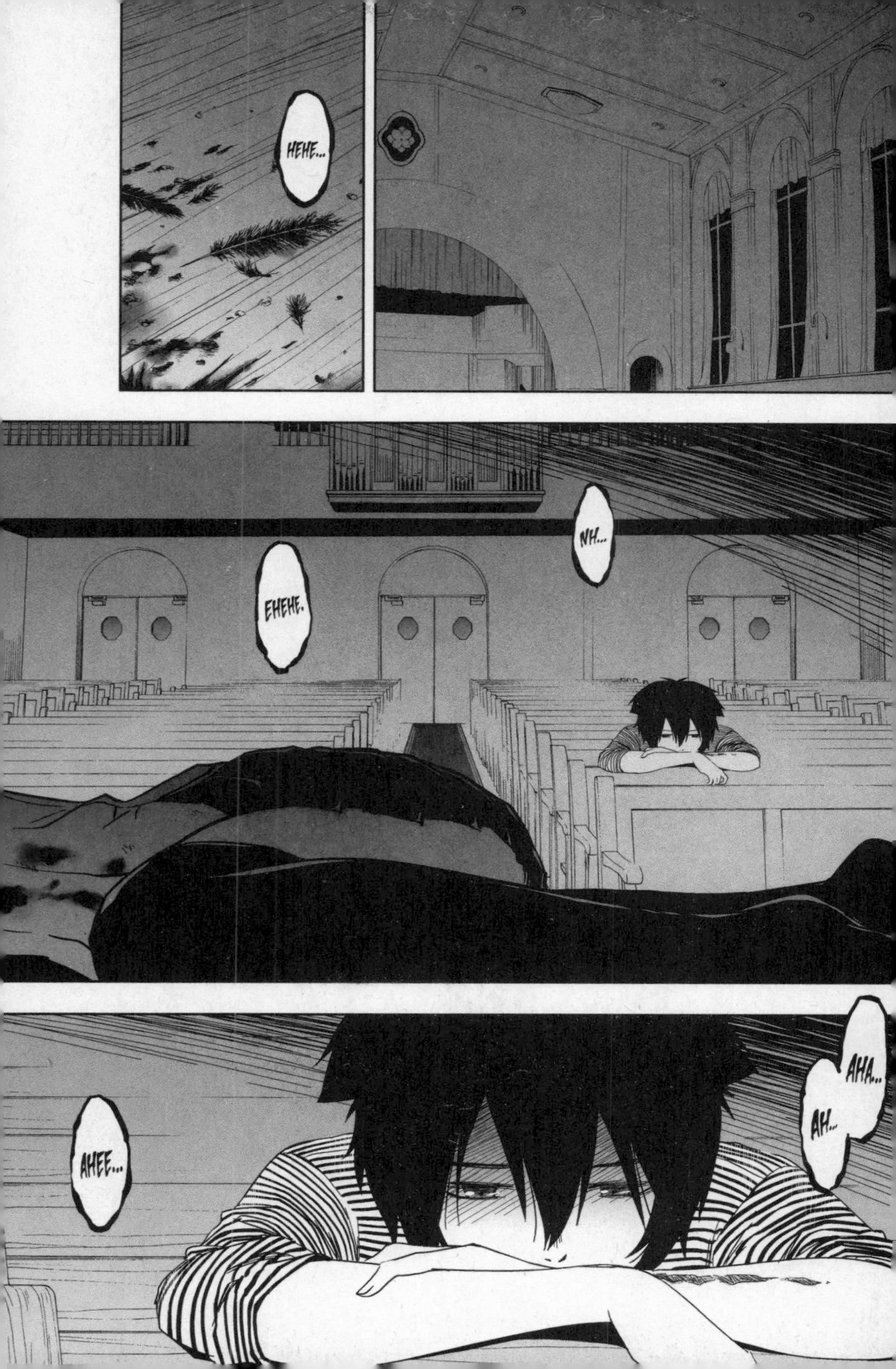
HEHE...
NH...
EHEHE.
AHA...
AH...
AHEE...

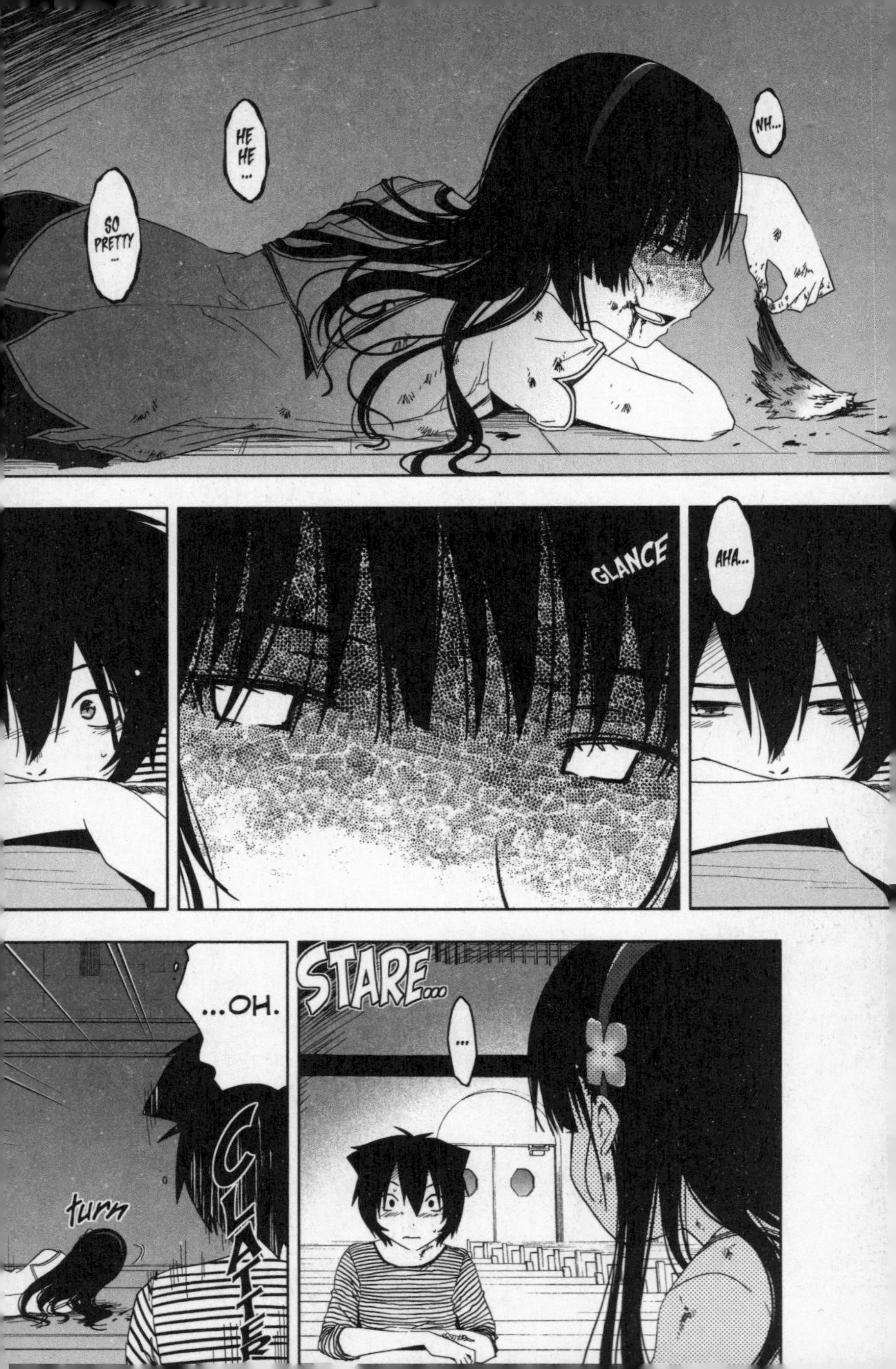
NH...
HE HE ...
SO PRETTY ...
AHA...
GLANCE
STARE...
...
...OH.
CLATTER
turn

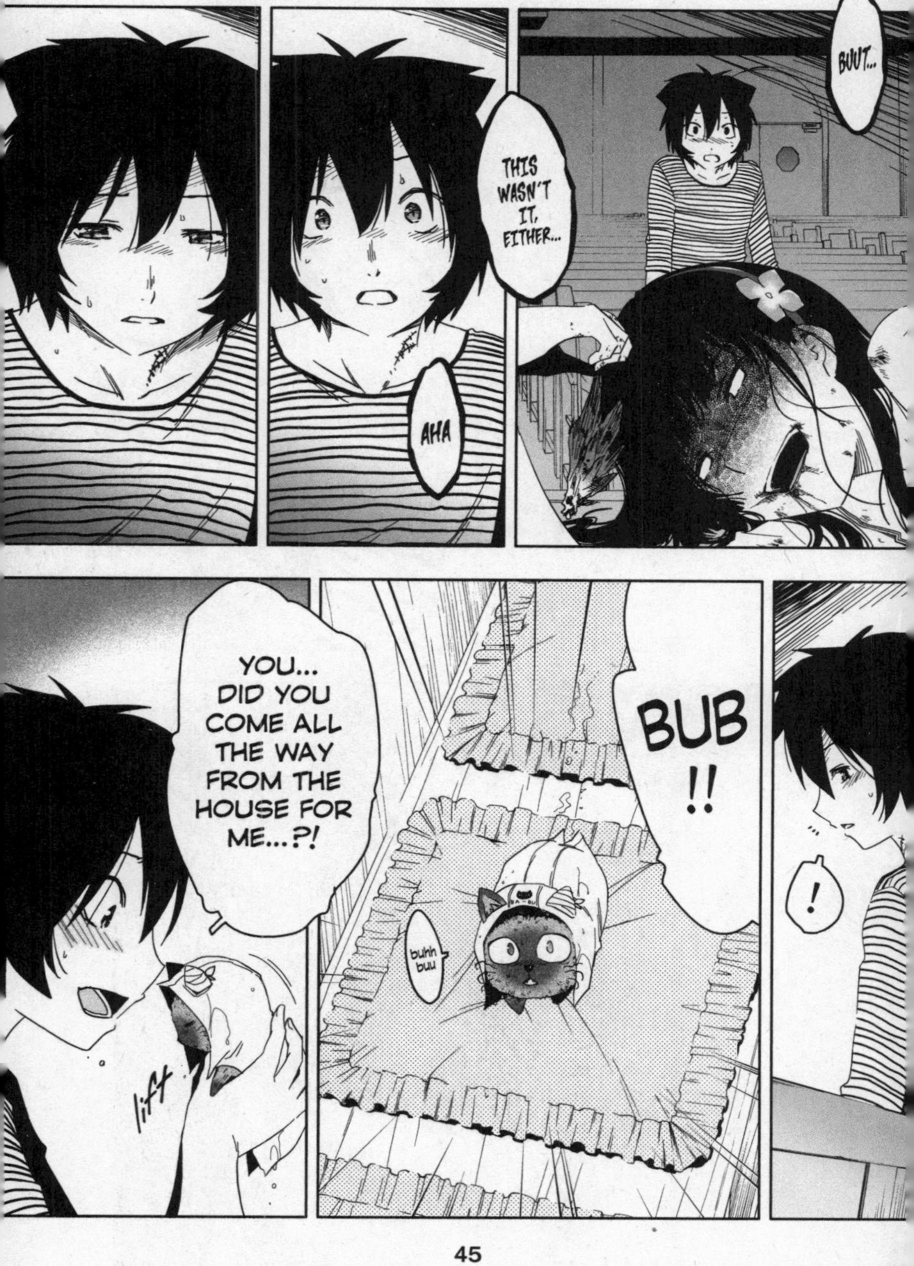
BUUT...
THIS WASN'T IT, EITHER...
AHA
!
BUB !!
buhh buu
YOU... DID YOU COME ALL THE WAY FROM THE HOUSE FOR ME...?!
lift

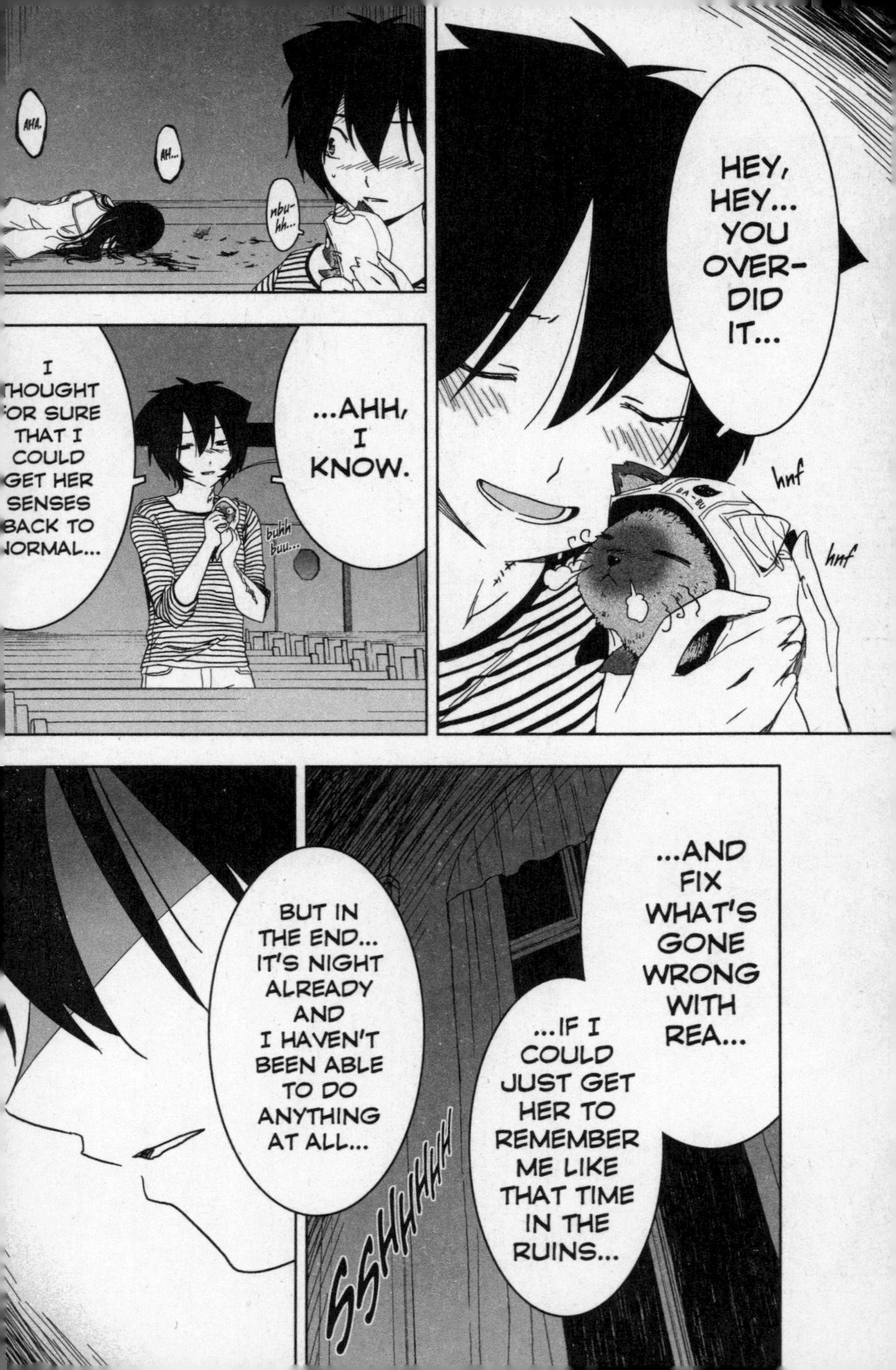
HEY, HEY... YOU OVER-DID IT...
hnf
hnf
AHA.
AH...
nbu-hh...
...AHH, I KNOW.
buhh buu...
I THOUGHT FOR SURE THAT I COULD GET HER SENSES BACK TO NORMAL...
...AND FIX WHAT'S GONE WRONG WITH REA...
...IF I COULD JUST GET HER TO REMEMBER ME LIKE THAT TIME IN THE RUINS...
SSHHHHH
BUT IN THE END... IT'S NIGHT ALREADY AND I HAVEN'T BEEN ABLE TO DO ANYTHING AT ALL...

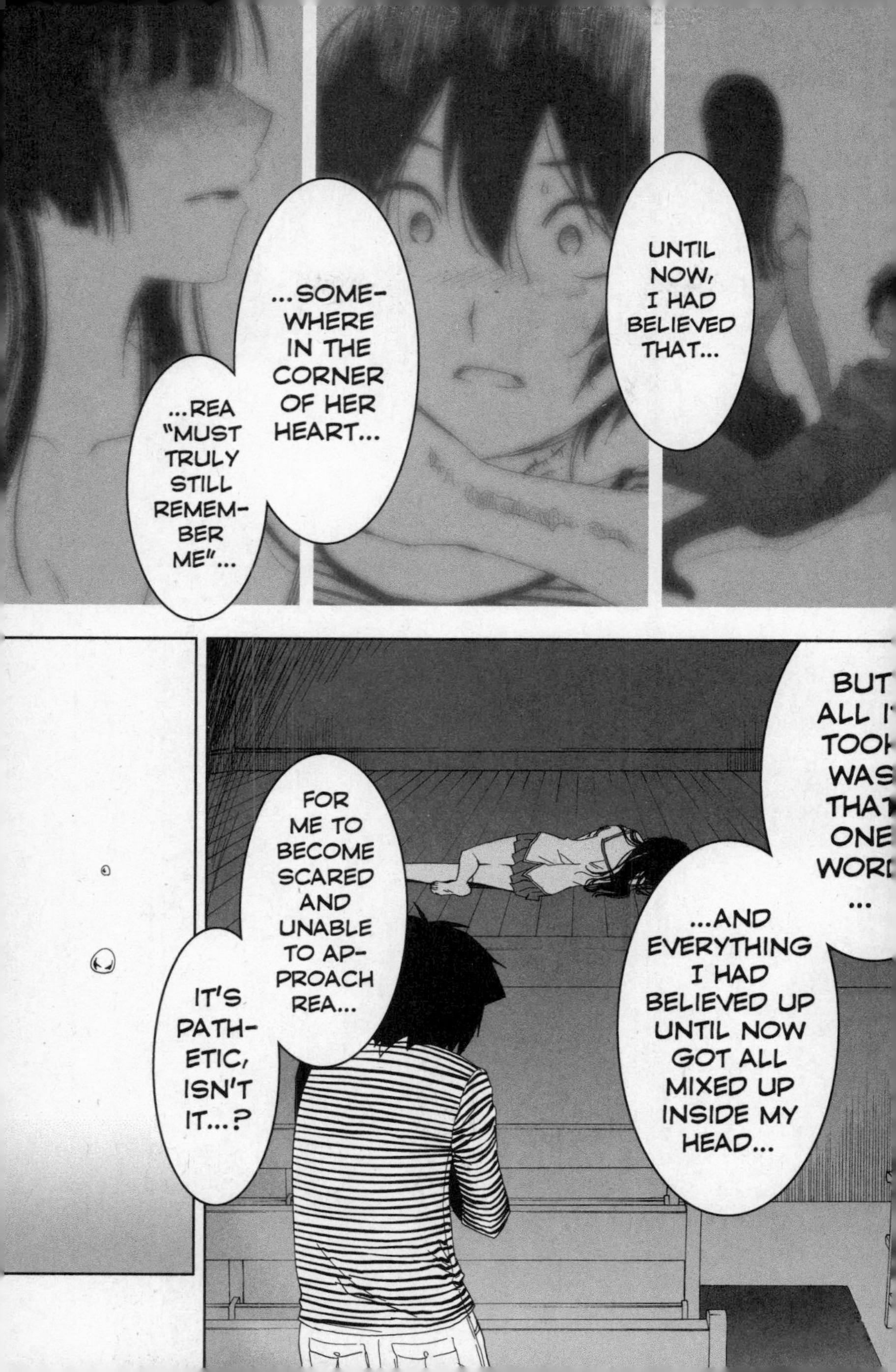
UNTIL NOW, I HAD BELIEVED THAT...
...SOMEWHERE IN THE CORNER OF HER HEART...
...REA "MUST TRULY STILL REMEMBER ME"...
BUT ALL I TOOK WAS THAT ONE WORD ...
...AND EVERYTHING I HAD BELIEVED UP UNTIL NOW GOT ALL MIXED UP INSIDE MY HEAD...
FOR ME TO BECOME SCARED AND UNABLE TO APPROACH REA...
IT'S PATHETIC, ISN'T IT...?

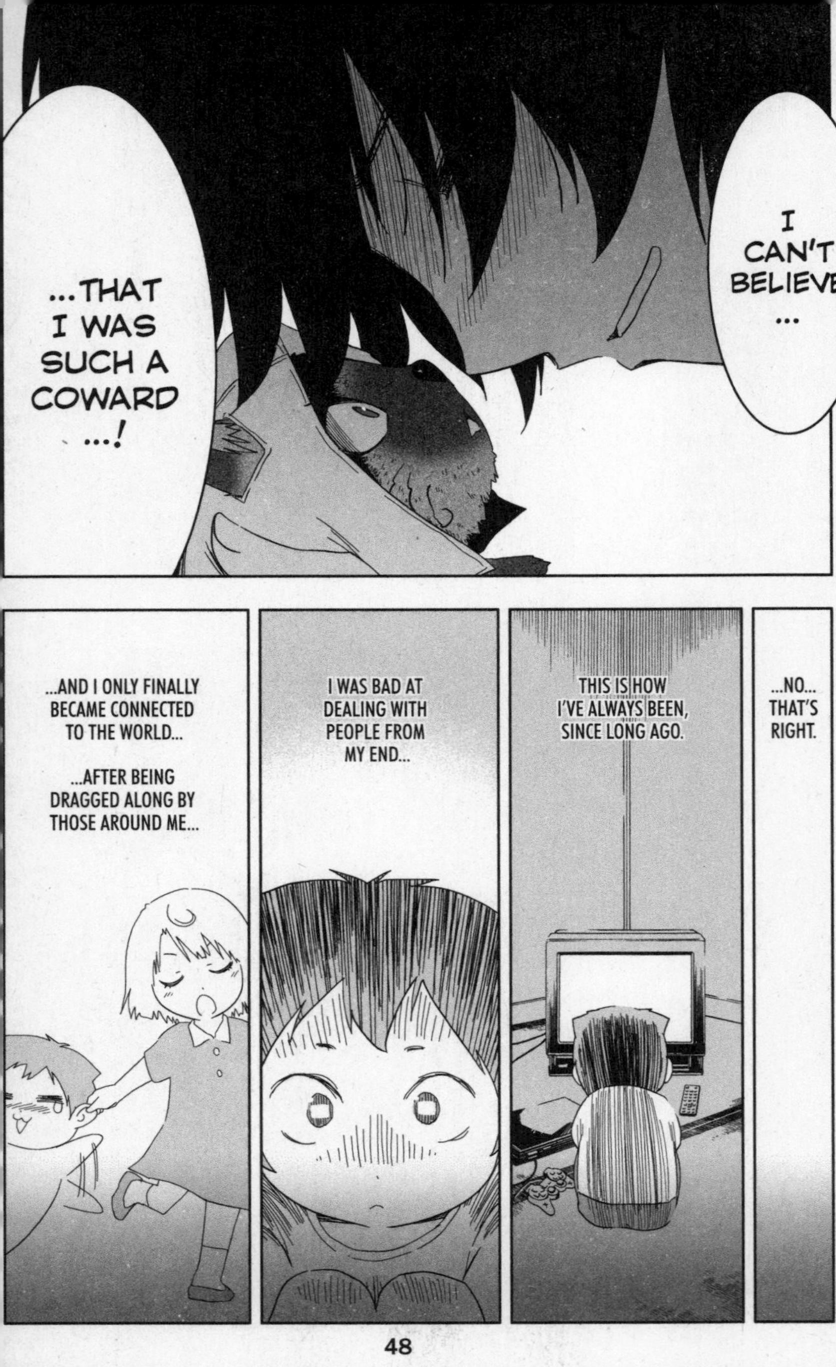
I CAN'T BELIEVE ...
...THAT I WAS SUCH A COWARD ...!
...NO... THAT'S RIGHT.
THIS IS HOW I'VE ALWAYS BEEN, SINCE LONG AGO.
I WAS BAD AT DEALING WITH PEOPLE FROM MY END...
...AND I ONLY FINALLY BECAME CONNECTED TO THE WORLD...
...AFTER BEING DRAGGED ALONG BY THOSE AROUND ME...

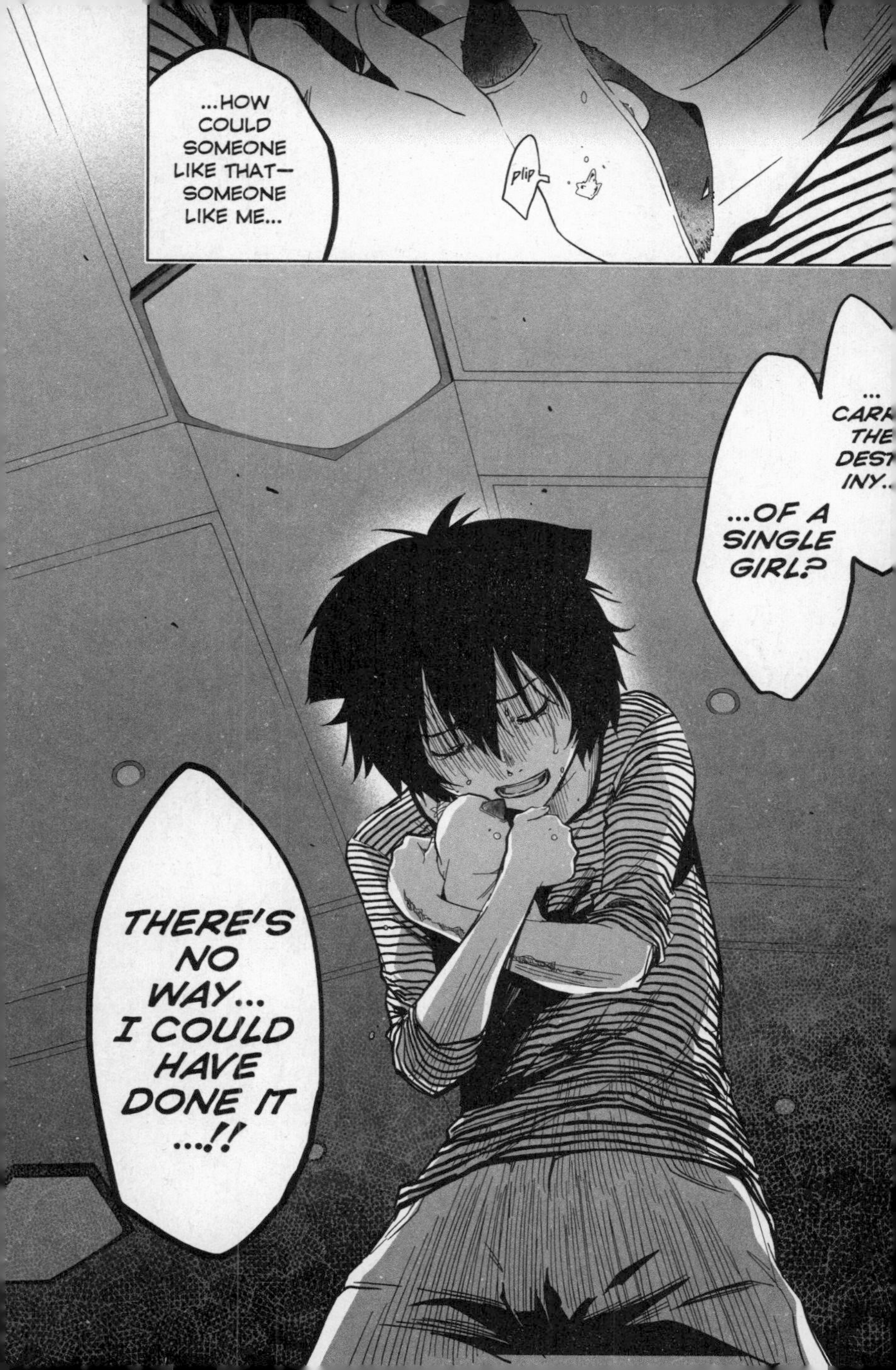
...HOW COULD SOMEONE LIKE THAT— SOMEONE LIKE ME...
plip
... CAR THE DEST INY..
...OF A SINGLE GIRL?
THERE'S NO WAY... I COULD HAVE DONE IT ...!!

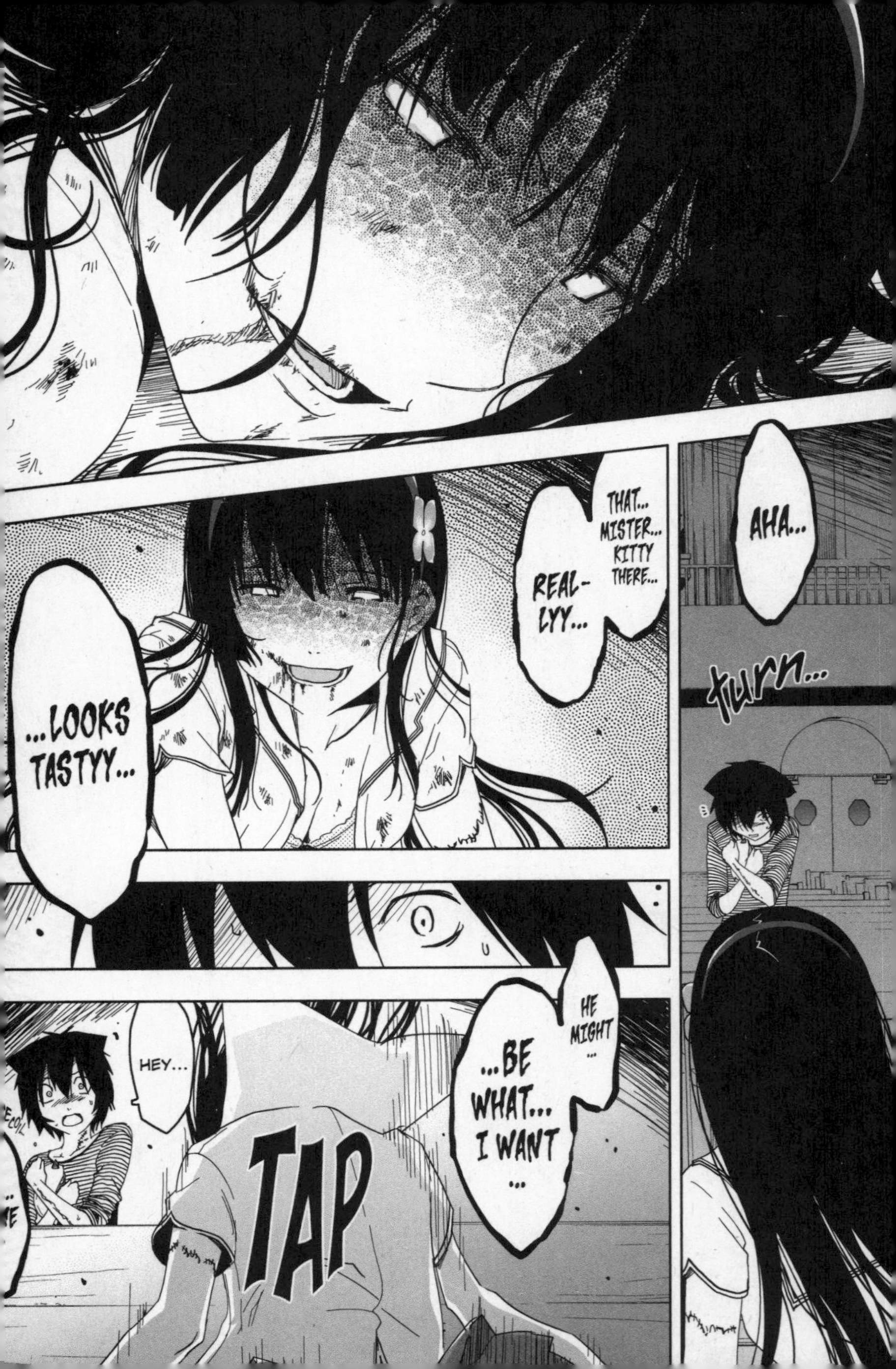
AHA...
turn...
THAT... MISTER... KITTY THERE...
REAL-LYY...
...LOOKS TASTYY...
HE MIGHT...
...BE WHAT... I WANT...
HEY...
TAP

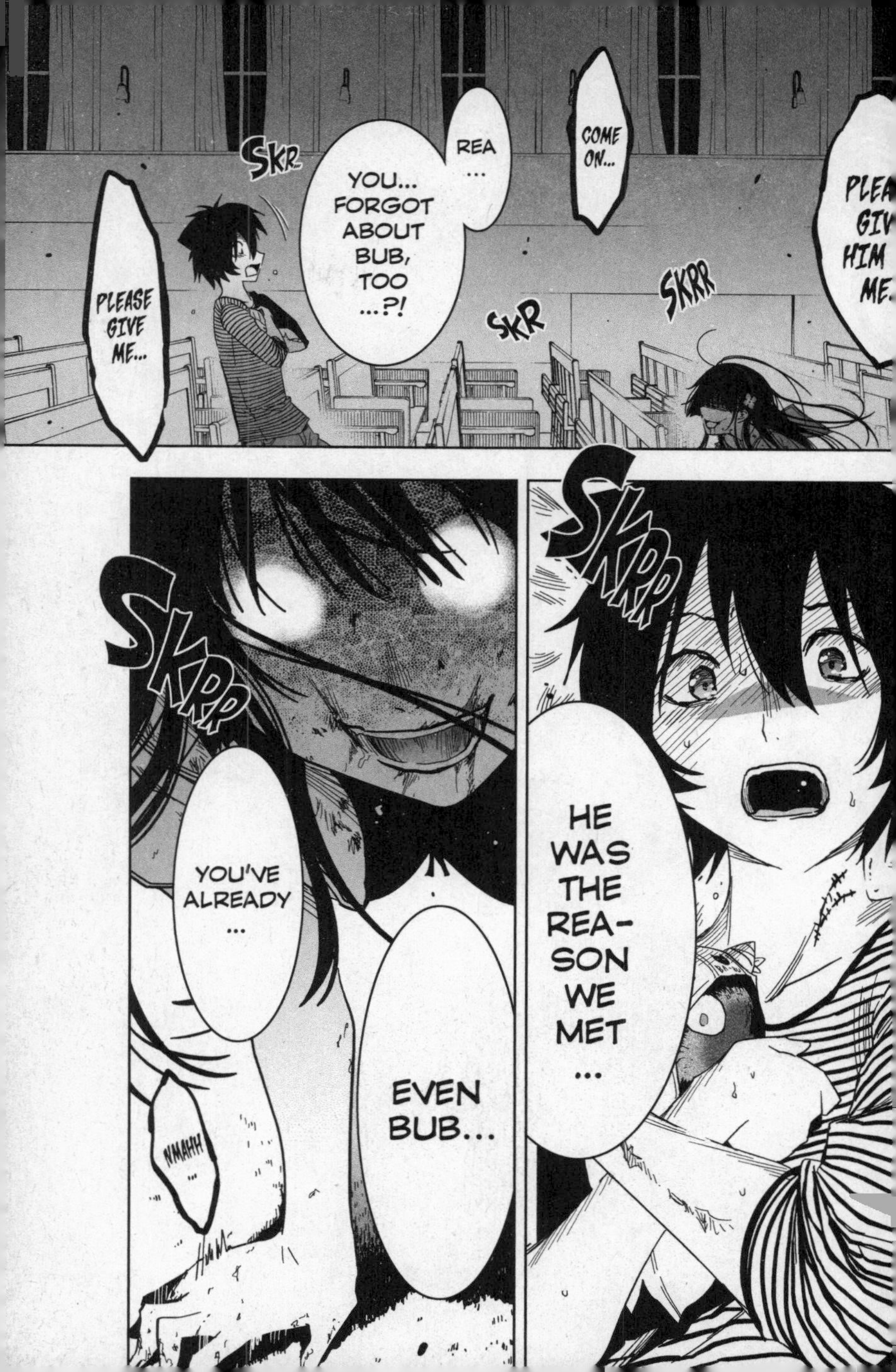
PLEA GIV HIM ME.
COME ON...
SKRR
SKR
REA ...
YOU... FORGOT ABOUT BUB, TOO ...?!
SKR
PLEASE GIVE ME...
SKRR
HE WAS THE REA-SON WE MET ...
SKRR
YOU'VE ALREADY ...
EVEN BUB...
NMAHH ...

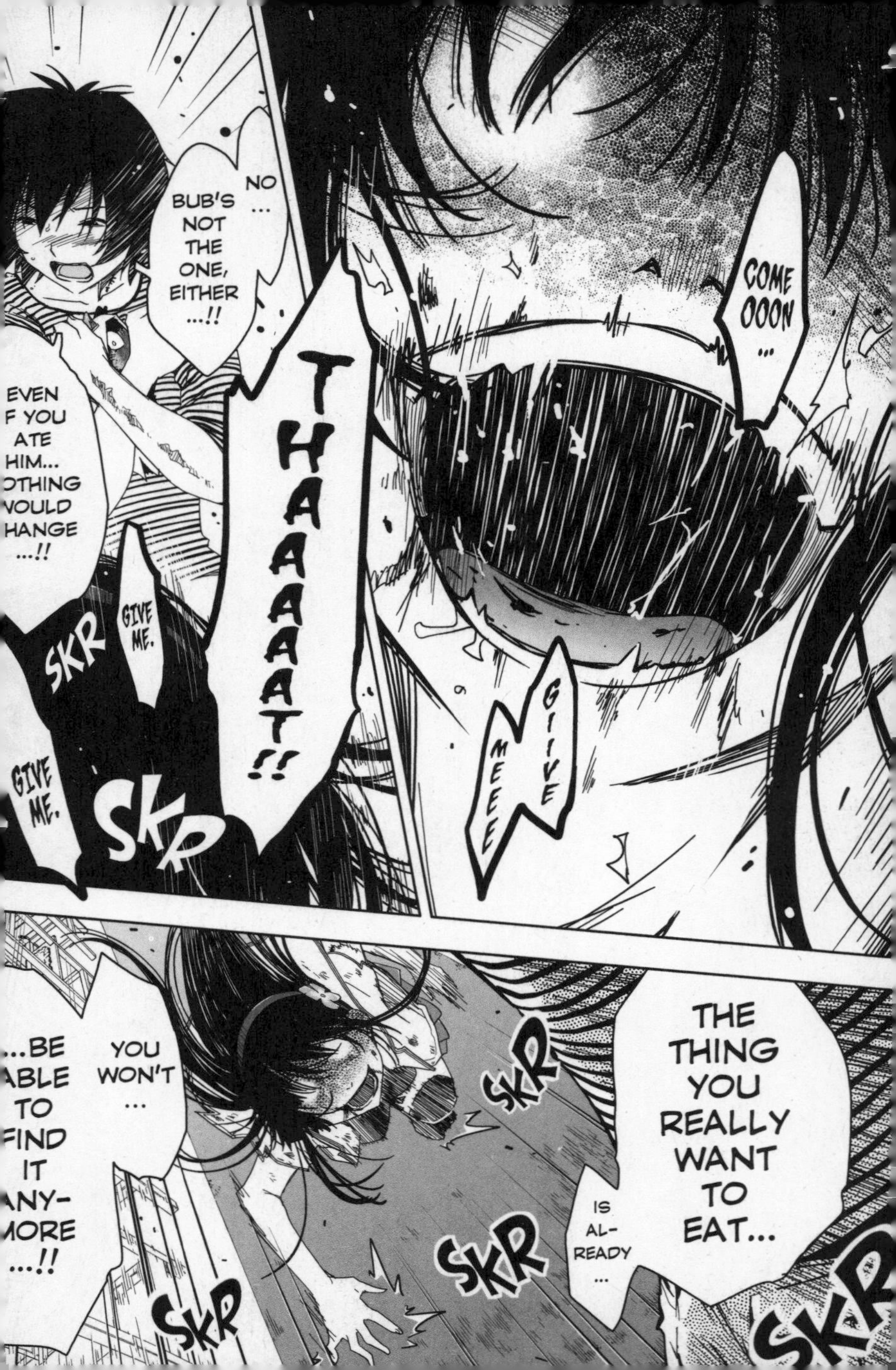
COME OOON ...
THAAAAAAT!!
GIIVE MEEE
NO ... BUB'S NOT THE ONE, EITHER ...!!
EVEN F YOU ATE HIM... OTHING VOULD HANGE ...!!
GIVE ME.
SKR
GIVE ME.
SKR
THE THING YOU REALLY WANT TO EAT...
IS AL-READY ...
SKR
SKR
SKR
YOU WON'T ...
...BE ABLE TO FIND IT NY-ORE ...!!
SKR

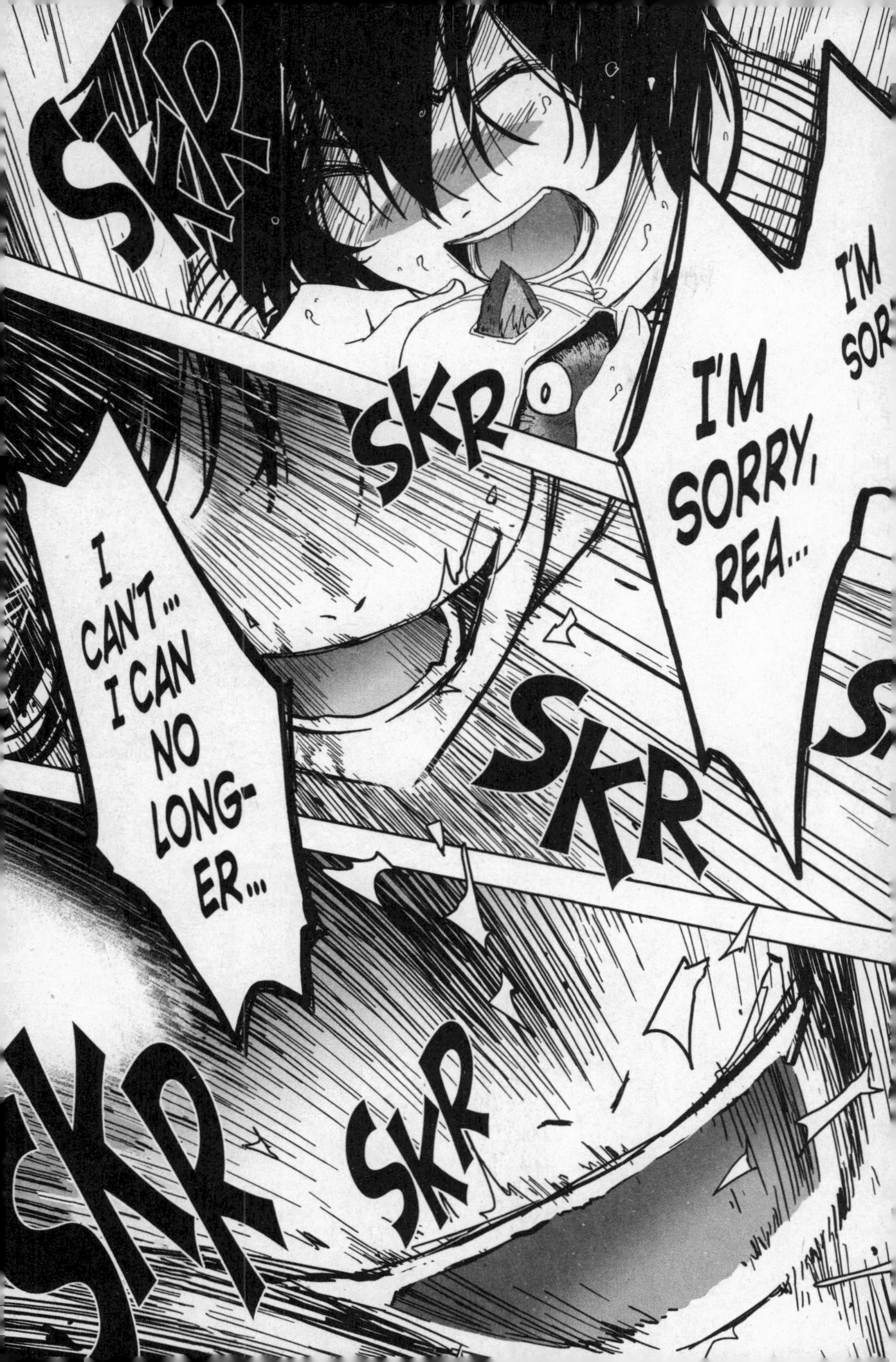
I'M SOR
I'M SORRY, REA...
SKR
SKR
SKR
I CAN'T... I CAN NO LONG-ER...
SKR
SKR

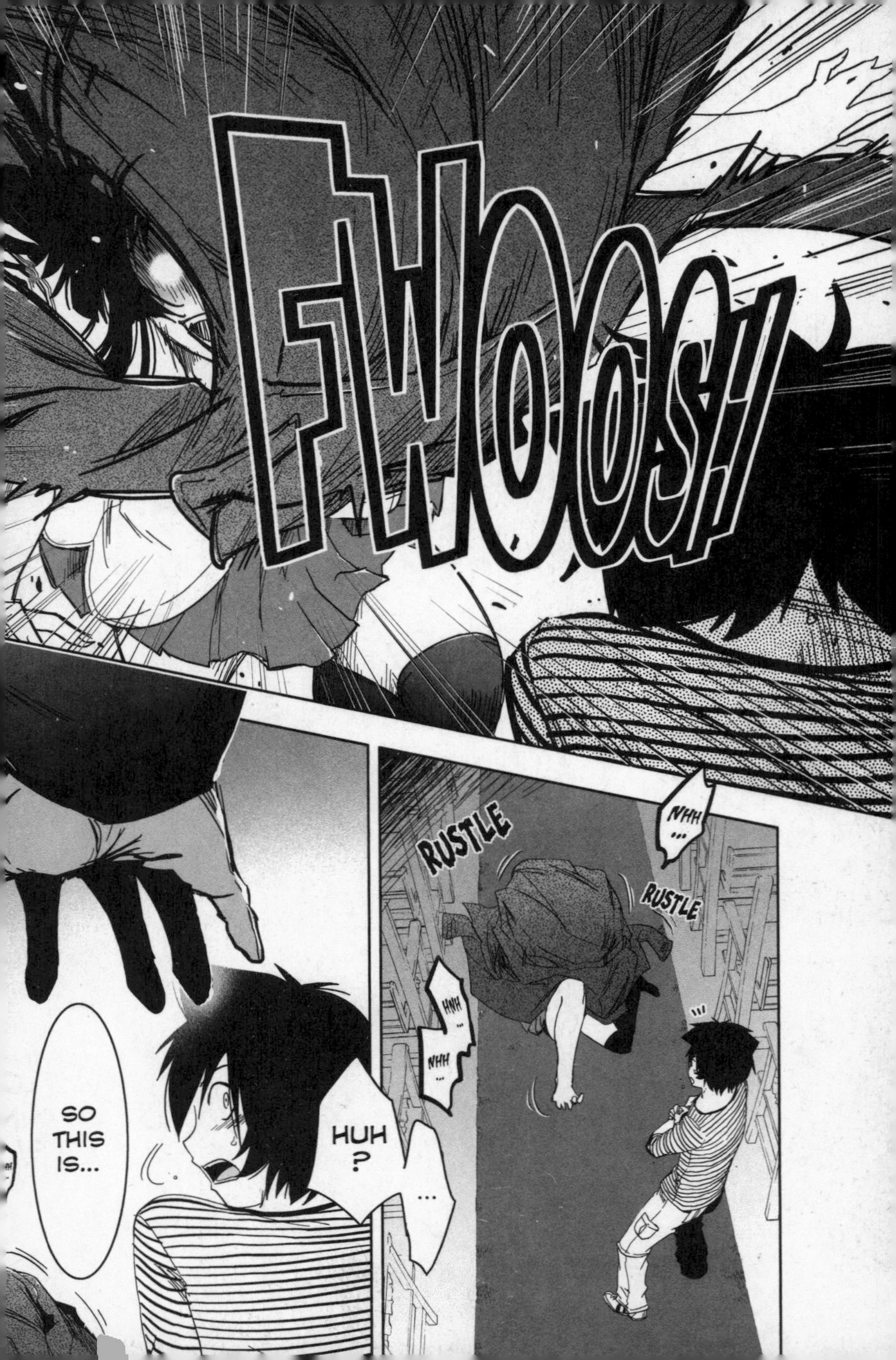
FWOOSH!
NHH ...
RUSTLE
RUSTLE
NHH ... NHH ...
...
HUH ?
...
SO THIS IS...

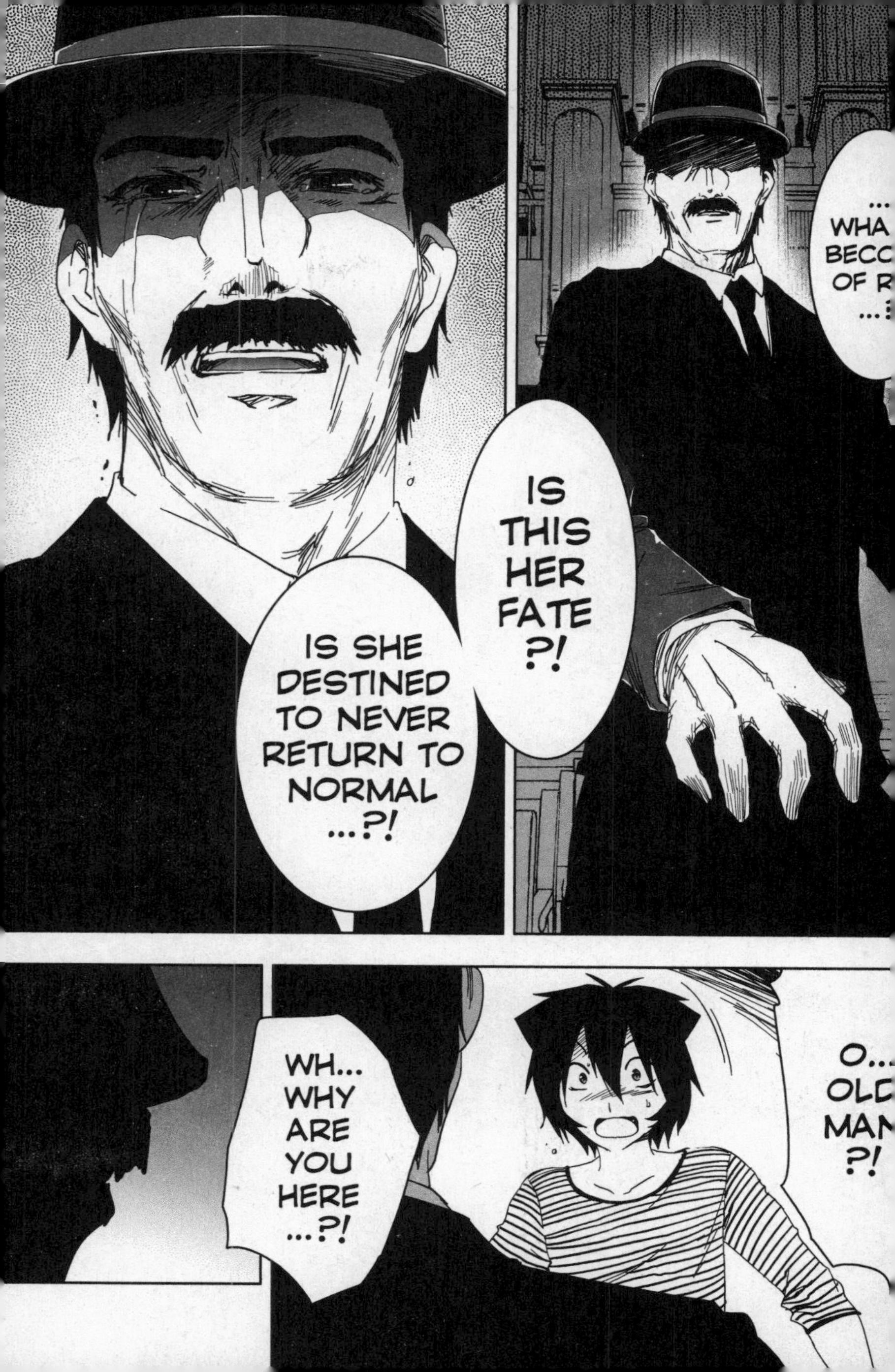
... WHA BECO OF R ...?
IS THIS HER FATE ?!
IS SHE DESTINED TO NEVER RETURN TO NORMAL ...?!
O... OLD MAN ?!
WH... WHY ARE YOU HERE ...?!

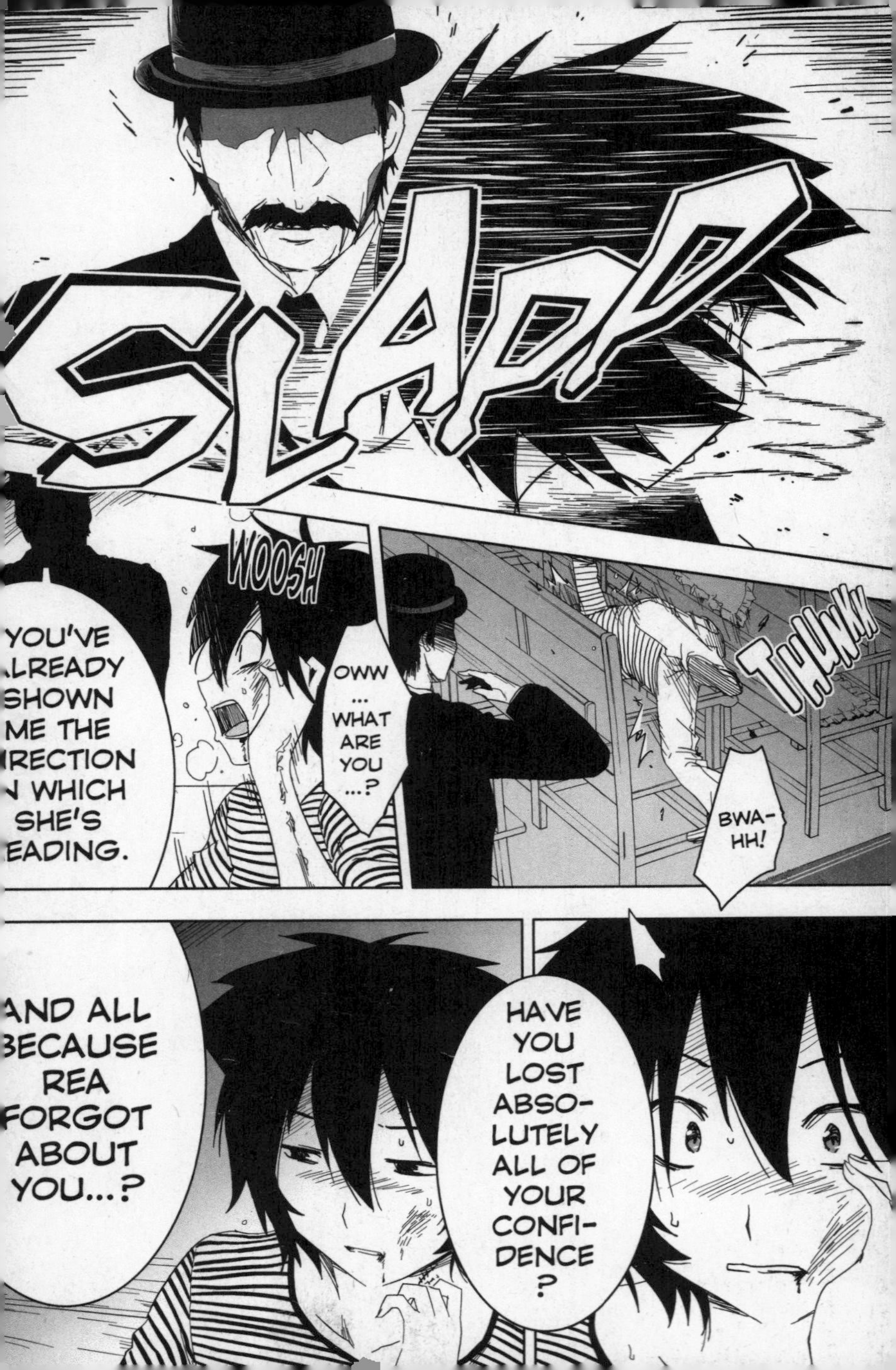
SLAP
THUNKK
BWA-HH!
WOOSH
OWW ... WHAT ARE YOU ...?
YOU'VE LREADY SHOWN ME THE RECTION N WHICH SHE'S EADING.
HAVE YOU LOST ABSO-LUTELY ALL OF YOUR CONFI-DENCE?
AND ALL BECAUSE REA FORGOT ABOUT YOU...?

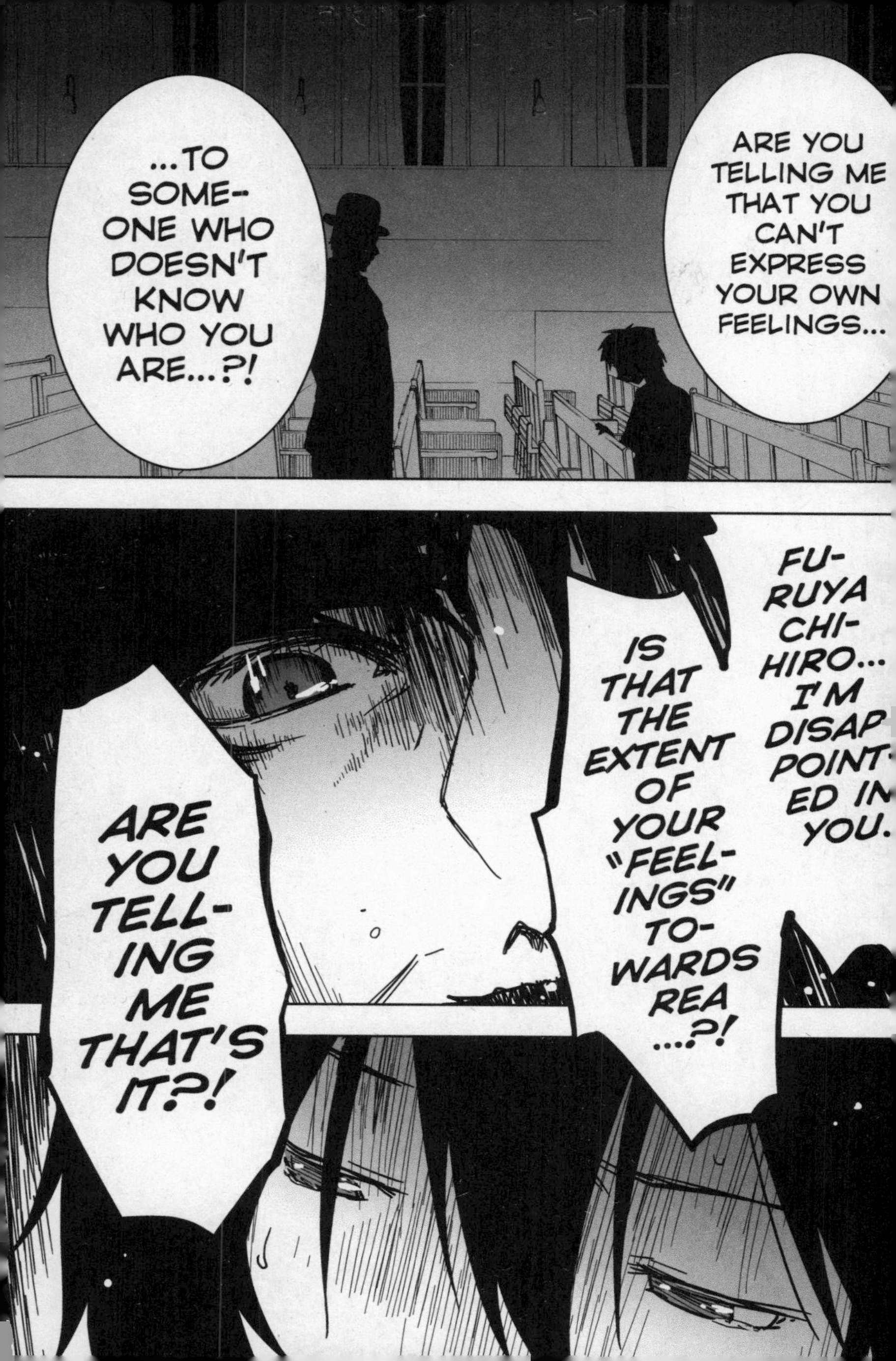
ARE YOU TELLING ME THAT YOU CAN'T EXPRESS YOUR OWN FEELINGS...
...TO SOME-ONE WHO DOESN'T KNOW WHO YOU ARE...?!
FU-RUYA CHI-HIRO... I'M DISAP-POINT-ED IN YOU.
IS THAT THE EXTENT OF YOUR "FEEL-INGS" TO-WARDS REA ...?!
ARE YOU TELL-ING ME THAT'S IT?!

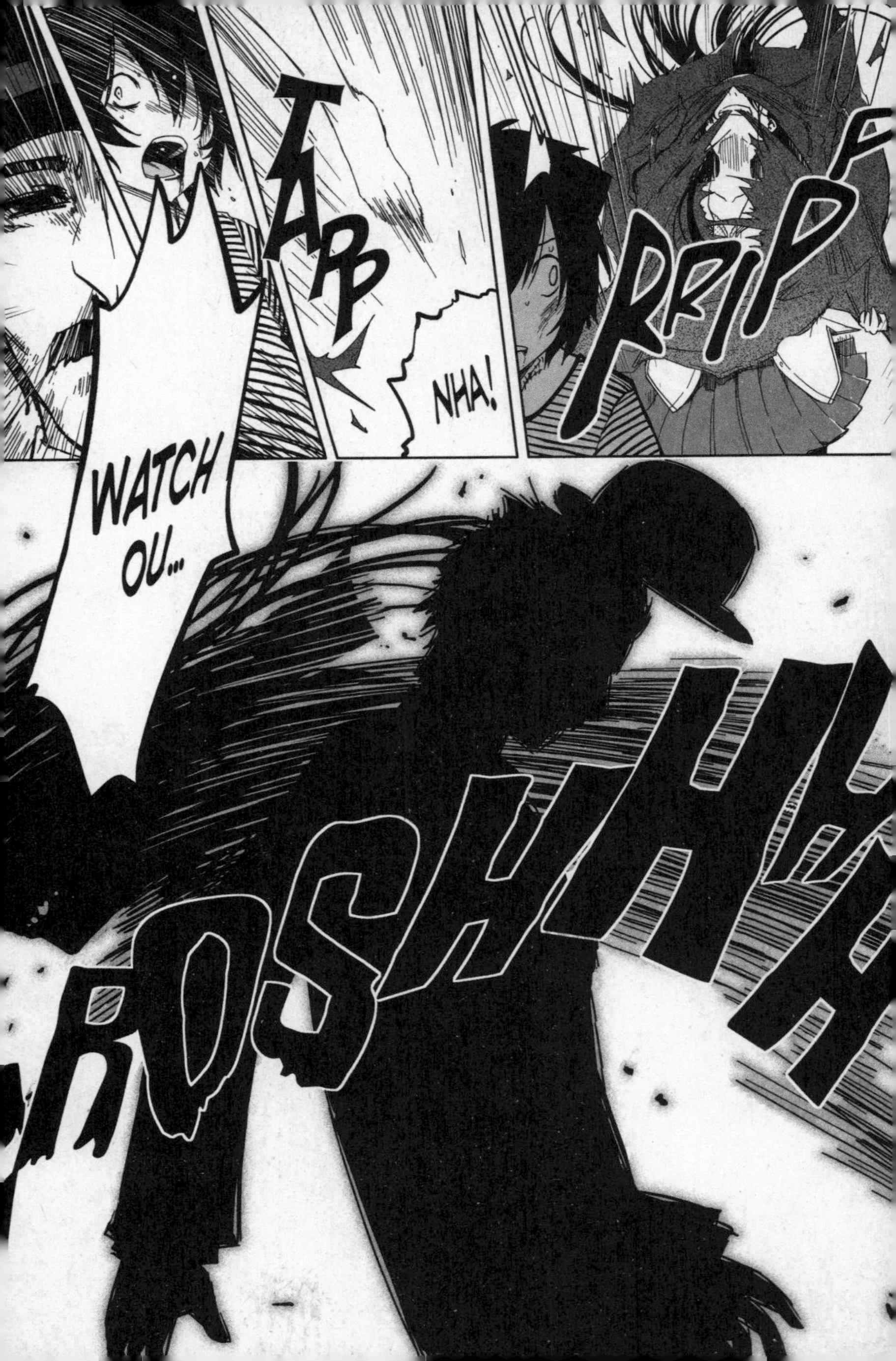
RRIP
TAP
NHA!
WATCH OU...
ROSHHHH

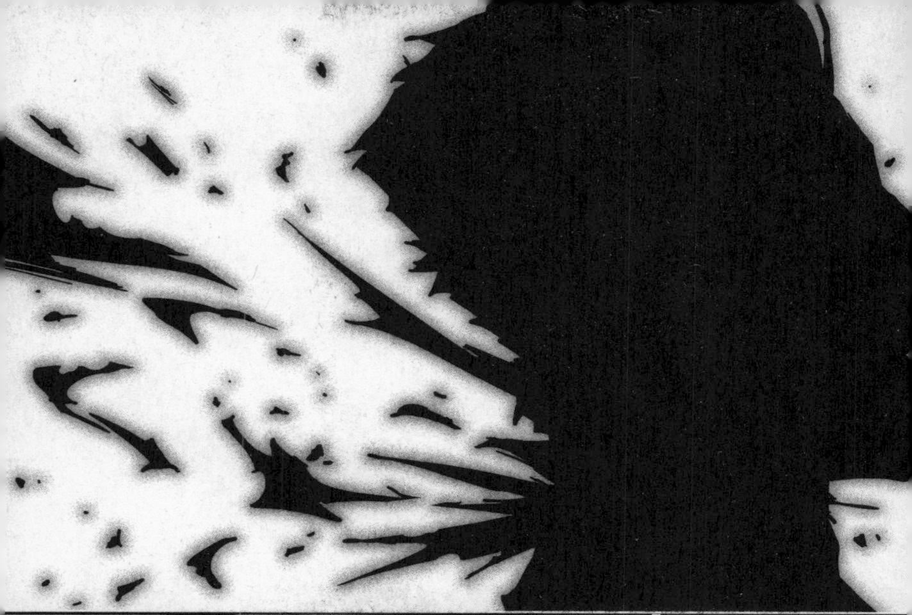

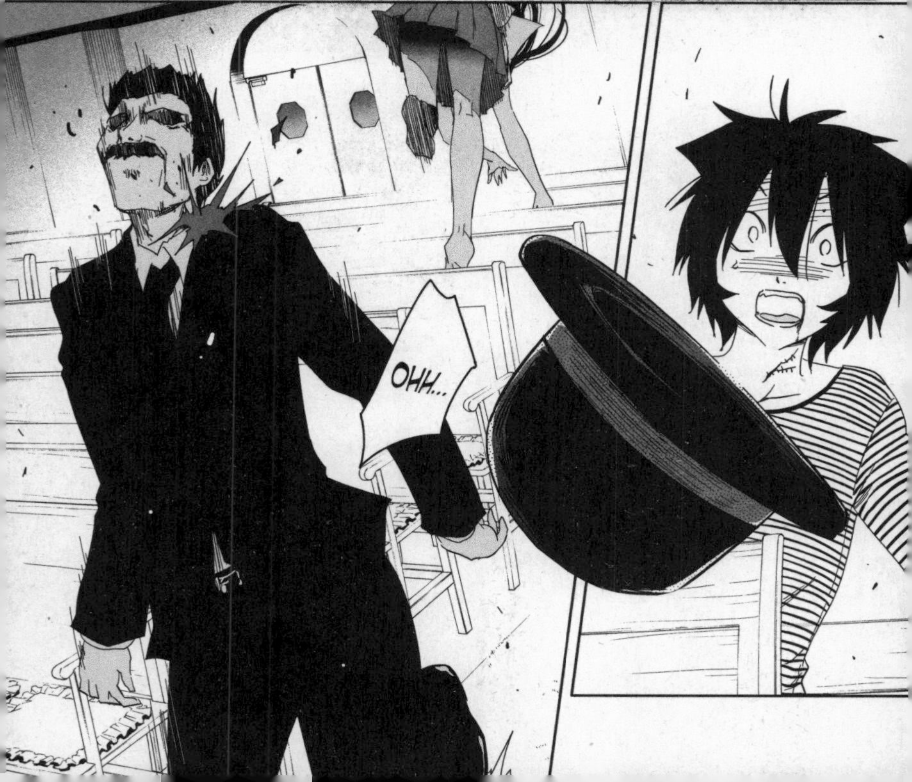
OHH...

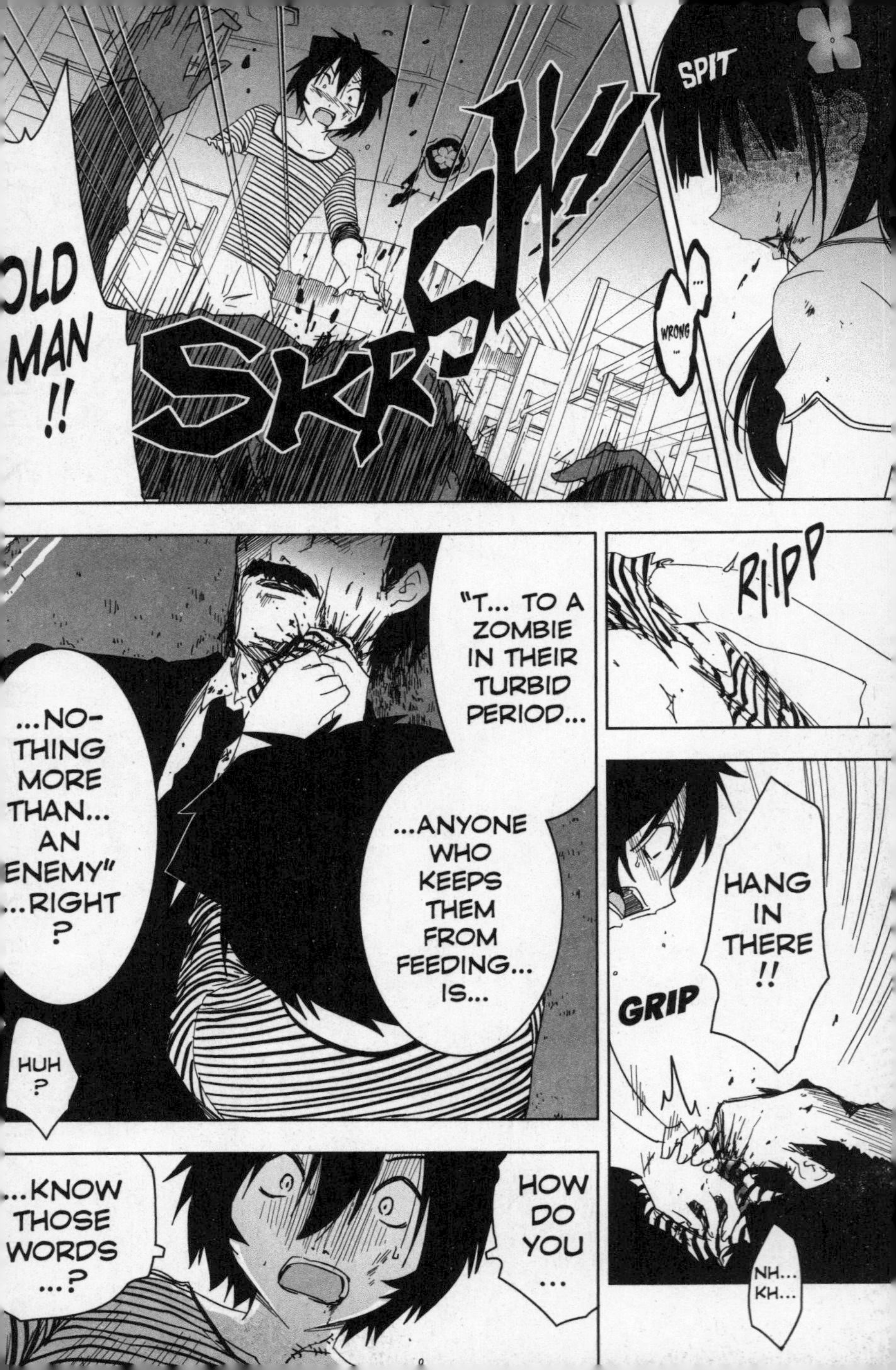
SPIT
... WRONG ...
SKRCHH
OLD MAN!!
RIPP
HANG IN THERE!!
GRIP
NH... KH...
"T... TO A ZOMBIE IN THEIR TURBID PERIOD...
...ANYONE WHO KEEPS THEM FROM FEEDING... IS...
...NO-THING MORE THAN... AN ENEMY" ...RIGHT?
HUH?
HOW DO YOU...
...KNOW THOSE WORDS...?

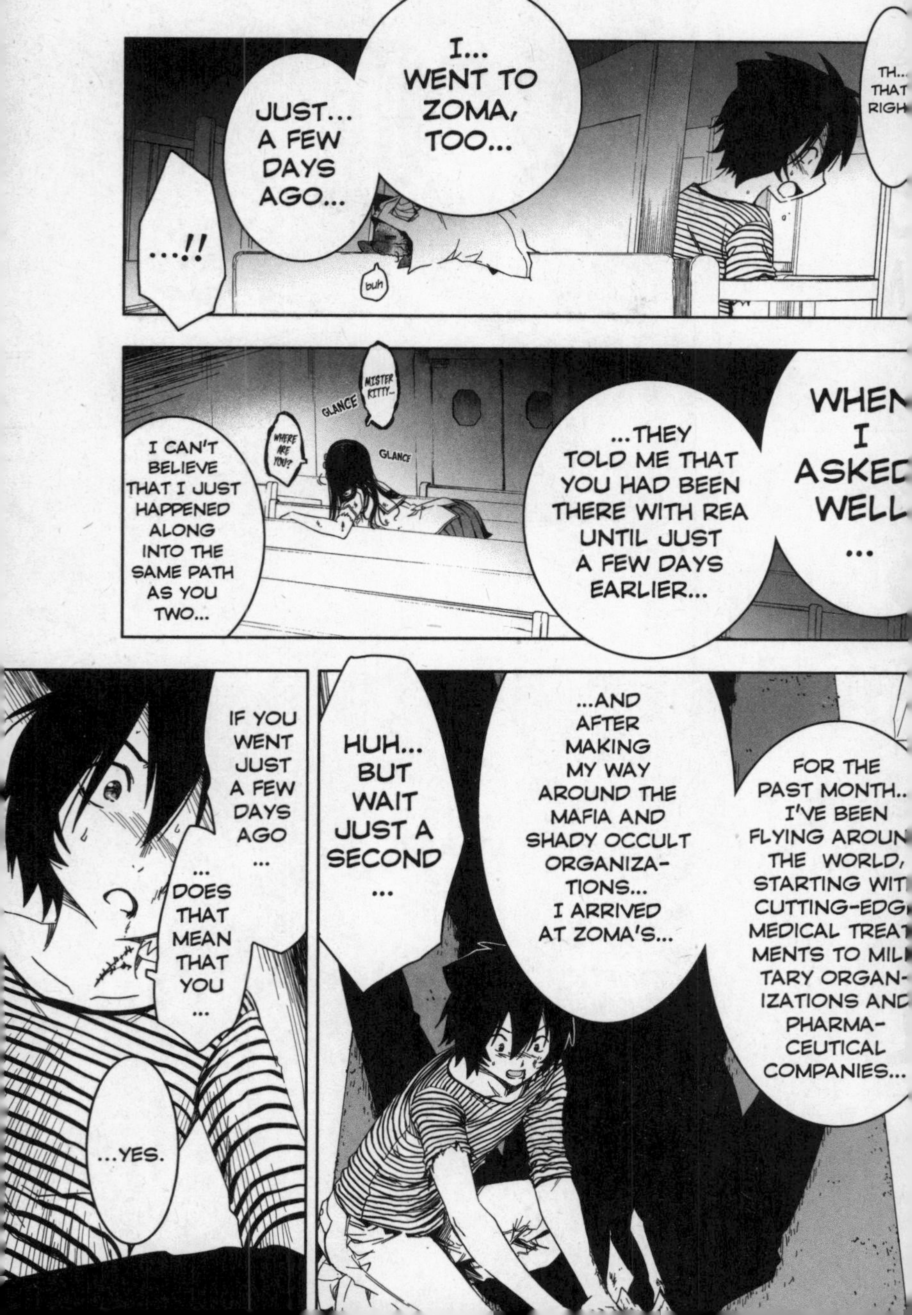
TH... THAT RIGH
I... WENT TO ZOMA, TOO...
JUST... A FEW DAYS AGO...
...!!
buh
WHEN I ASKED WELL ...
...THEY TOLD ME THAT YOU HAD BEEN THERE WITH REA UNTIL JUST A FEW DAYS EARLIER...
MISTER KITTY...
GLANCE
WHERE ARE YOU?
GLANCE
I CAN'T BELIEVE THAT I JUST HAPPENED ALONG INTO THE SAME PATH AS YOU TWO...
FOR THE PAST MONTH.. I'VE BEEN FLYING AROUN THE WORLD, STARTING WIT CUTTING-EDG MEDICAL TREAT MENTS TO MIL TARY ORGAN- IZATIONS AND PHARMA- CEUTICAL COMPANIES...
...AND AFTER MAKING MY WAY AROUND THE MAFIA AND SHADY OCCULT ORGANIZA- TIONS... I ARRIVED AT ZOMA'S...
HUH... BUT WAIT JUST A SECOND ...
IF YOU WENT JUST A FEW DAYS AGO ...
... DOES THAT MEAN THAT YOU ...
...YES.

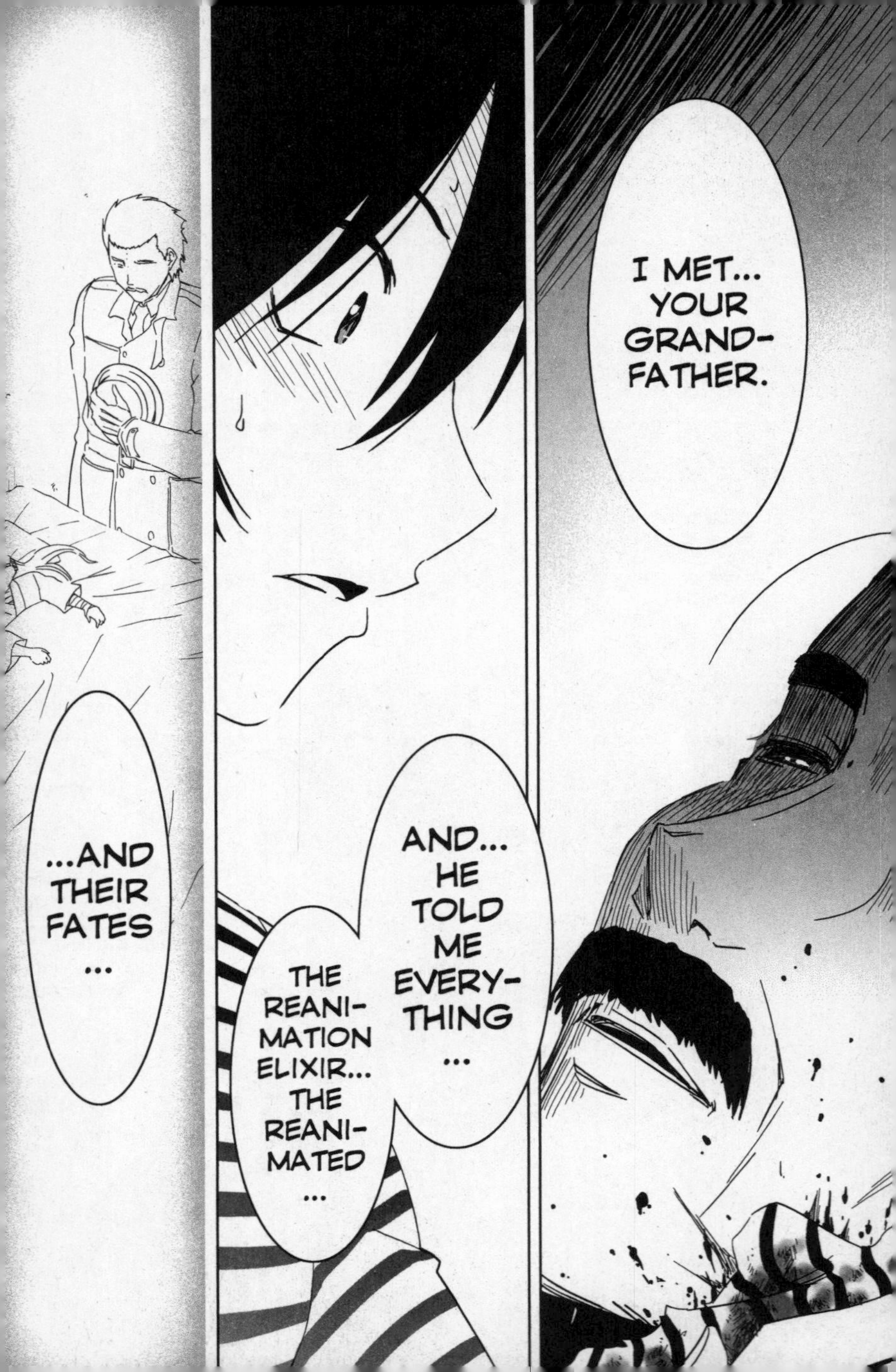
I MET... YOUR GRAND-FATHER.
AND... HE TOLD ME EVERY-THING...
THE REANI-MATION ELIXIR... THE REANI-MATED...
...AND THEIR FATES...

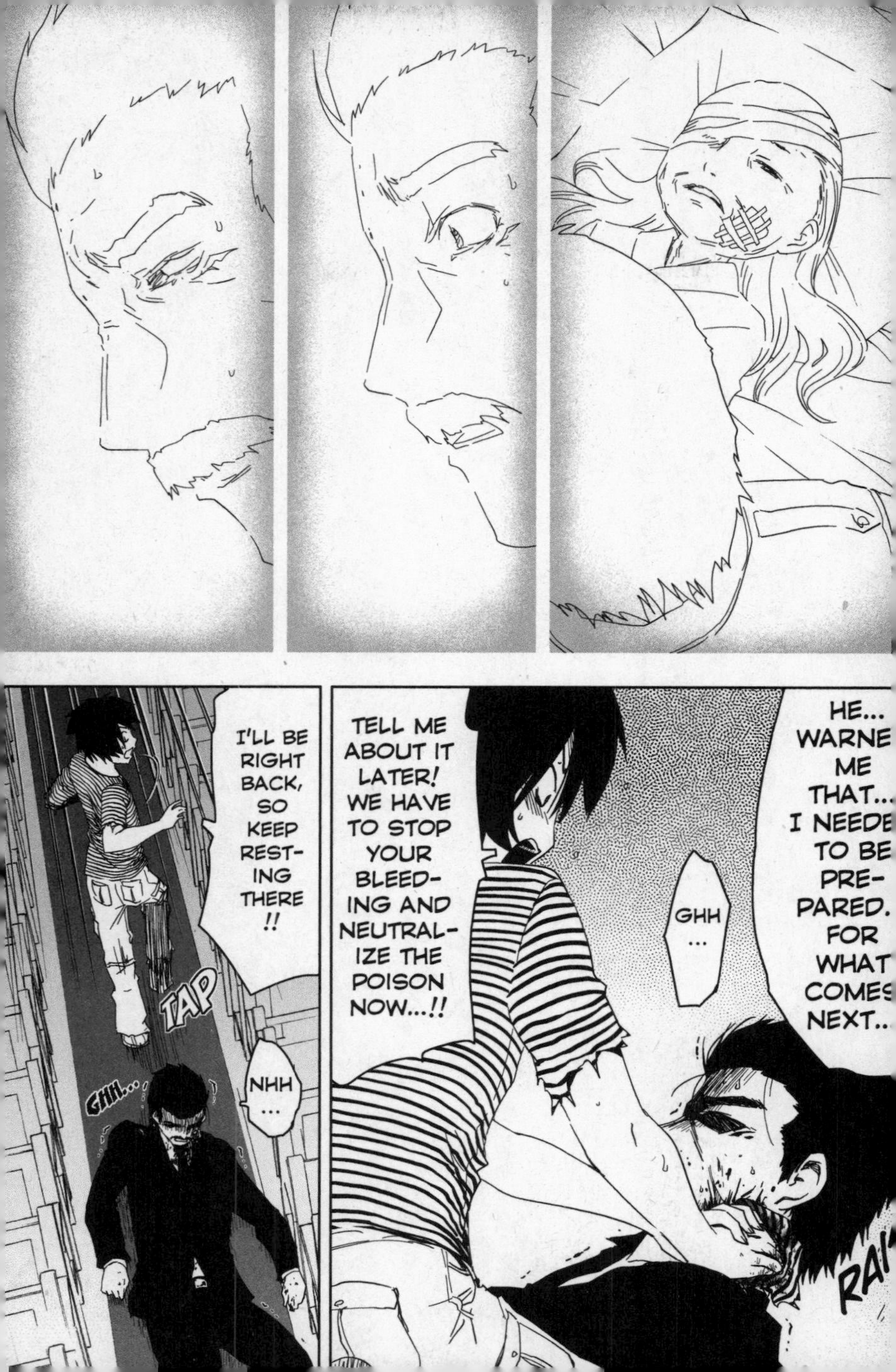
HE... WARNE ME THAT... I NEEDE TO BE PRE-PARED. FOR WHAT COMES NEXT...
GHH ...
TELL ME ABOUT IT LATER! WE HAVE TO STOP YOUR BLEED-ING AND NEUTRAL-IZE THE POISON NOW...!!
I'LL BE RIGHT BACK, SO KEEP REST-ING THERE!!
TAP
NHH ...
GHH...

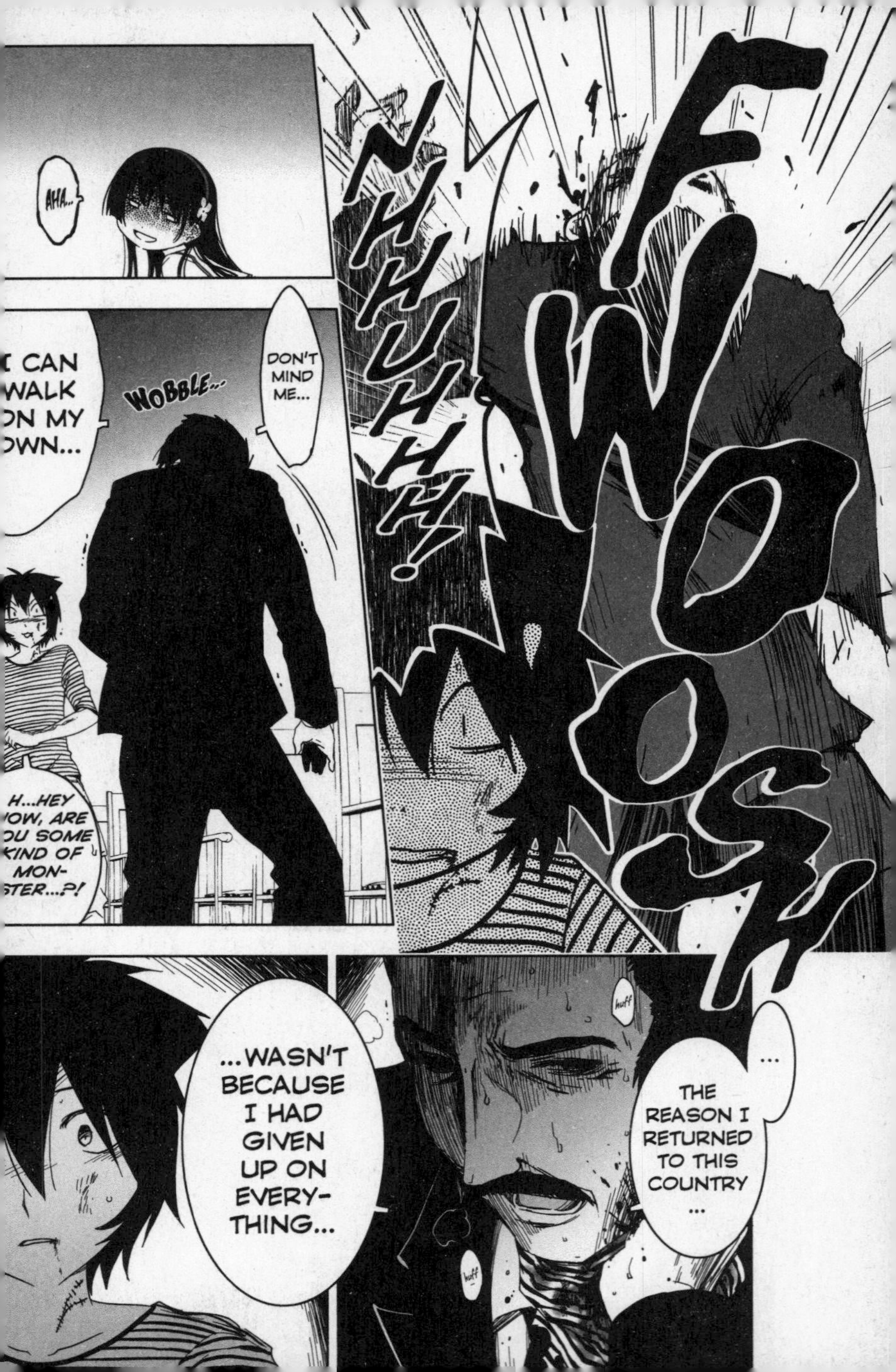
WHOOSH
NHHHHH!
AHA...
DON'T MIND ME...
WOBBLE...
I CAN WALK ON MY OWN...
H...HEY NOW, ARE YOU SOME KIND OF MON-STER...?!
huff
... THE REASON I RETURNED TO THIS COUNTRY ...
huff
...WASN'T BECAUSE I HAD GIVEN UP ON EVERY-THING...

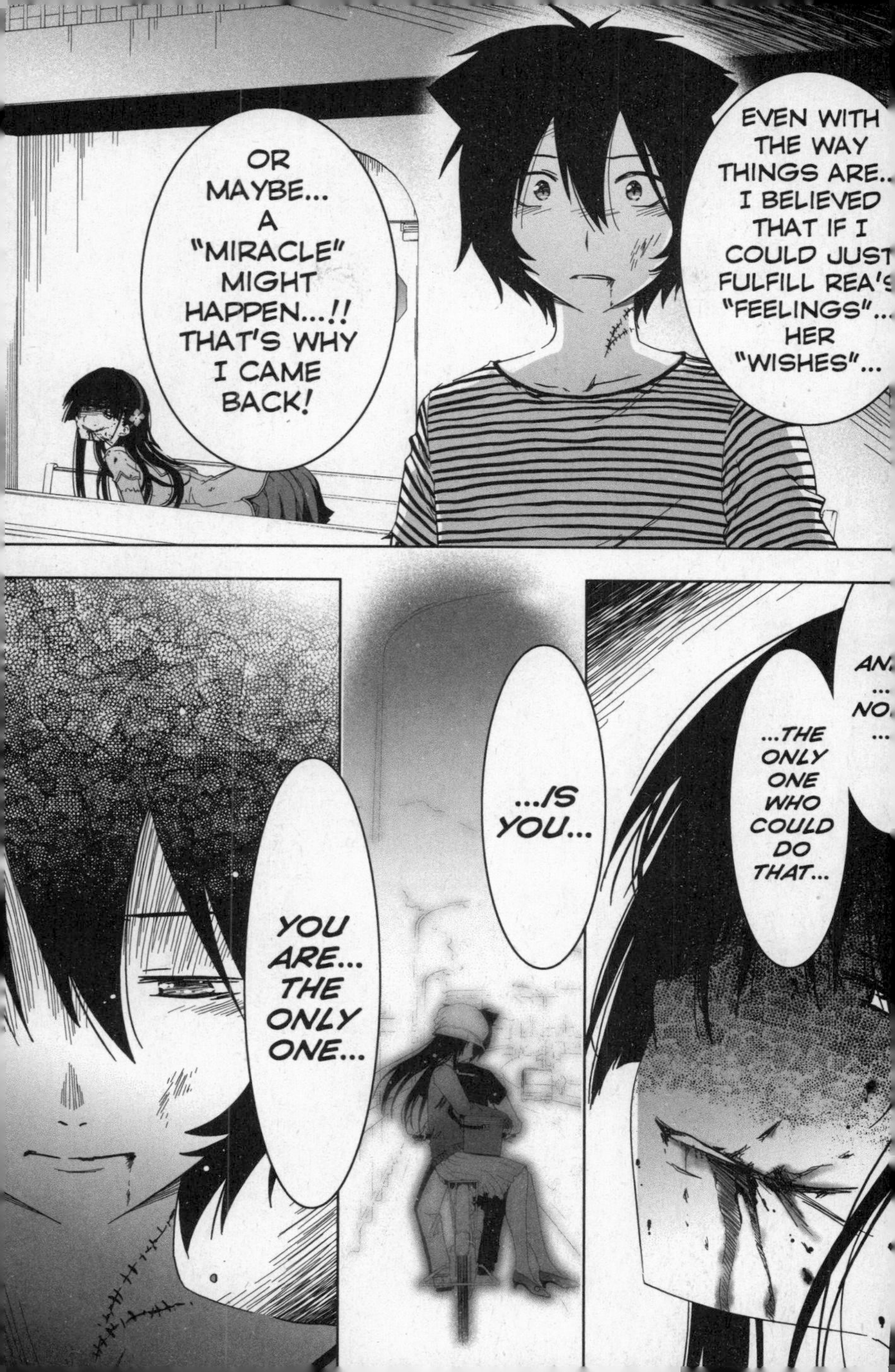
EVEN WITH THE WAY THINGS ARE... I BELIEVED THAT IF I COULD JUST FULFILL REA'S "FEELINGS"... HER "WISHES"...
OR MAYBE... A "MIRACLE" MIGHT HAPPEN...!! THAT'S WHY I CAME BACK!
...THE ONLY ONE WHO COULD DO THAT...
...IS YOU...
YOU ARE... THE ONLY ONE...

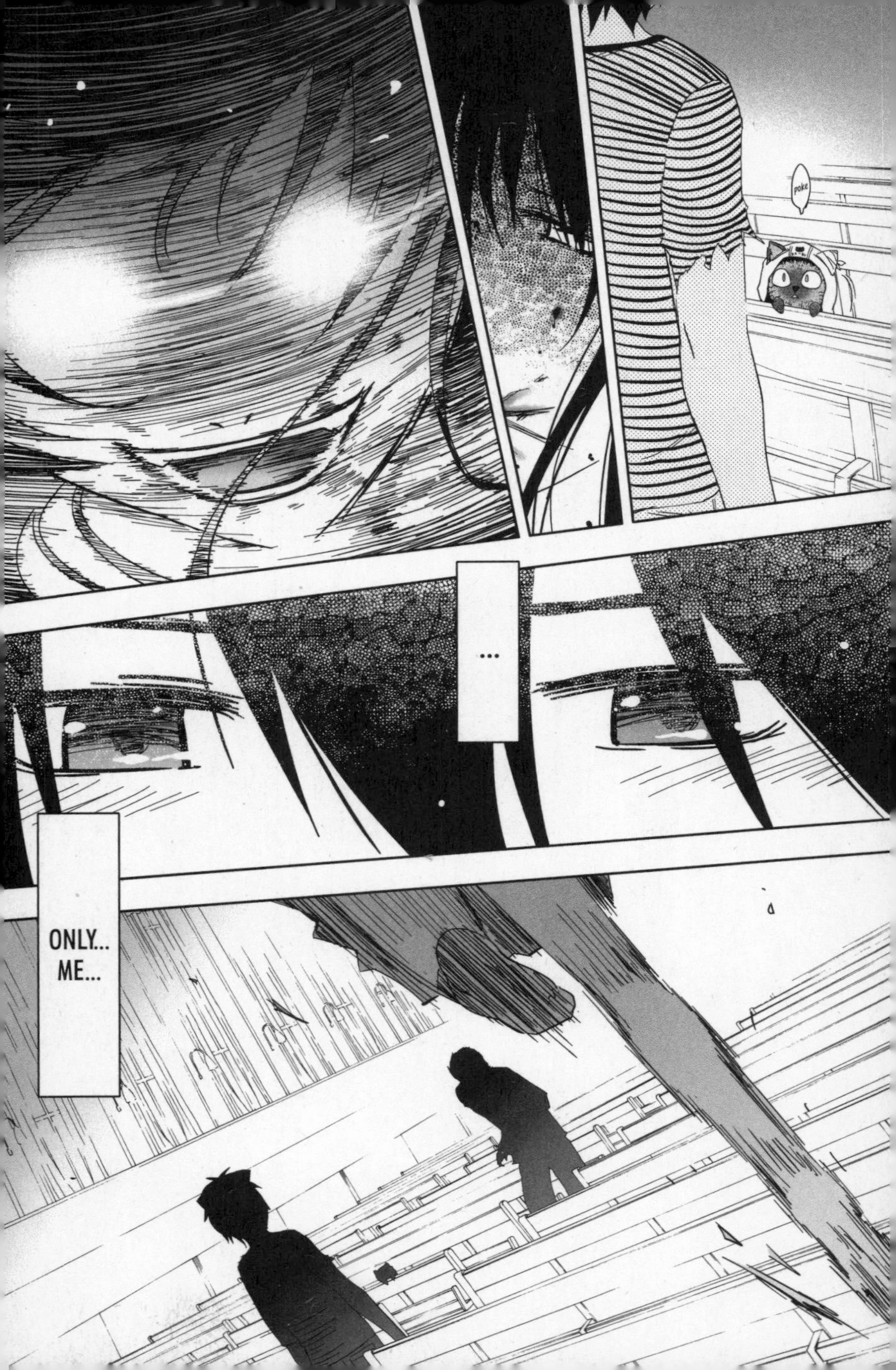
poke
...
ONLY... ME...

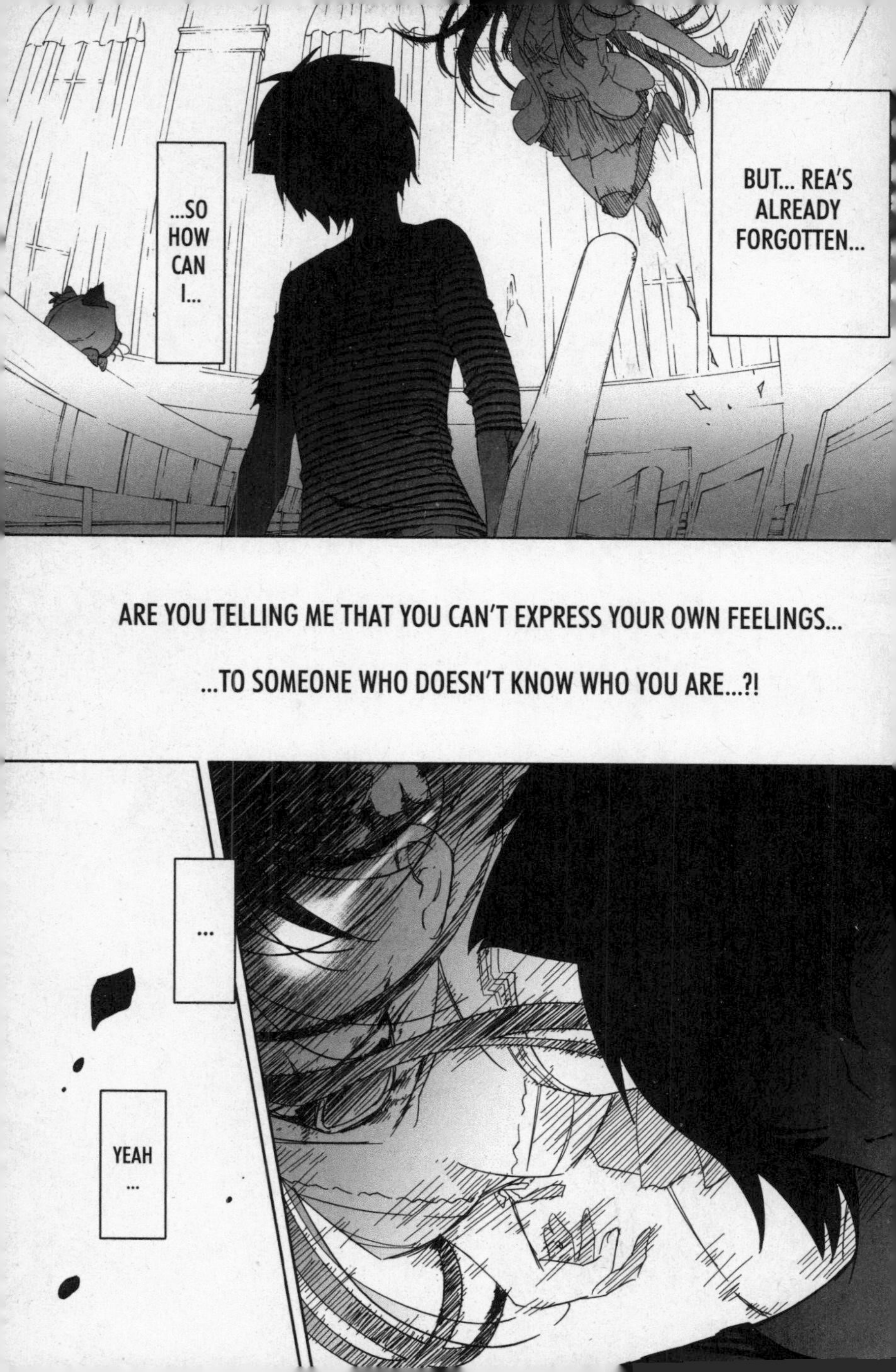
BUT... REA'S ALREADY FORGOTTEN...
...SO HOW CAN I...
ARE YOU TELLING ME THAT YOU CAN'T EXPRESS YOUR OWN FEELINGS...
...TO SOMEONE WHO DOESN'T KNOW WHO YOU ARE...?!
...
YEAH ...

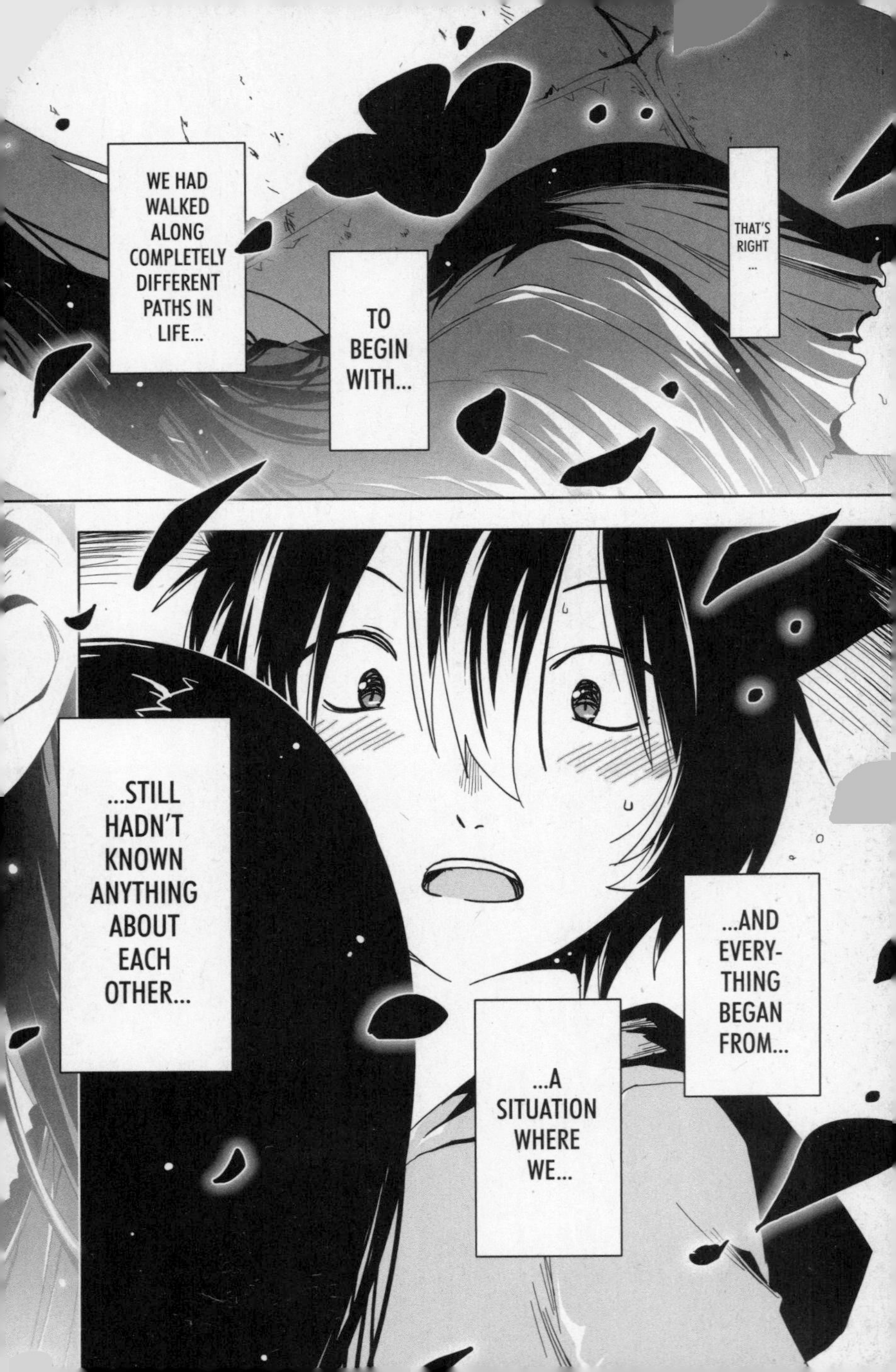
THAT'S RIGHT ...
TO BEGIN WITH...
WE HAD WALKED ALONG COMPLETELY DIFFERENT PATHS IN LIFE...
...AND EVERY-THING BEGAN FROM...
...A SITUATION WHERE WE...
...STILL HADN'T KNOWN ANYTHING ABOUT EACH OTHER...

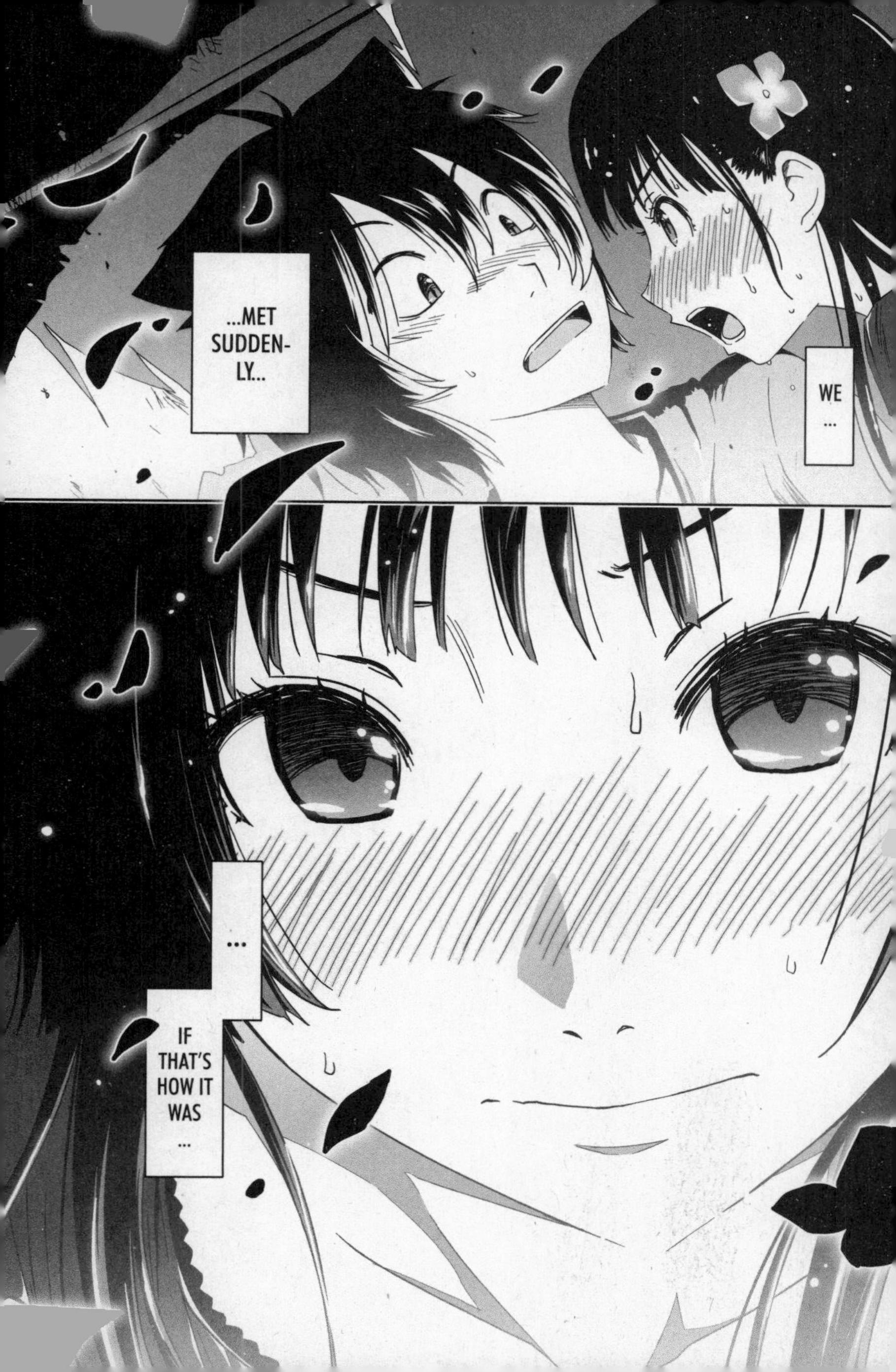
WE ...
...MET SUDDEN-LY...
...
IF THAT'S HOW IT WAS ...

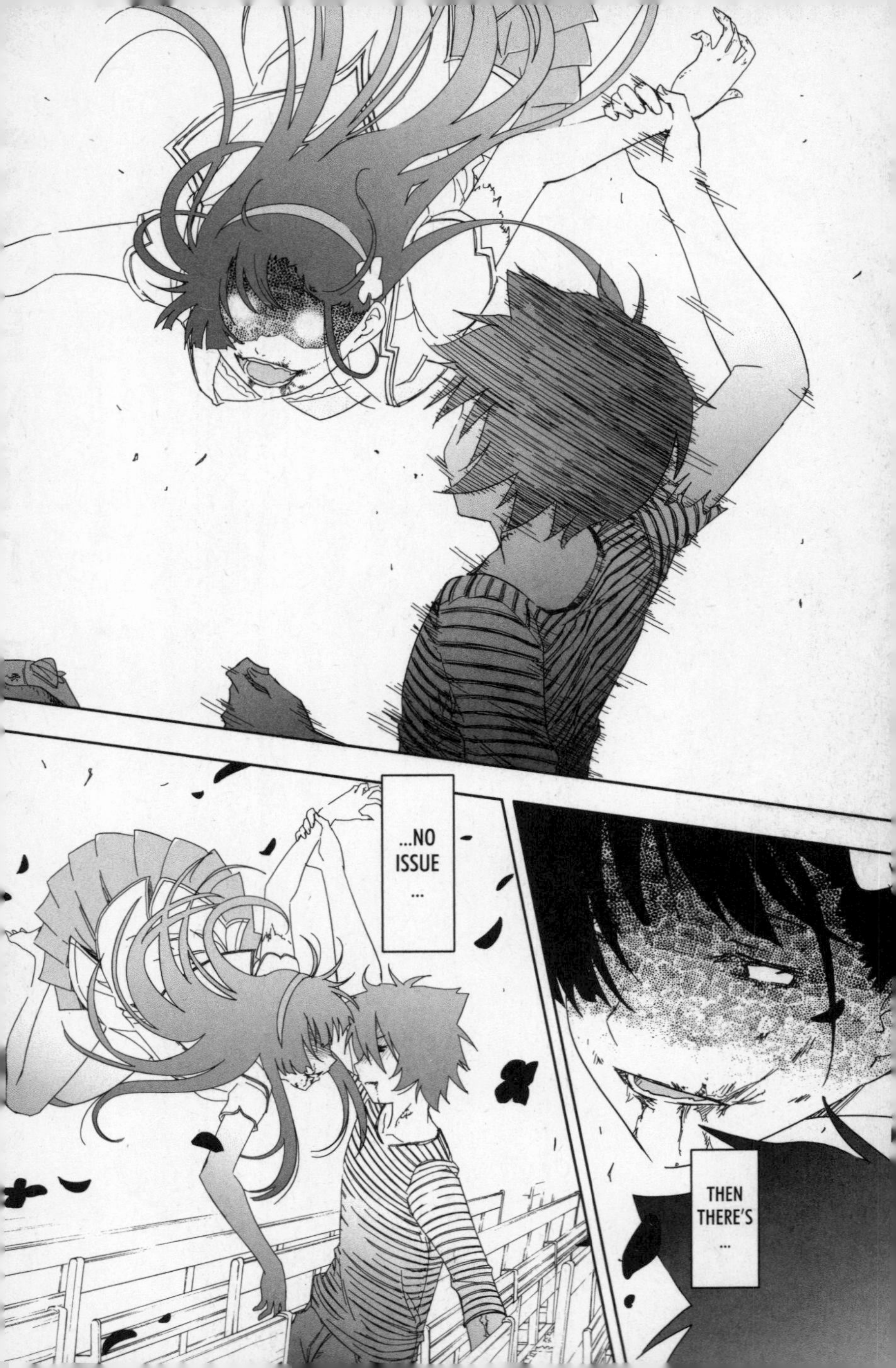
THEN THERE'S ...
...NO ISSUE ...

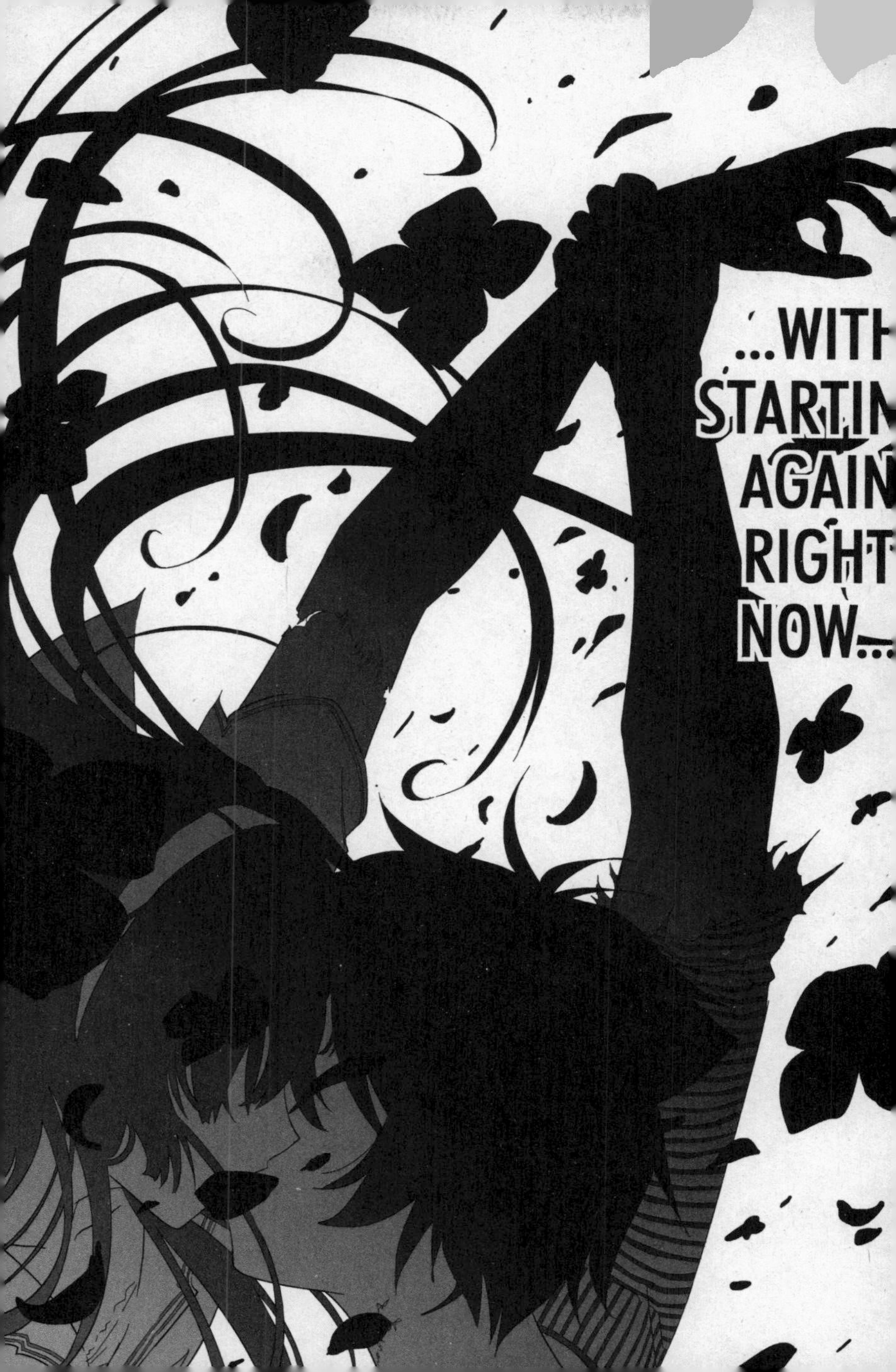
...WITH STARTIN AGAIN RIGHT NOW...

SANKAREA

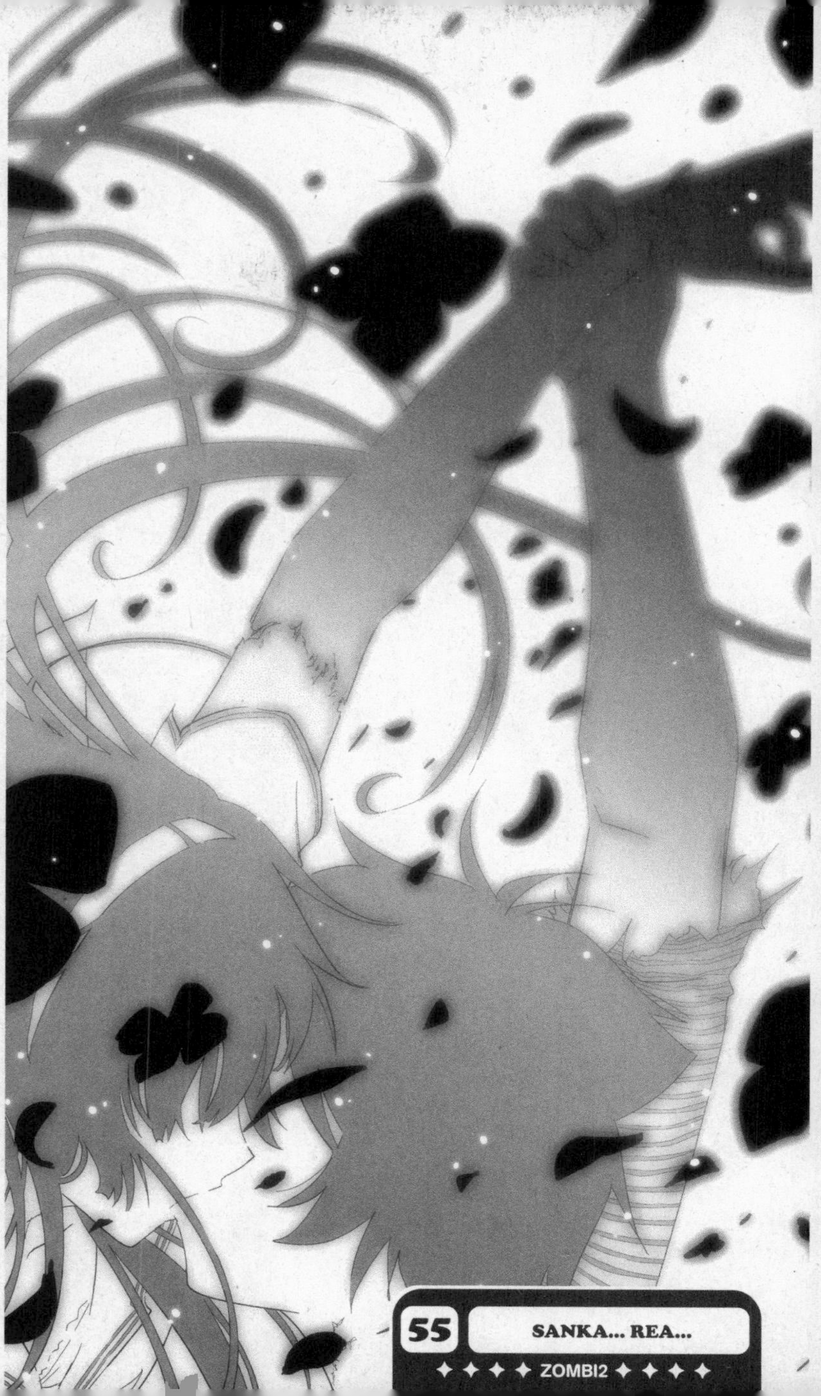
55
SANKA... REA...
ZOMBI2

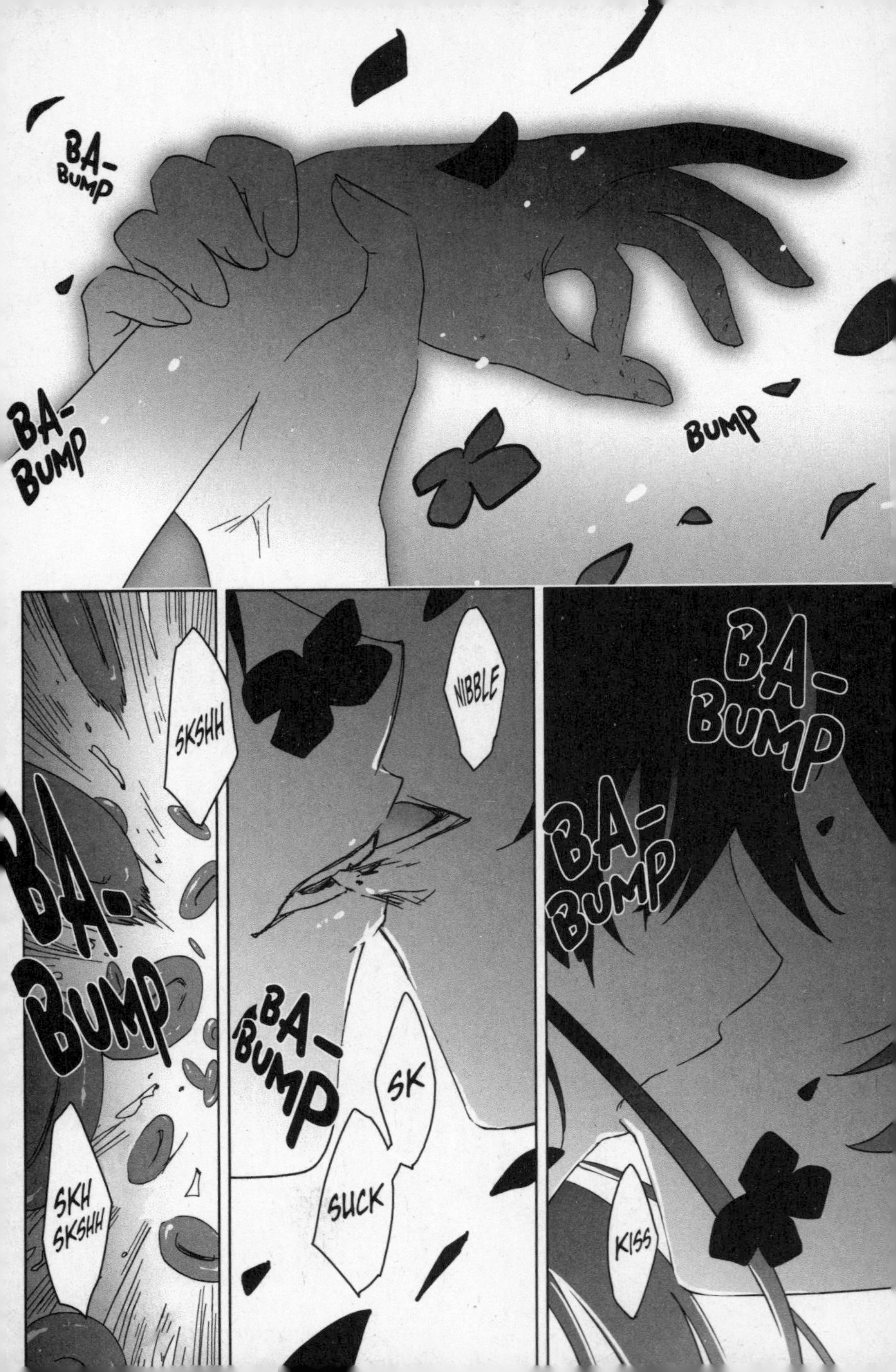
BA-BUMP
BUMP
BA-BUMP
BA-BUMP
BA-BUMP
KISS
NIBBLE
BA-BUMP
SK
SUCK
SKSHH
BA-BUMP
SKH SKSHH

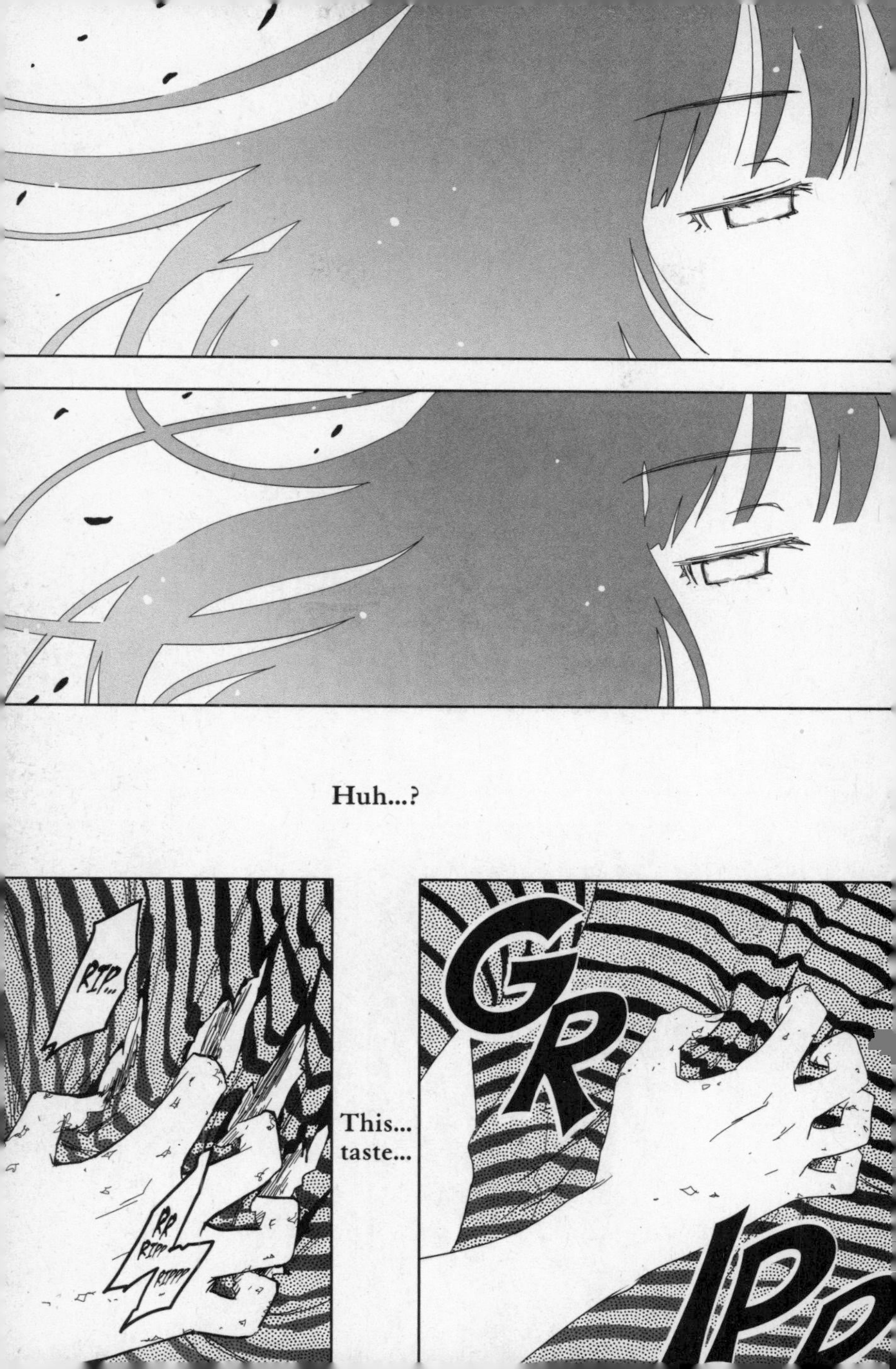
Huh...?
GR
IPP
This... taste...
RIP...
RR RIPP RIPPP

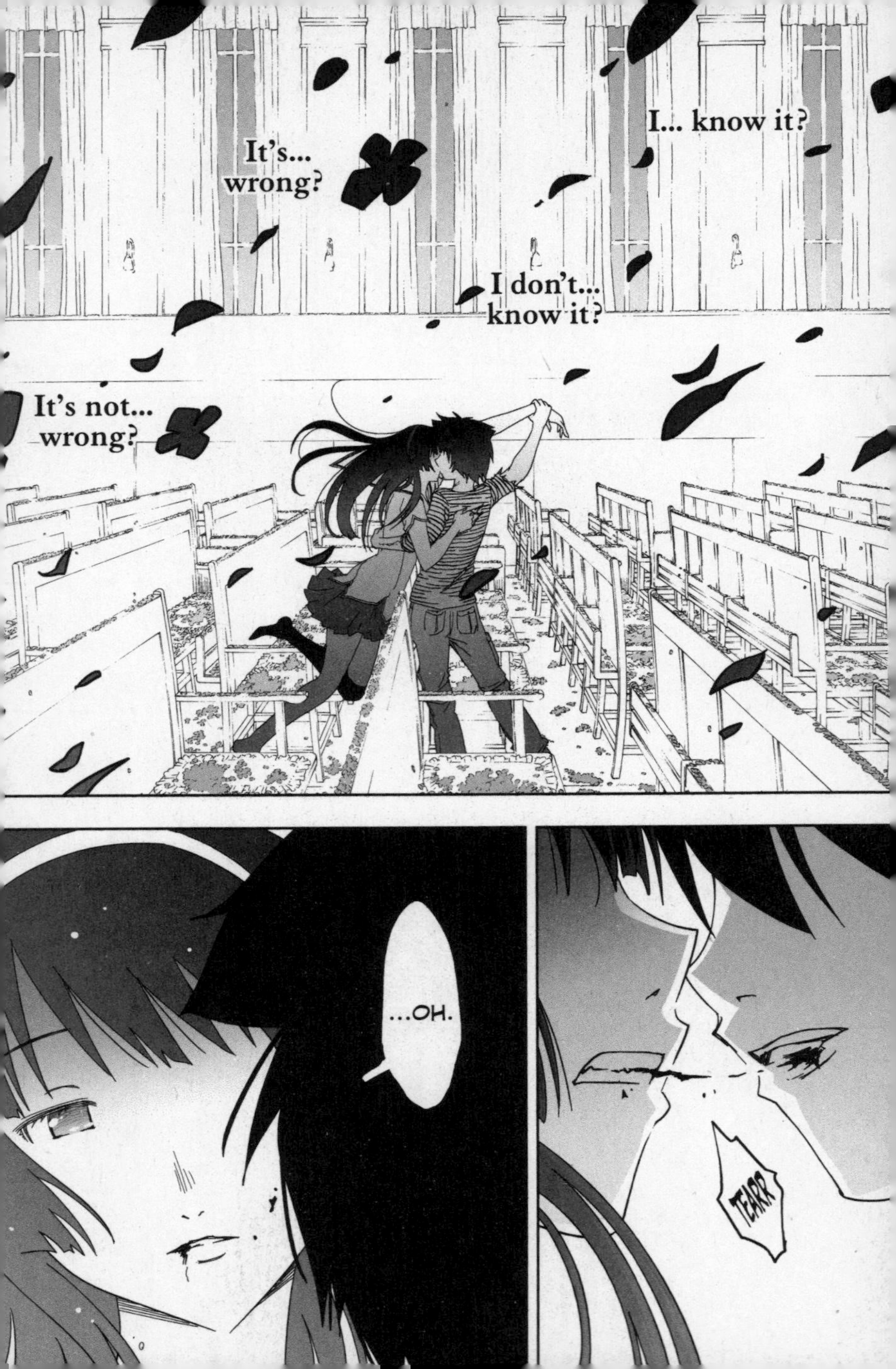
I... know it?
It's... wrong?
I don't... know it?
It's not... wrong?
TEARR
...OH.

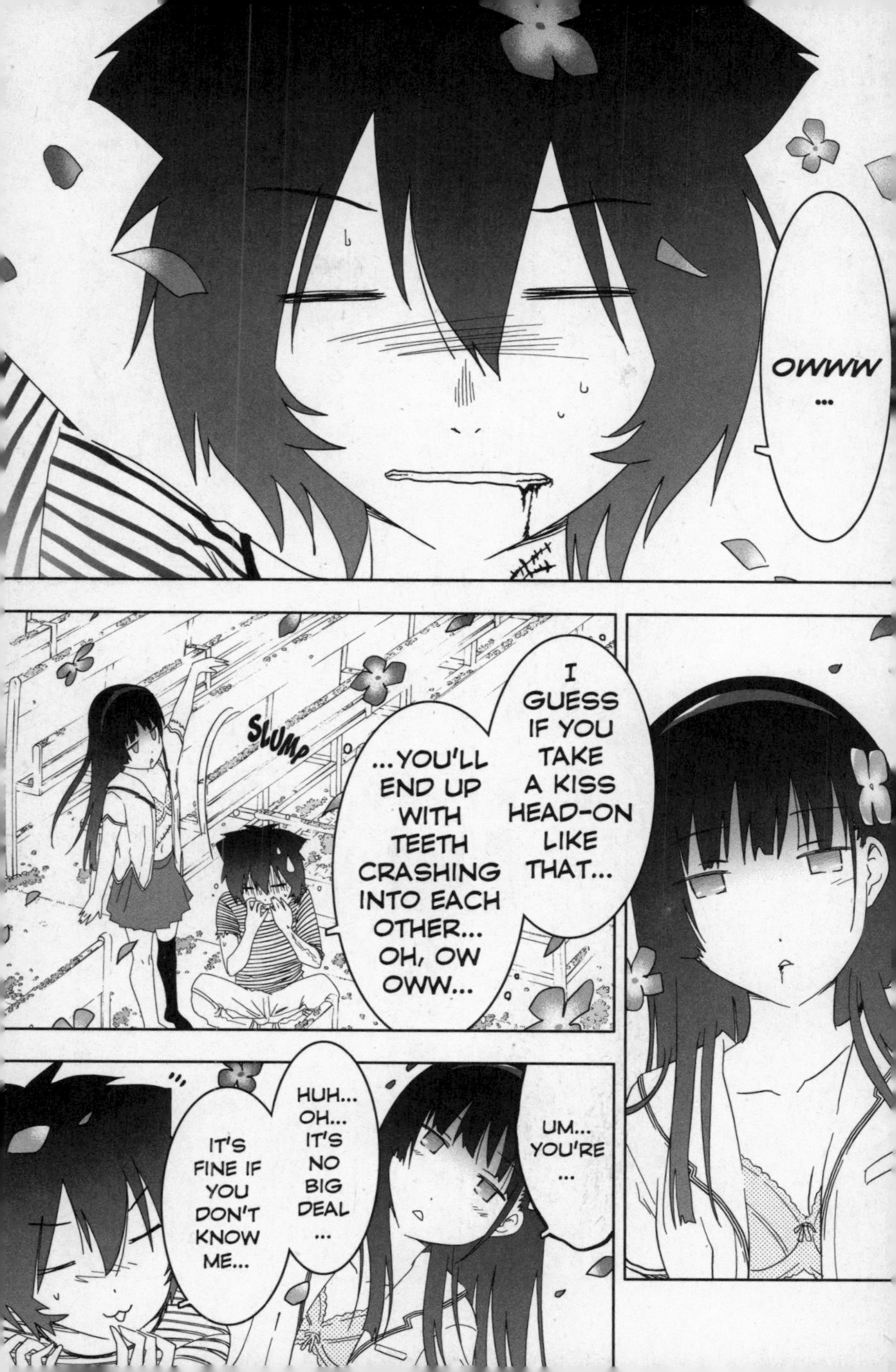
OWWW ...
I GUESS IF YOU TAKE A KISS HEAD-ON LIKE THAT...
...YOU'LL END UP WITH TEETH CRASHING INTO EACH OTHER... OH, OW OWW...
SLUMP
UM... YOU'RE ...
HUH... OH... IT'S NO BIG DEAL ...
IT'S FINE IF YOU DON'T KNOW ME...

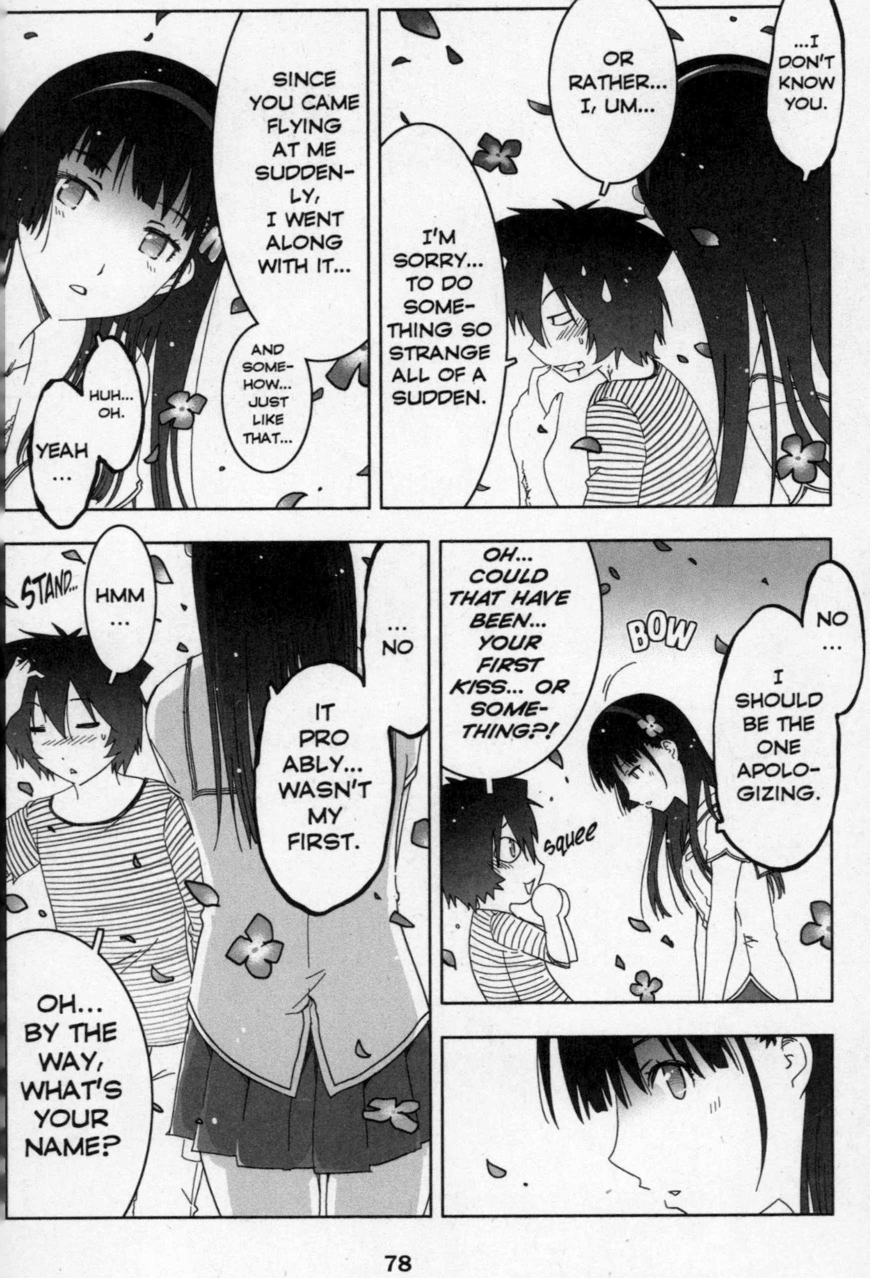
...I DON'T KNOW YOU.
OR RATHER... I, UM...
I'M SORRY... TO DO SOMETHING SO STRANGE ALL OF A SUDDEN.
SINCE YOU CAME FLYING AT ME SUDDENLY, I WENT ALONG WITH IT...
AND SOMEHOW... JUST LIKE THAT...
HUH... OH.
YEAH...
NO... I SHOULD BE THE ONE APOLOGIZING.
BOW
OH... COULD THAT HAVE BEEN... YOUR FIRST KISS... OR SOMETHING?!
squee
...NO
IT PRO ABLY... WASN'T MY FIRST.
HMM...
STAND...
OH... BY THE WAY, WHAT'S YOUR NAME?

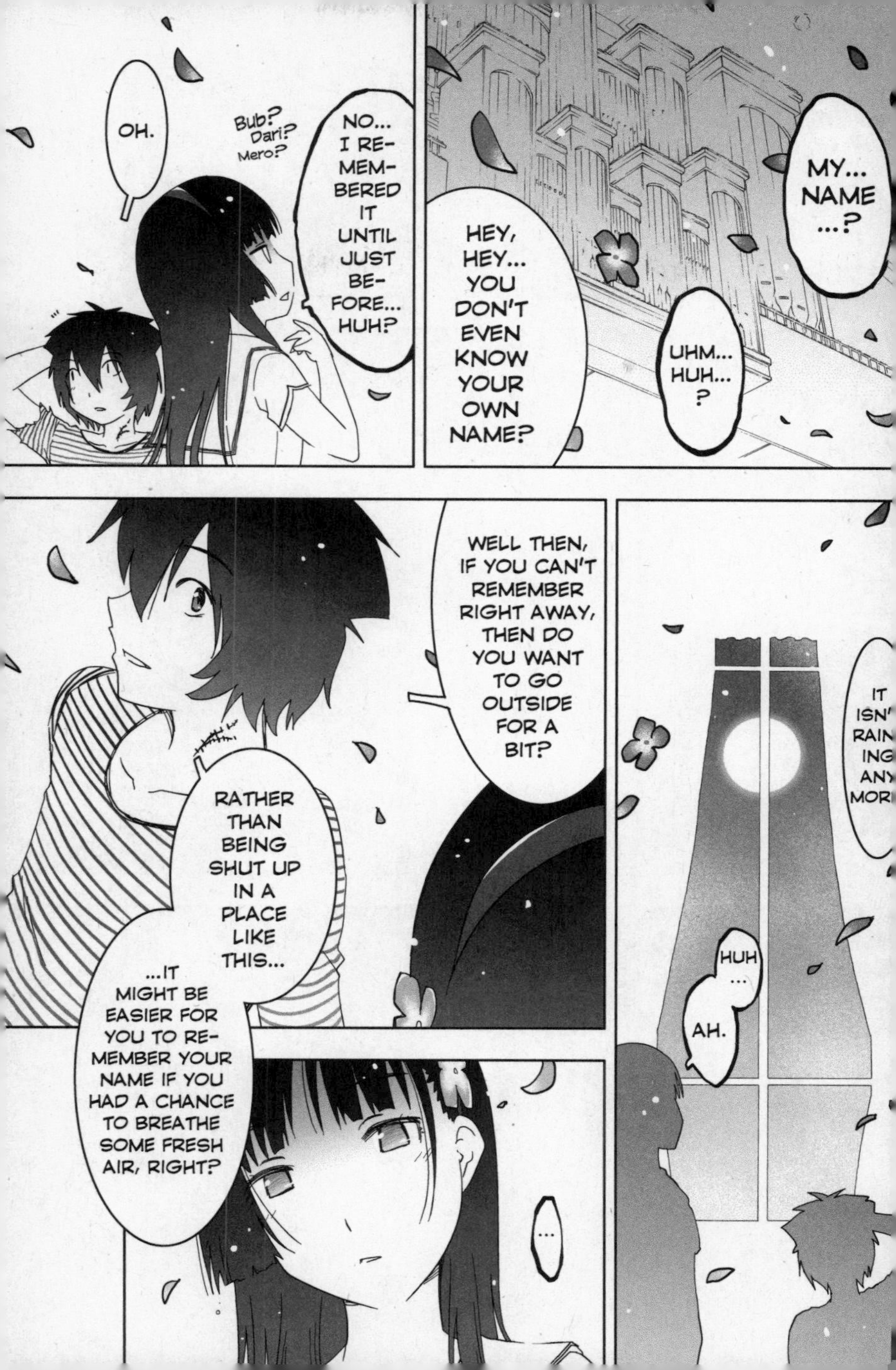
MY... NAME ...?
UHM... HUH... ?
HEY, HEY... YOU DON'T EVEN KNOW YOUR OWN NAME?
NO... I RE-MEM-BERED IT UNTIL JUST BE-FORE... HUH?
Bub? Dari? Mero?
OH.
IT ISN' RAIN ING ANY MOR
HUH ...
AH.
WELL THEN, IF YOU CAN'T REMEMBER RIGHT AWAY, THEN DO YOU WANT TO GO OUTSIDE FOR A BIT?
RATHER THAN BEING SHUT UP IN A PLACE LIKE THIS...
...IT MIGHT BE EASIER FOR YOU TO RE-MEMBER YOUR NAME IF YOU HAD A CHANCE TO BREATHE SOME FRESH AIR, RIGHT?
...

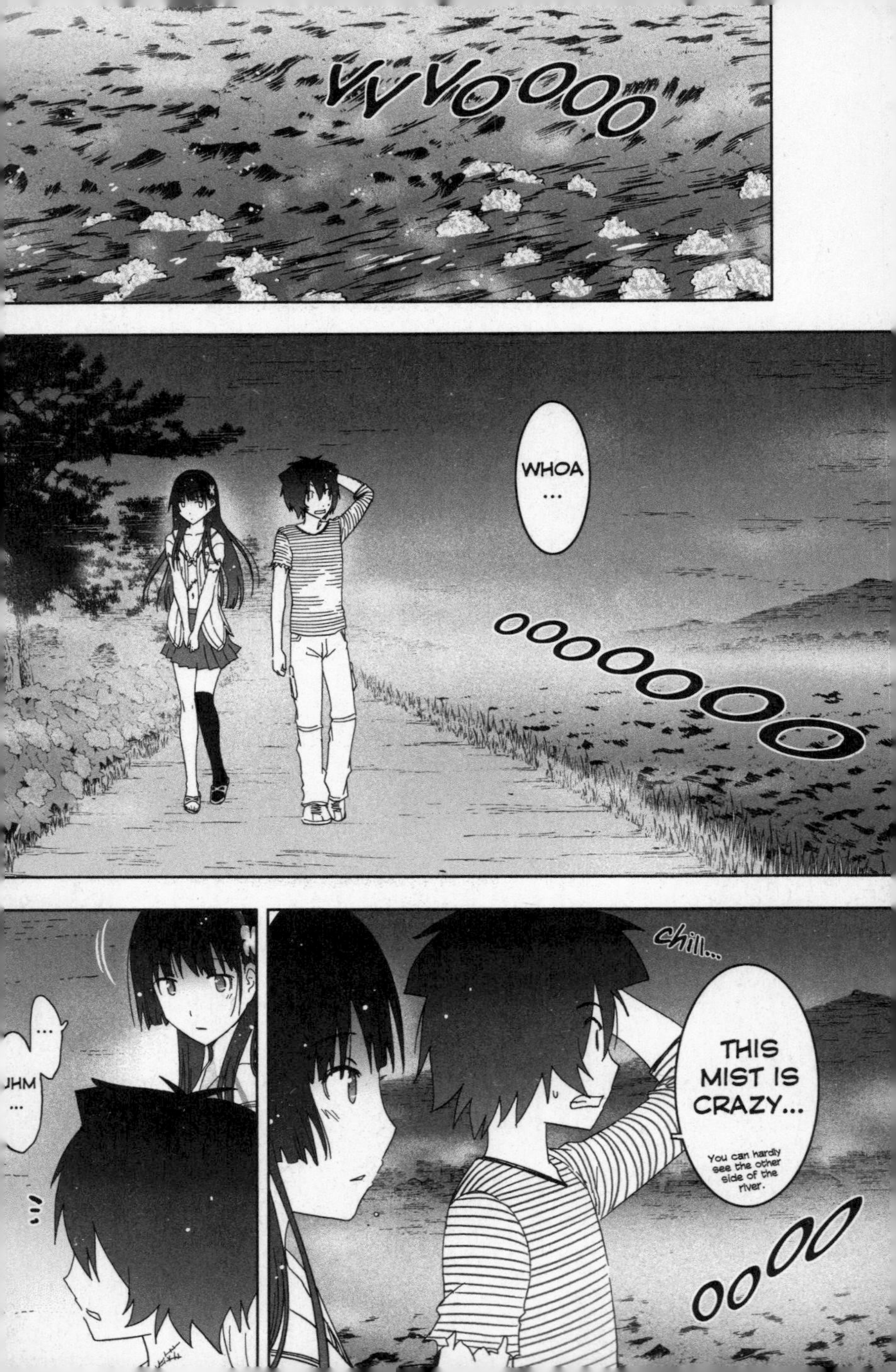
VVVOOOO
WHOA ...
OOOOOOOOO
chill...
THIS MIST IS CRAZY...
You can hardly see the other side of the river.
OOOO
... UHM ...

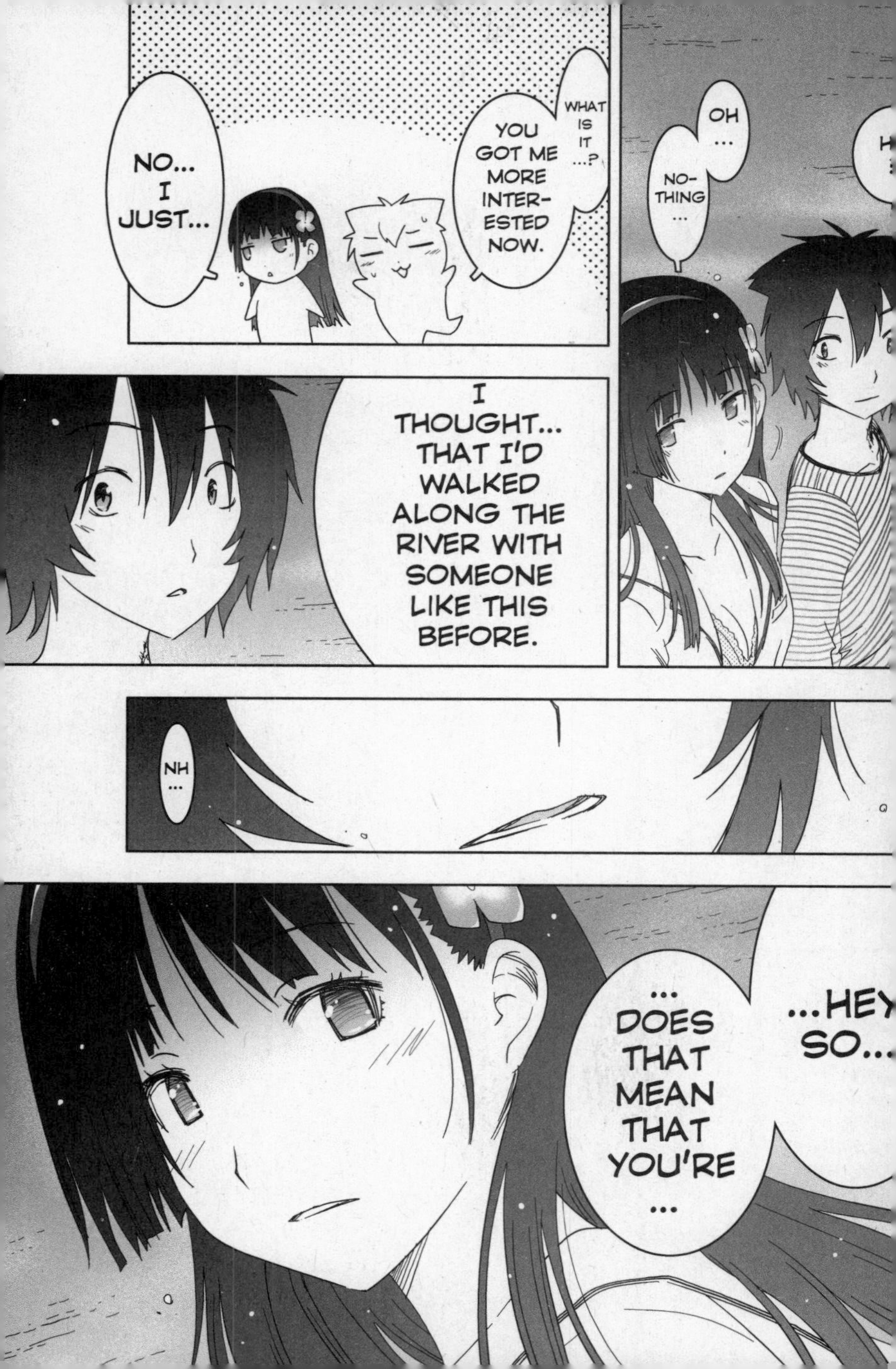
OH ...
NO-THING ...
WHAT IS IT ...?
YOU GOT ME MORE INTER-ESTED NOW.
NO... I JUST...
I THOUGHT... THAT I'D WALKED ALONG THE RIVER WITH SOMEONE LIKE THIS BEFORE.
NH ...
...HEY SO...
... DOES THAT MEAN THAT YOU'RE ...

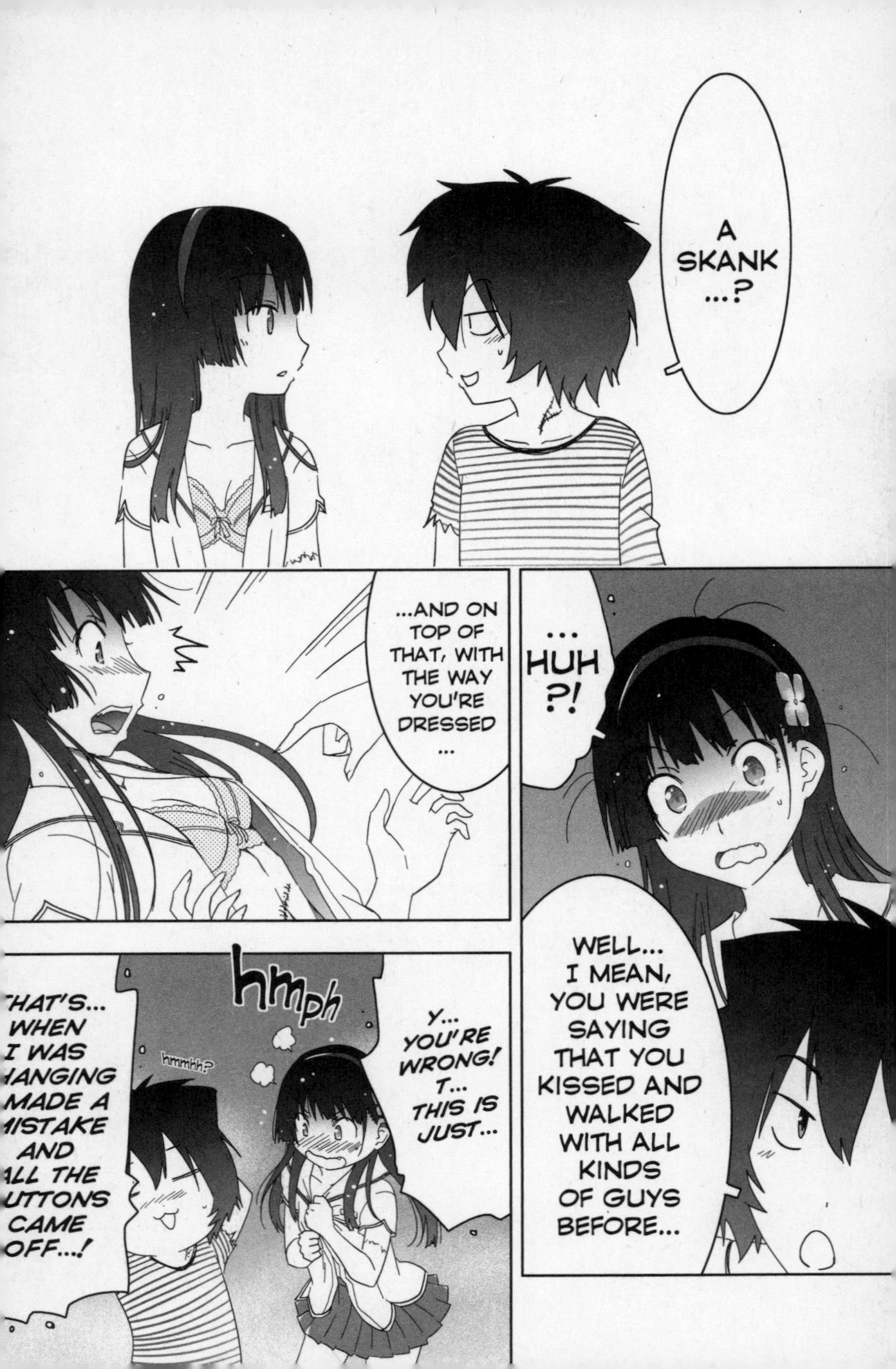
A SKANK ...?
... HUH ?!
WELL... I MEAN, YOU WERE SAYING THAT YOU KISSED AND WALKED WITH ALL KINDS OF GUYS BEFORE...
...AND ON TOP OF THAT, WITH THE WAY YOU'RE DRESSED ...
hmph
Y... YOU'RE WRONG! T... THIS IS JUST...
hmmhh?
HAT'S... WHEN I WAS HANGING MADE A ISTAKE AND LL THE UTTONS CAME OFF...!

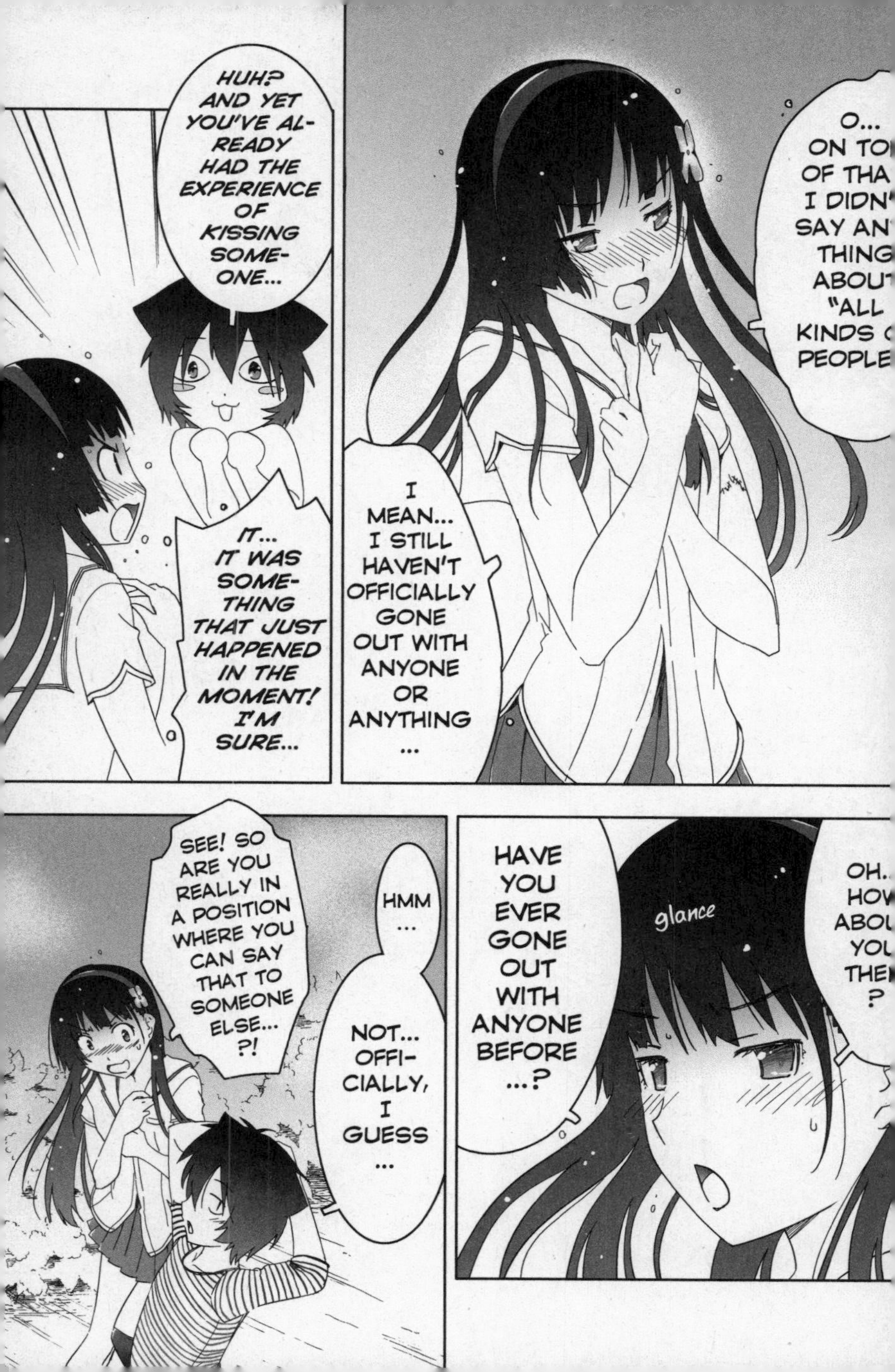

O... ON TO OF THA I DIDN' SAY AN THING ABOU "ALL KINDS PEOPLE
I MEAN... I STILL HAVEN'T OFFICIALLY GONE OUT WITH ANYONE OR ANYTHING ...
HUH? AND YET YOU'VE AL-READY HAD THE EXPERIENCE OF KISSING SOME-ONE...
IT... IT WAS SOME-THING THAT JUST HAPPENED IN THE MOMENT! I'M SURE...
OH... HOW ABOU YOU THE ?
HAVE YOU EVER GONE OUT WITH ANYONE BEFORE ...?
glance
HMM ...
NOT... OFFI-CIALLY, I GUESS ...
SEE! SO ARE YOU REALLY IN A POSITION WHERE YOU CAN SAY THAT TO SOMEONE ELSE... ?!

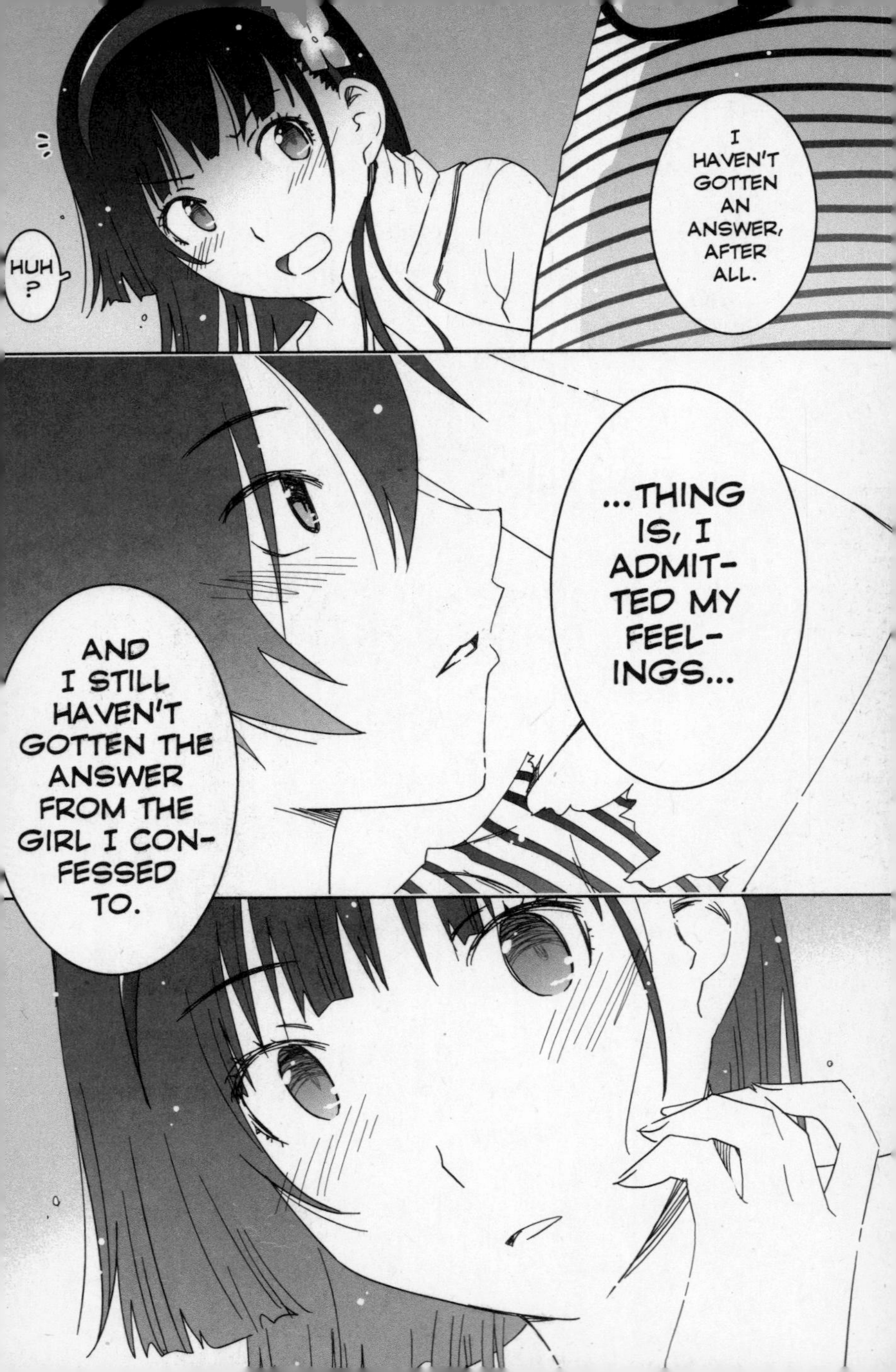

I HAVEN'T GOTTEN AN ANSWER, AFTER ALL.
HUH?
...THING IS, I ADMIT-TED MY FEEL-INGS...
AND I STILL HAVEN'T GOTTEN THE ANSWER FROM THE GIRL I CON-FESSED TO.

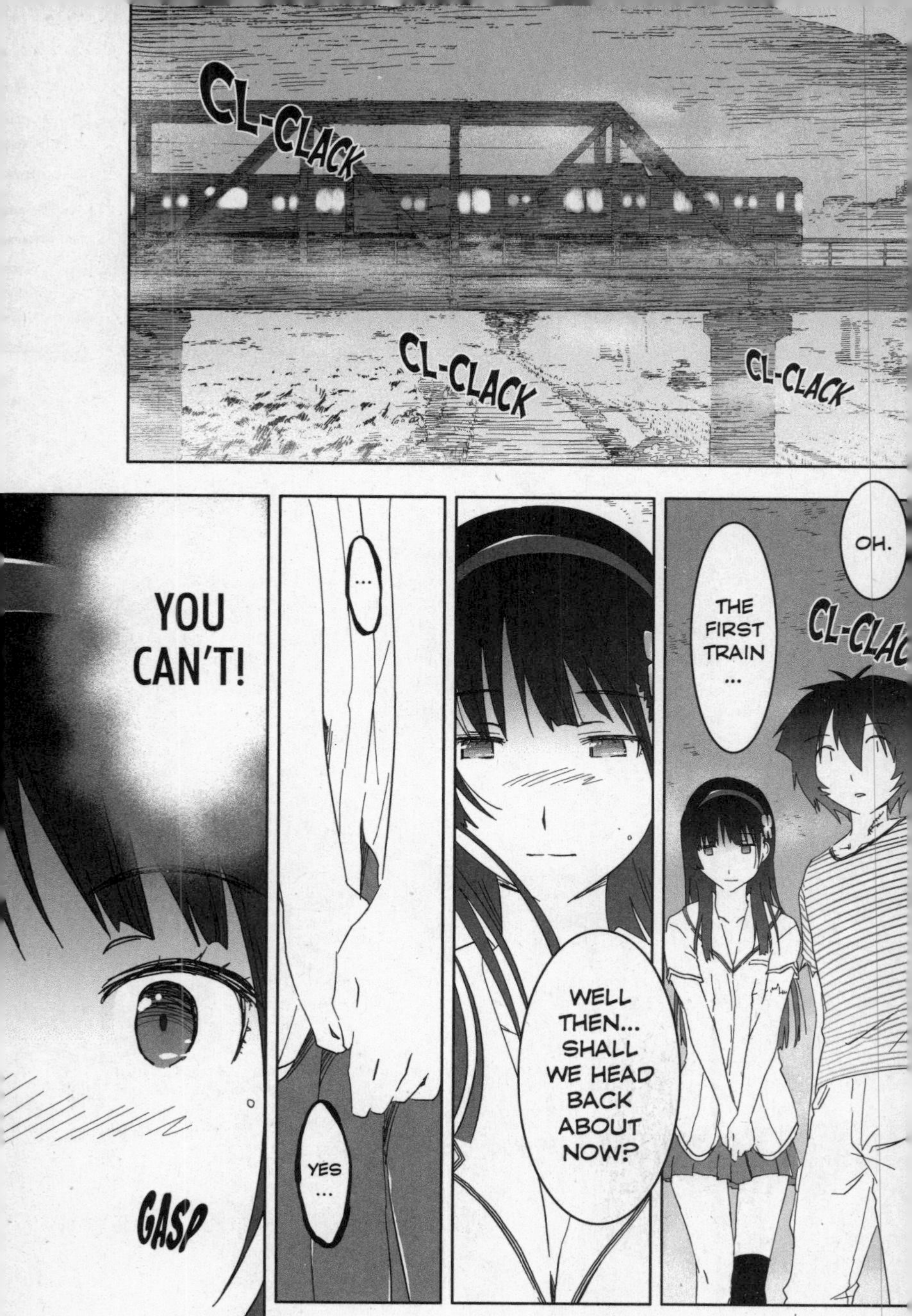
CL-CLACK
CL-CLACK
CL-CLACK
OH.
CL-CLAC
THE FIRST TRAIN ...
WELL THEN... SHALL WE HEAD BACK ABOUT NOW?
...
YES ...
YOU CAN'T!
GASP

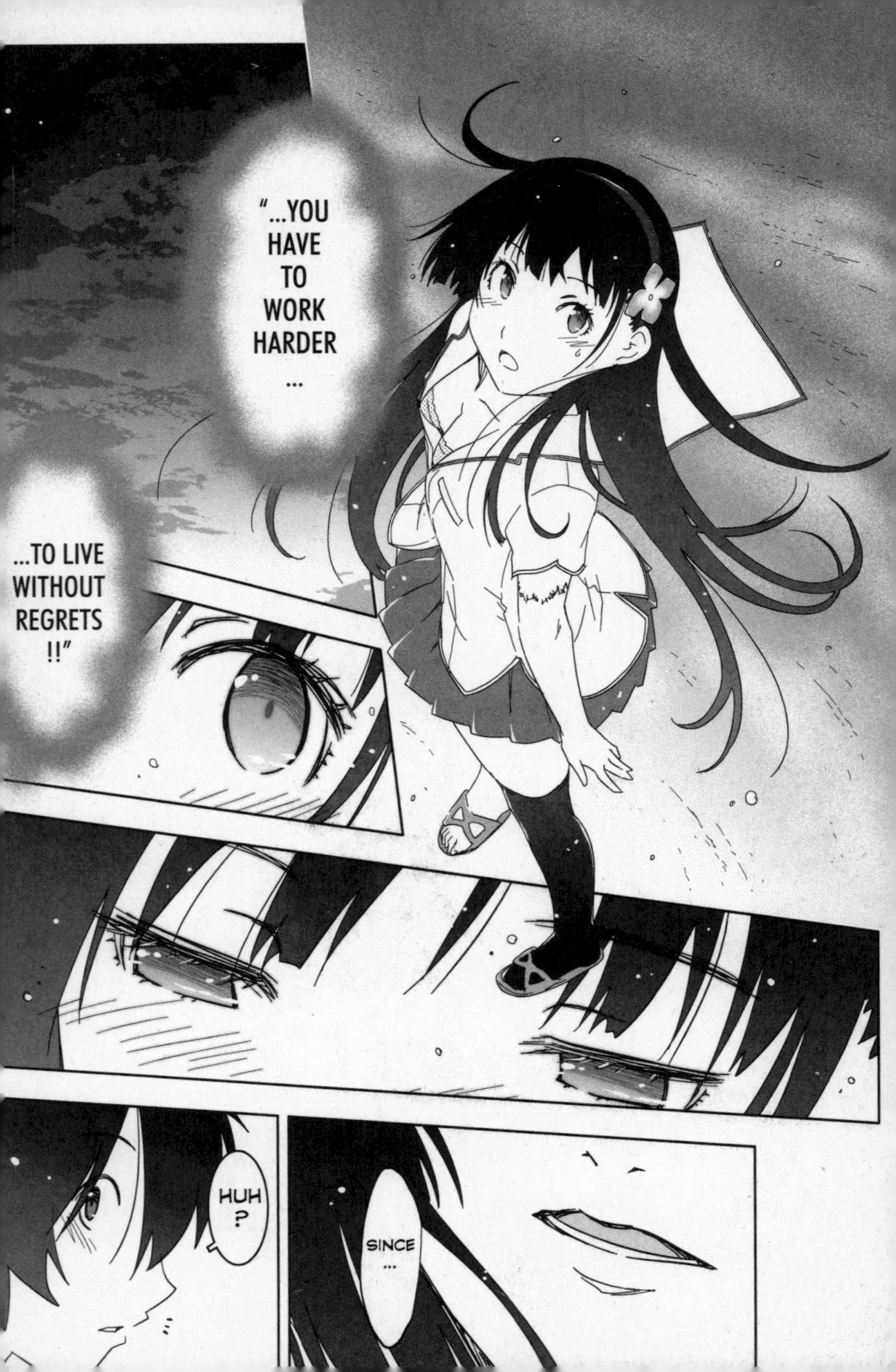
"...YOU HAVE TO WORK HARDER ...
...TO LIVE WITHOUT REGRETS !!"
SINCE ...
HUH ?

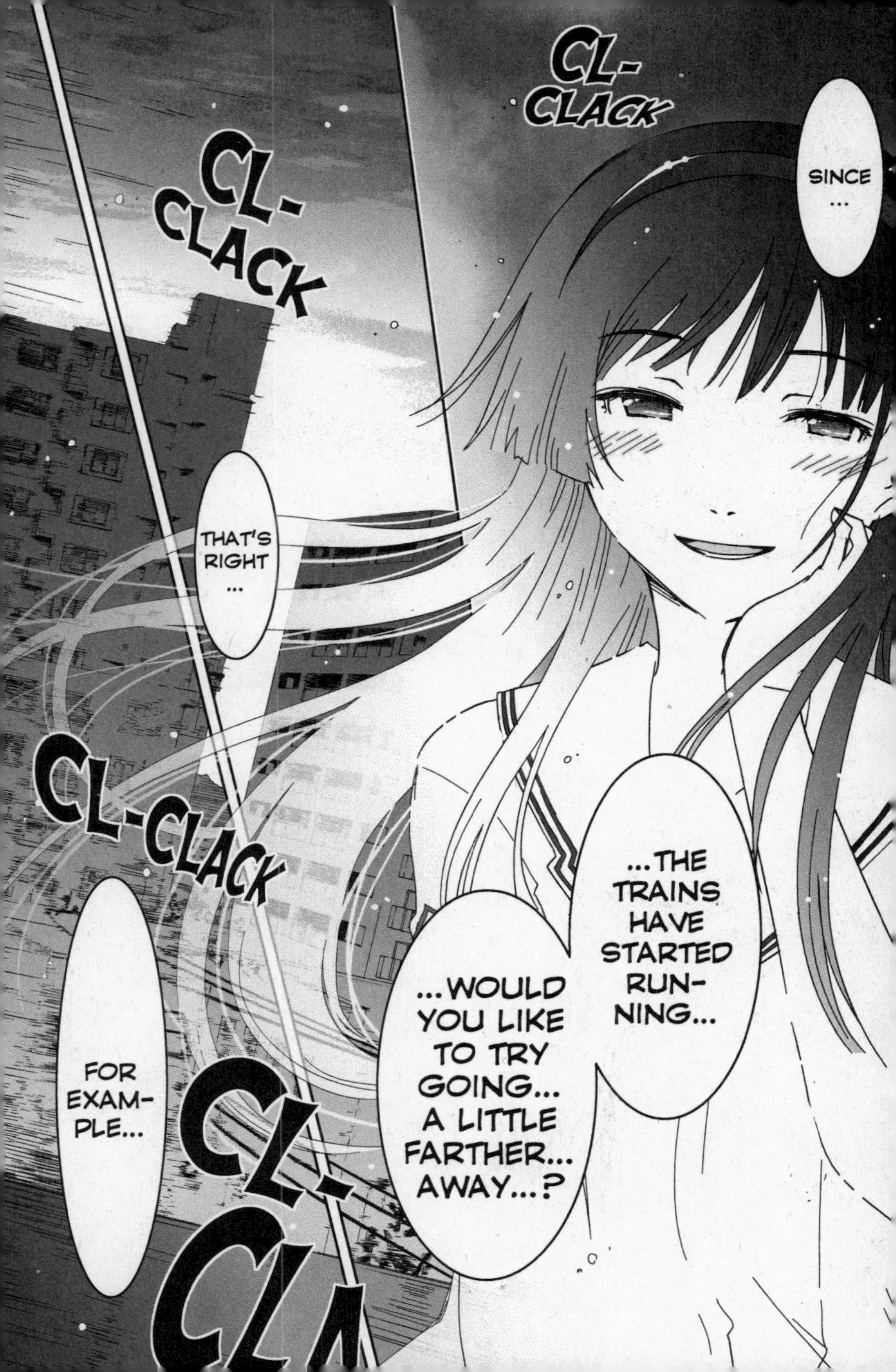
CL-CLACK
SINCE...
...THE TRAINS HAVE STARTED RUNNING...
CL-CLACK
THAT'S RIGHT...
CL-CLACK
FOR EXAMPLE...
...WOULD YOU LIKE TO TRY GOING... A LITTLE FARTHER... AWAY...?
CL-CLA

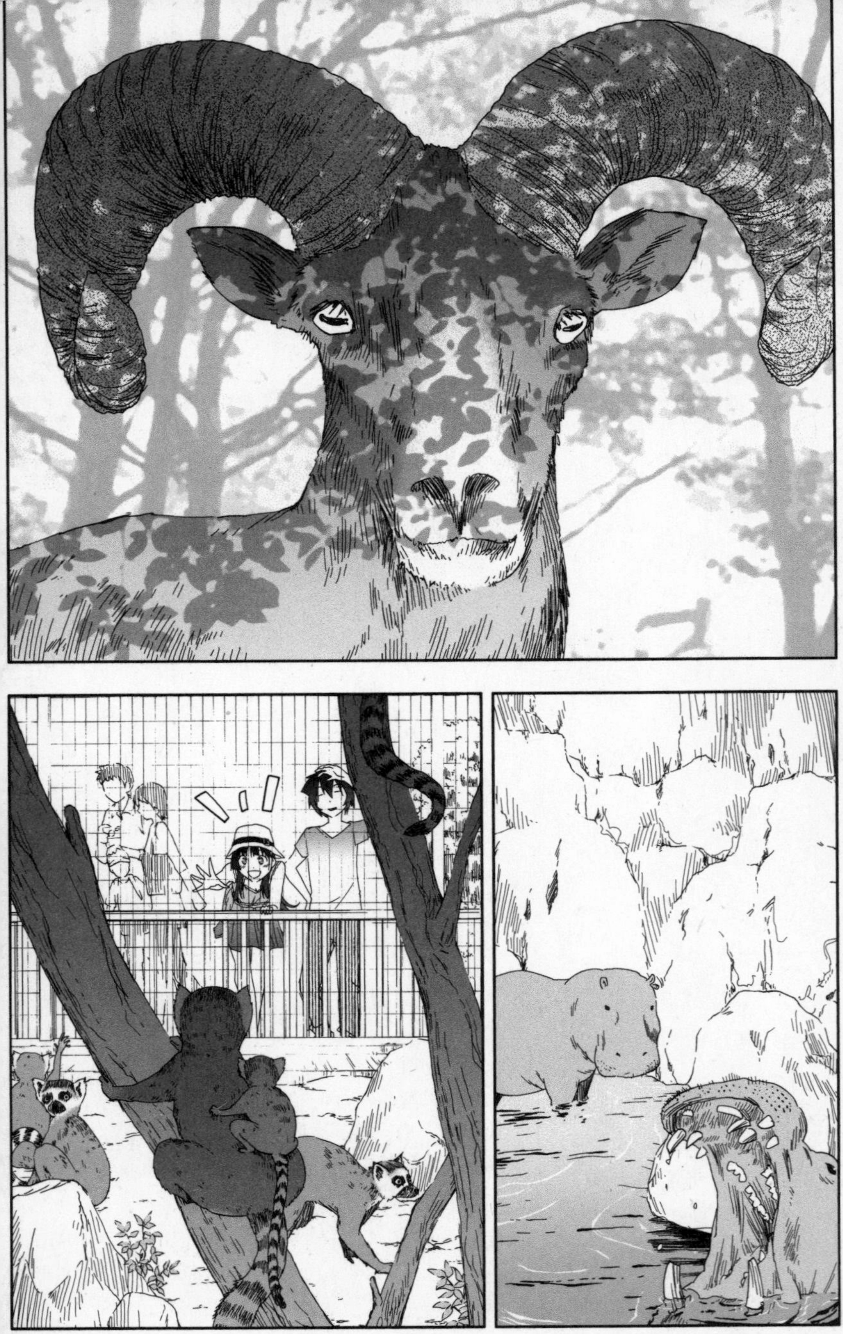

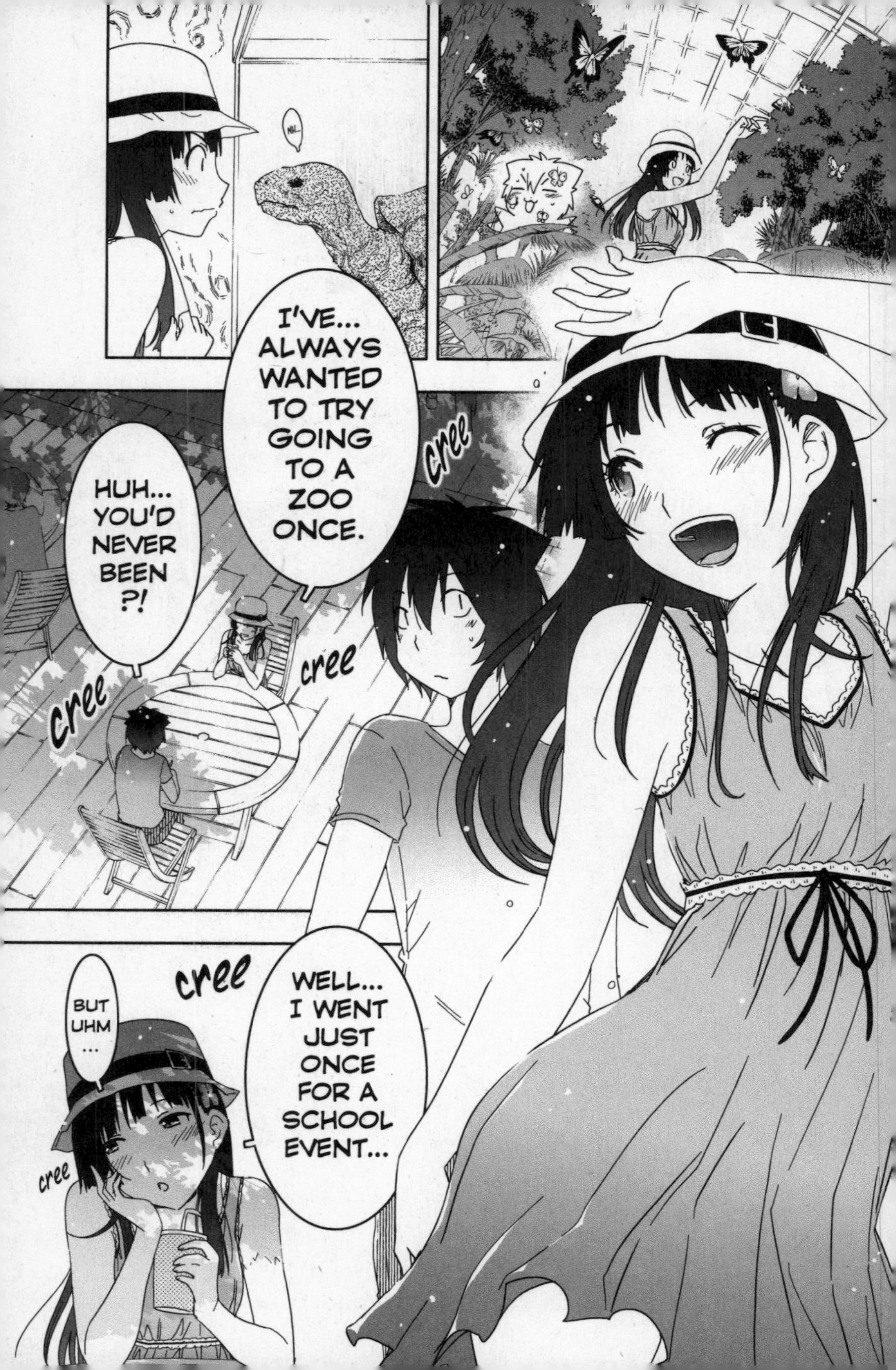
I'VE... ALWAYS WANTED TO TRY GOING TO A ZOO ONCE.
cree
HUH... YOU'D NEVER BEEN ?!
cree
cree
cree
WELL... I WENT JUST ONCE FOR A SCHOOL EVENT...
BUT UHM ...
cree

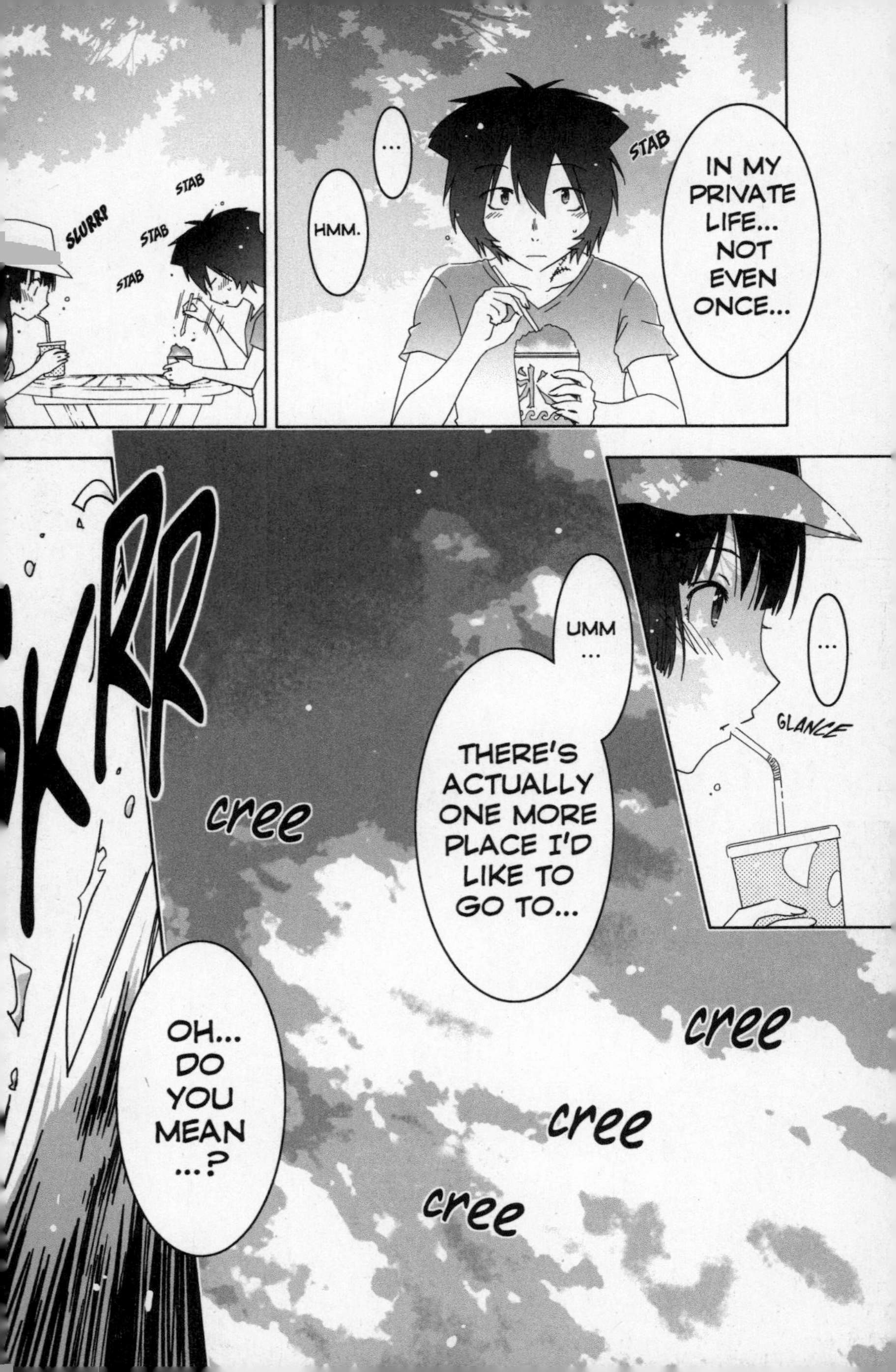
IN MY PRIVATE LIFE... NOT EVEN ONCE...
STAB
...
HMM.
STAB
SLURRP
STAB
STAB
...
GLANCE
UMM ...
THERE'S ACTUALLY ONE MORE PLACE I'D LIKE TO GO TO...
cree
cree
cree
cree
OH... DO YOU MEAN ...?
SKRR

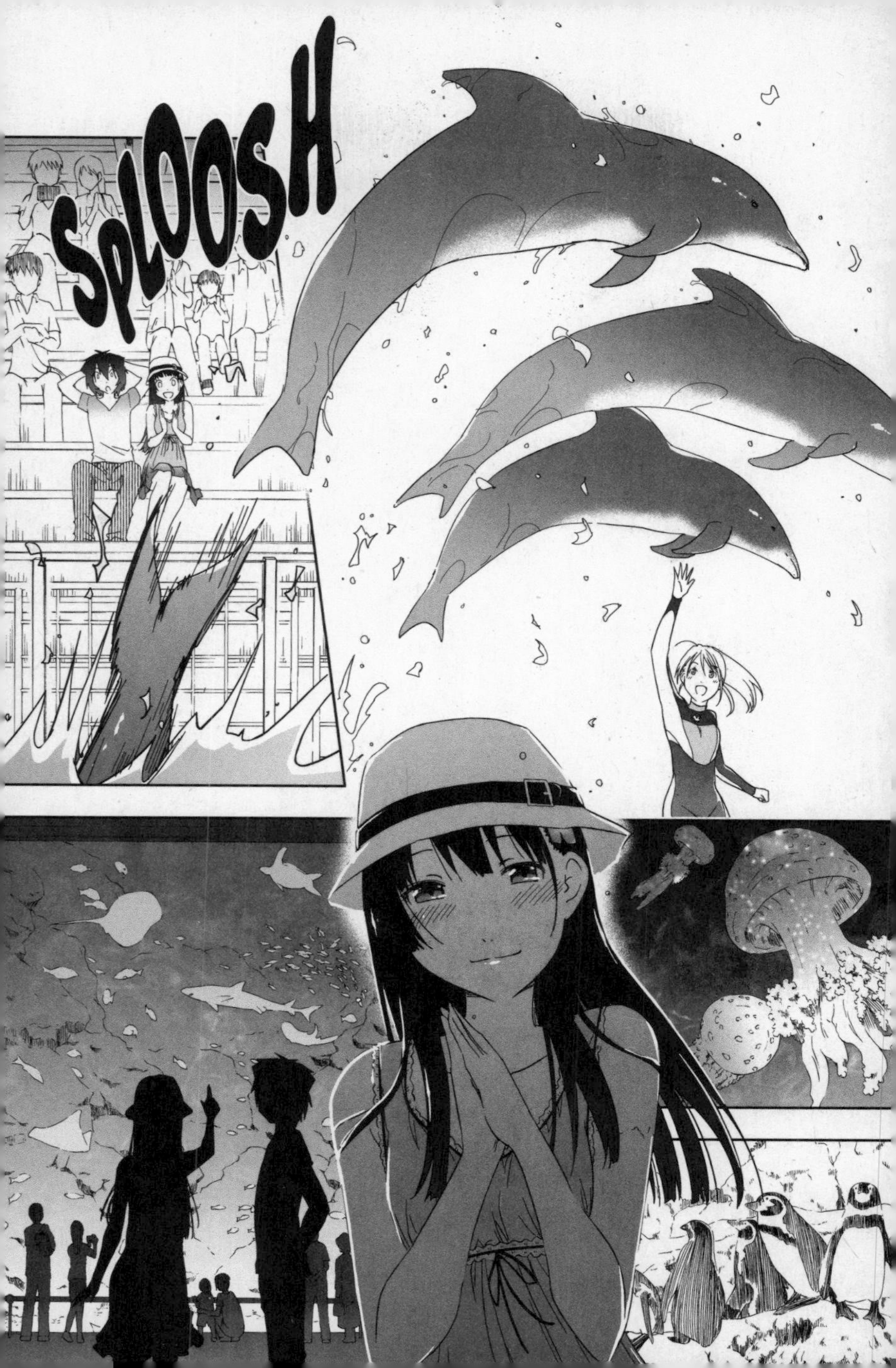
SPLOOSH

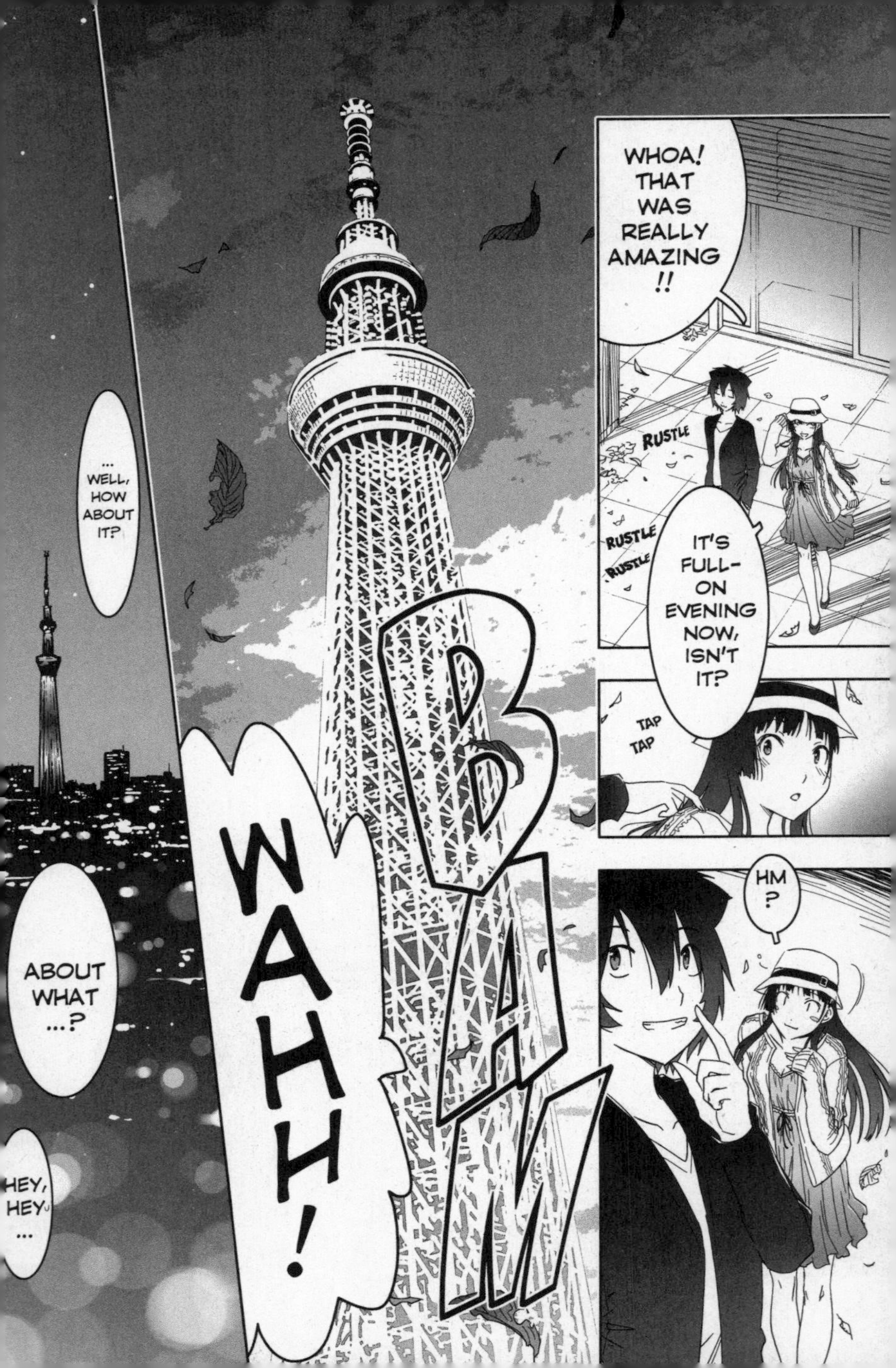
WHOA! THAT WAS REALLY AMAZING!!
RUSTLE
RUSTLE
RUSTLE
IT'S FULL-ON EVENING NOW, ISN'T IT?
TAP TAP
HM?
BAM
WAHH!
...WELL, HOW ABOUT IT?
ABOUT WHAT...?
HEY, HEY...

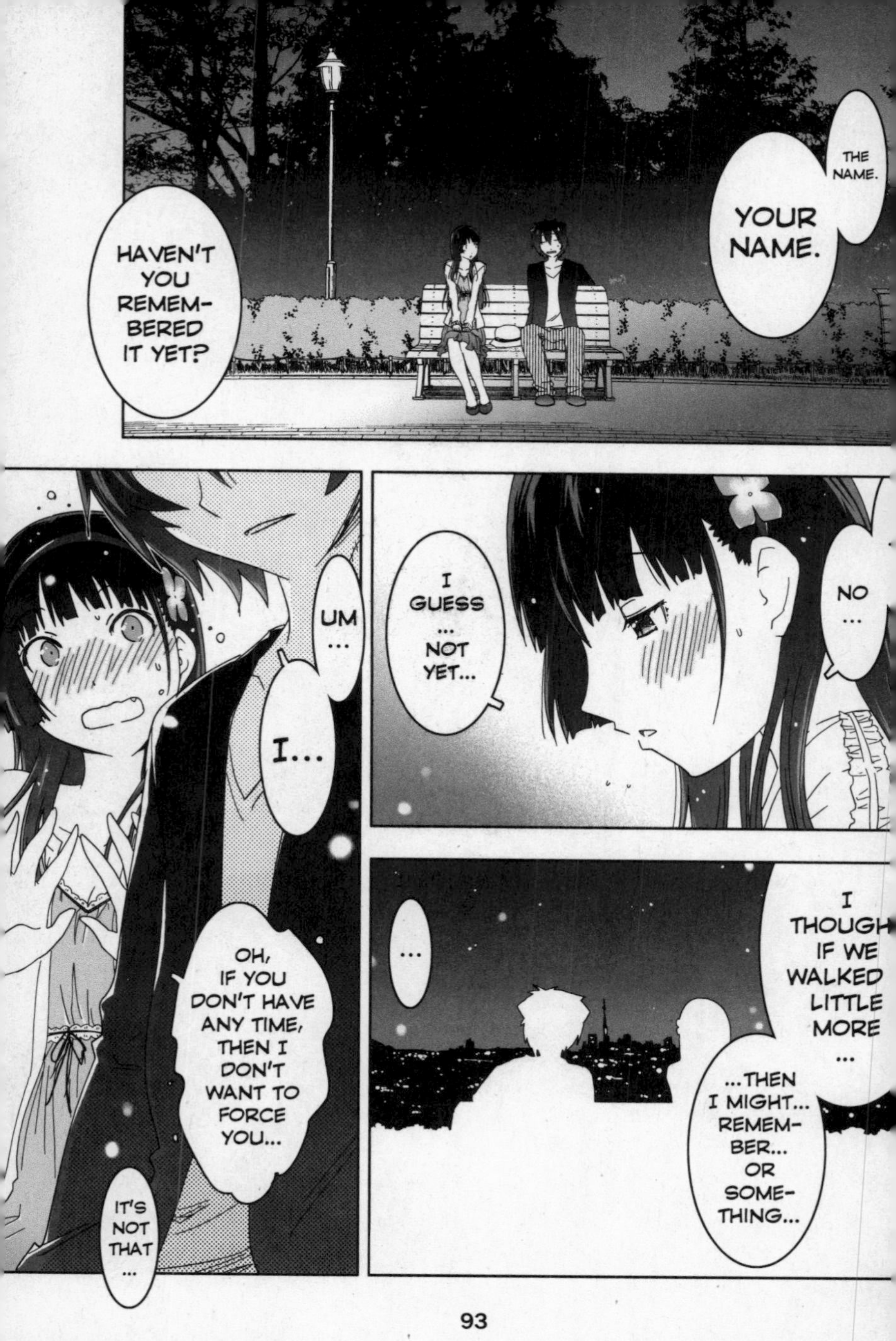
THE NAME.
YOUR NAME.
HAVEN'T YOU REMEMBERED IT YET?
NO ...
I GUESS ... NOT YET...
I THOUGH IF WE WALKED LITTLE MORE ...
...THEN I MIGHT... REMEMBER... OR SOMETHING...
...
UM ...
I...
OH, IF YOU DON'T HAVE ANY TIME, THEN I DON'T WANT TO FORCE YOU...
IT'S NOT THAT ...

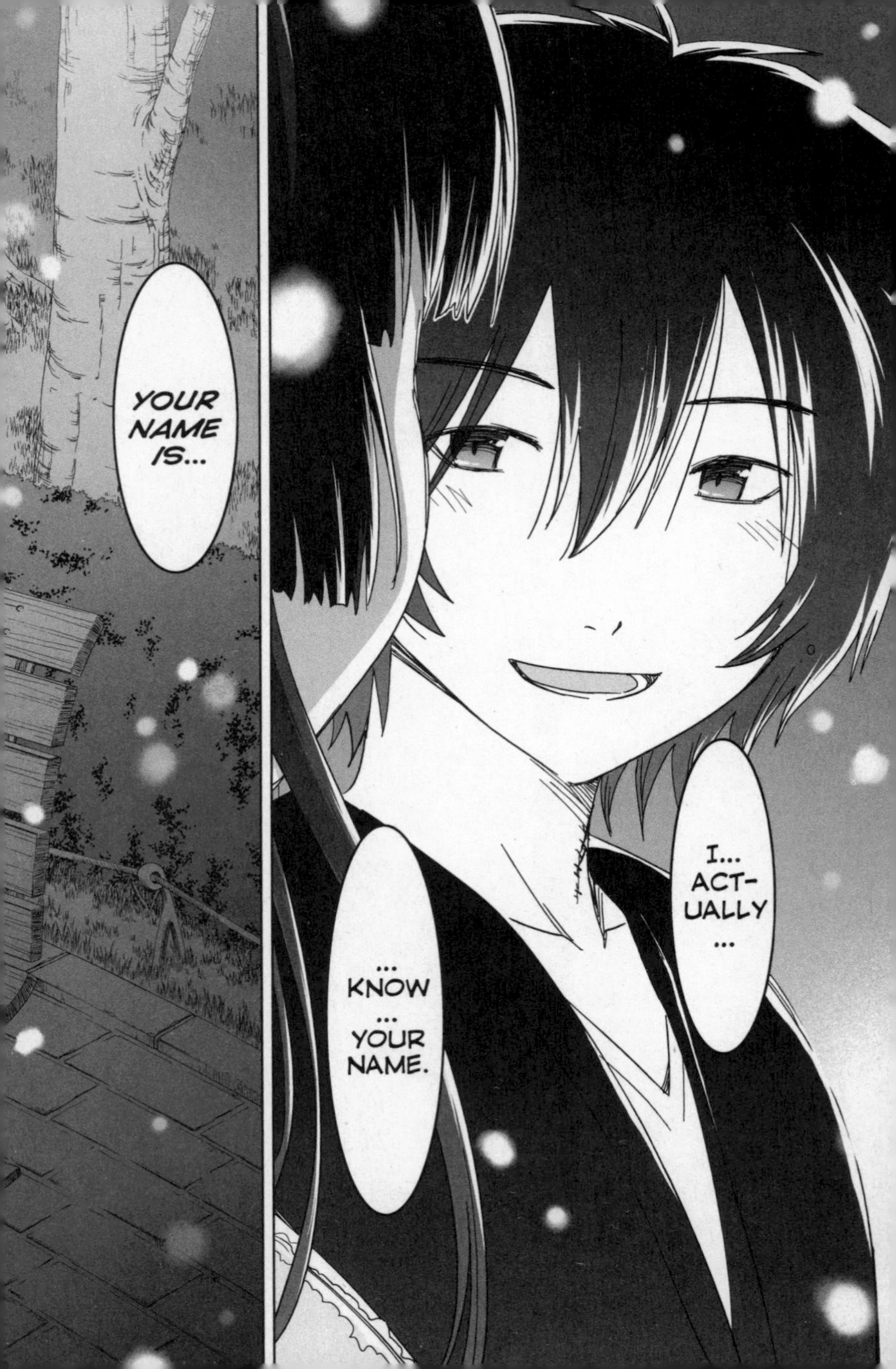
I... ACT-UALLY ...
... KNOW ... YOUR NAME.
YOUR NAME IS...

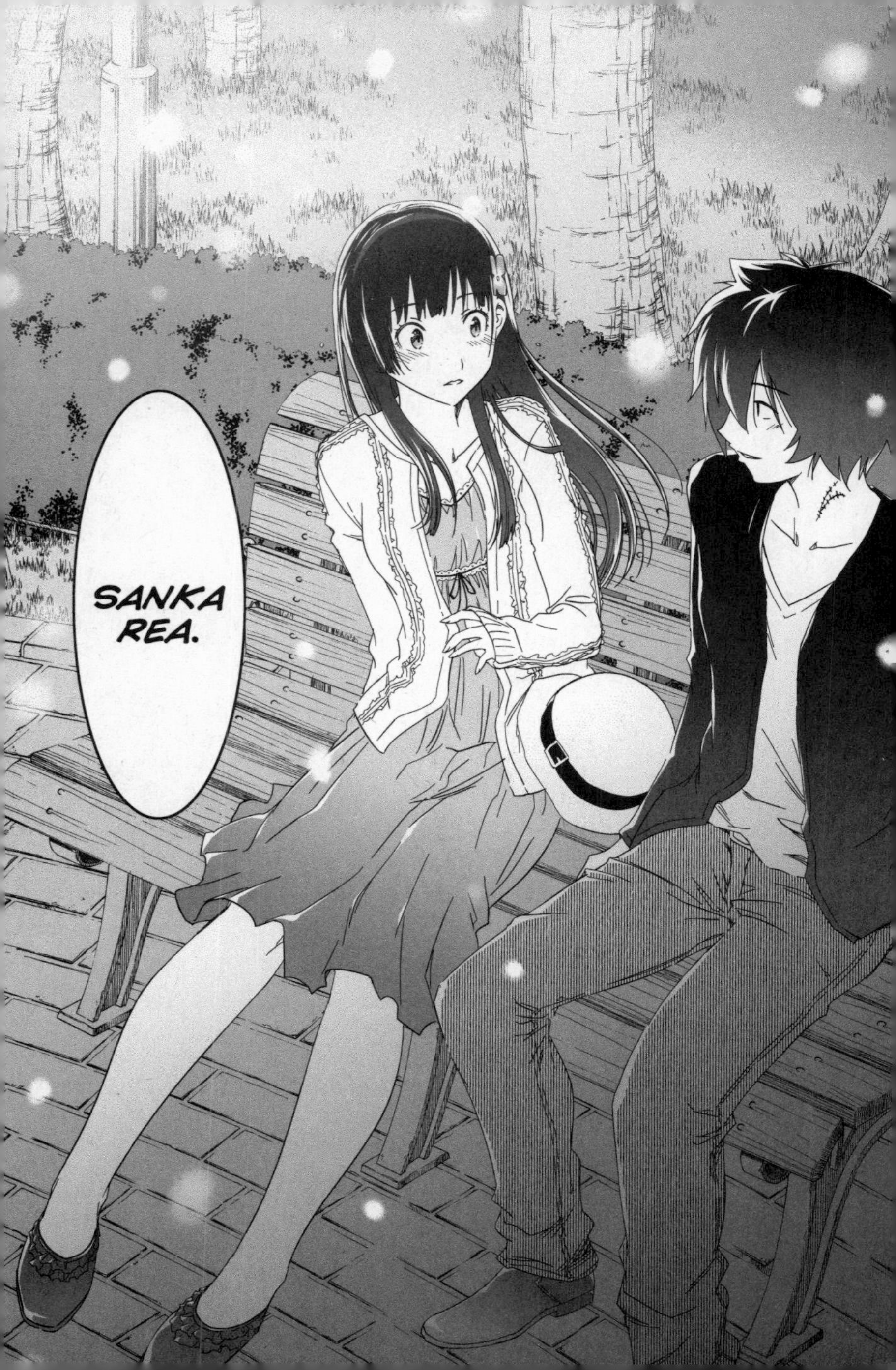
SANKA REA.

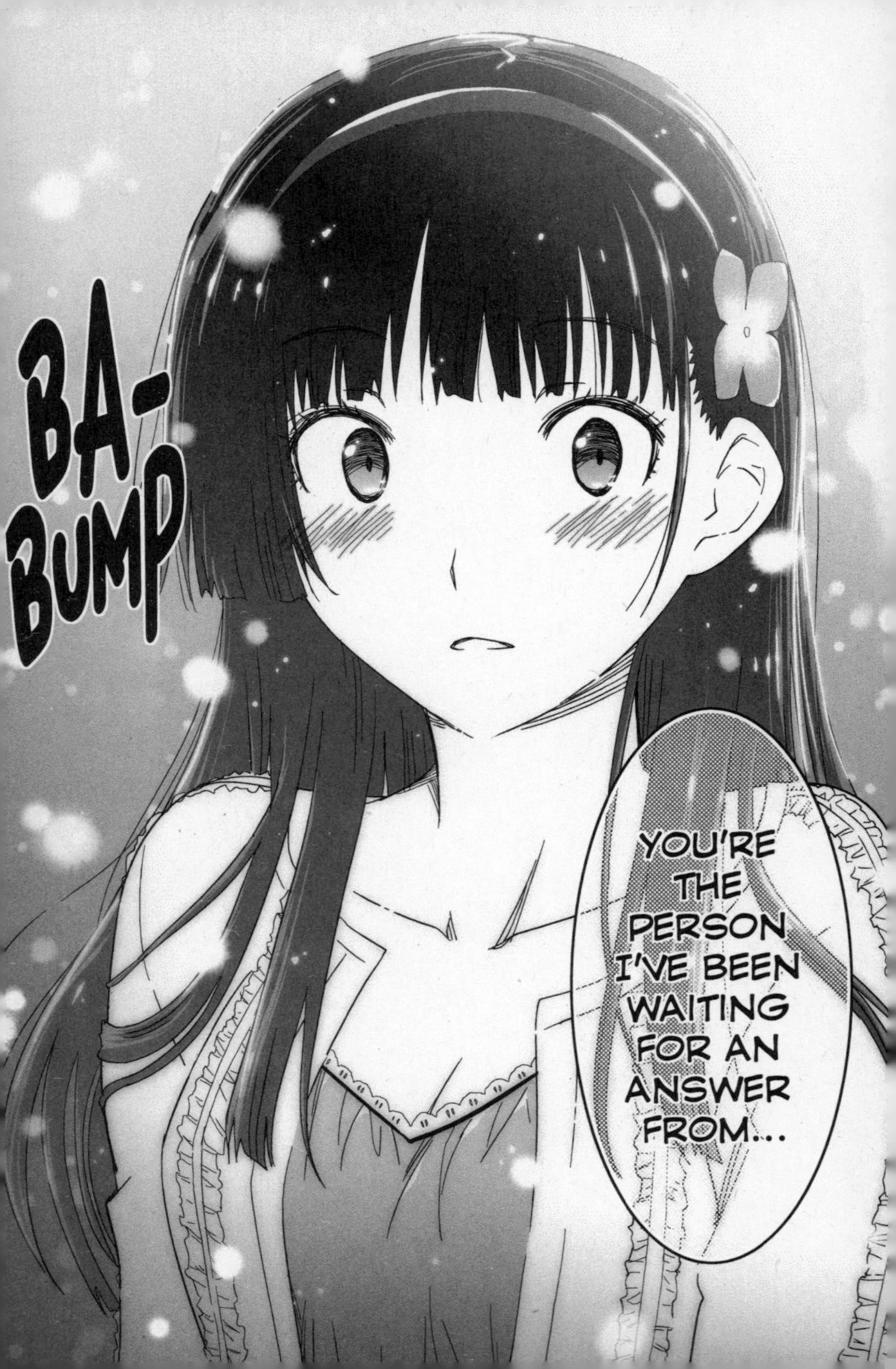
BA-BUMP
YOU'RE THE PERSON I'VE BEEN WAITING FOR AN ANSWER FROM...

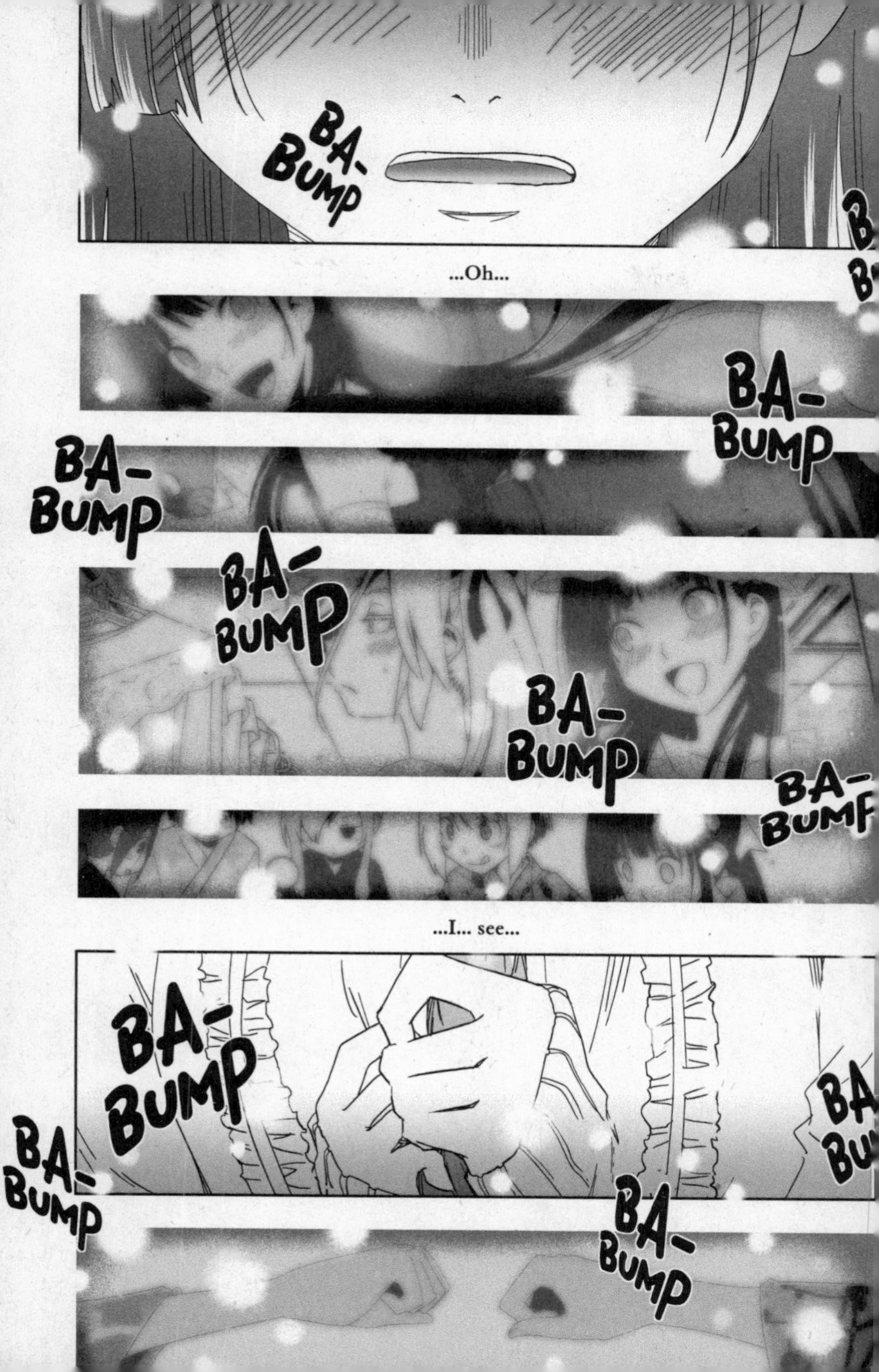

BA-BUMP
...Oh...
BA-BUMP
BA-BUMP
BA-BUMP
BA-BUMP
BA-BUMP
...I... see...
BA-BUMP
BA-BUMP
BA-BUMP

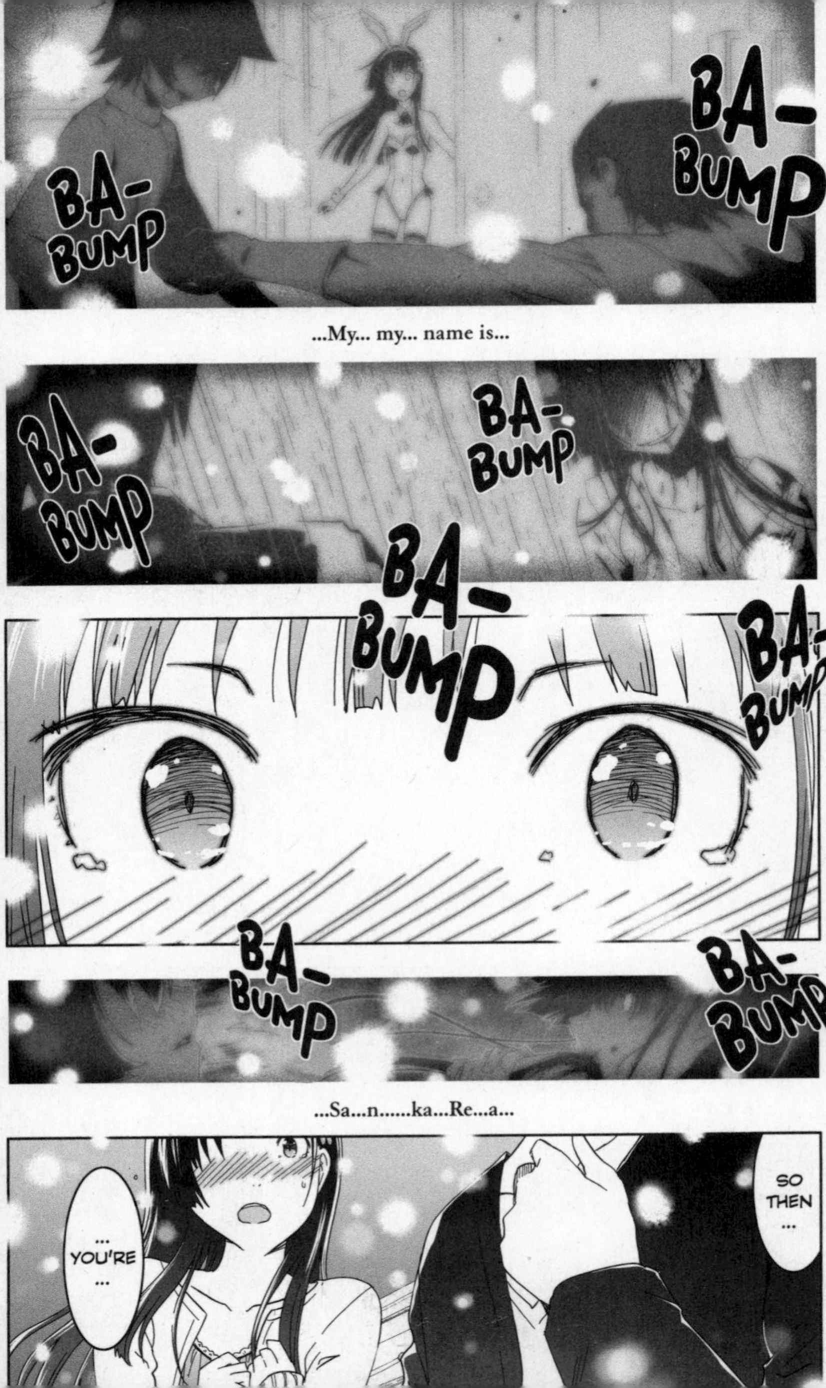

BA-BUMP
BA-BUMP
...My... my... name is...
BA-BUMP
BA-BUMP
BA-BUMP
BA-BUMP
BA-BUMP
BA-BUMP
...Sa...n......ka...Re...a...
SO THEN ...
... YOU'RE ...

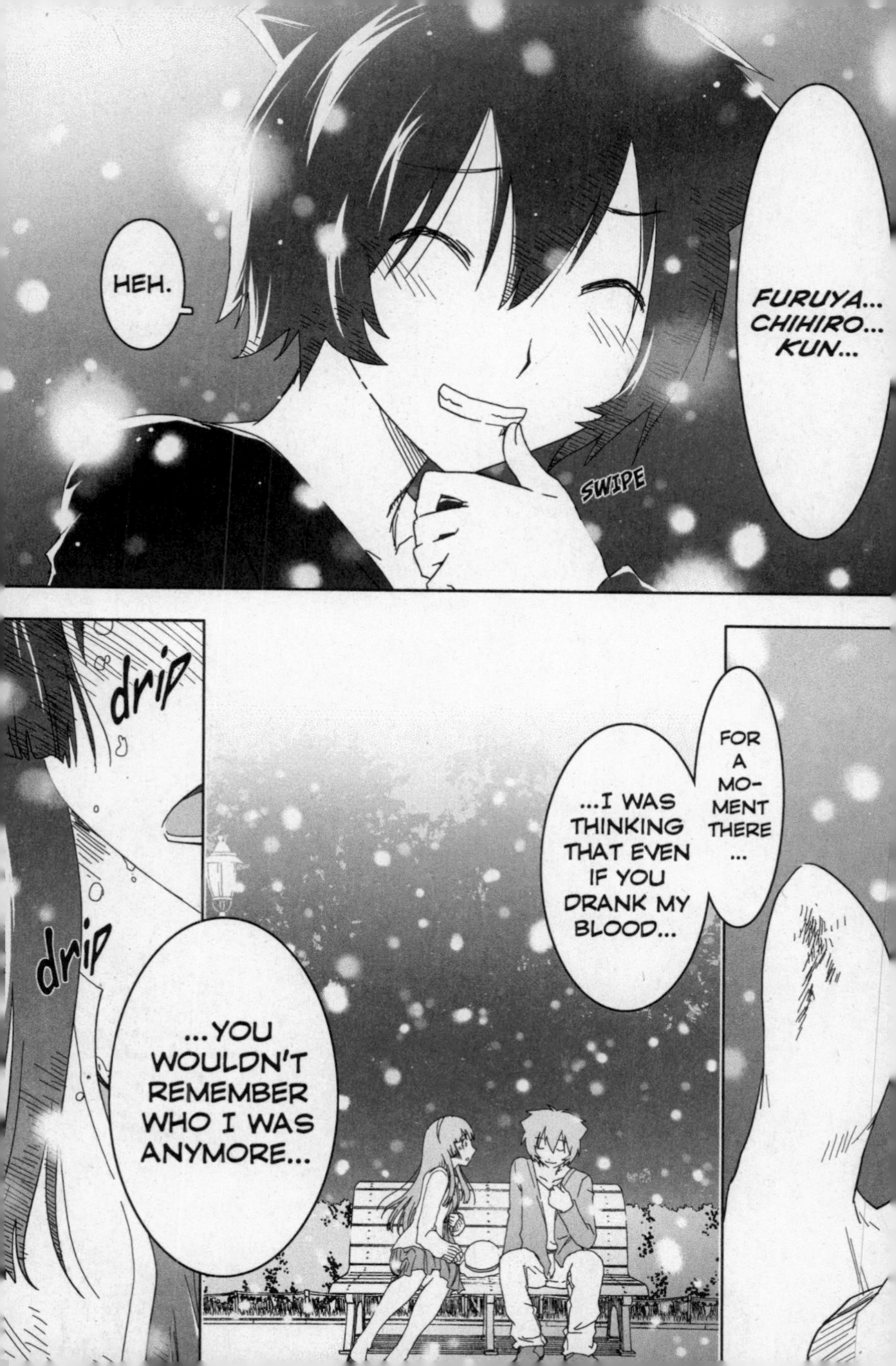

FURUYA... CHIHIRO... KUN...
HEH.
SWIPE
FOR A MOMENT THERE...
...I WAS THINKING THAT EVEN IF YOU DRANK MY BLOOD...
...YOU WOULDN'T REMEMBER WHO I WAS ANYMORE...
drip
drip

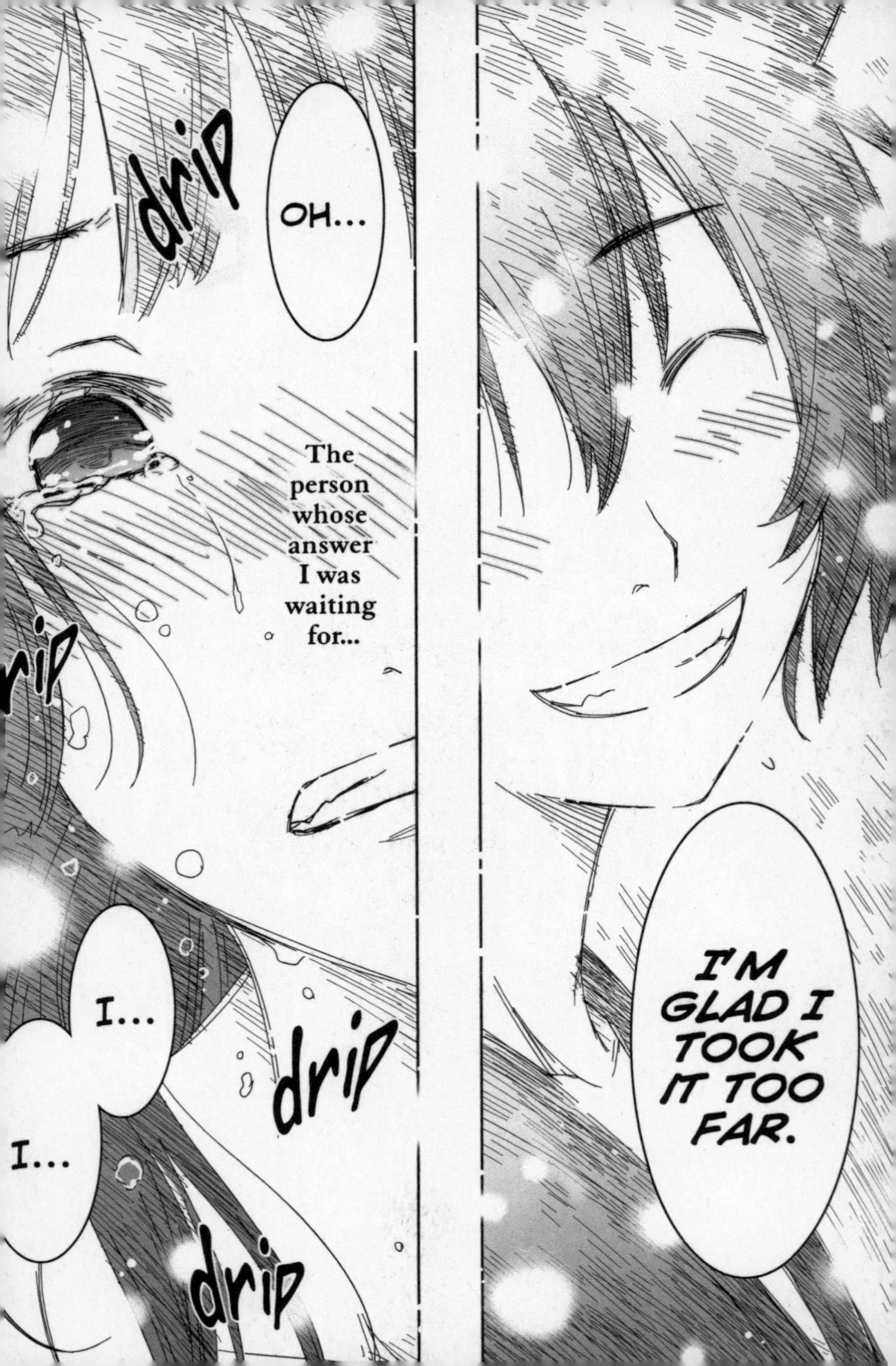
I'M GLAD I TOOK IT TOO FAR.
OH...
drip
The person whose answer I was waiting for...
drip
drip
I...
I...
drip

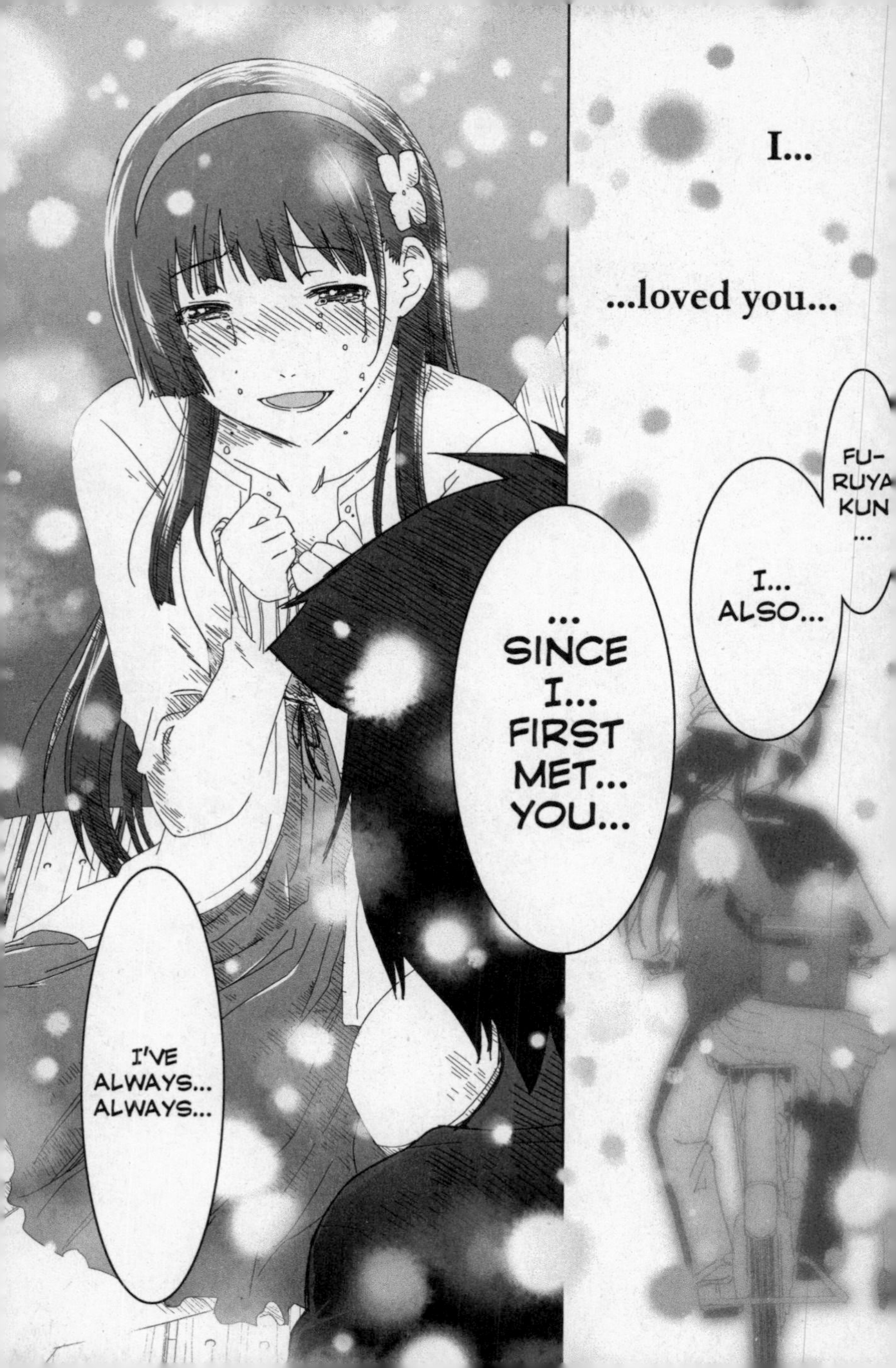
I...
...loved you...
FU-RUYA KUN ... I... ALSO...
... SINCE I... FIRST MET... YOU...
I'VE ALWAYS... ALWAYS...

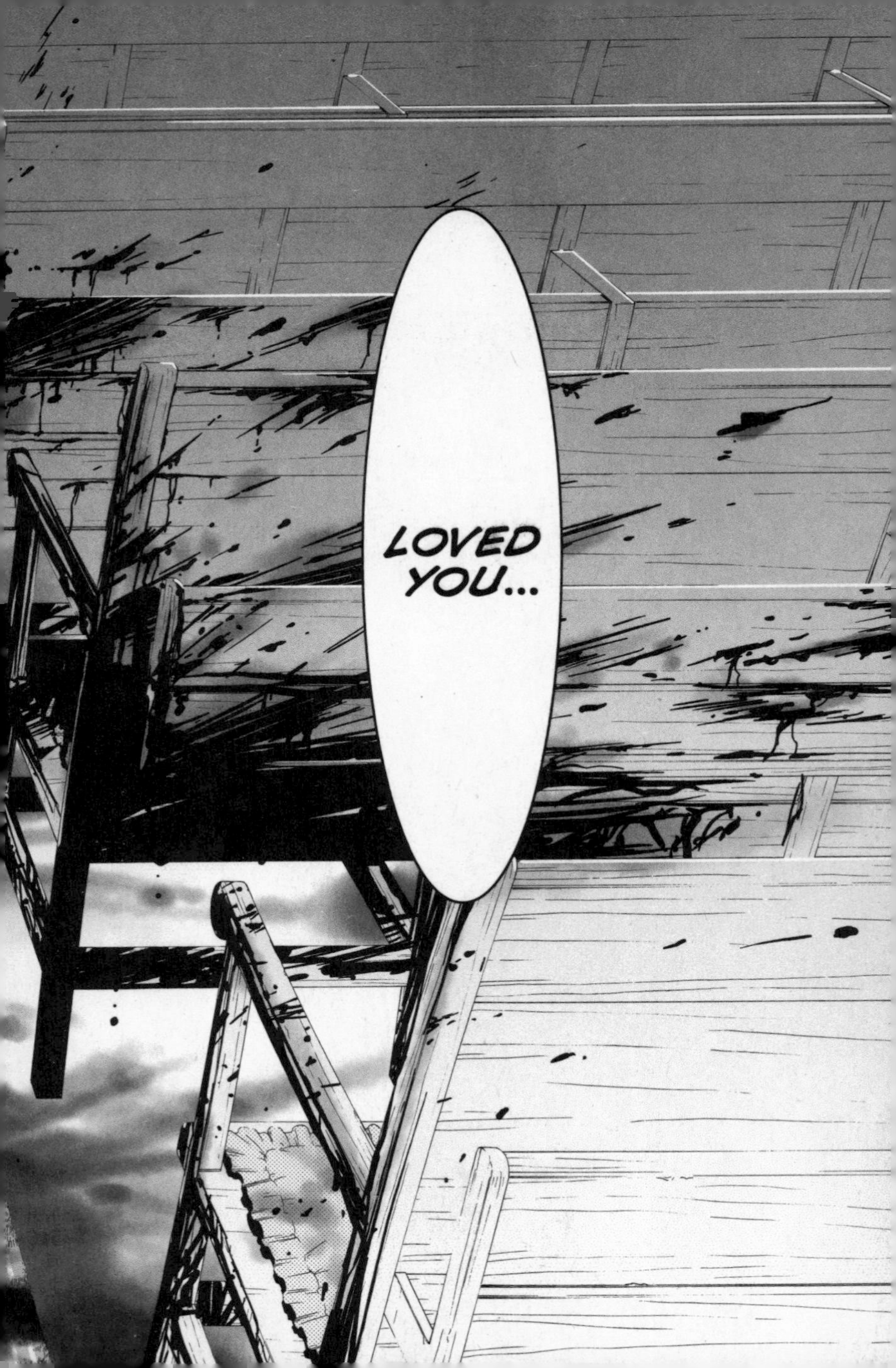
LOVED YOU...

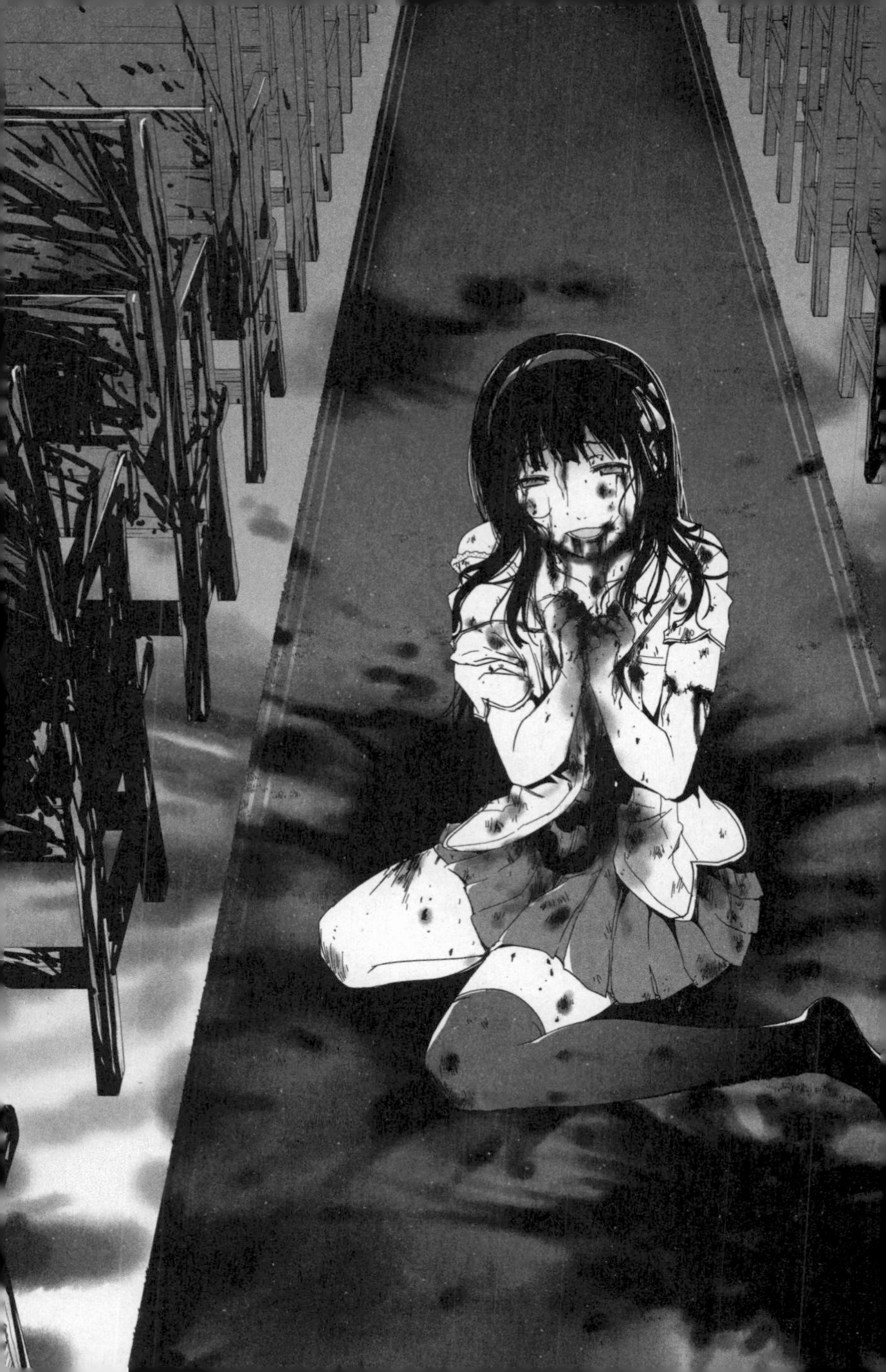

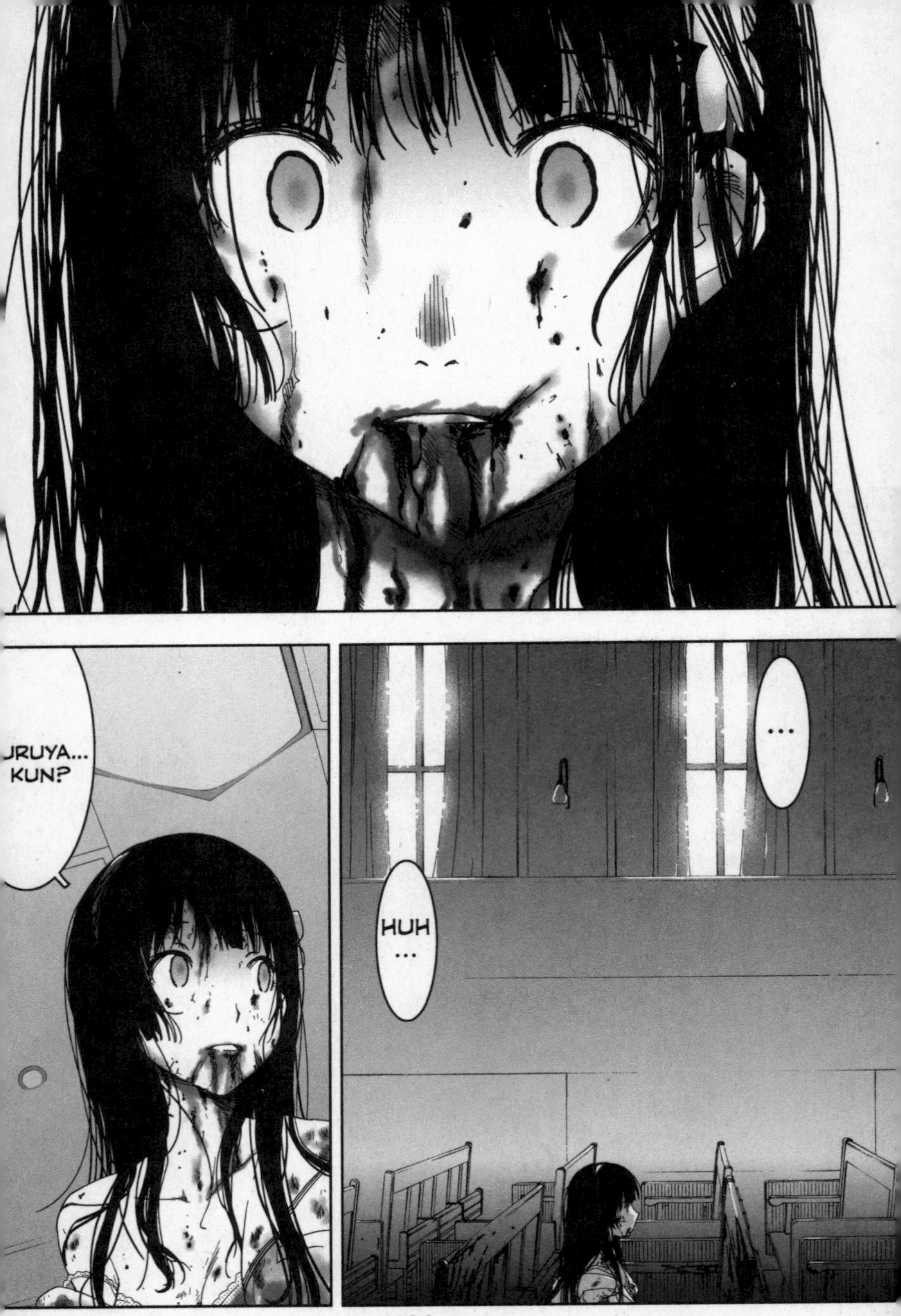
...
HUH ...
URUYA... KUN?

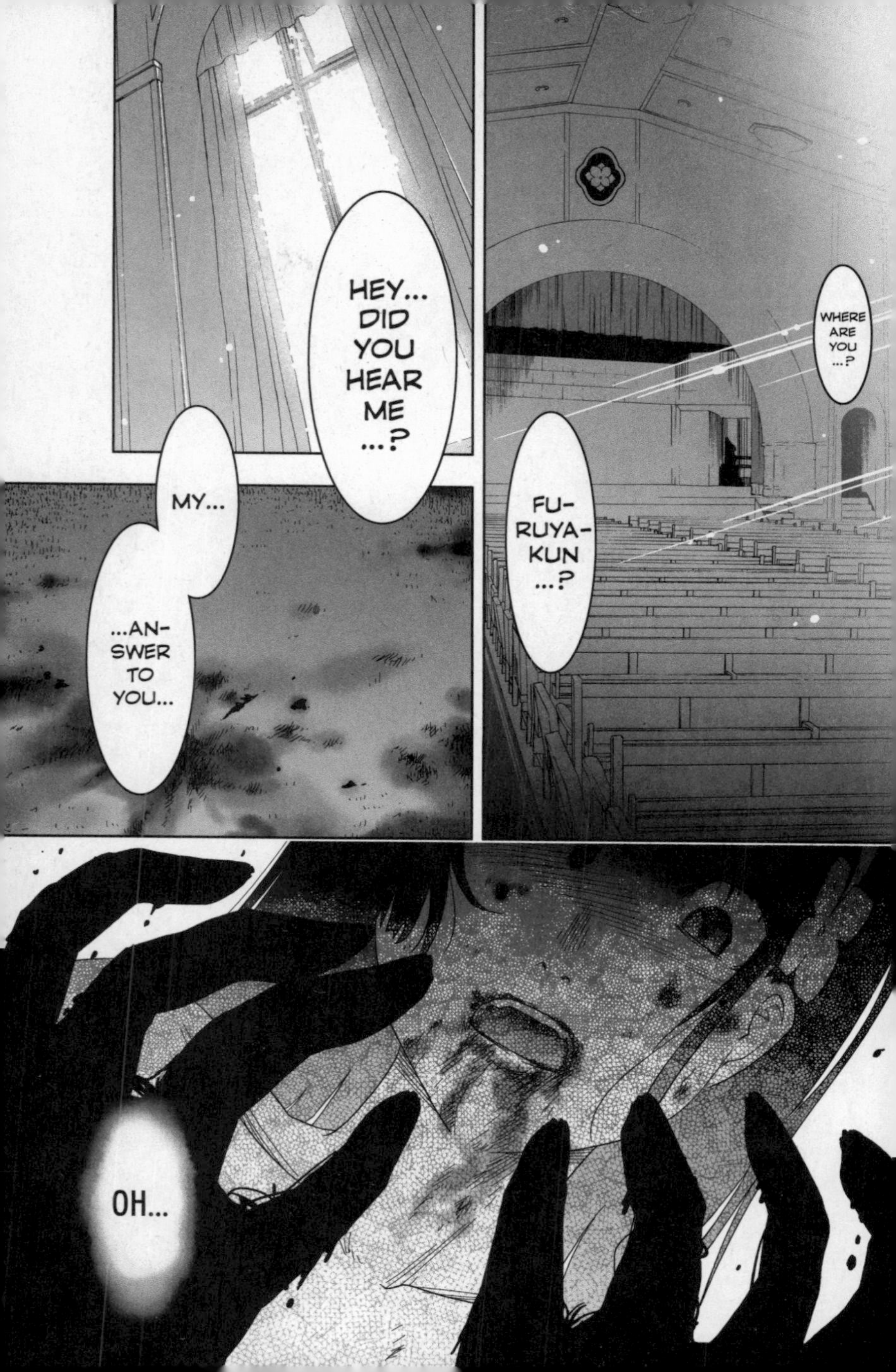
WHERE ARE YOU ...?
FU-RUYA-KUN ...?
HEY... DID YOU HEAR ME ...?
MY...
...AN-SWER TO YOU...
OH...

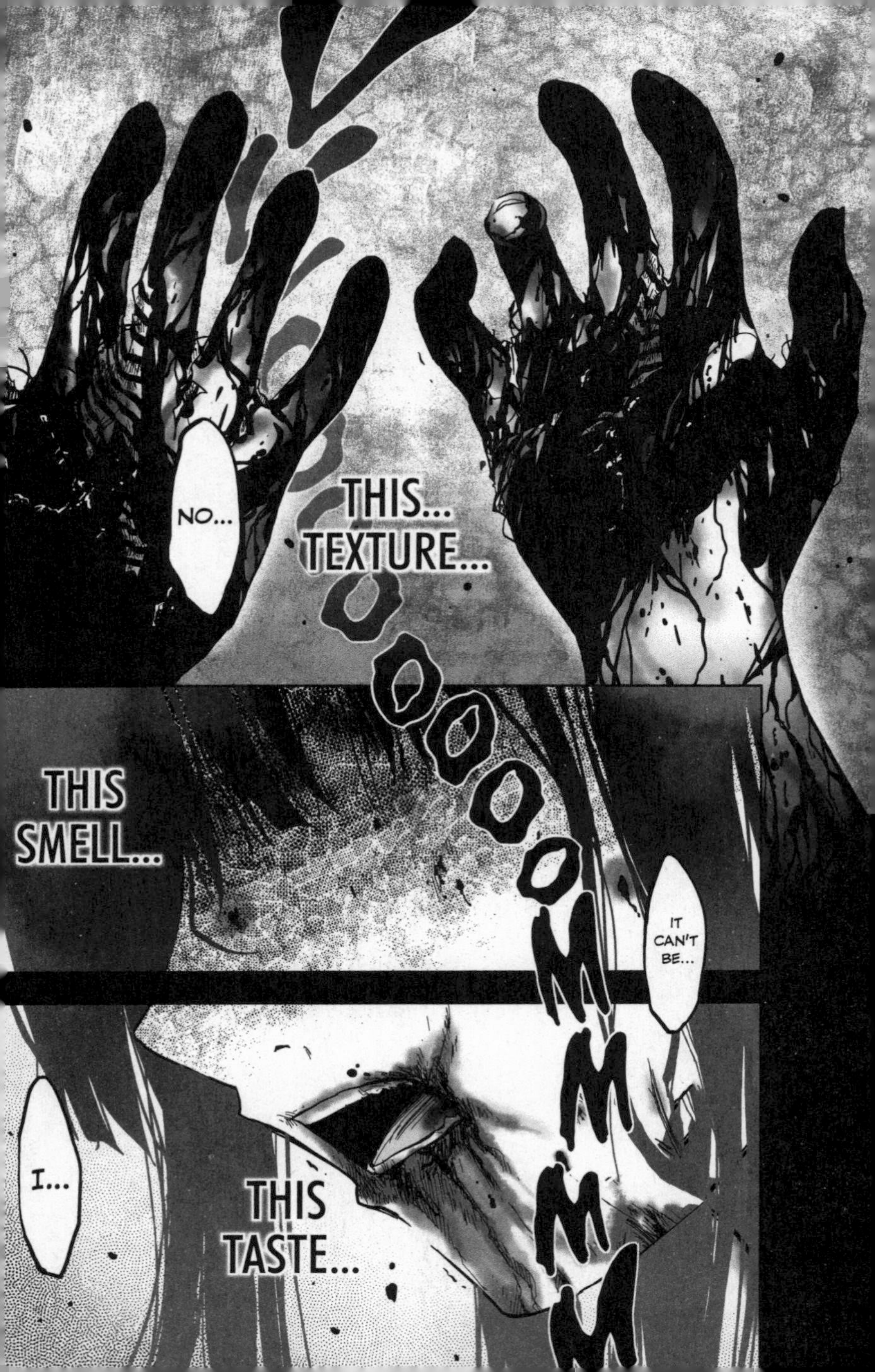
THIS... TEXTURE...
NO...
IT CAN'T BE...
THIS SMELL...
THIS TASTE...
I...

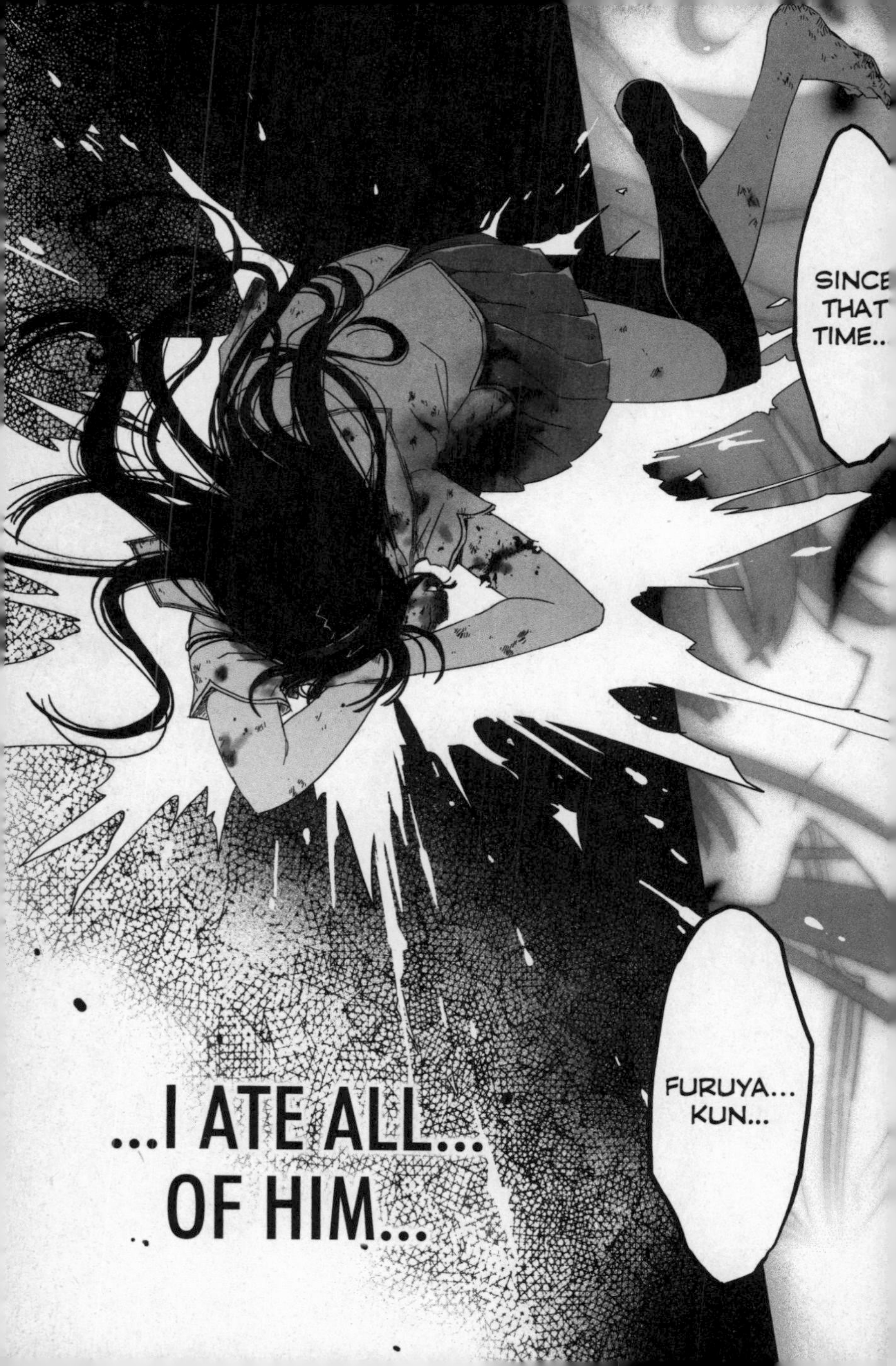
SINCE THAT TIME...
FURUYA... KUN...
...I ATE ALL... OF HIM...

SANKAREA

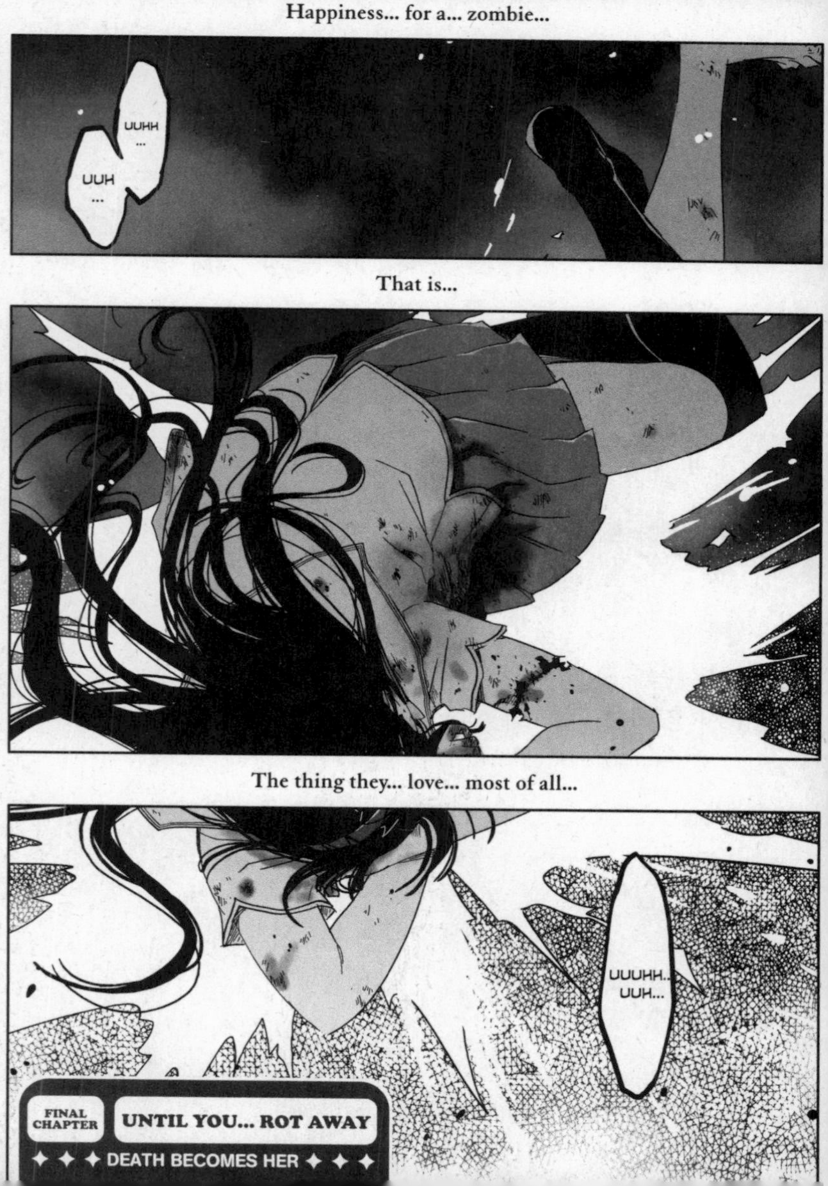
Happiness... for a... zombie...
UUHH...
UUH...
That is...
The thing they... love... most of all...
UUUHH.. UUH...
FINAL CHAPTER
UNTIL YOU... ROT AWAY
DEATH BECOMES HER

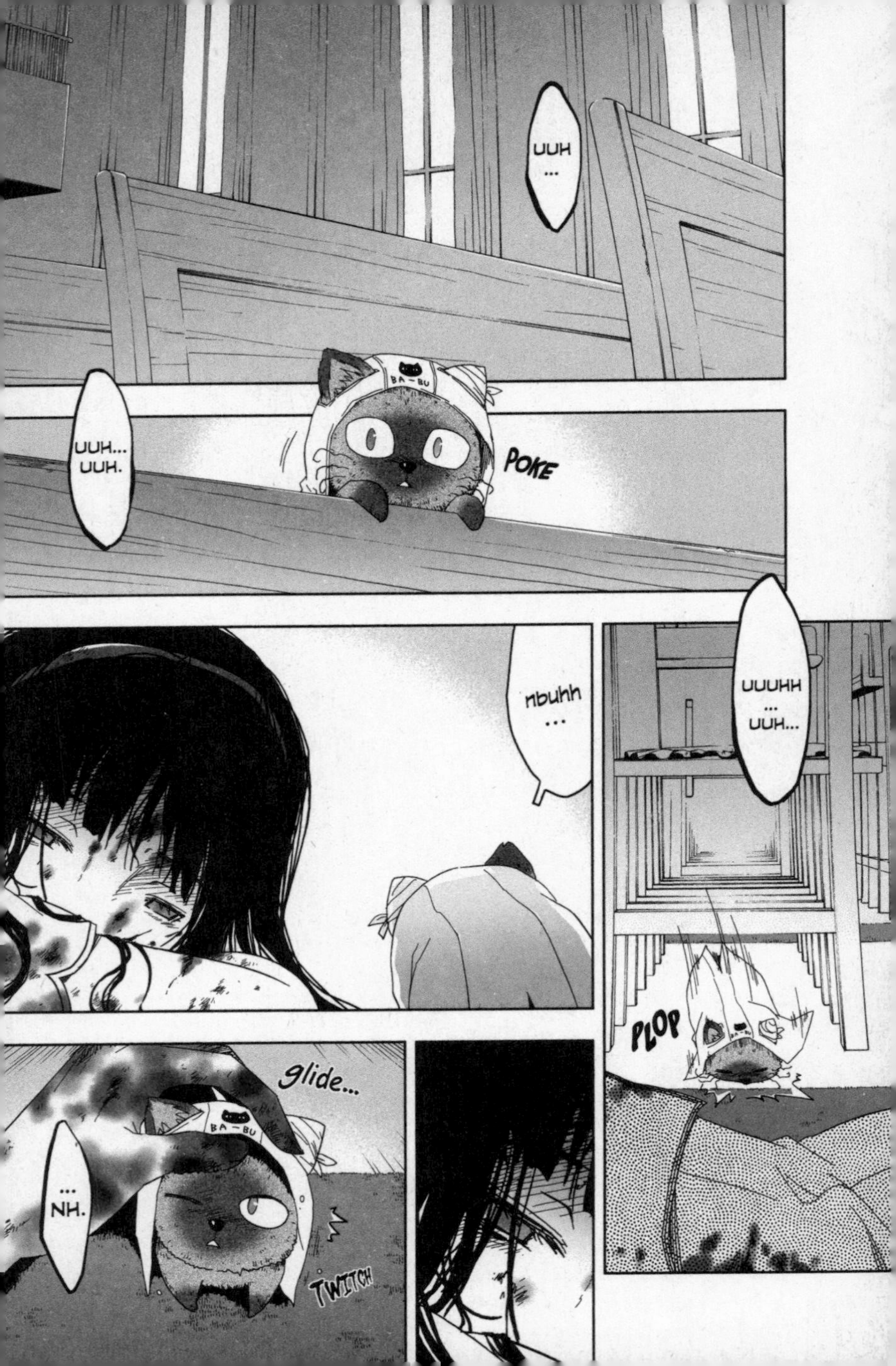
UUH ...
UUH... UUH.
POKE
UUUHH ... UUH...
PLOP
nbuhh ...
glide...
... NH.
TWITCH

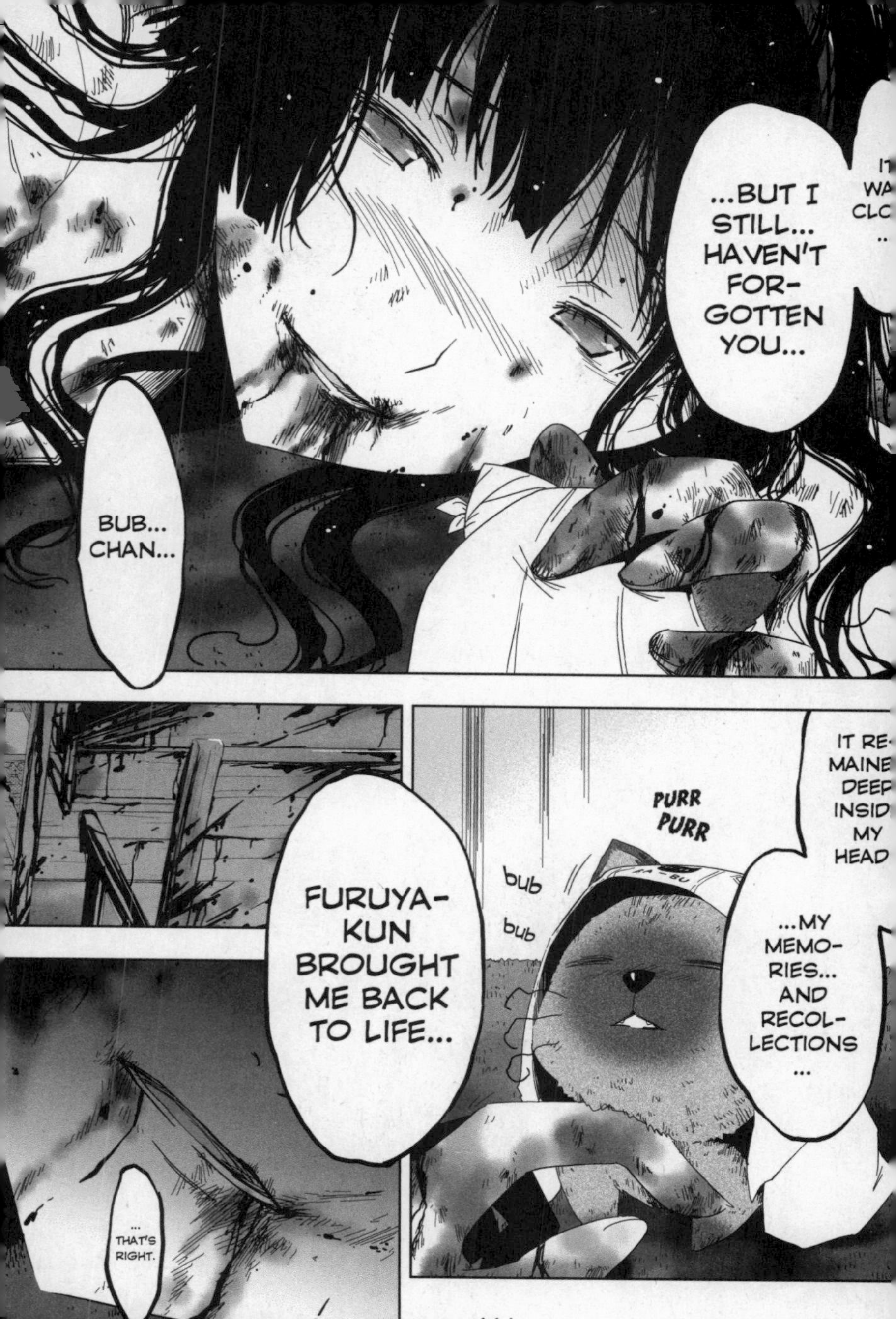
IT WA CLC ..
...BUT I STILL... HAVEN'T FOR-GOTTEN YOU...
BUB... CHAN...
IT RE- MAINE DEEP INSID MY HEAD
PURR PURR
...MY MEMO-RIES... AND RECOL-LECTIONS ...
bub bub
FURUYA-KUN BROUGHT ME BACK TO LIFE...
... THAT'S RIGHT.

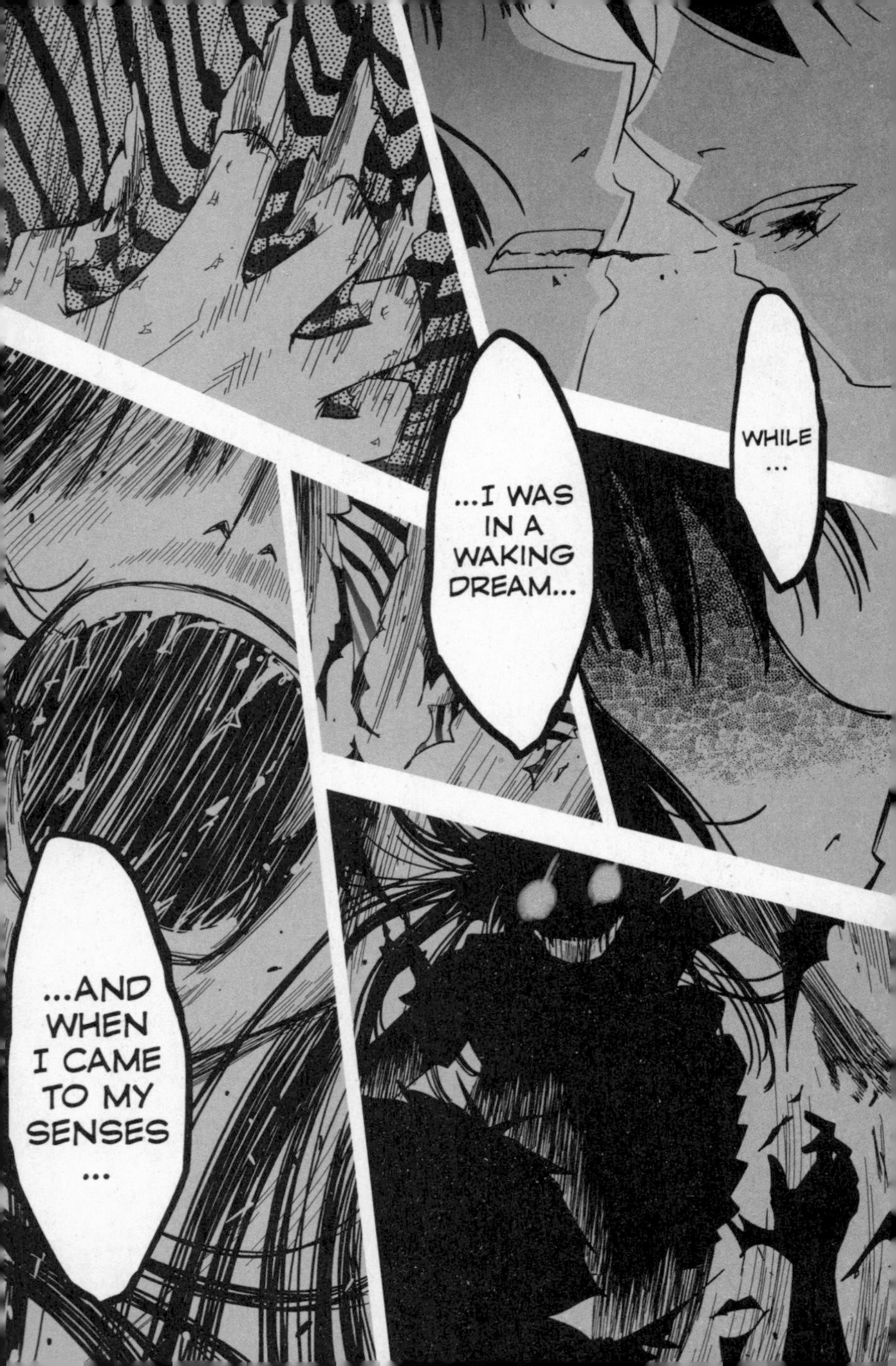
WHILE
...
...I WAS
IN A
WAKING
DREAM...
...AND
WHEN
I CAME
TO MY
SENSES
...

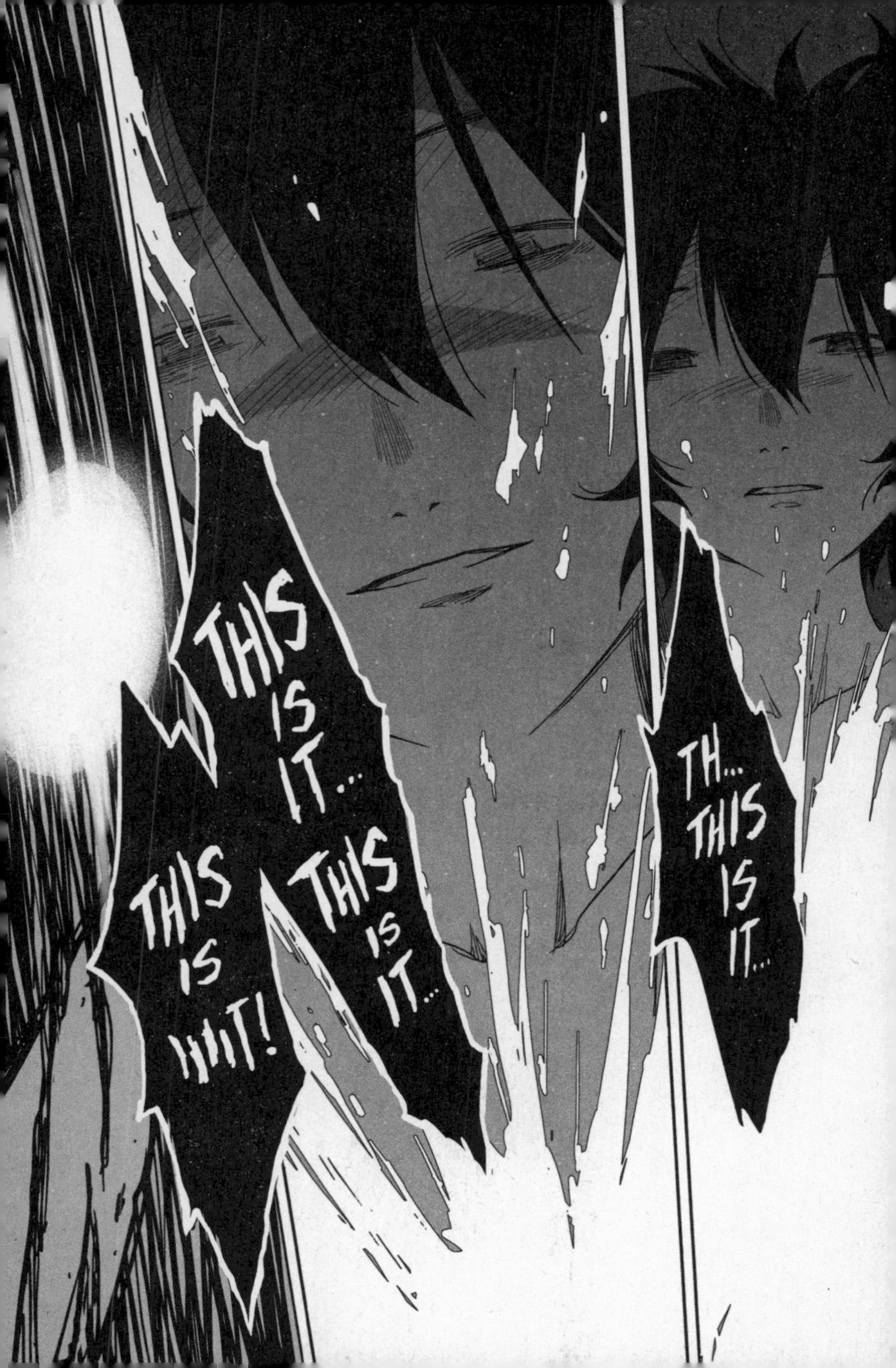

TH... THIS IS IT...
THIS IS IT... THIS IS IT... THIS IS IIIIT!

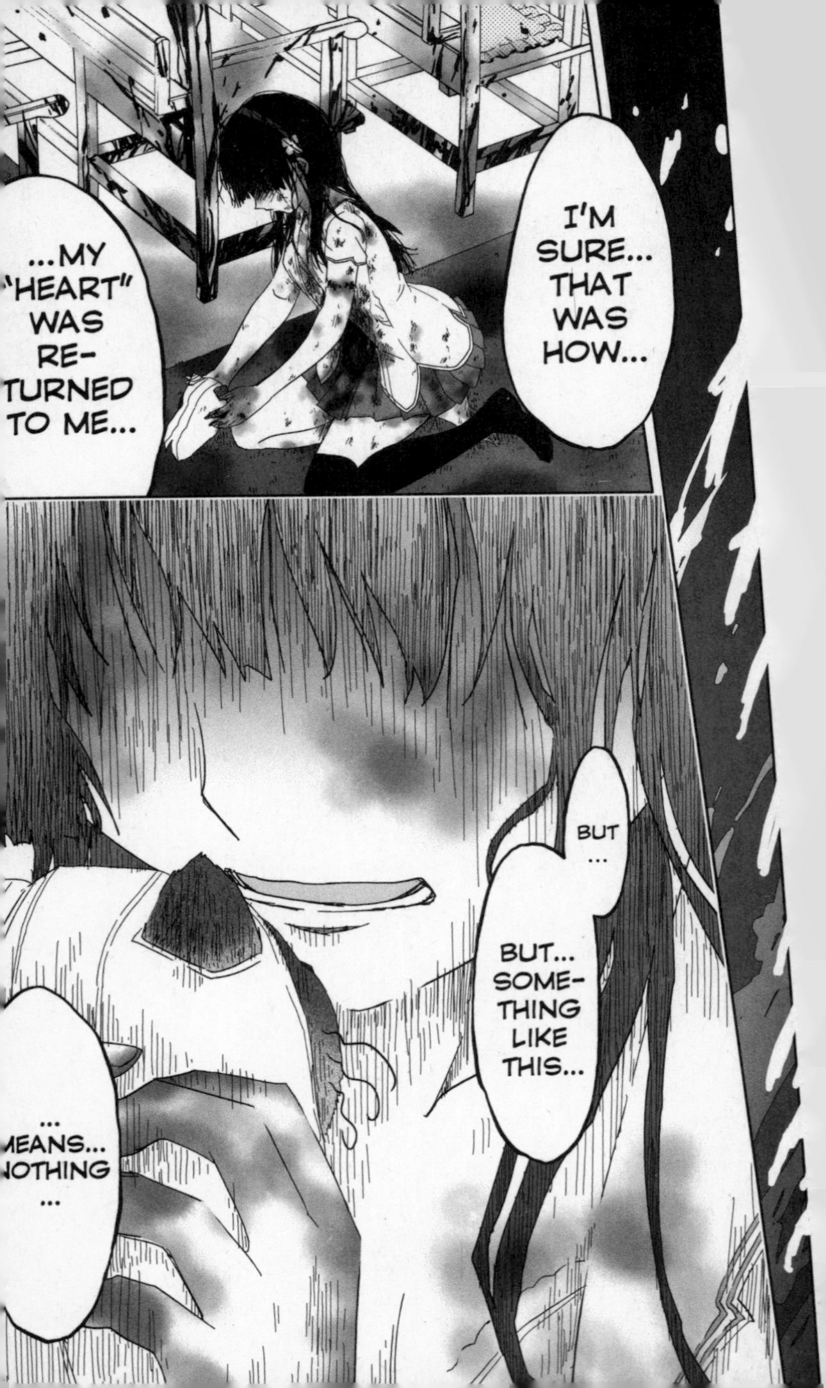
I'M SURE... THAT WAS HOW...
...MY "HEART" WAS RE-TURNED TO ME...
BUT ...
BUT... SOMETHING LIKE THIS...
... MEANS... NOTHING ...

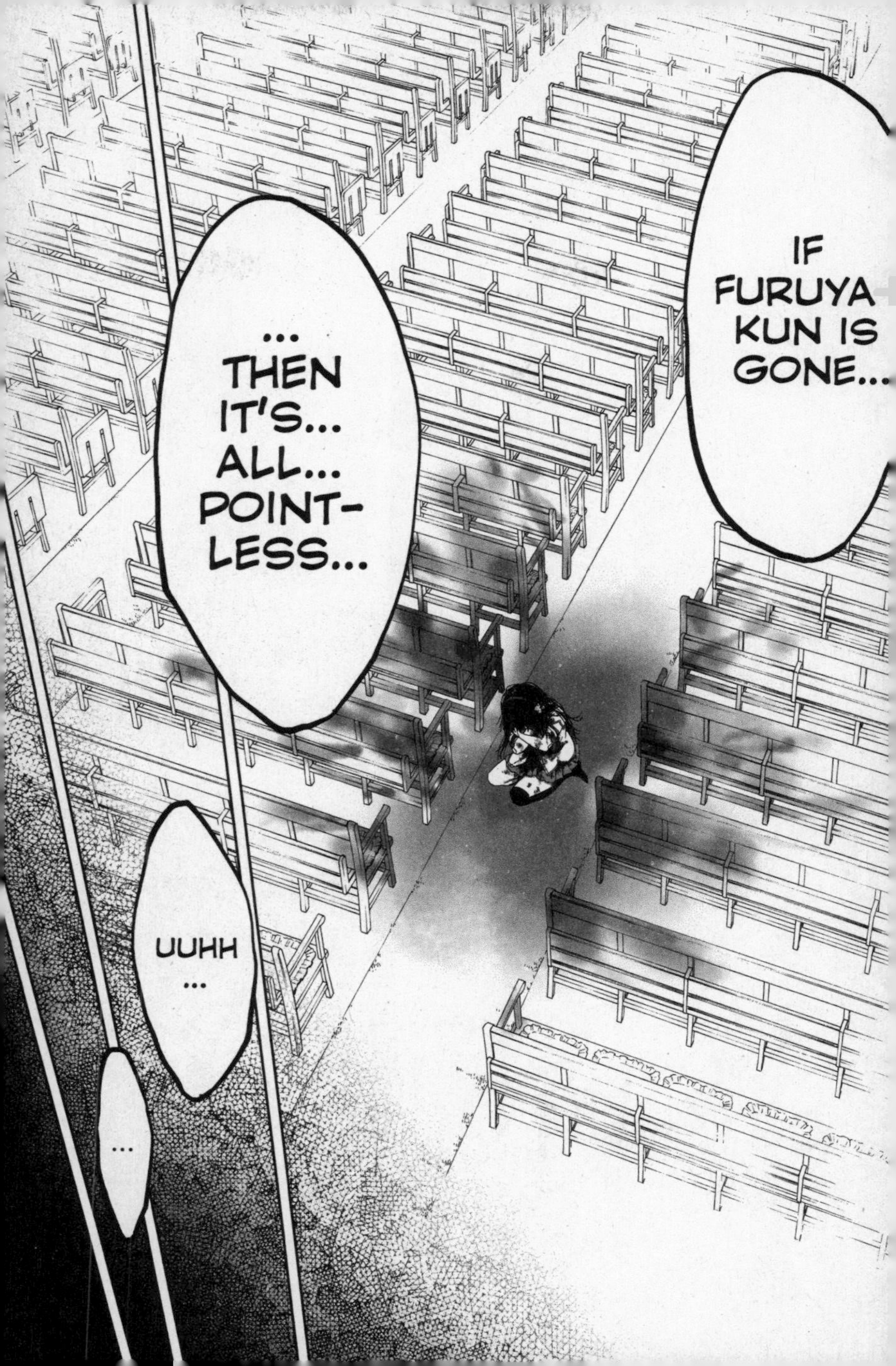
IF FURUYA KUN IS GONE...
... THEN IT'S... ALL... POINT-LESS...
UUHH ...
...

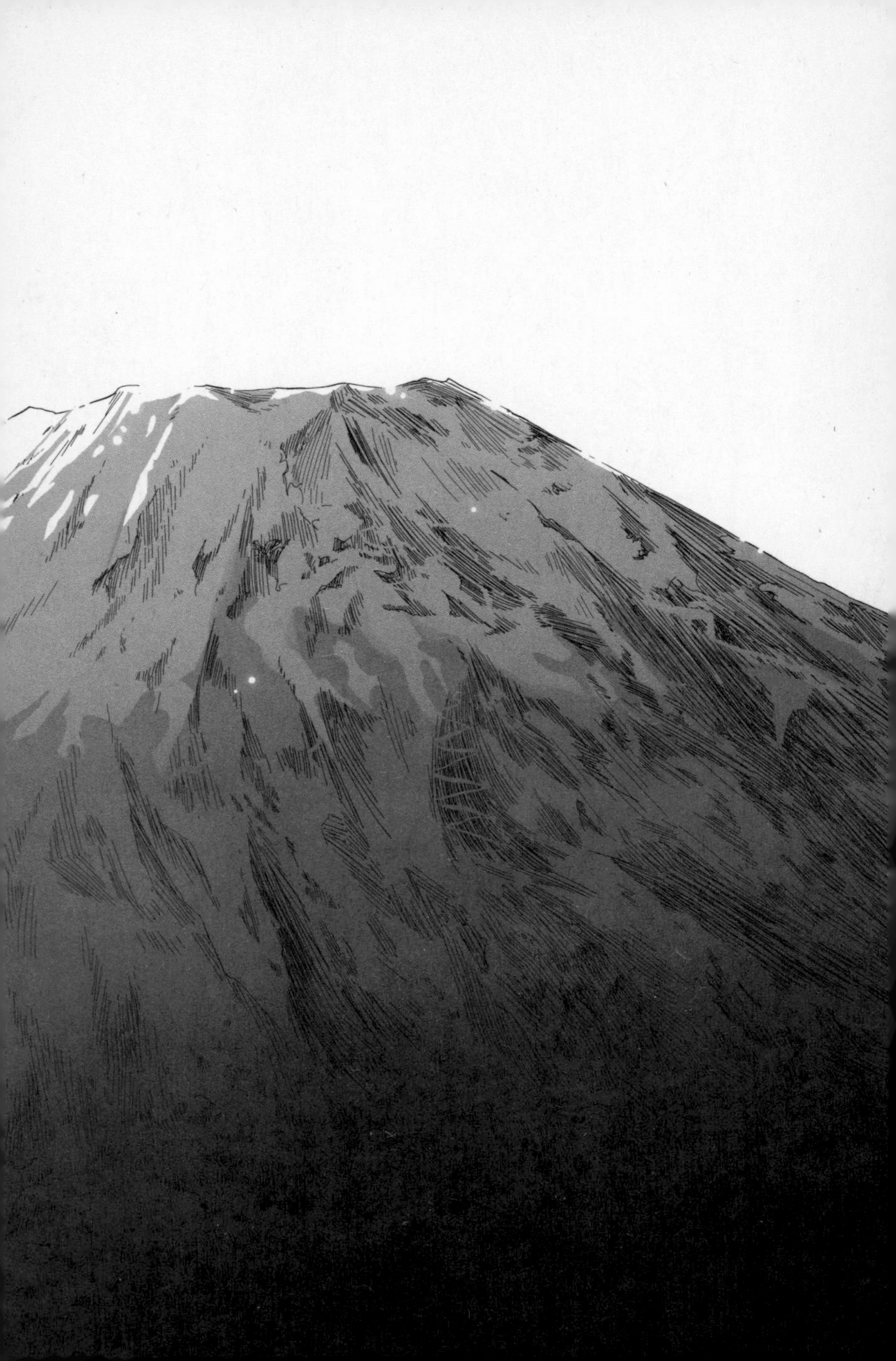

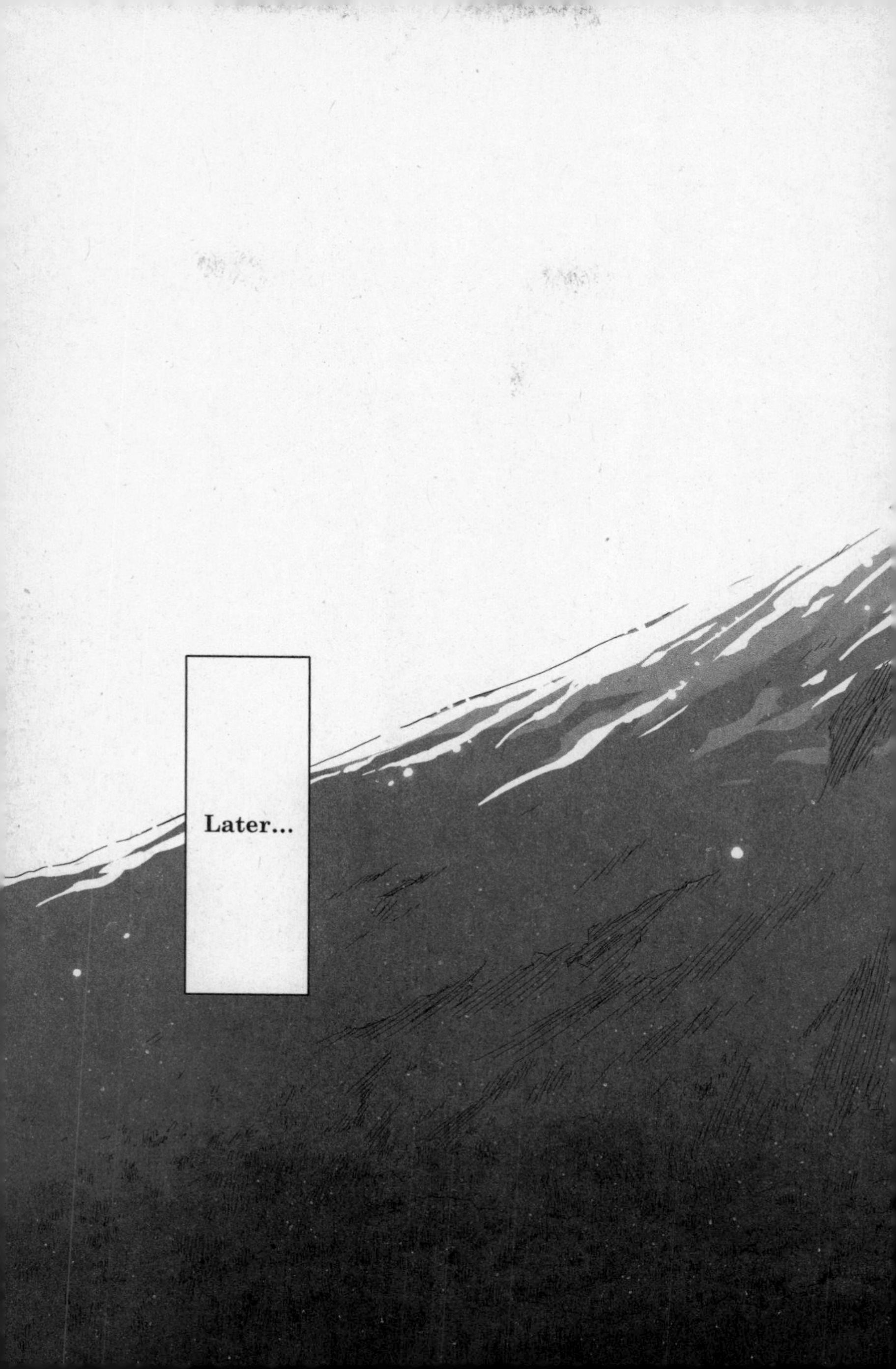
Later...

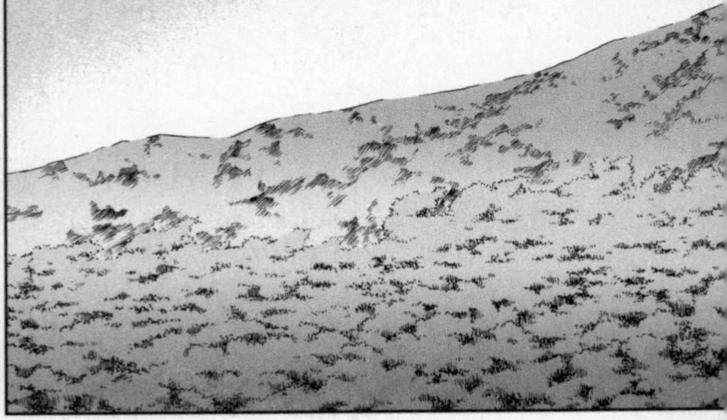

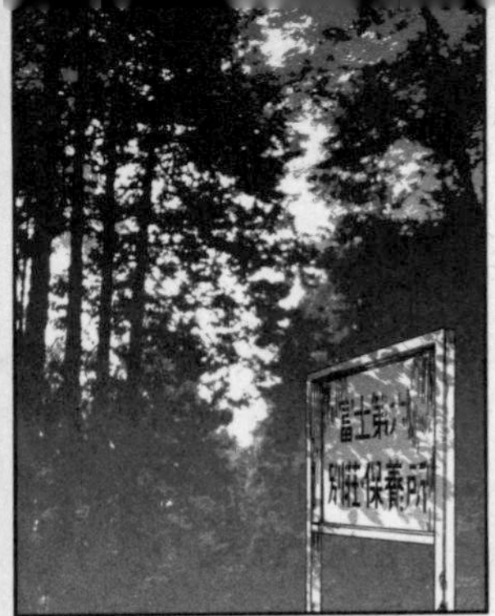

SIGN: Fuji No. 6 Villa & Recreation Center

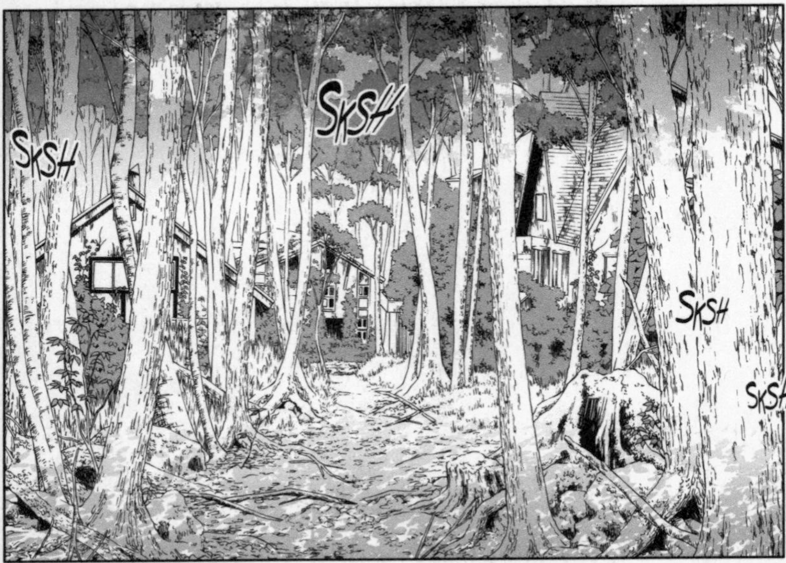
SKSH
SKSH
SKSH
SKSH

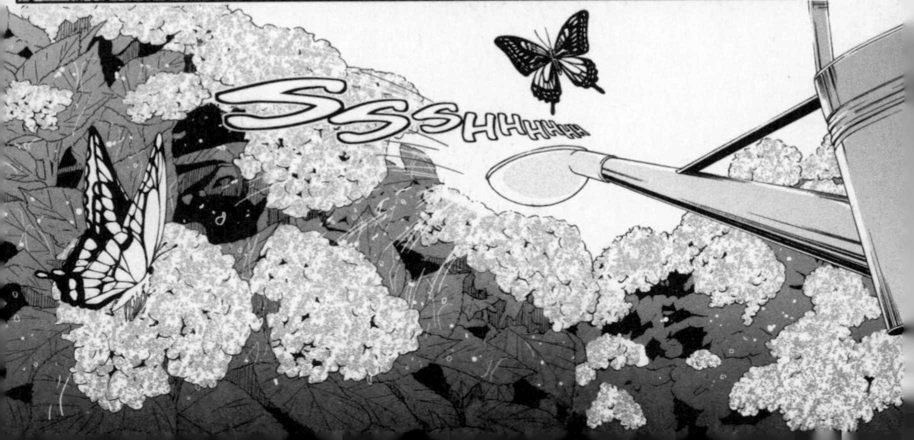
SSSHHHHH

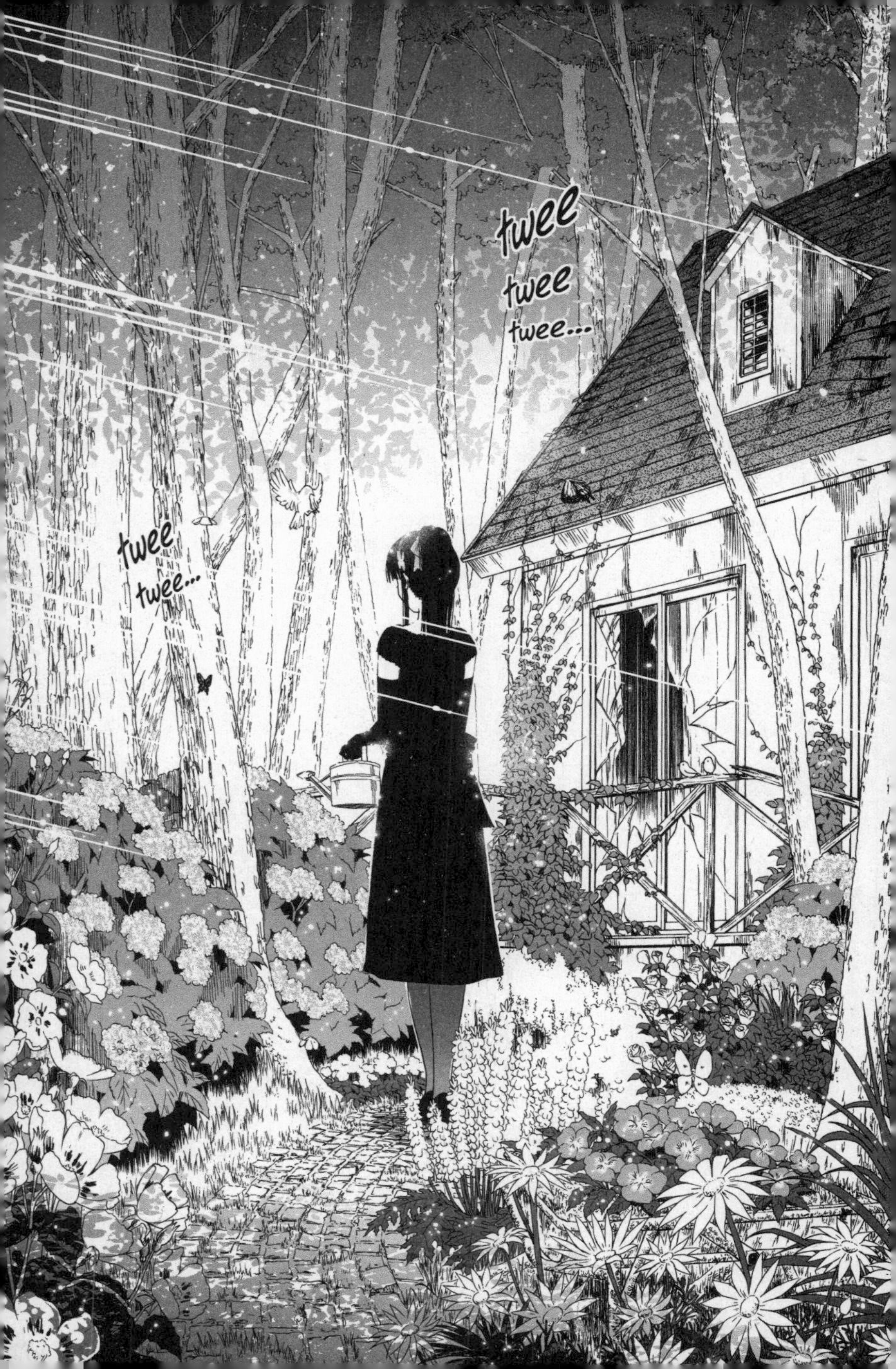
twee
twee
twee...
twee
twee...

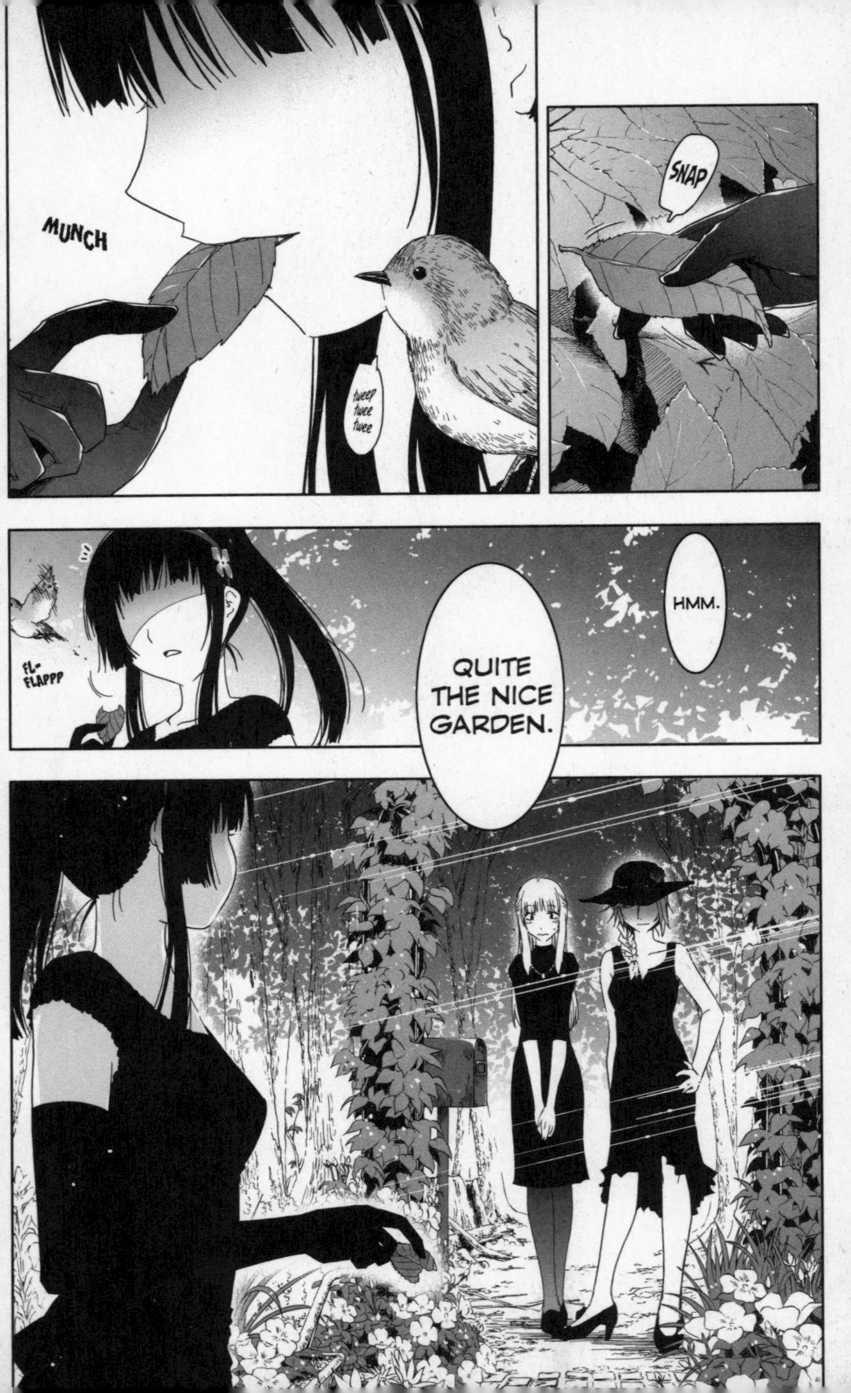
SNAP
MUNCH
tweep twee twee
HMM.
QUITE THE NICE GARDEN.
FL-FLAPPP

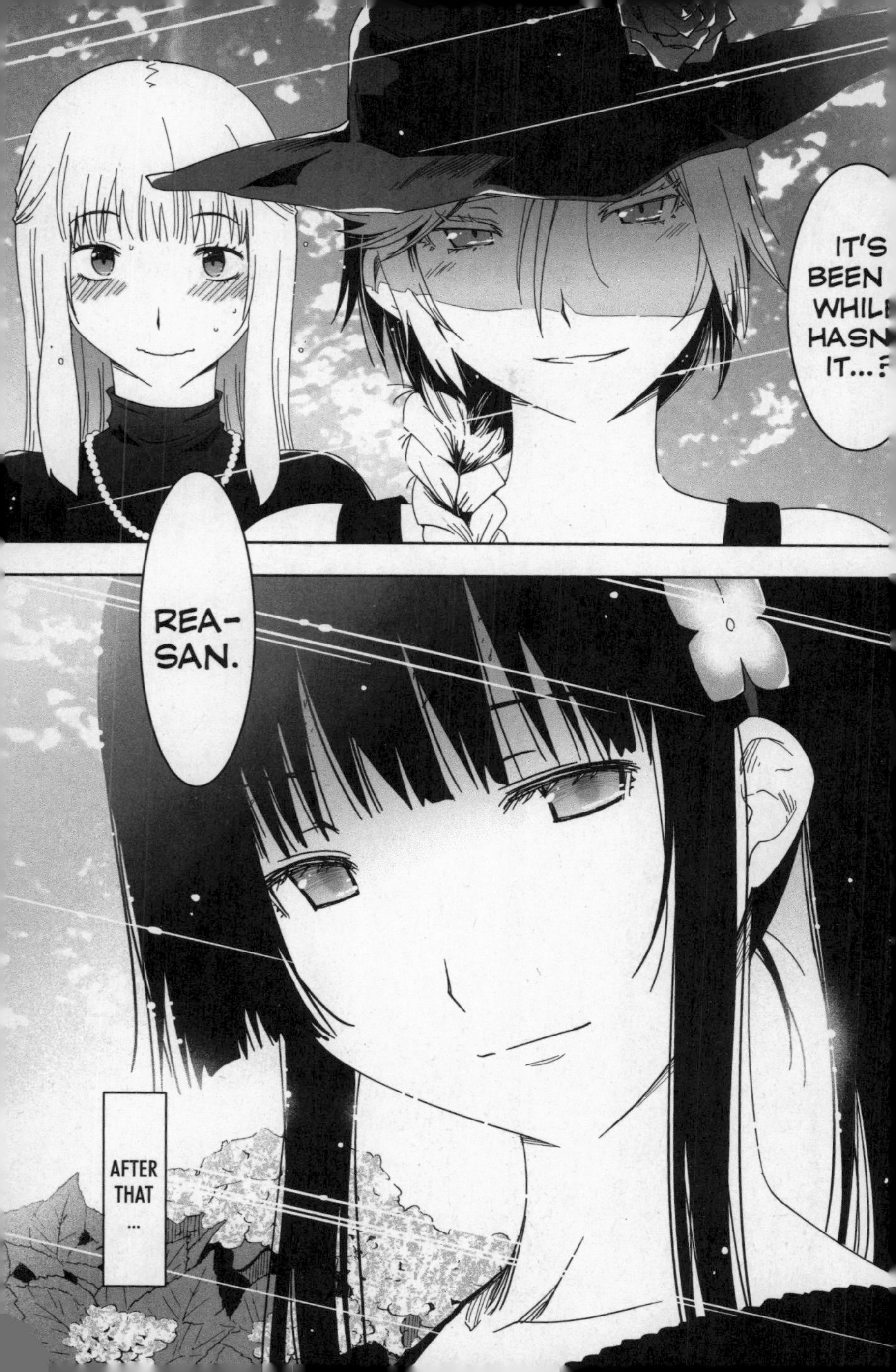

IT'S BEEN WHIL HASN IT...?
REA-SAN.
AFTER THAT ...

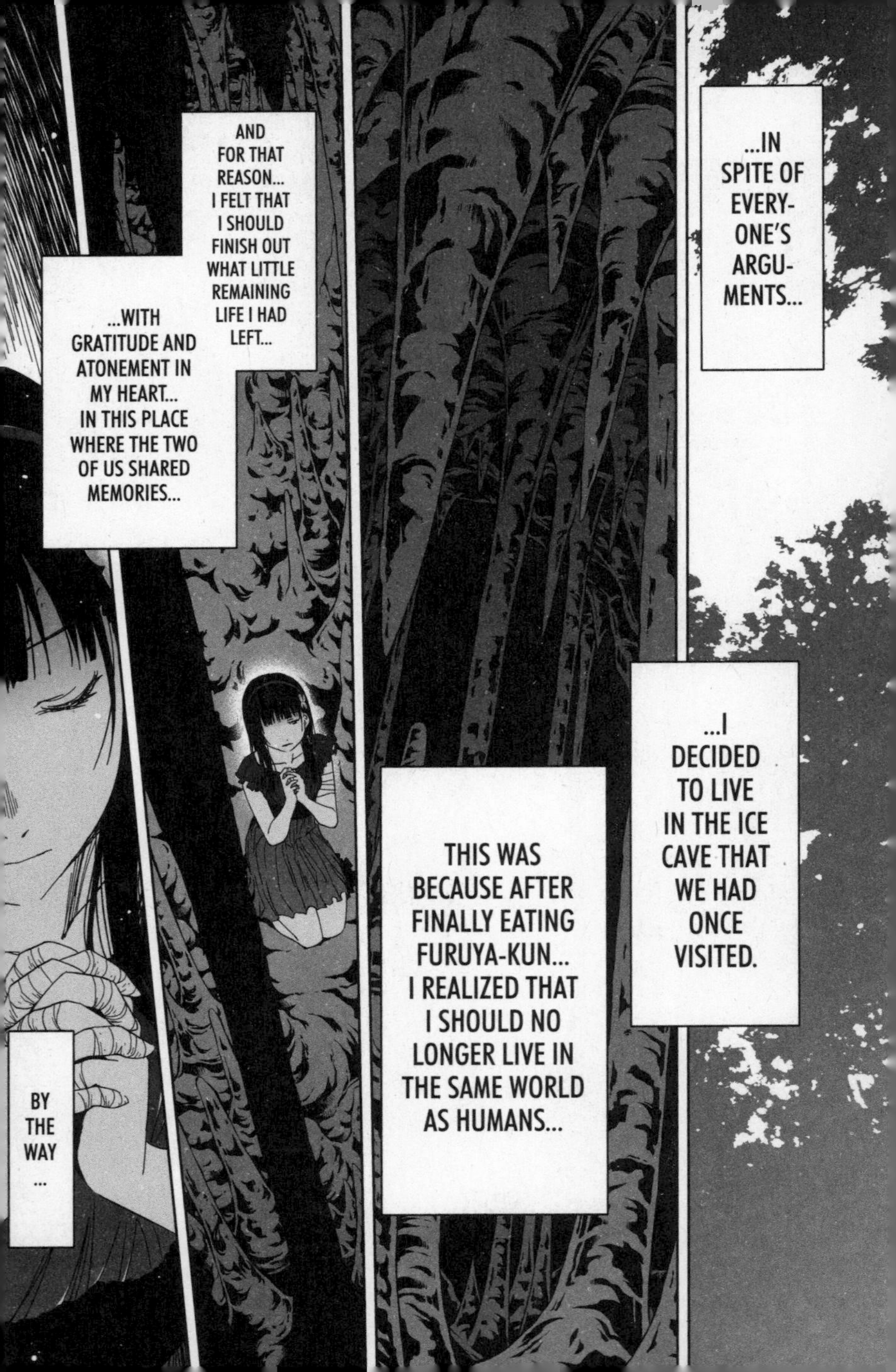
...IN SPITE OF EVERY-ONE'S ARGUMENTS...
...I DECIDED TO LIVE IN THE ICE CAVE THAT WE HAD ONCE VISITED.
THIS WAS BECAUSE AFTER FINALLY EATING FURUYA-KUN... I REALIZED THAT I SHOULD NO LONGER LIVE IN THE SAME WORLD AS HUMANS...
AND FOR THAT REASON... I FELT THAT I SHOULD FINISH OUT WHAT LITTLE REMAINING LIFE I HAD LEFT...
...WITH GRATITUDE AND ATONEMENT IN MY HEART... IN THIS PLACE WHERE THE TWO OF US SHARED MEMORIES...
BY THE WAY...

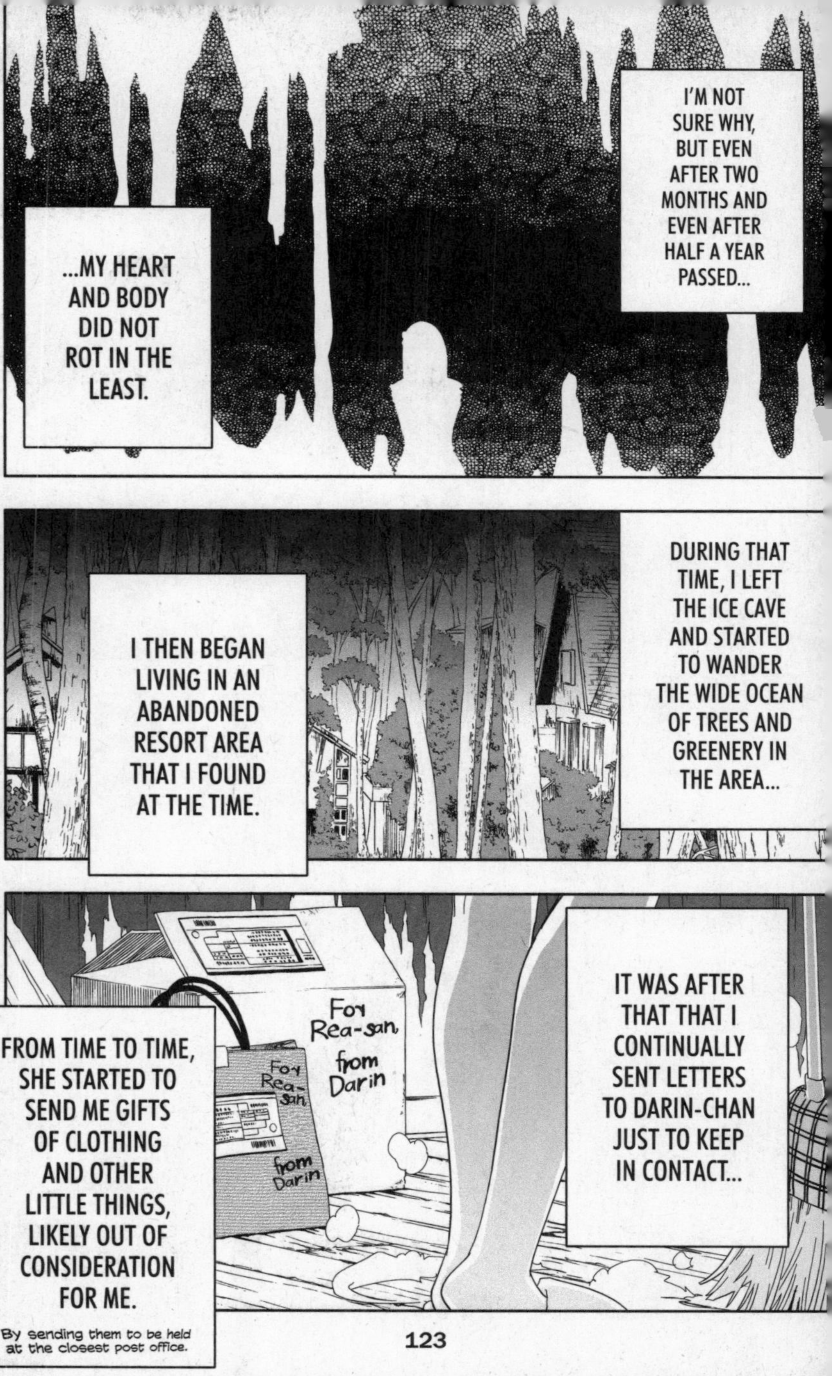
I'M NOT SURE WHY, BUT EVEN AFTER TWO MONTHS AND EVEN AFTER HALF A YEAR PASSED...
...MY HEART AND BODY DID NOT ROT IN THE LEAST.
DURING THAT TIME, I LEFT THE ICE CAVE AND STARTED TO WANDER THE WIDE OCEAN OF TREES AND GREENERY IN THE AREA...
I THEN BEGAN LIVING IN AN ABANDONED RESORT AREA THAT I FOUND AT THE TIME.
IT WAS AFTER THAT THAT I CONTINUALLY SENT LETTERS TO DARIN-CHAN JUST TO KEEP IN CONTACT...
For Rea-san, from Darin
For Rea-san from Darin
FROM TIME TO TIME, SHE STARTED TO SEND ME GIFTS OF CLOTHING AND OTHER LITTLE THINGS, LIKELY OUT OF CONSIDERATION FOR ME.
By sending them to be held at the closest post office.

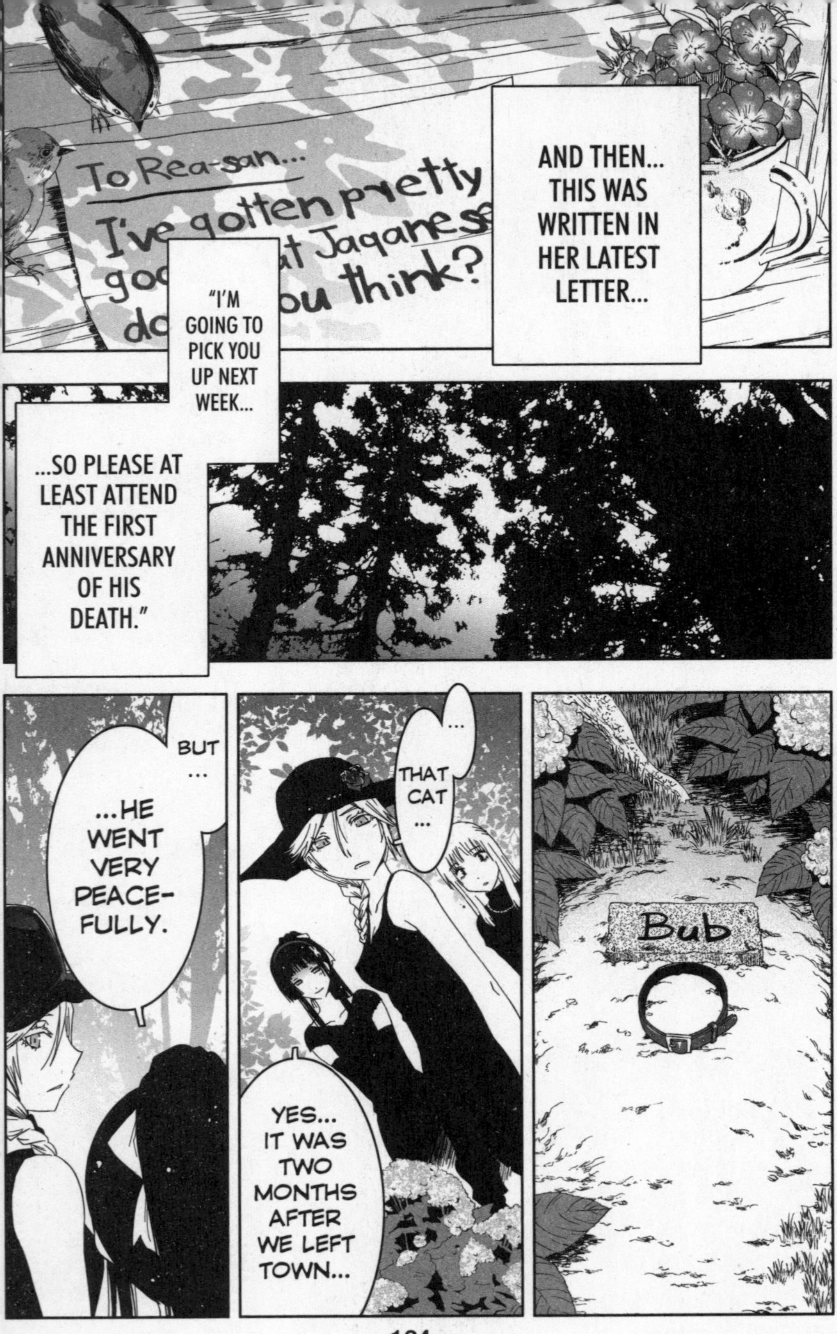
To Rea-san...
I've gotten pretty
at Jaqanese
ou think?
AND THEN... THIS WAS WRITTEN IN HER LATEST LETTER...
"I'M GOING TO PICK YOU UP NEXT WEEK...
...SO PLEASE AT LEAST ATTEND THE FIRST ANNIVERSARY OF HIS DEATH."
Bub
... THAT CAT ...
YES... IT WAS TWO MONTHS AFTER WE LEFT TOWN...
BUT ...
...HE WENT VERY PEACE-FULLY.

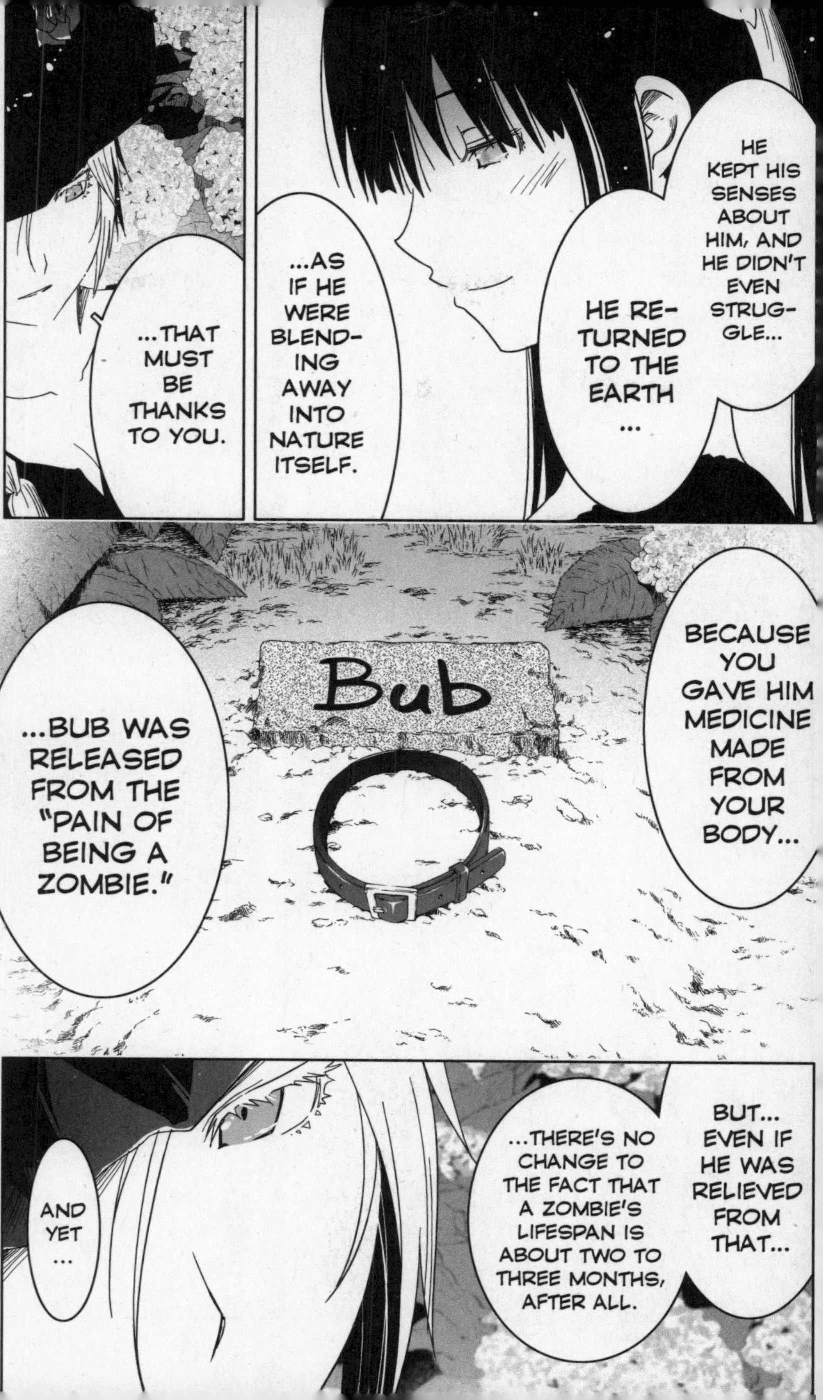
HE KEPT HIS SENSES ABOUT HIM, AND HE DIDN'T EVEN STRUGGLE...
HE RETURNED TO THE EARTH...
...AS IF HE WERE BLENDING AWAY INTO NATURE ITSELF.
...THAT MUST BE THANKS TO YOU.
BECAUSE YOU GAVE HIM MEDICINE MADE FROM YOUR BODY...
Bub
...BUB WAS RELEASED FROM THE "PAIN OF BEING A ZOMBIE."
BUT... EVEN IF HE WAS RELIEVED FROM THAT...
...THERE'S NO CHANGE TO THE FACT THAT A ZOMBIE'S LIFESPAN IS ABOUT TWO TO THREE MONTHS, AFTER ALL.
AND YET...

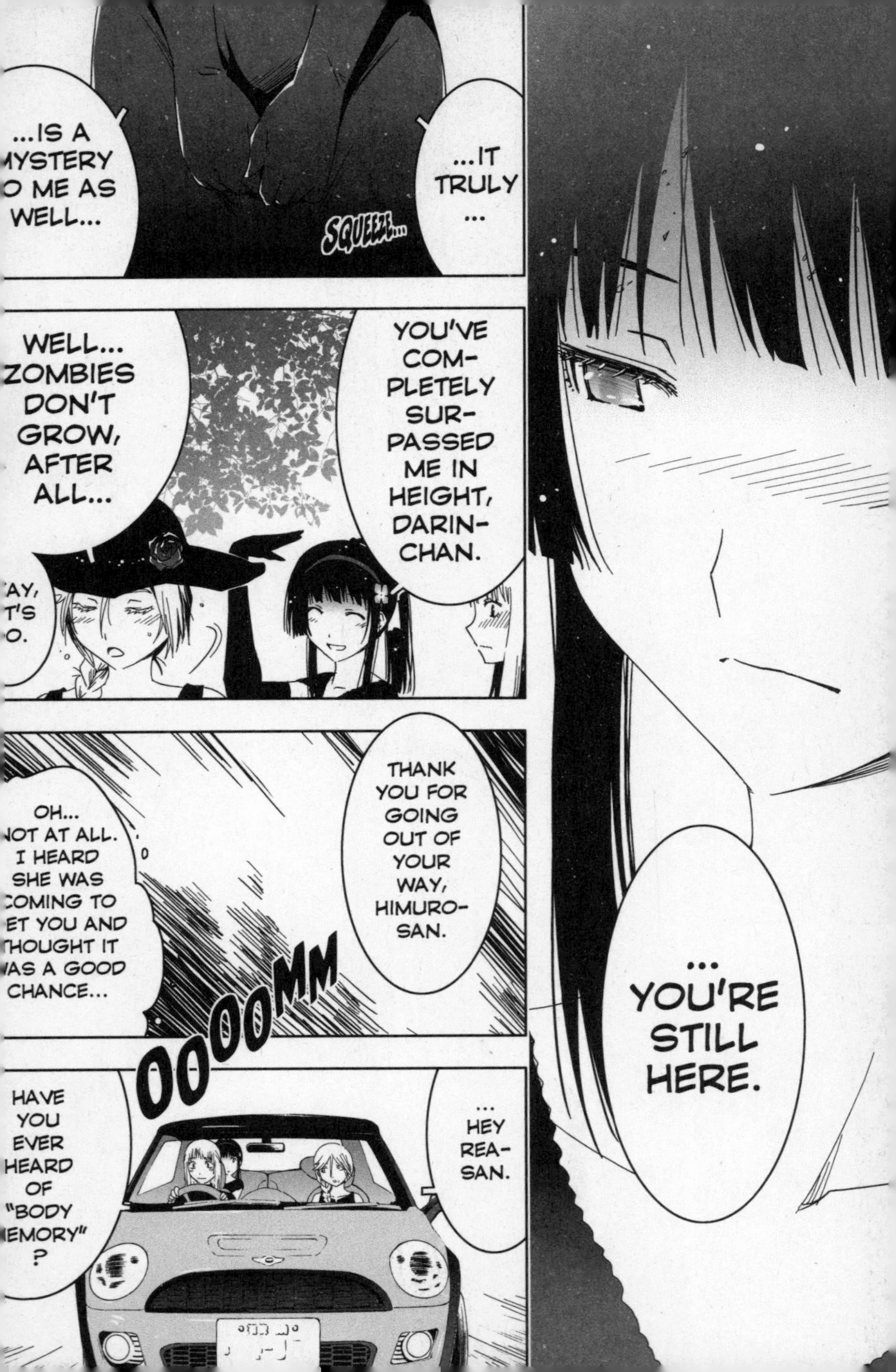

... YOU'RE STILL HERE.
...IT TRULY ...
...IS A MYSTERY O ME AS WELL...
SQUEEZE...
YOU'VE COM-PLETELY SUR-PASSED ME IN HEIGHT, DARIN-CHAN.
WELL... ZOMBIES DON'T GROW, AFTER ALL...
AY, T'S O.
THANK YOU FOR GOING OUT OF YOUR WAY, HIMURO-SAN.
OH... NOT AT ALL. I HEARD SHE WAS COMING TO ET YOU AND THOUGHT IT AS A GOOD CHANCE...
OOOOOOMM
... HEY REA-SAN.
HAVE YOU EVER HEARD OF "BODY EMORY" ?

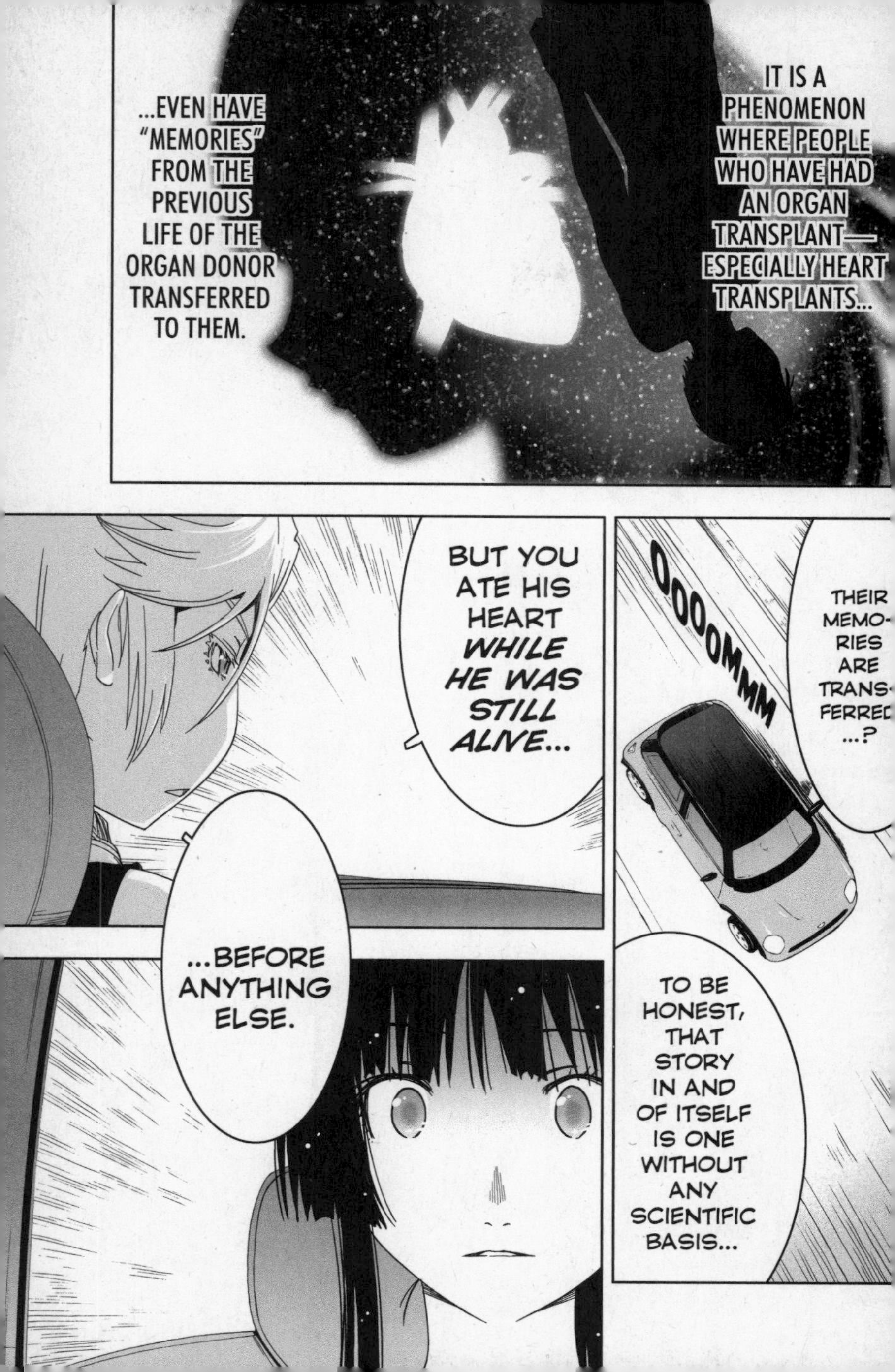
IT IS A PHENOMENON WHERE PEOPLE WHO HAVE HAD AN ORGAN TRANSPLANT—ESPECIALLY HEART TRANSPLANTS...
...EVEN HAVE "MEMORIES" FROM THE PREVIOUS LIFE OF THE ORGAN DONOR TRANSFERRED TO THEM.
OOOOMMM
THEIR MEMORIES ARE TRANSFERRED ...?
TO BE HONEST, THAT STORY IN AND OF ITSELF IS ONE WITHOUT ANY SCIENTIFIC BASIS...
BUT YOU ATE HIS HEART WHILE HE WAS STILL ALIVE...
...BEFORE ANYTHING ELSE.

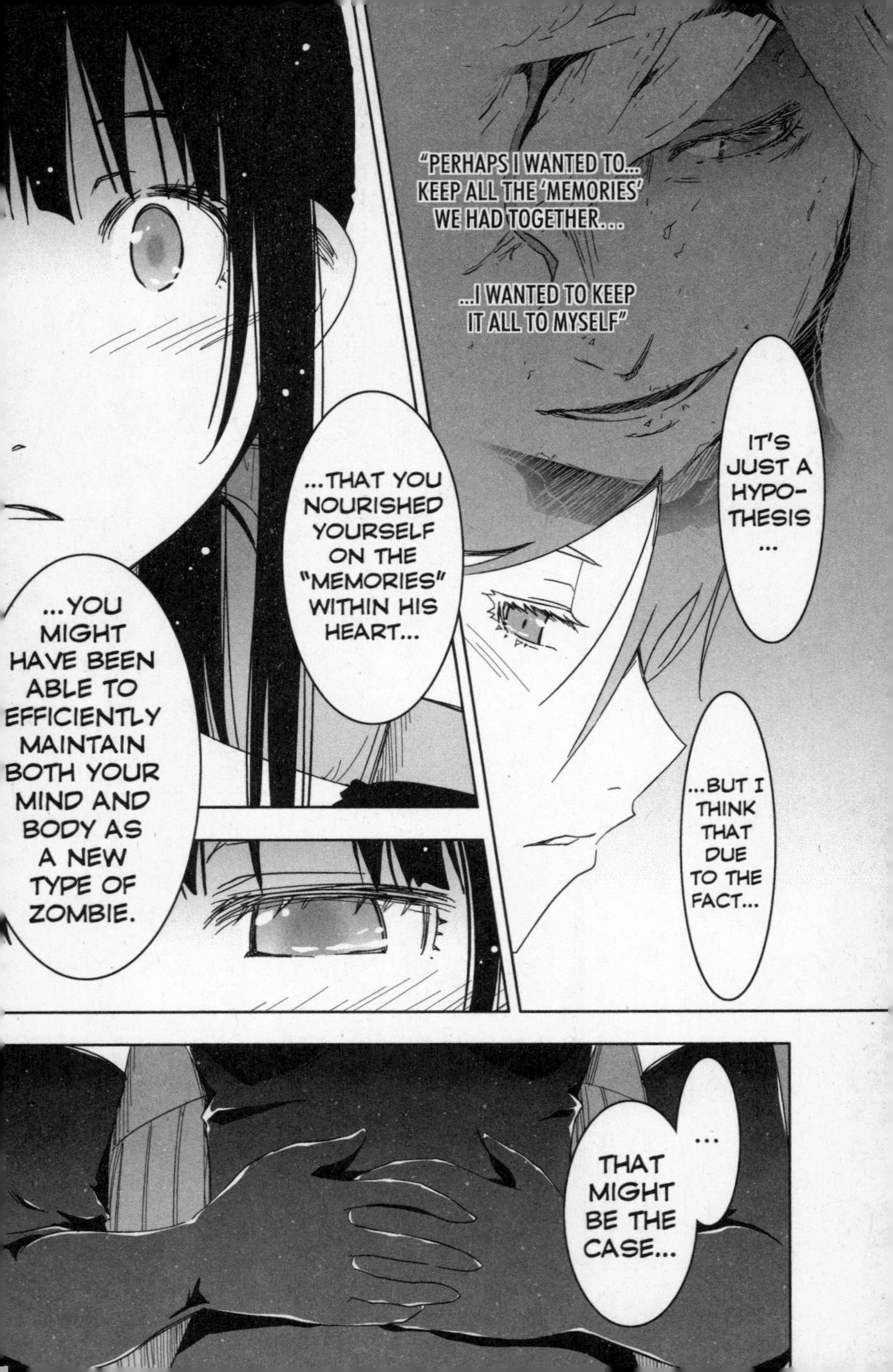
"PERHAPS I WANTED TO... KEEP ALL THE 'MEMORIES' WE HAD TOGETHER...
...I WANTED TO KEEP IT ALL TO MYSELF"
IT'S JUST A HYPO-THESIS...
...BUT I THINK THAT DUE TO THE FACT...
...THAT YOU NOURISHED YOURSELF ON THE "MEMORIES" WITHIN HIS HEART...
...YOU MIGHT HAVE BEEN ABLE TO EFFICIENTLY MAINTAIN BOTH YOUR MIND AND BODY AS A NEW TYPE OF ZOMBIE.
... THAT MIGHT BE THE CASE...

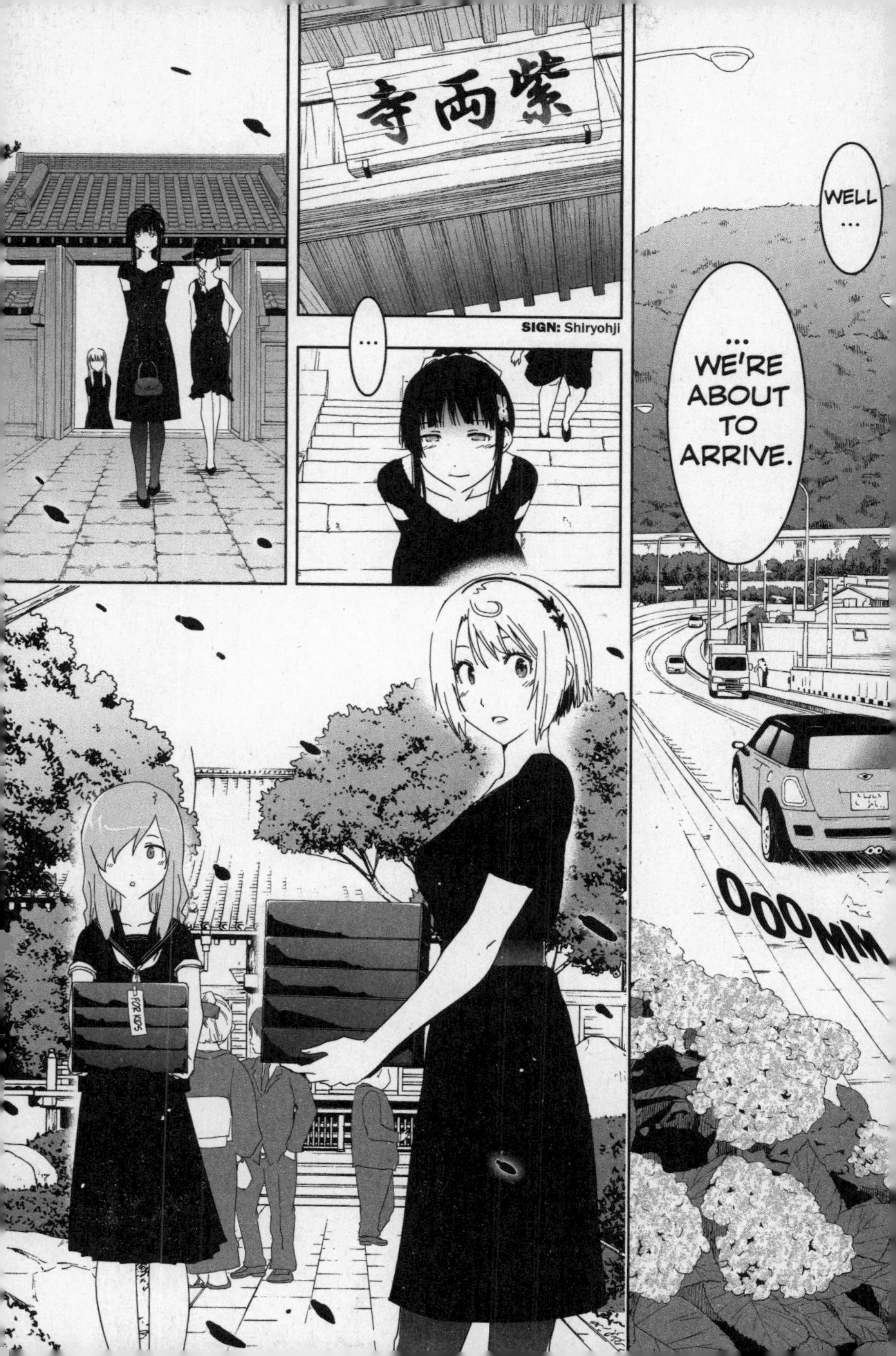
WELL...
... WE'RE ABOUT TO ARRIVE.
OOOMM
紫両寺
SIGN: Shiryohji
...
FOR KIDS

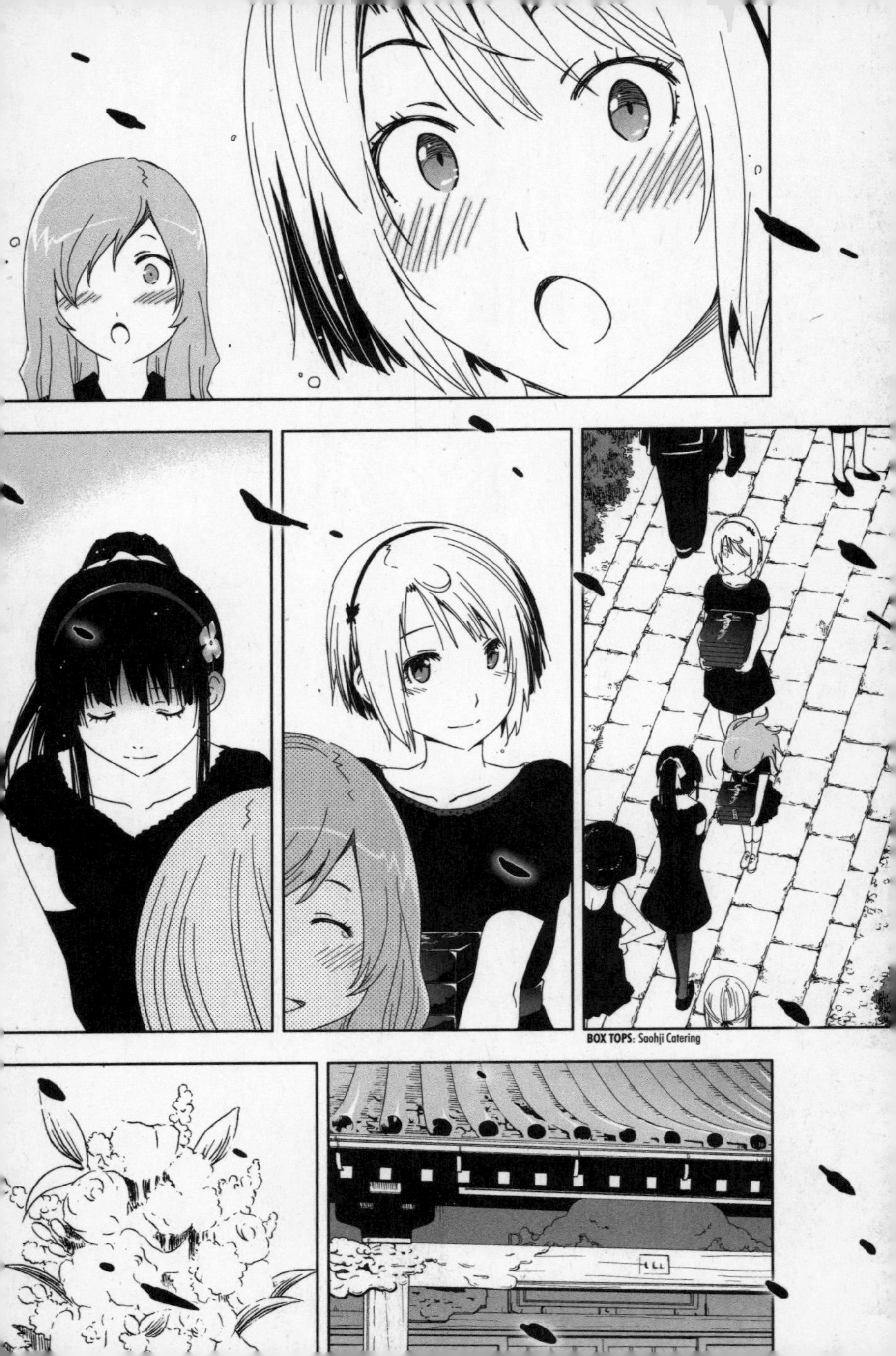
BOX TOPS: Saohji Catering

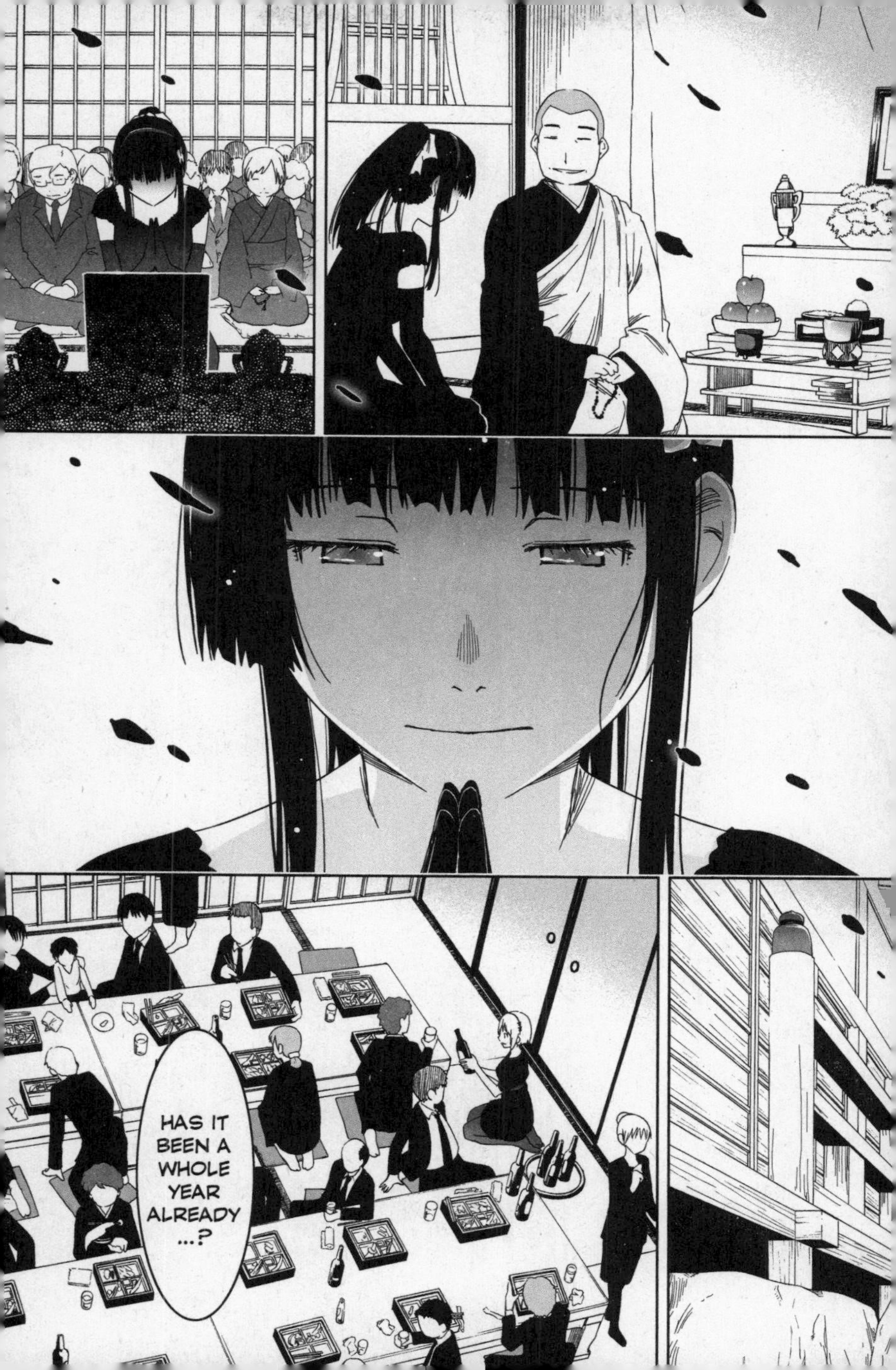
HAS IT BEEN A WHOLE YEAR ALREADY ...?

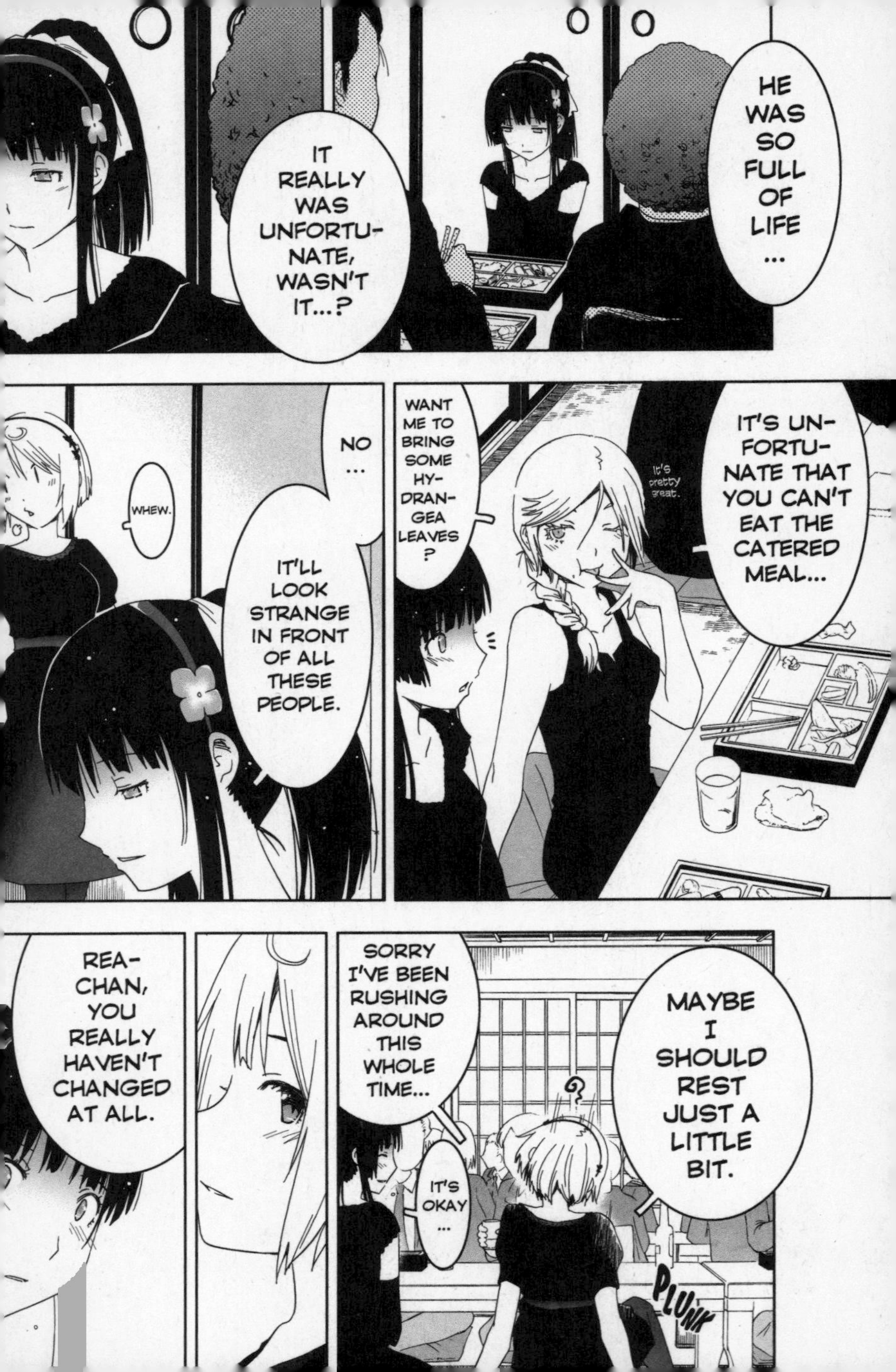
HE WAS SO FULL OF LIFE ...
IT REALLY WAS UNFORTUNATE, WASN'T IT...?
IT'S UNFORTUNATE THAT YOU CAN'T EAT THE CATERED MEAL...
It's pretty great.
WANT ME TO BRING SOME HYDRANGEA LEAVES?
NO ...
IT'LL LOOK STRANGE IN FRONT OF ALL THESE PEOPLE.
WHEW.
MAYBE I SHOULD REST JUST A LITTLE BIT.
SORRY I'VE BEEN RUSHING AROUND THIS WHOLE TIME...
IT'S OKAY ...
PLUNK
REA-CHAN, YOU REALLY HAVEN'T CHANGED AT ALL.

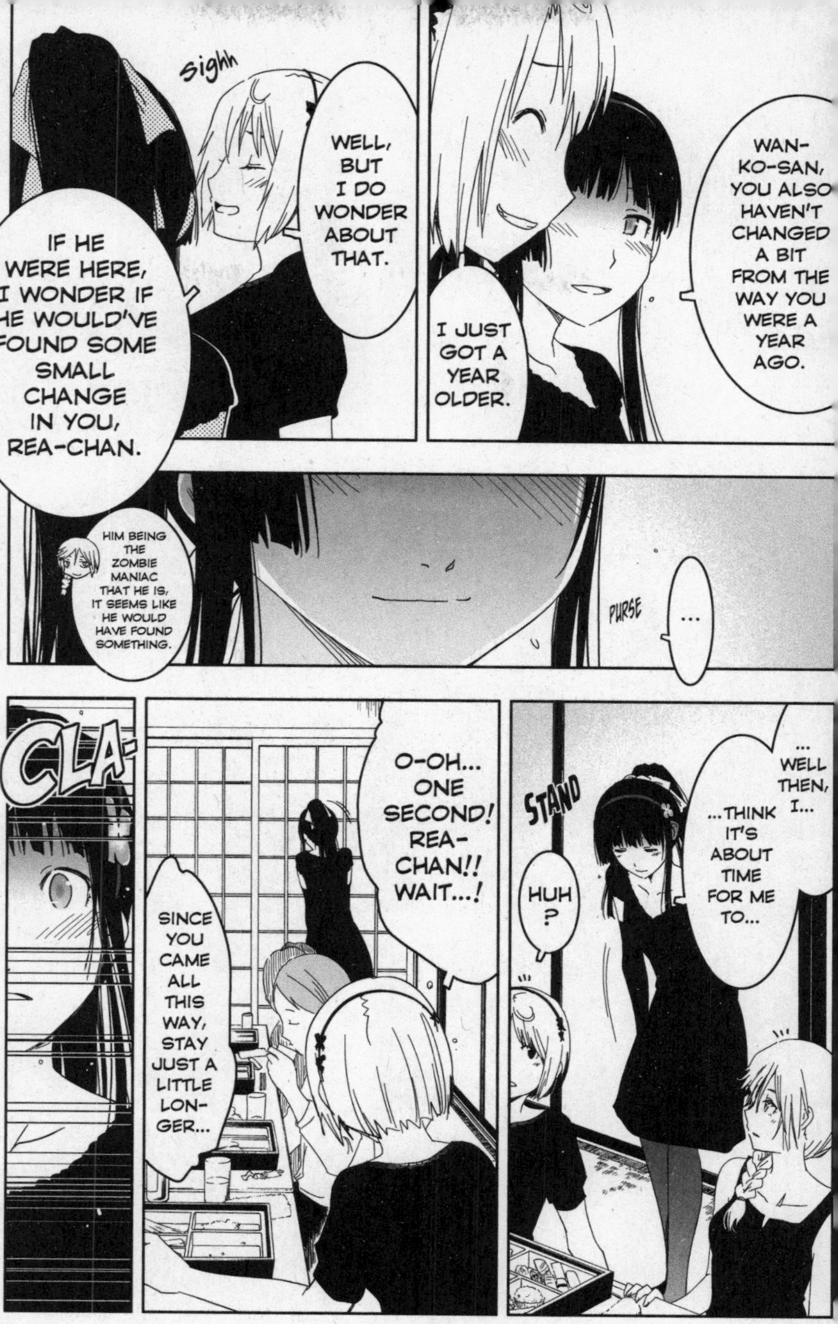
WAN-KO-SAN, YOU ALSO HAVEN'T CHANGED A BIT FROM THE WAY YOU WERE A YEAR AGO.
I JUST GOT A YEAR OLDER.
Sighh
WELL, BUT I DO WONDER ABOUT THAT.
IF HE WERE HERE, I WONDER IF HE WOULD'VE FOUND SOME SMALL CHANGE IN YOU, REA-CHAN.
...
PURSE
HIM BEING THE ZOMBIE MANIAC THAT HE IS, IT SEEMS LIKE HE WOULD HAVE FOUND SOMETHING.
... WELL THEN, I...
...THINK IT'S ABOUT TIME FOR ME TO...
STAND
HUH?
O-OH... ONE SECOND! REA-CHAN!! WAIT...!
SINCE YOU CAME ALL THIS WAY, STAY JUST A LITTLE LONGER...
CLA-

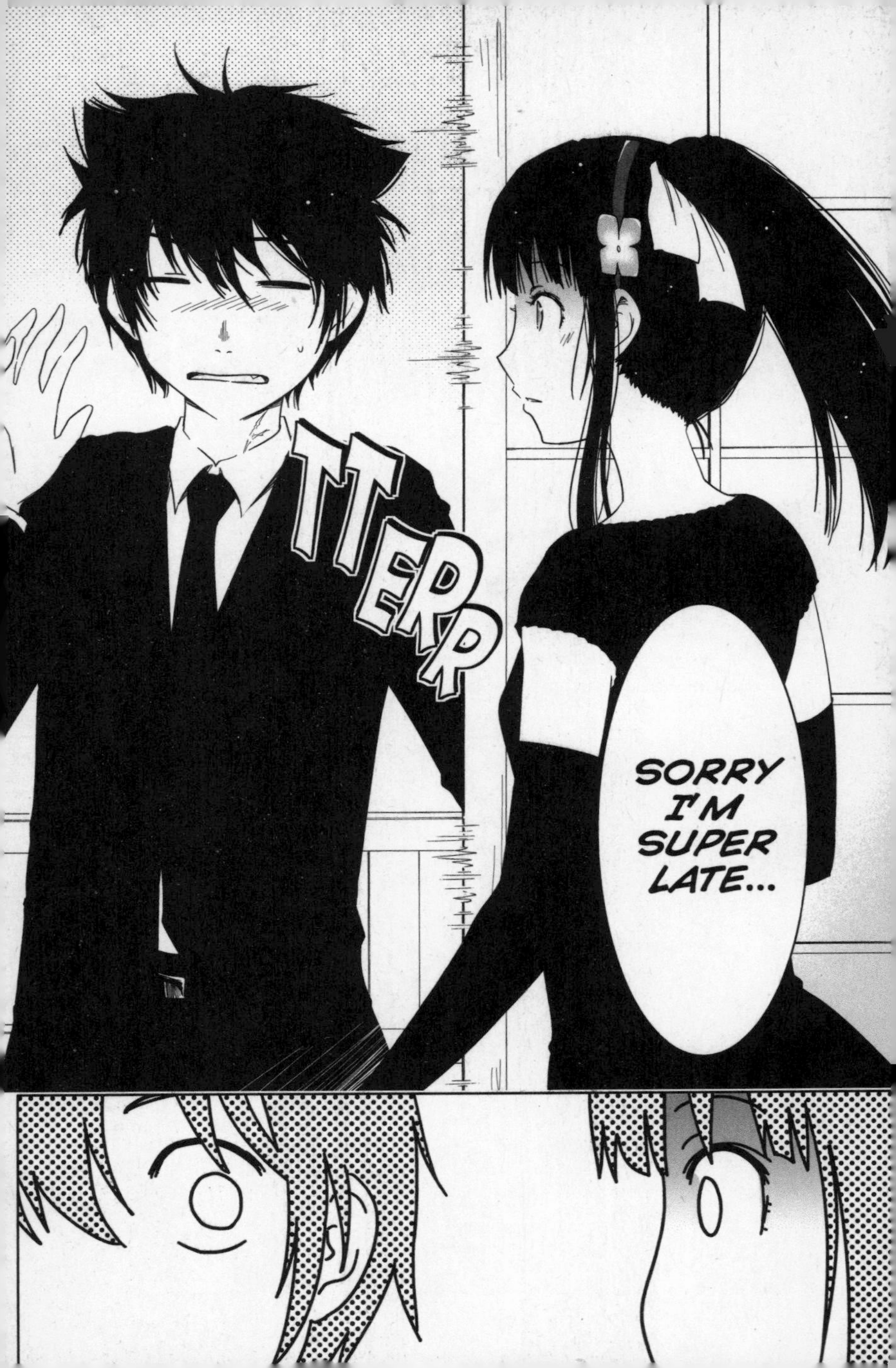
SORRY I'M SUPER LATE...
TTERR

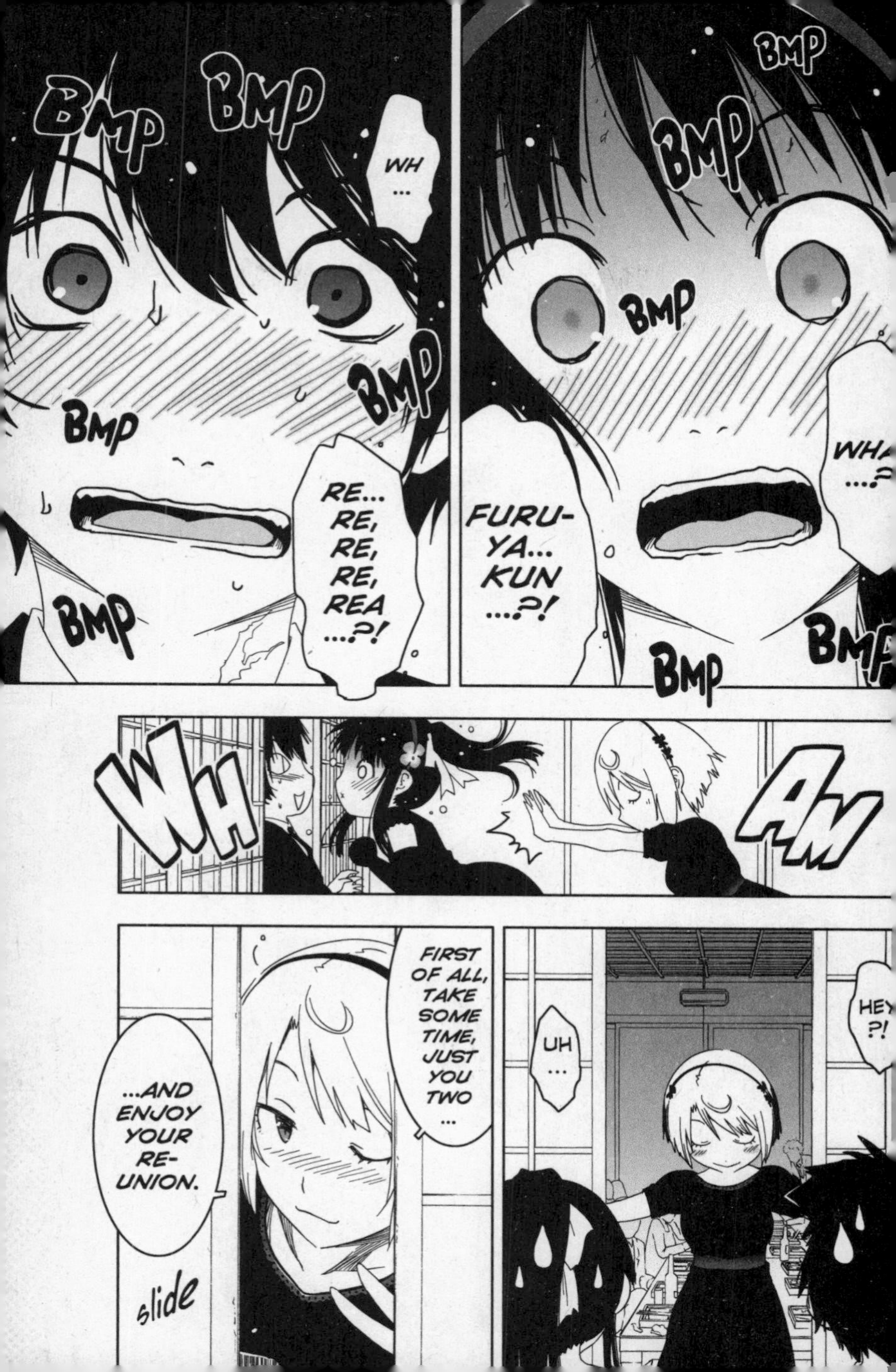
BMP
BMP
BMP
WHA ...?!
FURU-YA... KUN ...?!
BMP
BMP
BMP
BMP
WH ...
BMP
BMP
RE... RE, RE, RE, REA ...?!
BMP
AM
WH
HEY ?!
UH ...
FIRST OF ALL, TAKE SOME TIME, JUST YOU TWO ...
...AND ENJOY YOUR RE-UNION.
slide

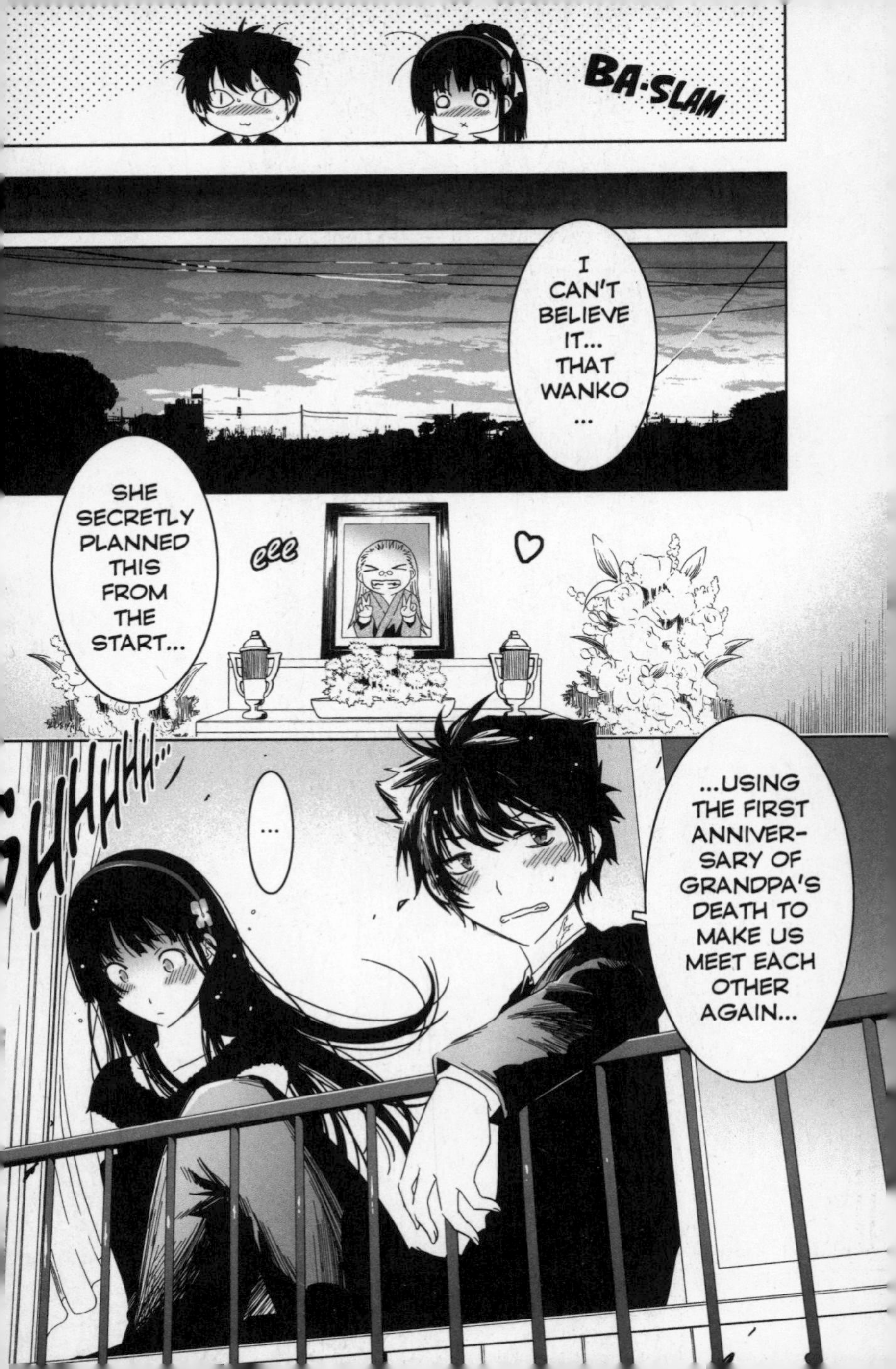
BA-SLAM
I CAN'T BELIEVE IT... THAT WANKO ...
SHE SECRETLY PLANNED THIS FROM THE START...
eee
...USING THE FIRST ANNIVER-SARY OF GRANDPA'S DEATH TO MAKE US MEET EACH OTHER AGAIN...
...
SHHHHH...

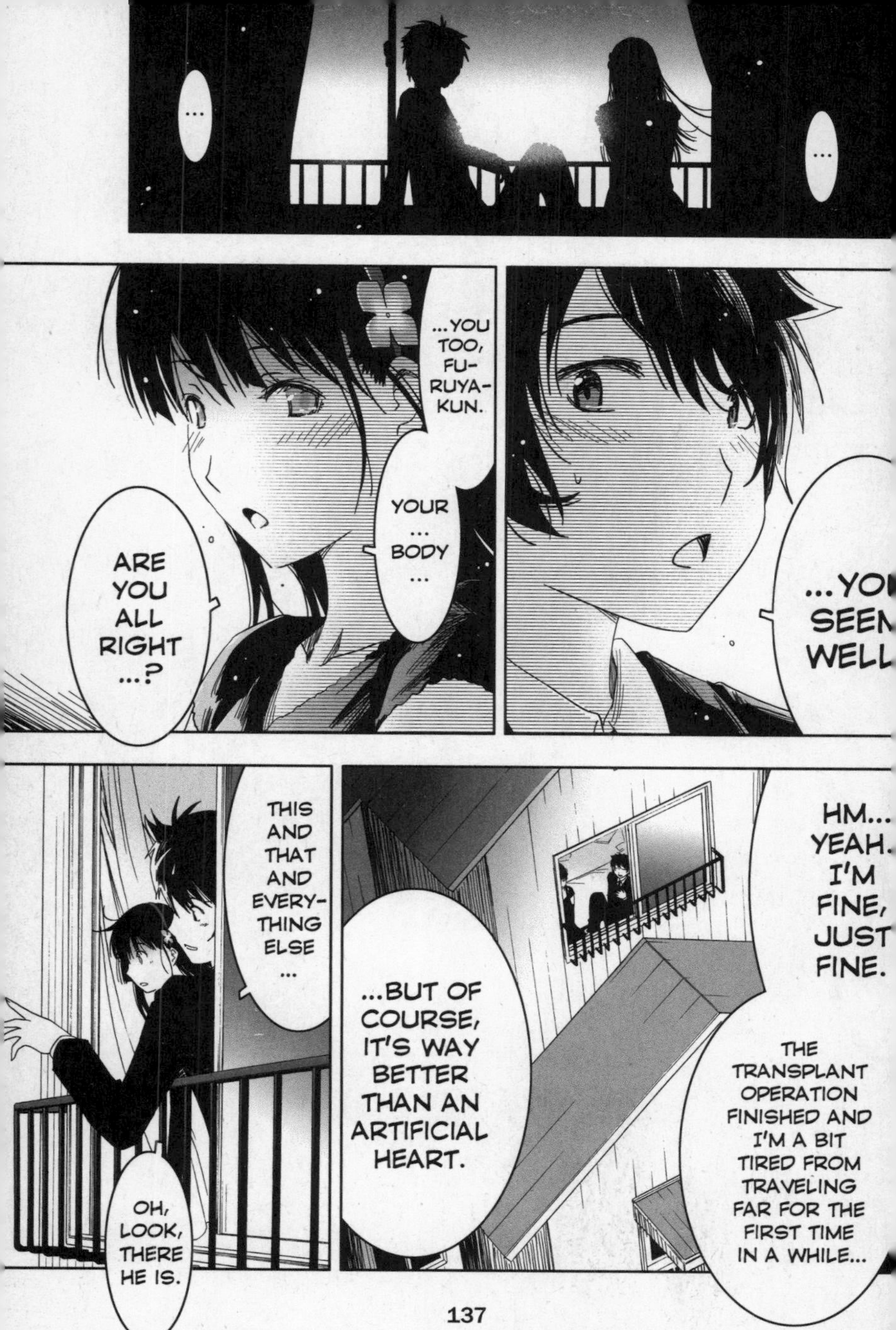
...
...
...YO SEEM WELL
...YOU TOO, FU-RUYA-KUN.
YOUR ... BODY ...
ARE YOU ALL RIGHT ...?
HM... YEAH. I'M FINE, JUST FINE.
THE TRANSPLANT OPERATION FINISHED AND I'M A BIT TIRED FROM TRAVELING FAR FOR THE FIRST TIME IN A WHILE...
...BUT OF COURSE, IT'S WAY BETTER THAN AN ARTIFICIAL HEART.
THIS AND THAT AND EVERY-THING ELSE ...
OH, LOOK, THERE HE IS.

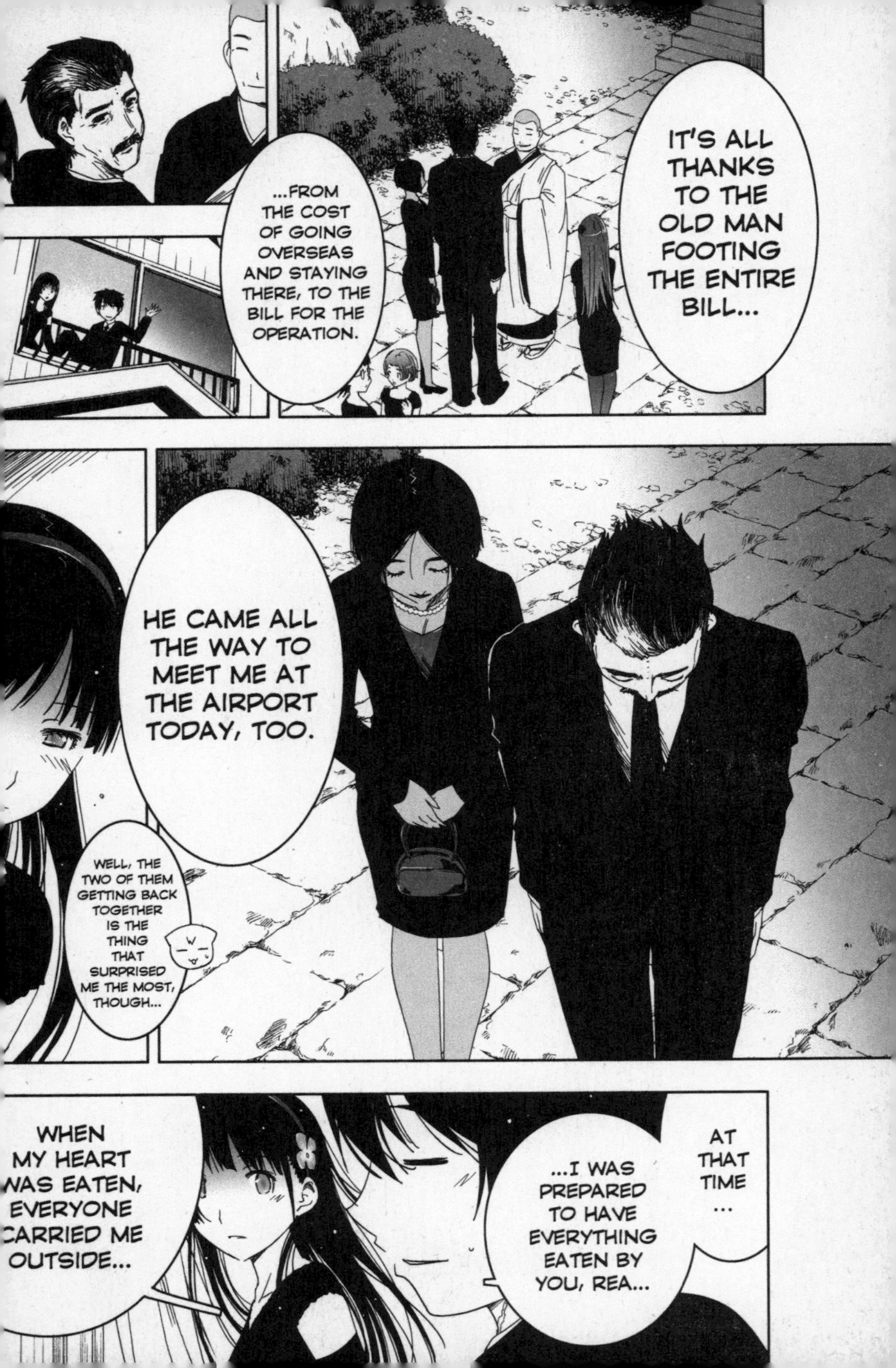
IT'S ALL THANKS TO THE OLD MAN FOOTING THE ENTIRE BILL...
...FROM THE COST OF GOING OVERSEAS AND STAYING THERE, TO THE BILL FOR THE OPERATION.
HE CAME ALL THE WAY TO MEET ME AT THE AIRPORT TODAY, TOO.
WELL, THE TWO OF THEM GETTING BACK TOGETHER IS THE THING THAT SURPRISED ME THE MOST, THOUGH...
AT THAT TIME...
...I WAS PREPARED TO HAVE EVERYTHING EATEN BY YOU, REA...
WHEN MY HEART WAS EATEN, EVERYONE CARRIED ME OUTSIDE...

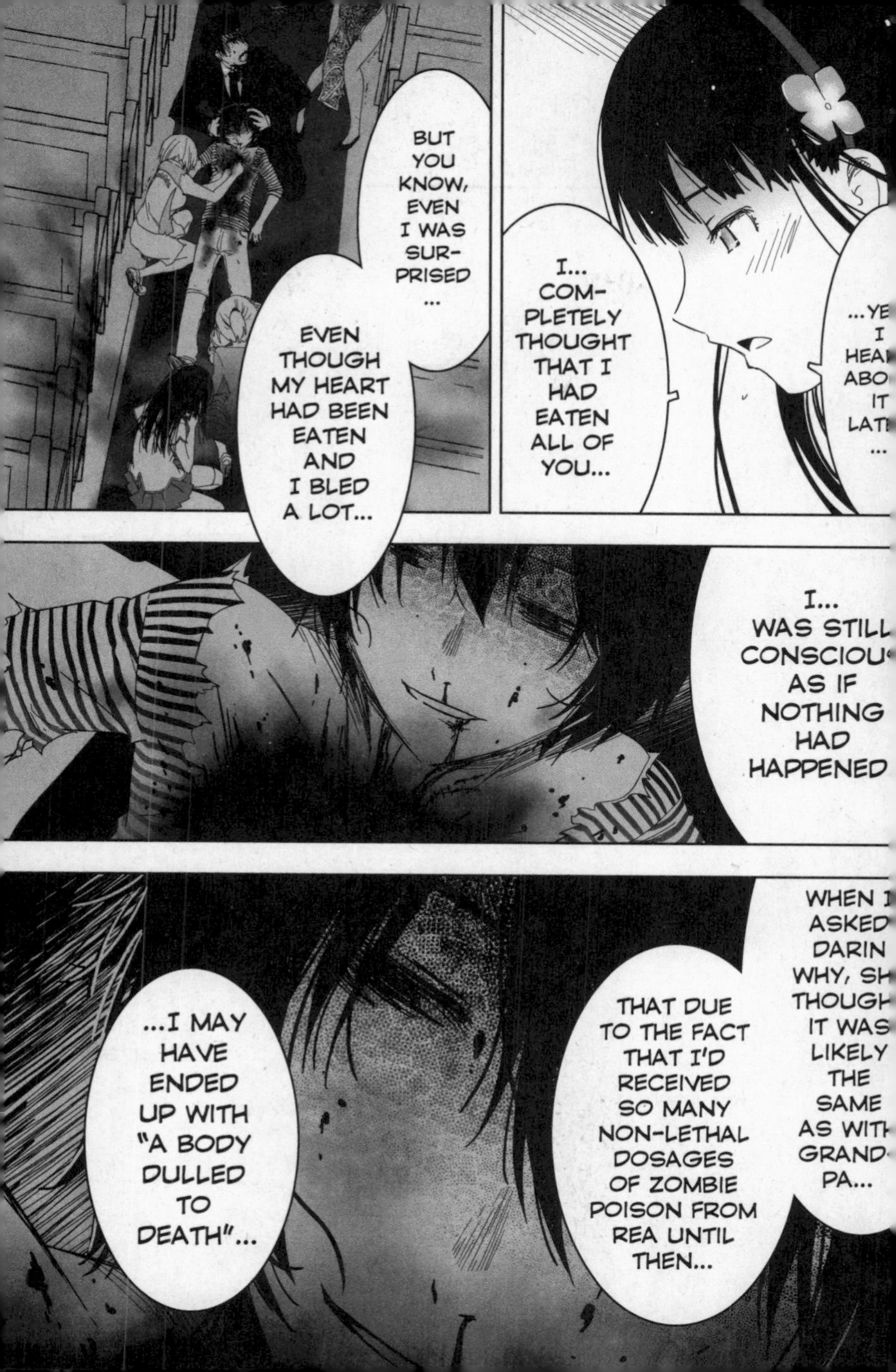
...YE I HEA ABO IT LAT ...
I... COMPLETELY THOUGHT THAT I HAD EATEN ALL OF YOU...
BUT YOU KNOW, EVEN I WAS SURPRISED ...
EVEN THOUGH MY HEART HAD BEEN EATEN AND I BLED A LOT...
I... WAS STILL CONSCIOU AS IF NOTHING HAD HAPPENED
WHEN I ASKED DARIN WHY, SH THOUGH IT WAS LIKELY THE SAME AS WITH GRANDPA...
THAT DUE TO THE FACT THAT I'D RECEIVED SO MANY NON-LETHAL DOSAGES OF ZOMBIE POISON FROM REA UNTIL THEN...
...I MAY HAVE ENDED UP WITH "A BODY DULLED TO DEATH"...

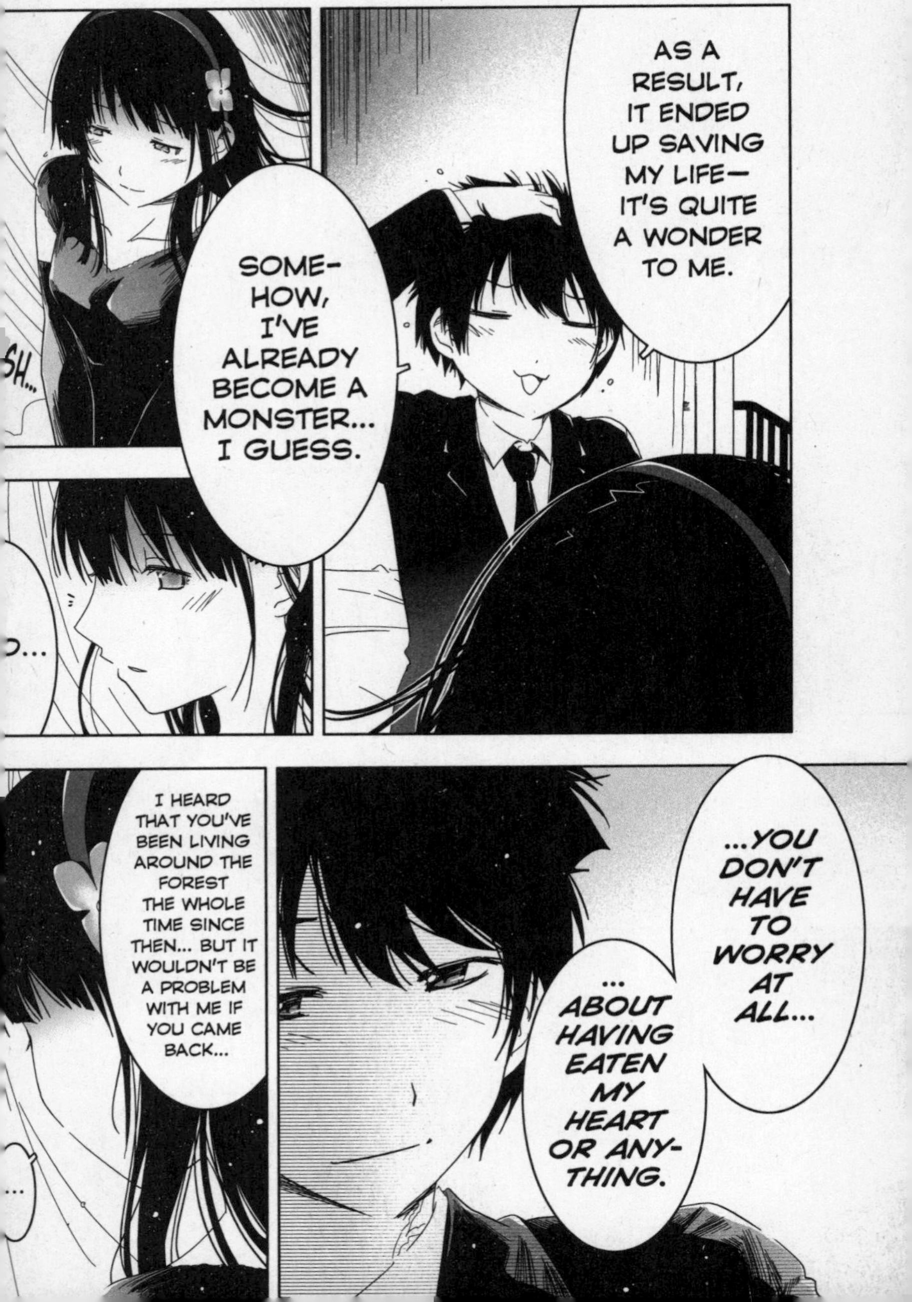
AS A RESULT, IT ENDED UP SAVING MY LIFE— IT'S QUITE A WONDER TO ME.
SOME-HOW, I'VE ALREADY BECOME A MONSTER... I GUESS.
...YOU DON'T HAVE TO WORRY AT ALL...
...ABOUT HAVING EATEN MY HEART OR ANY-THING.
I HEARD THAT YOU'VE BEEN LIVING AROUND THE FOREST THE WHOLE TIME SINCE THEN... BUT IT WOULDN'T BE A PROBLEM WITH ME IF YOU CAME BACK...

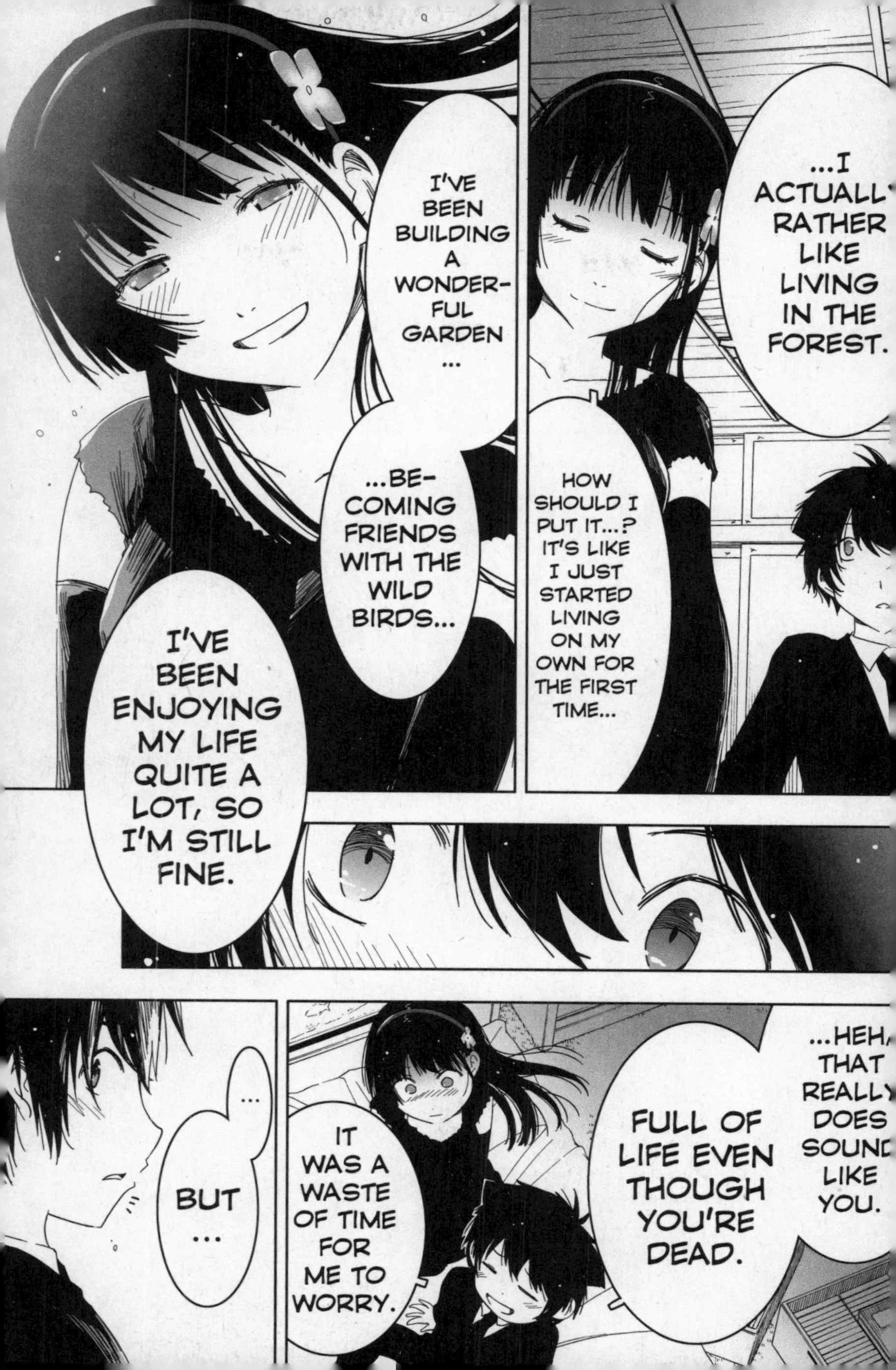
...I ACTUALL RATHER LIKE LIVING IN THE FOREST.
HOW SHOULD I PUT IT...? IT'S LIKE I JUST STARTED LIVING ON MY OWN FOR THE FIRST TIME...
I'VE BEEN BUILDING A WONDER-FUL GARDEN...
...BE-COMING FRIENDS WITH THE WILD BIRDS...
I'VE BEEN ENJOYING MY LIFE QUITE A LOT, SO I'M STILL FINE.
...HEH, THAT REALLY DOES SOUND LIKE YOU.
FULL OF LIFE EVEN THOUGH YOU'RE DEAD.
IT WAS A WASTE OF TIME FOR ME TO WORRY.
...
BUT...

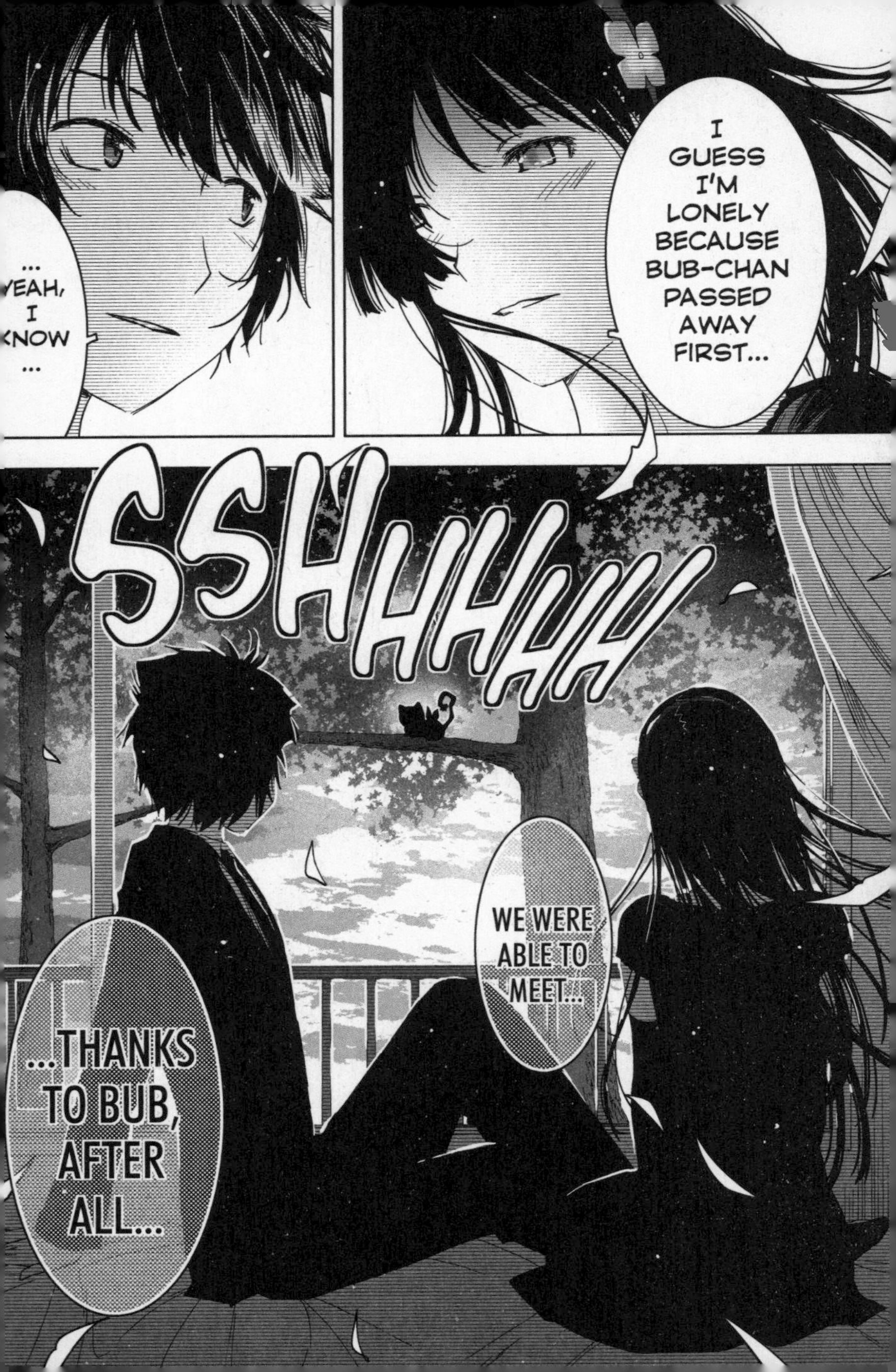
I GUESS I'M LONELY BECAUSE BUB-CHAN PASSED AWAY FIRST...
...YEAH, I KNOW...
SSHHHHHH
WE WERE ABLE TO MEET...
...THANKS TO BUB, AFTER ALL...

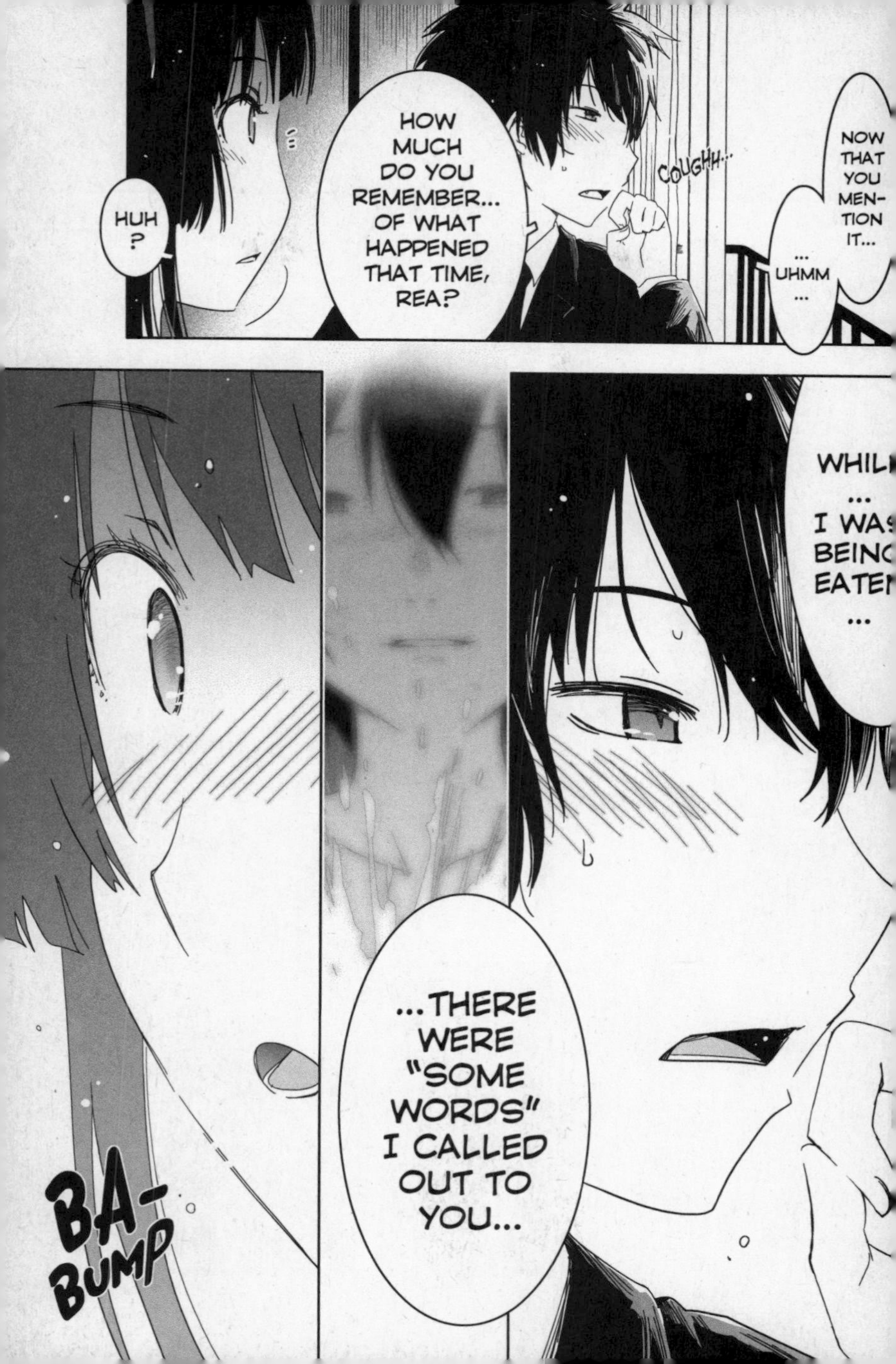
NOW THAT YOU MEN-TION IT...
... UHMM ...
COUGHH...
HOW MUCH DO YOU REMEMBER... OF WHAT HAPPENED THAT TIME, REA?
HUH?
WHIL ... I WA BEIN EATE ...
...THERE WERE "SOME WORDS" I CALLED OUT TO YOU...
BA-BUMP

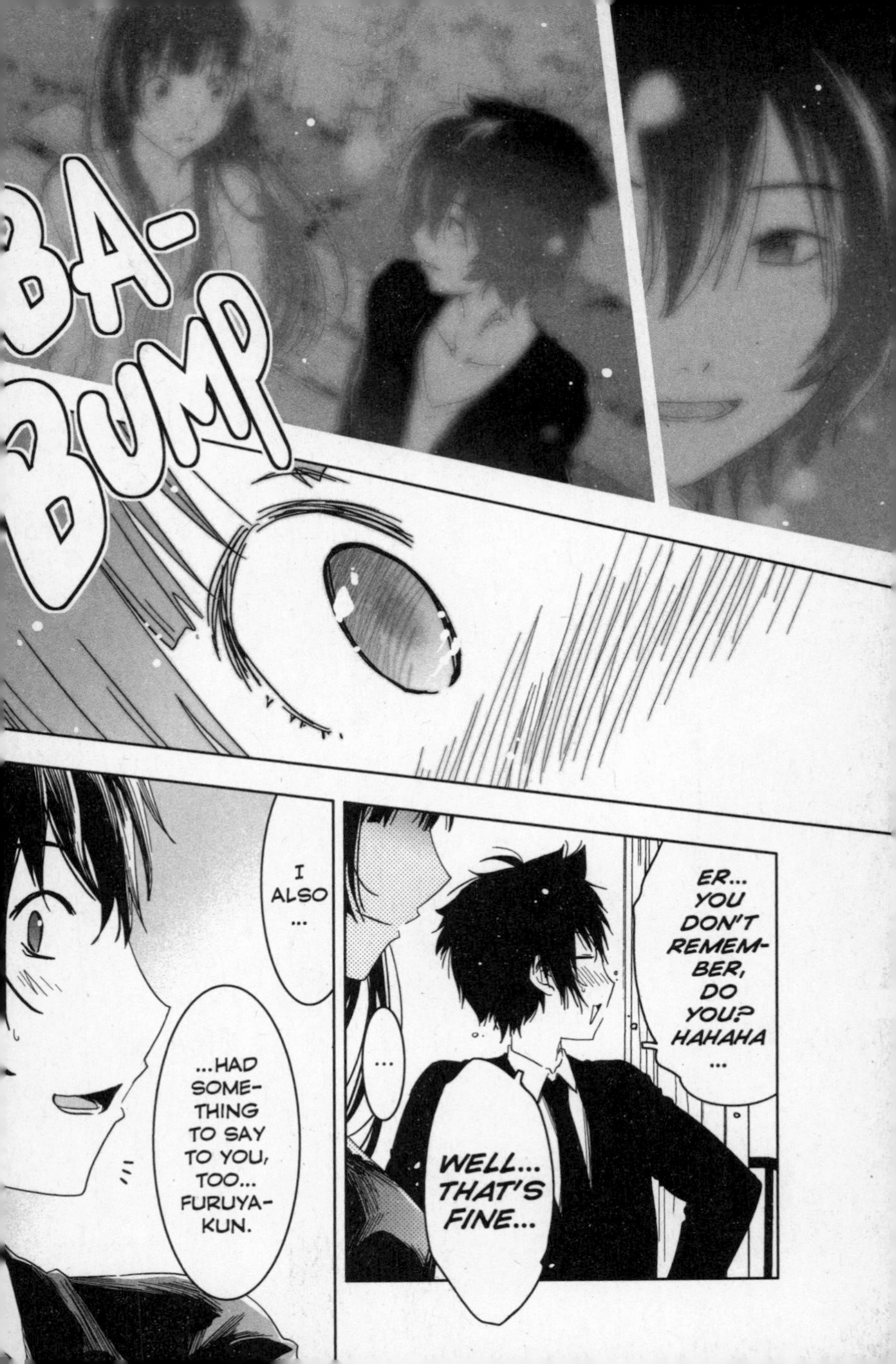
BA-BUMP
ER... YOU DON'T REMEMBER, DO YOU? HAHAHA...
...
WELL... THAT'S FINE...
I ALSO...
...HAD SOMETHING TO SAY TO YOU, TOO... FURUYA-KUN.

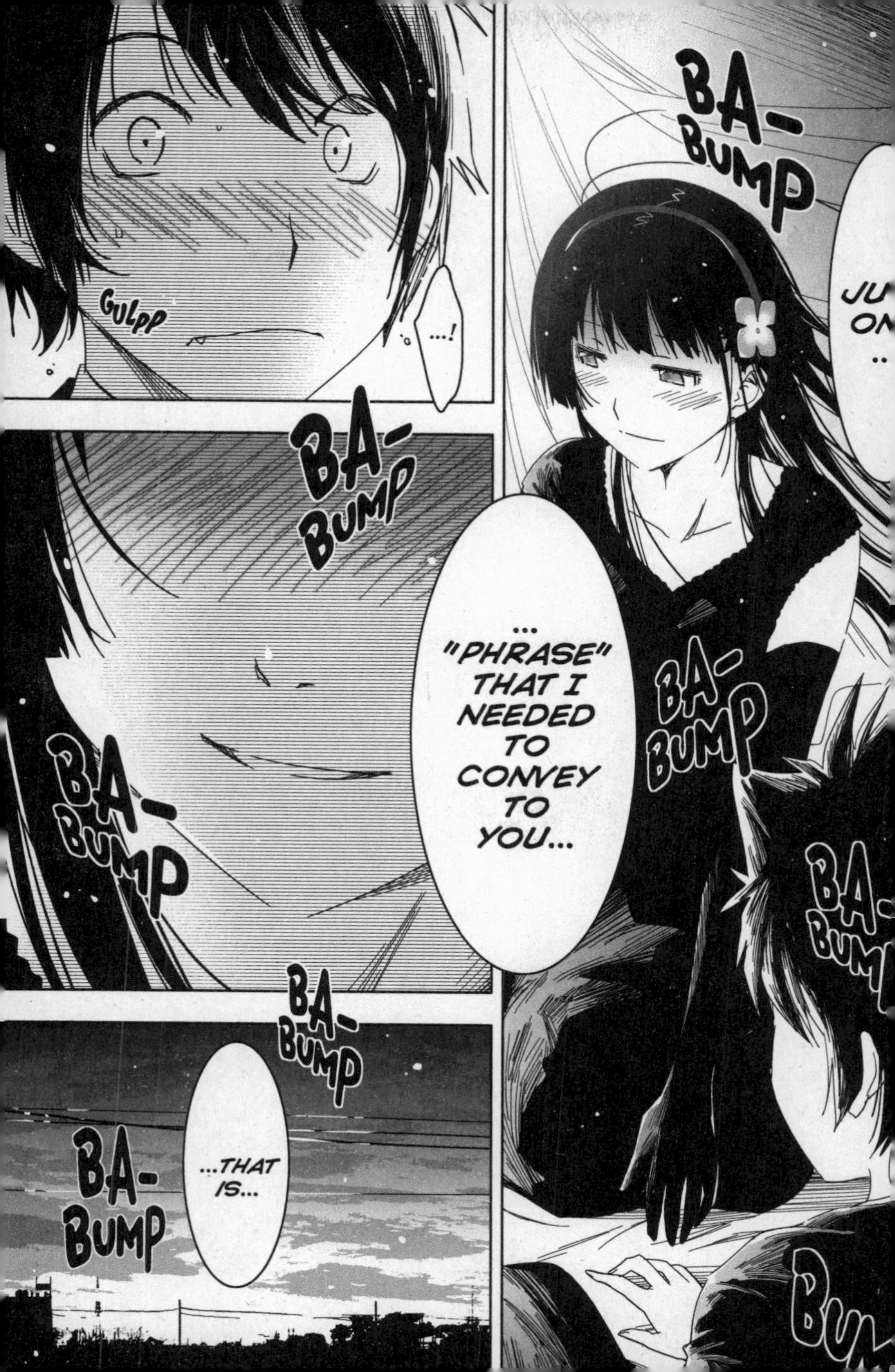
BA-BUMP
... "PHRASE" THAT I NEEDED TO CONVEY TO YOU...
BA-BUMP
GULPP
...!
BA-BUMP
BA-BUMP
BA-BUMP
...THAT IS...
BA-BUMP

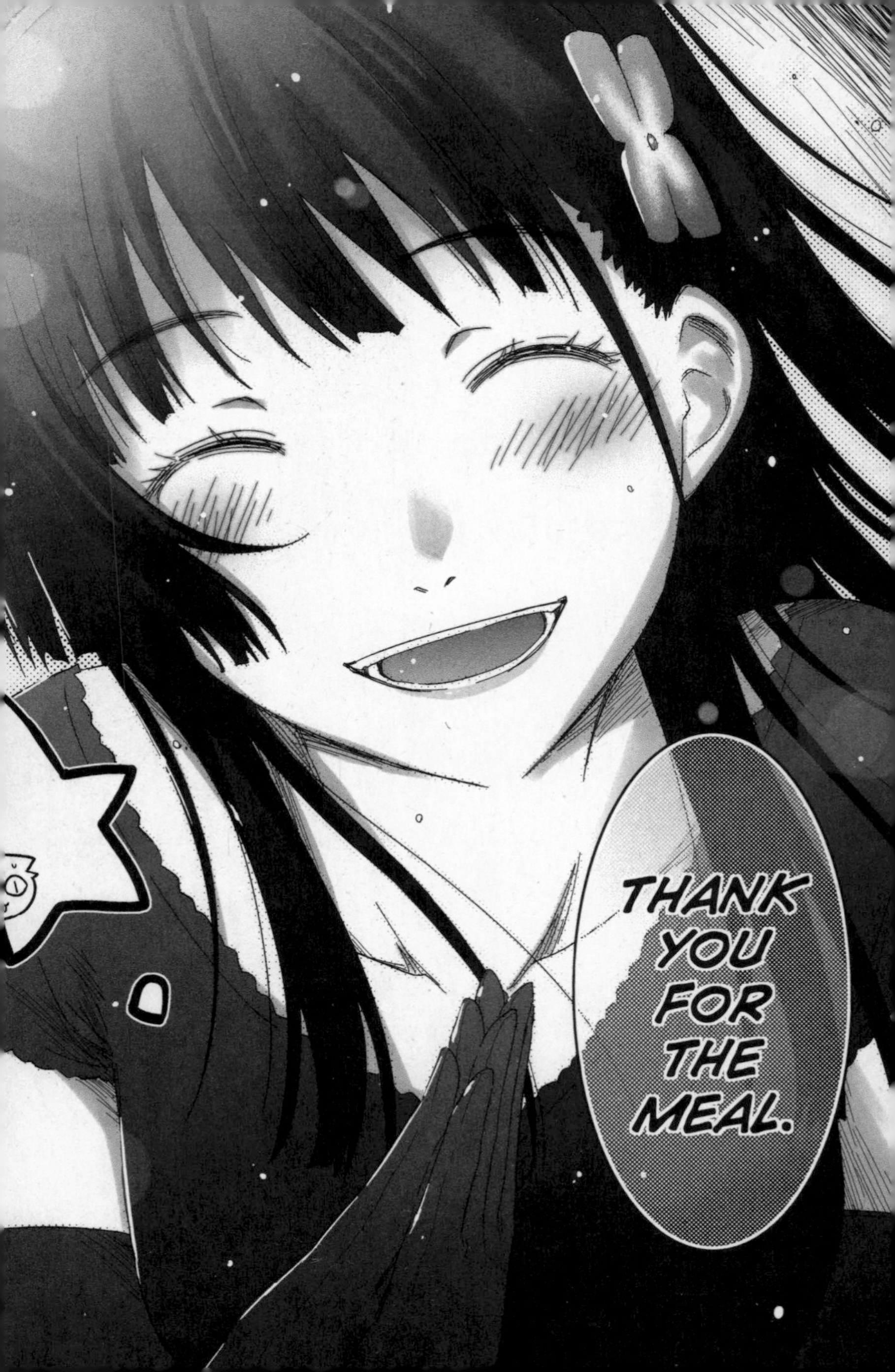
THANK YOU FOR THE MEAL.

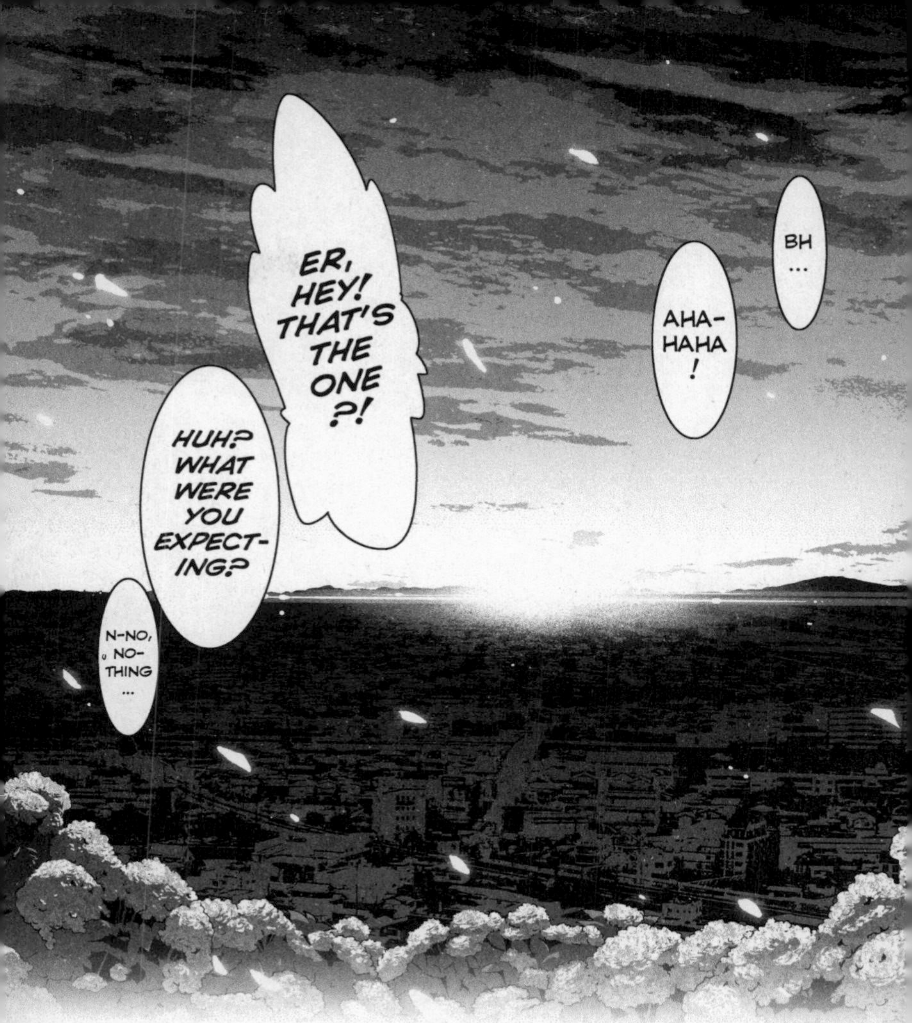
BH...
AHA-HAHA!
ER, HEY! THAT'S THE ONE?!
HUH? WHAT WERE YOU EXPECTING?
N-NO, NOTHING...

From here on...
Forever more...
Wherever you'll be...
Until you rot away...

The end

Something like an afterword

My sincere thanks for staying with me through to the final, 11th volume. This ended up being in serialization quite a bit longer than I had planned in the beginning, but somehow, I was able to end it without issue.

Among all of the serialized manga I've written up to this point, this one ended up on the dark side, content-wise, and I ended it without bringing it to a depressing end. That said, I also kept a balance in which it wasn't overly happy, too.

As for how long Rea and Chihiro were able to be together... I'll leave that to your imagination.

I can't thank you enough for your passionate readership.

By the way, starting on the next page, I've put together a side story that borrows the settings from the main book, and in a way it's drawn as a play on a parallel-world kind of thing. Please enjoy it without thinking too deeply.

Well then, let's meet again in my new work.

Hattori Mitsuru.

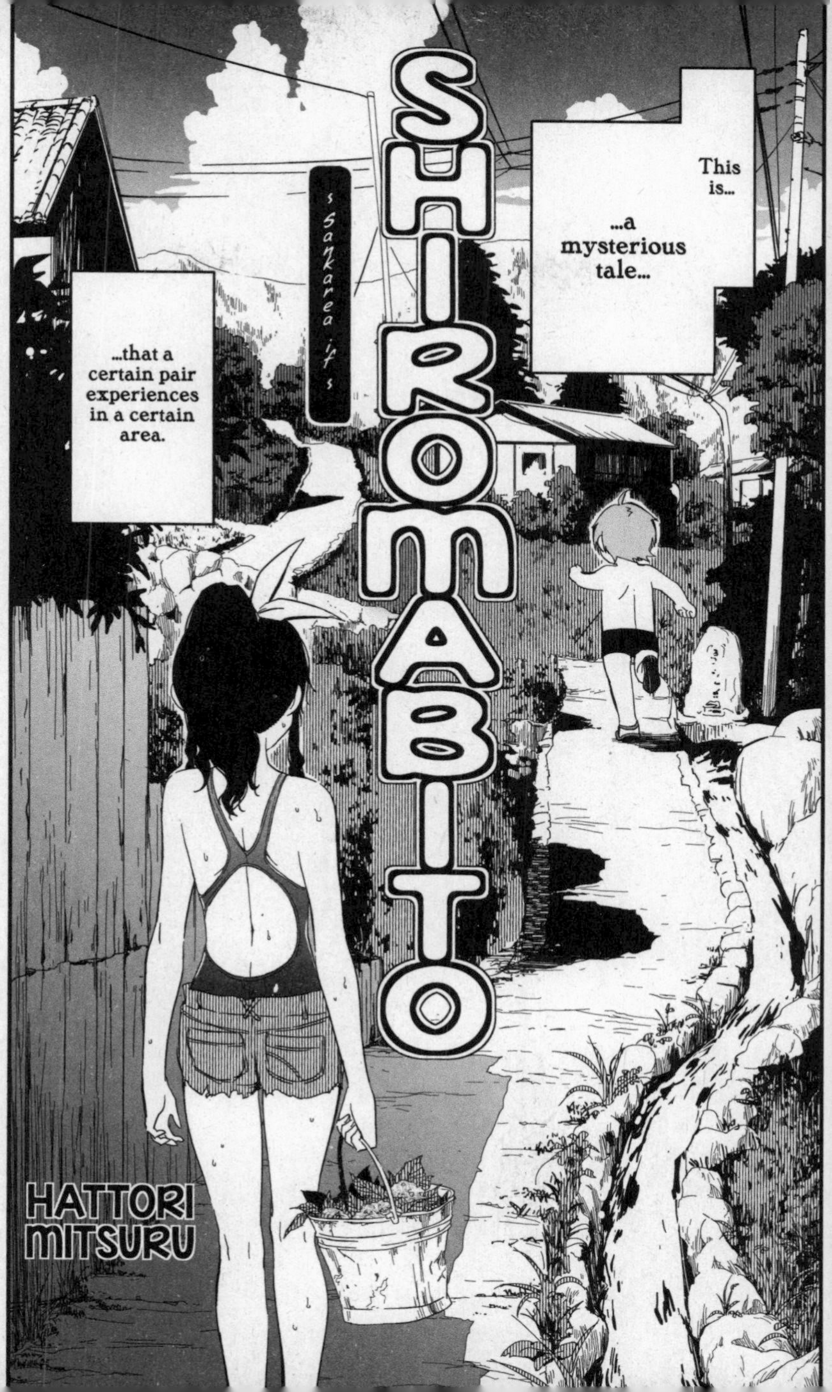
SHIROMABITO
Sankarea if's
This is...
...a mysterious tale...
...that a certain pair experiences in a certain area.
HATTORI MITSURU

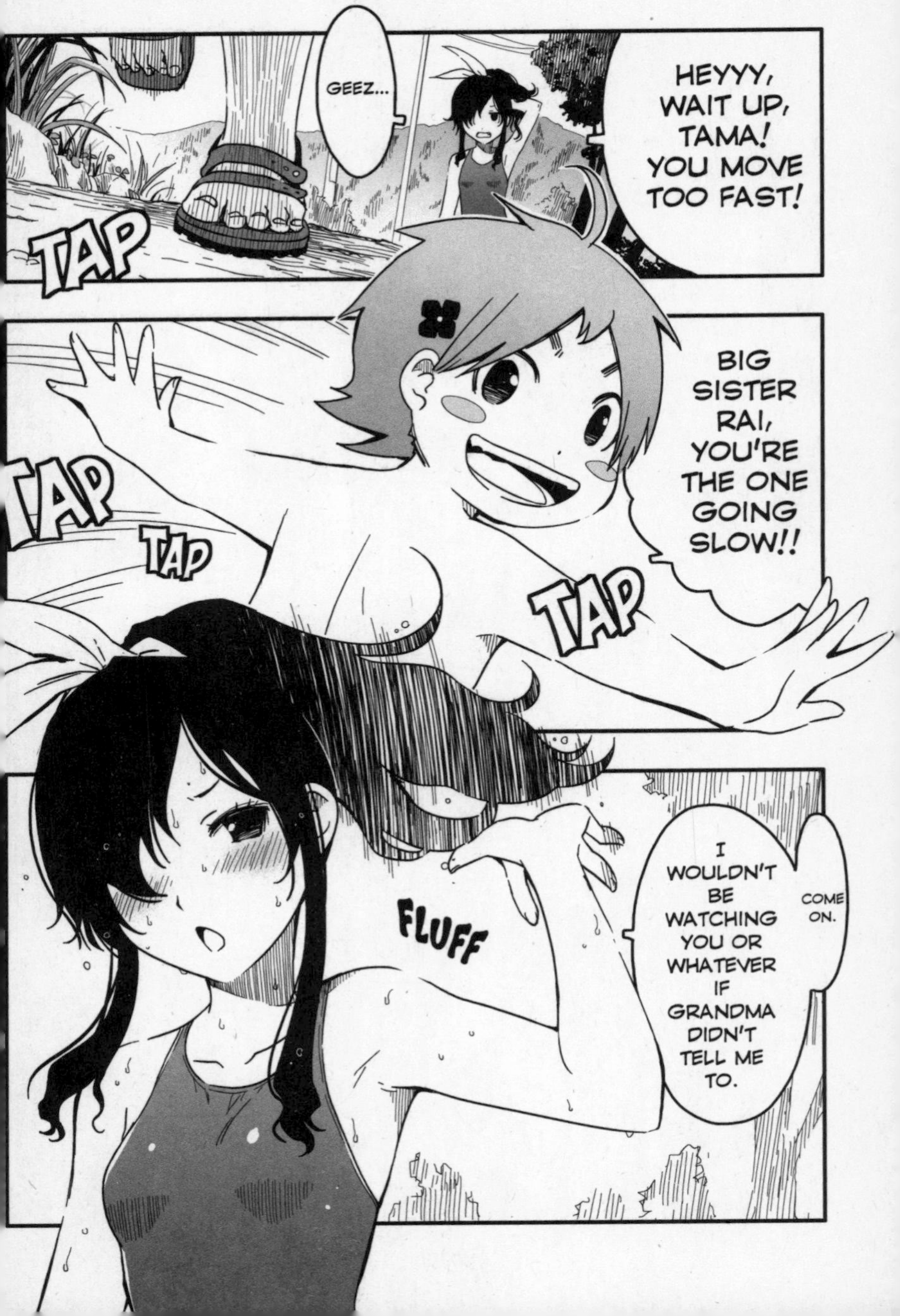
HEYYY, WAIT UP, TAMA! YOU MOVE TOO FAST!
GEEZ...
TAP
BIG SISTER RAI, YOU'RE THE ONE GOING SLOW!!
TAP
TAP
TAP
COME ON.
I WOULDN'T BE WATCHING YOU OR WHATEVER IF GRANDMA DIDN'T TELL ME TO.
FLUFF

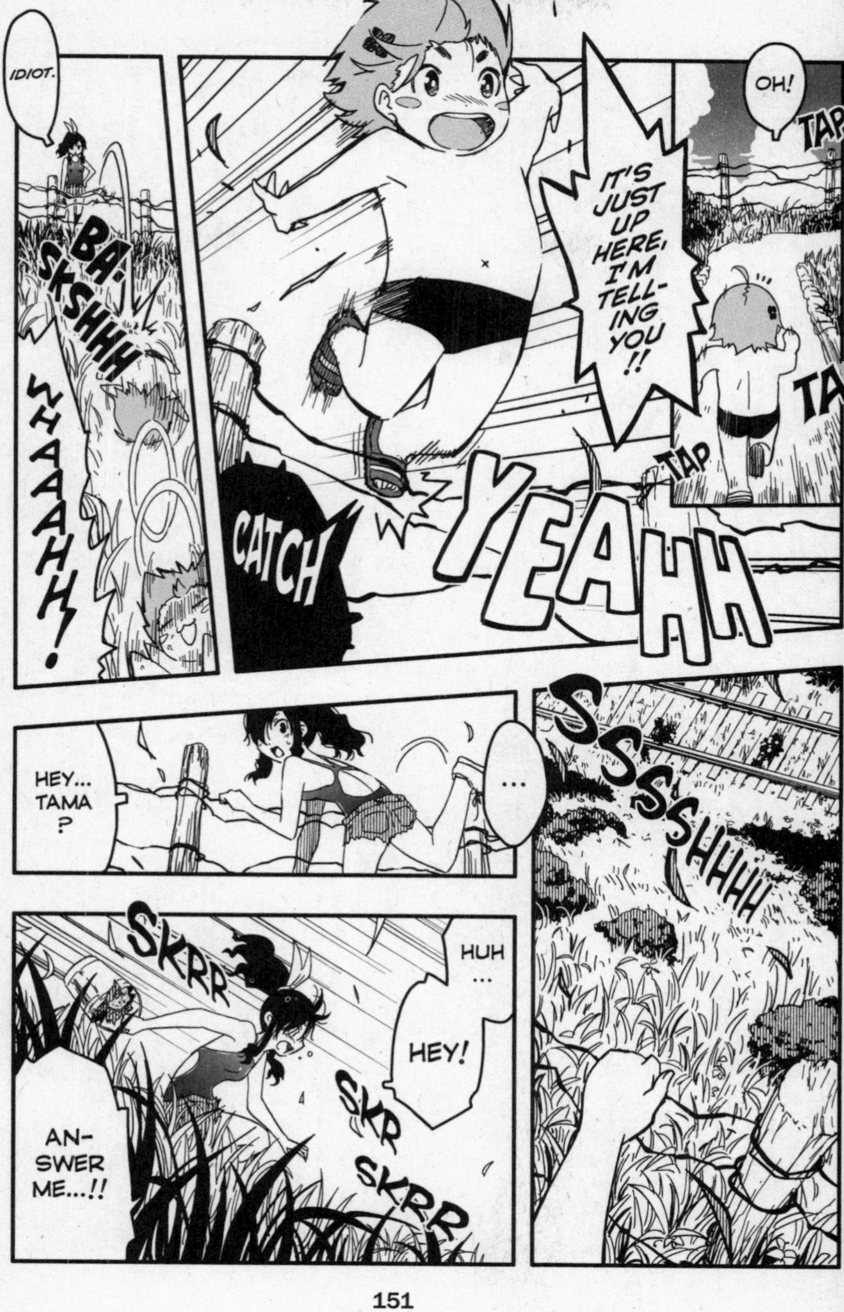
OH!
TAP
TA
TAP
IT'S JUST UP HERE, I'M TELL-ING YOU!!
YEAHH
CATCH
IDIOT.
BA-SKSHHH
WHAAAAHH!
SSSSSHHHH
...
HEY... TAMA?
HUH...
HEY!
SKRR
SKR
SKRR
AN-SWER ME...!!

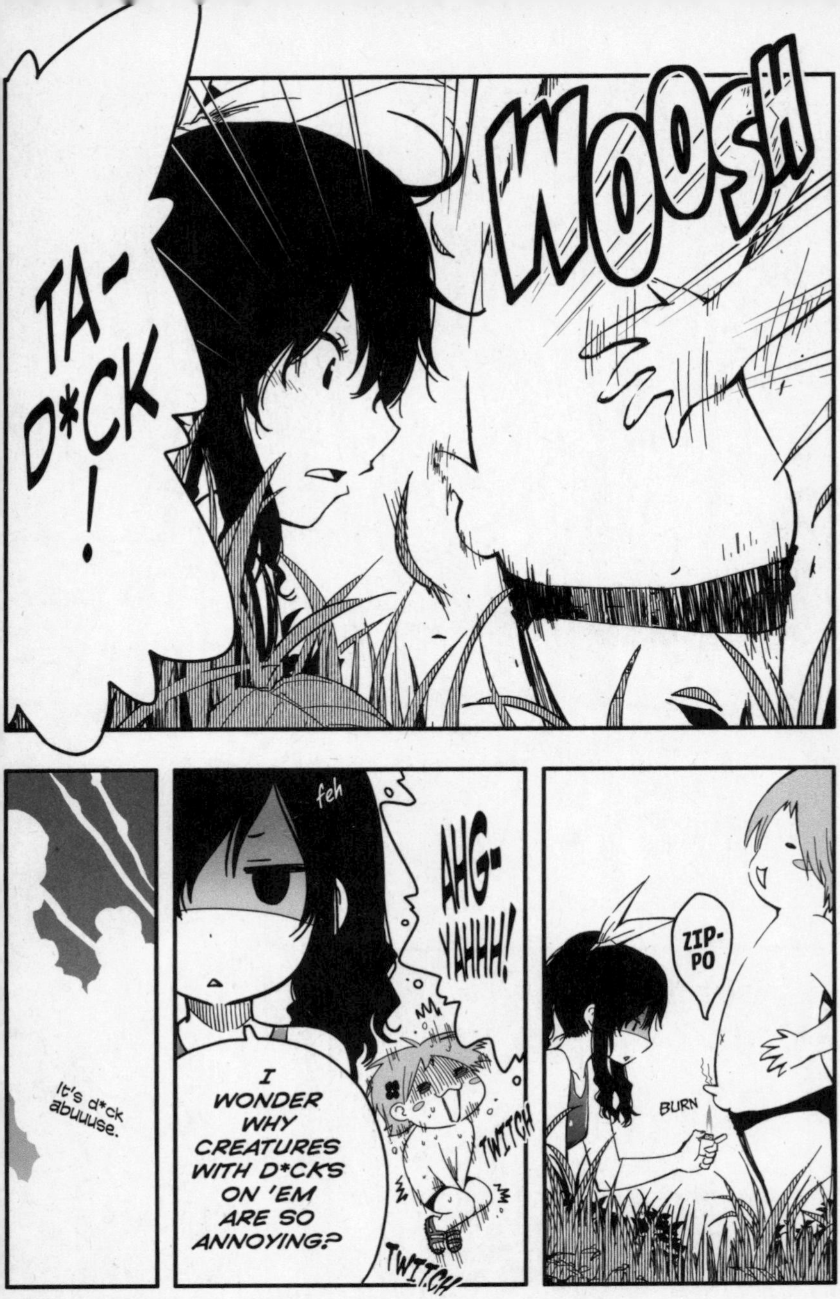
WOOSH
TA-D*CK!
ZIP-PO
BURN
feh
AHG-YAHHH!
I WONDER WHY CREATURES WITH D*CKS ON 'EM ARE SO ANNOYING?
TWITCH
TWITCH
It's d*ck abuuuse.

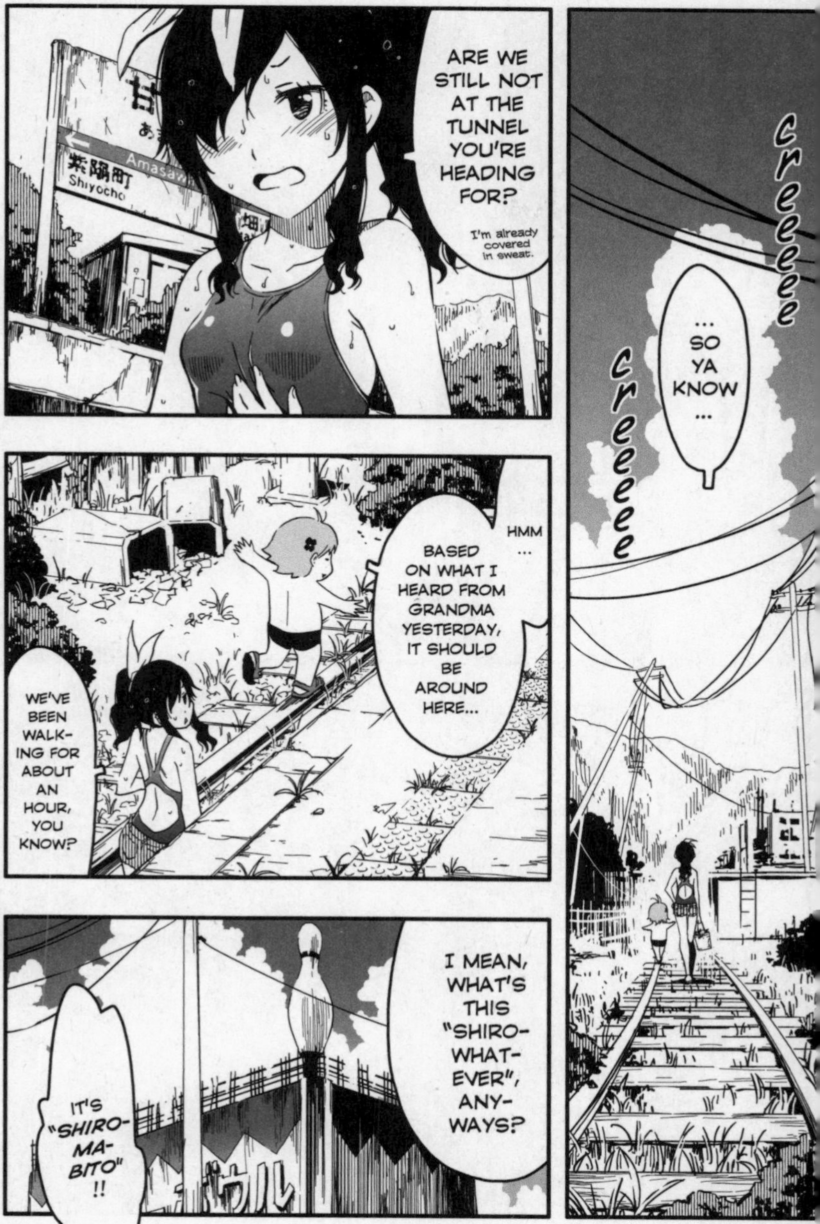
creeeeee
... SO YA KNOW ...
creeeeee
紫陽町
Shiyocho
ARE WE STILL NOT AT THE TUNNEL YOU'RE HEADING FOR?
I'm already covered in sweat.
HMM ...
BASED ON WHAT I HEARD FROM GRANDMA YESTERDAY, IT SHOULD BE AROUND HERE...
WE'VE BEEN WALKING FOR ABOUT AN HOUR, YOU KNOW?
I MEAN, WHAT'S THIS "SHIRO-WHATEVER", ANYWAYS?
IT'S "SHIROMABITO"!!

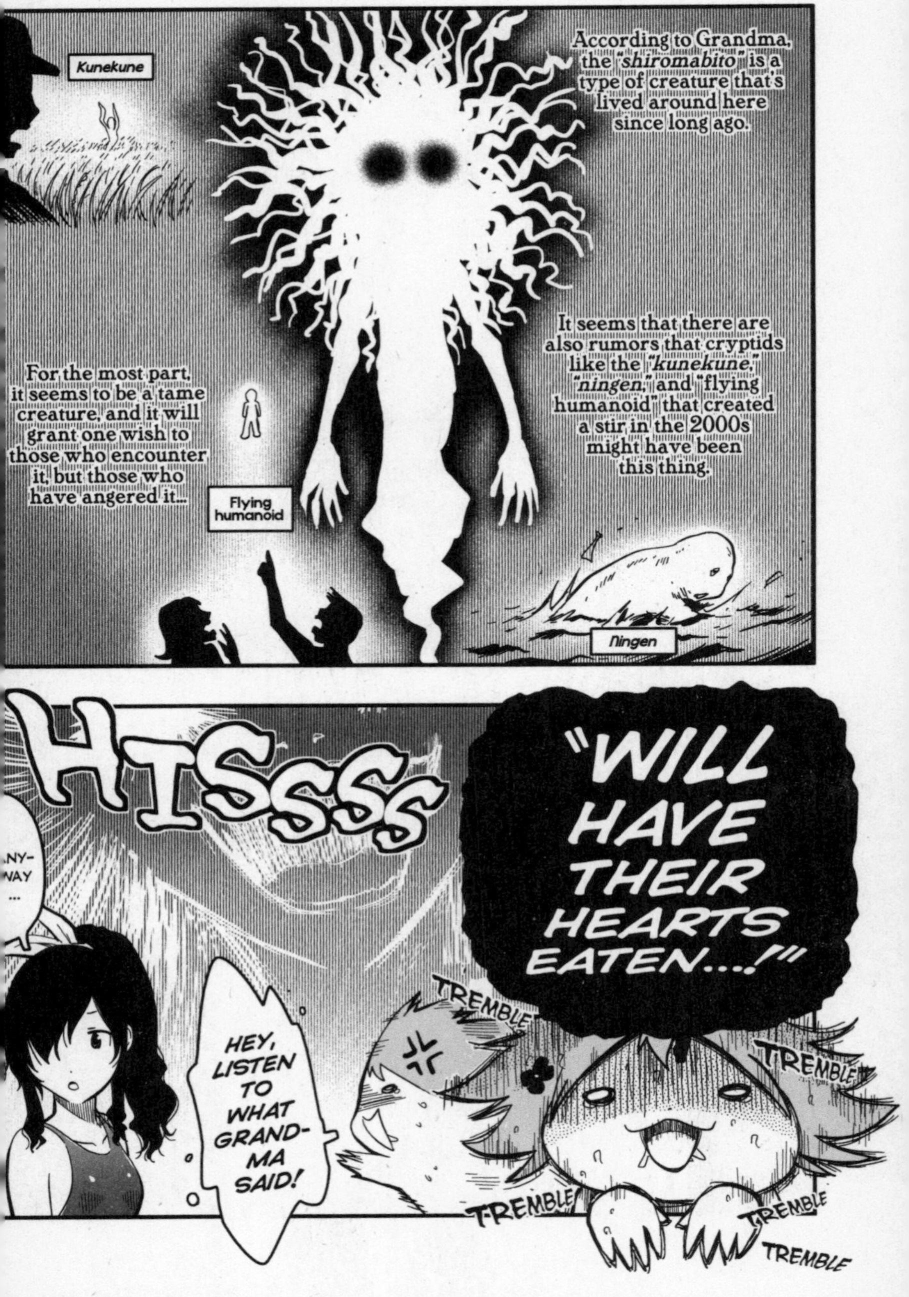
According to Grandma, the "shiromabito" is a type of creature that's lived around here since long ago.
Kunekune
It seems that there are also rumors that cryptids like the "kunekune," "ningen," and "flying humanoid" that created a stir in the 2000s might have been this thing.
For the most part, it seems to be a tame creature, and it will grant one wish to those who encounter it, but those who have angered it...
Flying humanoid
Ningen
"WILL HAVE THEIR HEARTS EATEN...!"
HISSSS
TREMBLE
TREMBLE
TREMBLE
TREMBLE
TREMBLE
HEY, LISTEN TO WHAT GRAND-MA SAID!

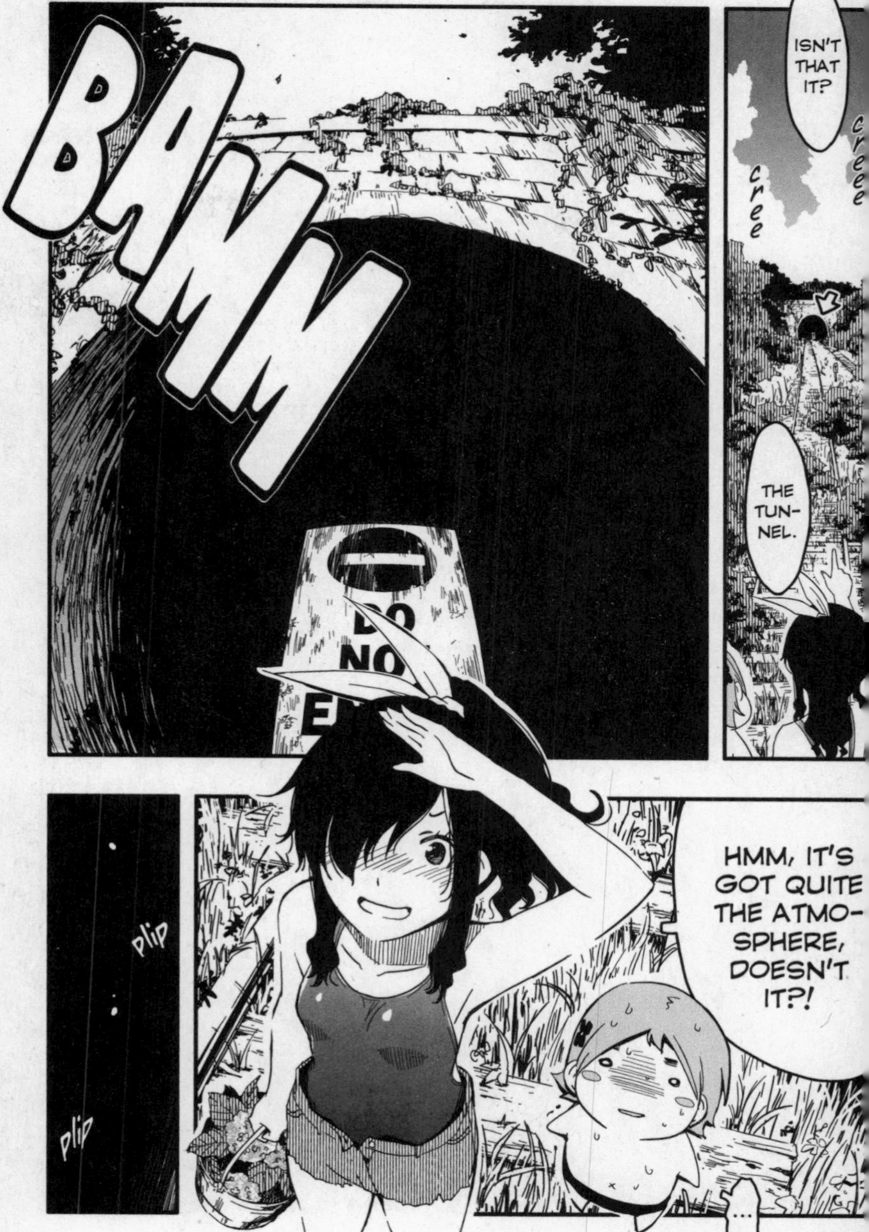
ISN'T THAT IT?
cree
creee
THE TUN-NEL.
BAMM
HMM, IT'S GOT QUITE THE ATMO-SPHERE, DOESN'T IT?!
...
plip
plip

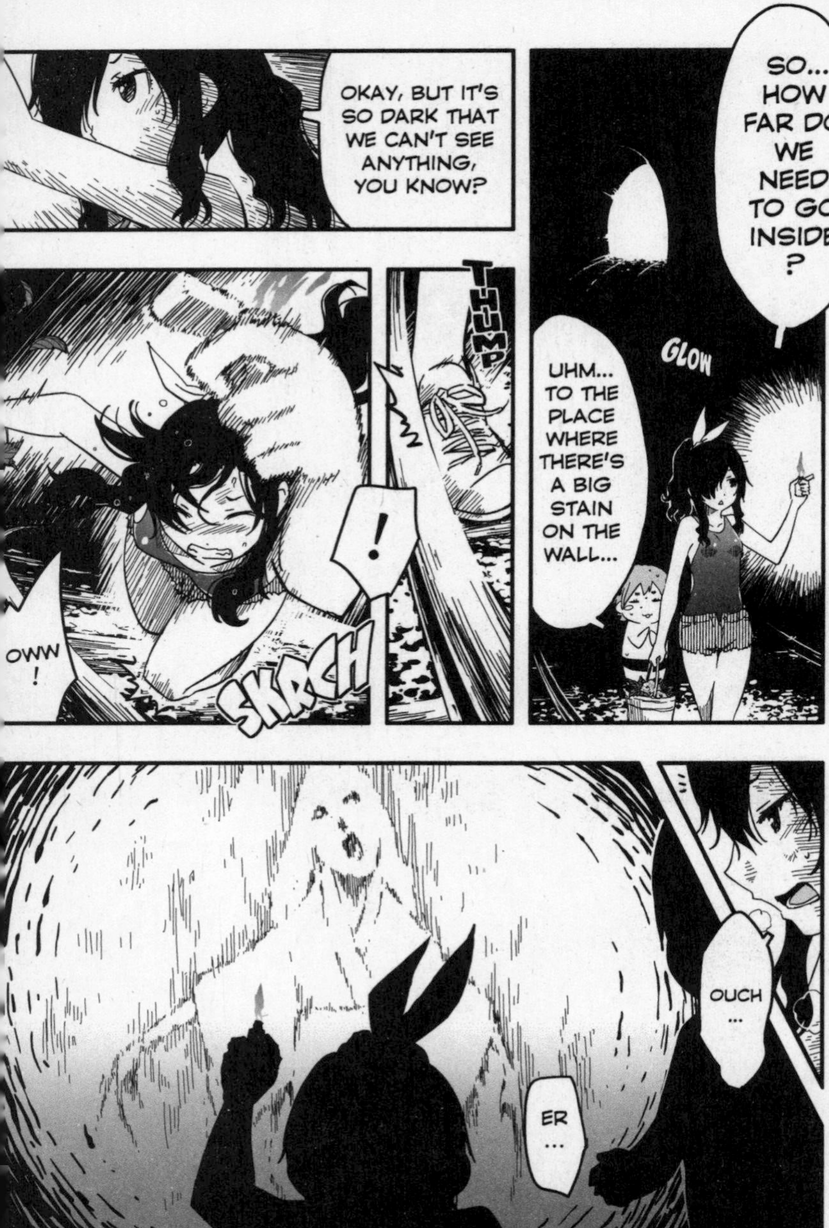
SO... HOW FAR DO WE NEED TO GO INSIDE?
GLOW
UHM... TO THE PLACE WHERE THERE'S A BIG STAIN ON THE WALL...
OKAY, BUT IT'S SO DARK THAT WE CAN'T SEE ANYTHING, YOU KNOW?
THUMP
!
SKRCH
OWW!
OUCH...
ER...

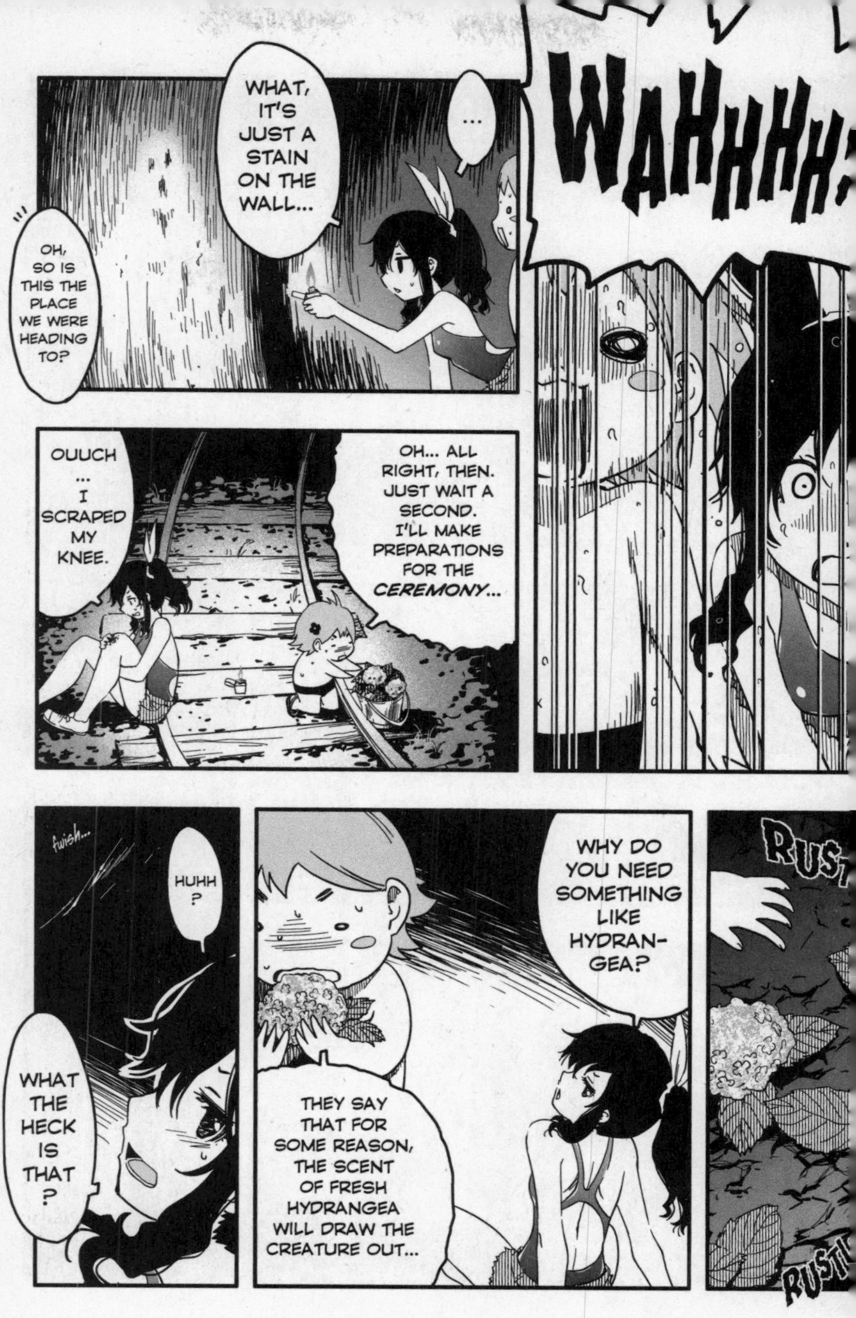
WAHHHH
...
WHAT, IT'S JUST A STAIN ON THE WALL...
OH, SO IS THIS THE PLACE WE WERE HEADING TO?
OH... ALL RIGHT, THEN. JUST WAIT A SECOND. I'LL MAKE PREPARATIONS FOR THE *CEREMONY*...
OUUCH ... I SCRAPED MY KNEE.
RUST
RUST
WHY DO YOU NEED SOMETHING LIKE HYDRAN-GEA?
THEY SAY THAT FOR SOME REASON, THE SCENT OF FRESH HYDRANGEA WILL DRAW THE CREATURE OUT...
fwish...
HUHH ?
WHAT THE HECK IS THAT ?

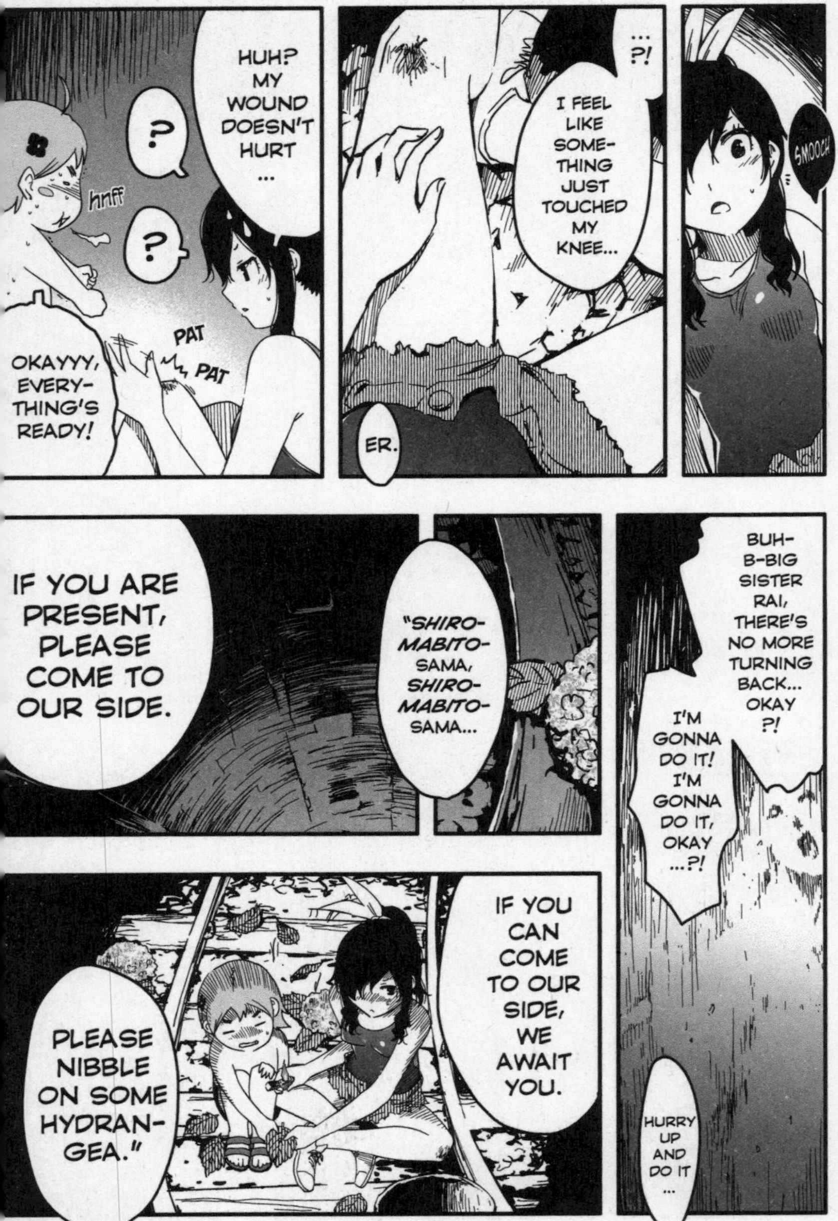
SMOOCH
...?!
I FEEL LIKE SOME-THING JUST TOUCHED MY KNEE...
ER.
HUH? MY WOUND DOESN'T HURT ...
?
?
hnff
PAT PAT
OKAYYY, EVERY-THING'S READY!
BUH-B-BIG SISTER RAI, THERE'S NO MORE TURNING BACK... OKAY ?!
I'M GONNA DO IT! I'M GONNA DO IT, OKAY ...?!
HURRY UP AND DO IT ...
"SHIRO-MABITO-SAMA, SHIRO-MABITO-SAMA...
IF YOU ARE PRESENT, PLEASE COME TO OUR SIDE.
IF YOU CAN COME TO OUR SIDE, WE AWAIT YOU.
PLEASE NIBBLE ON SOME HYDRAN-GEA."

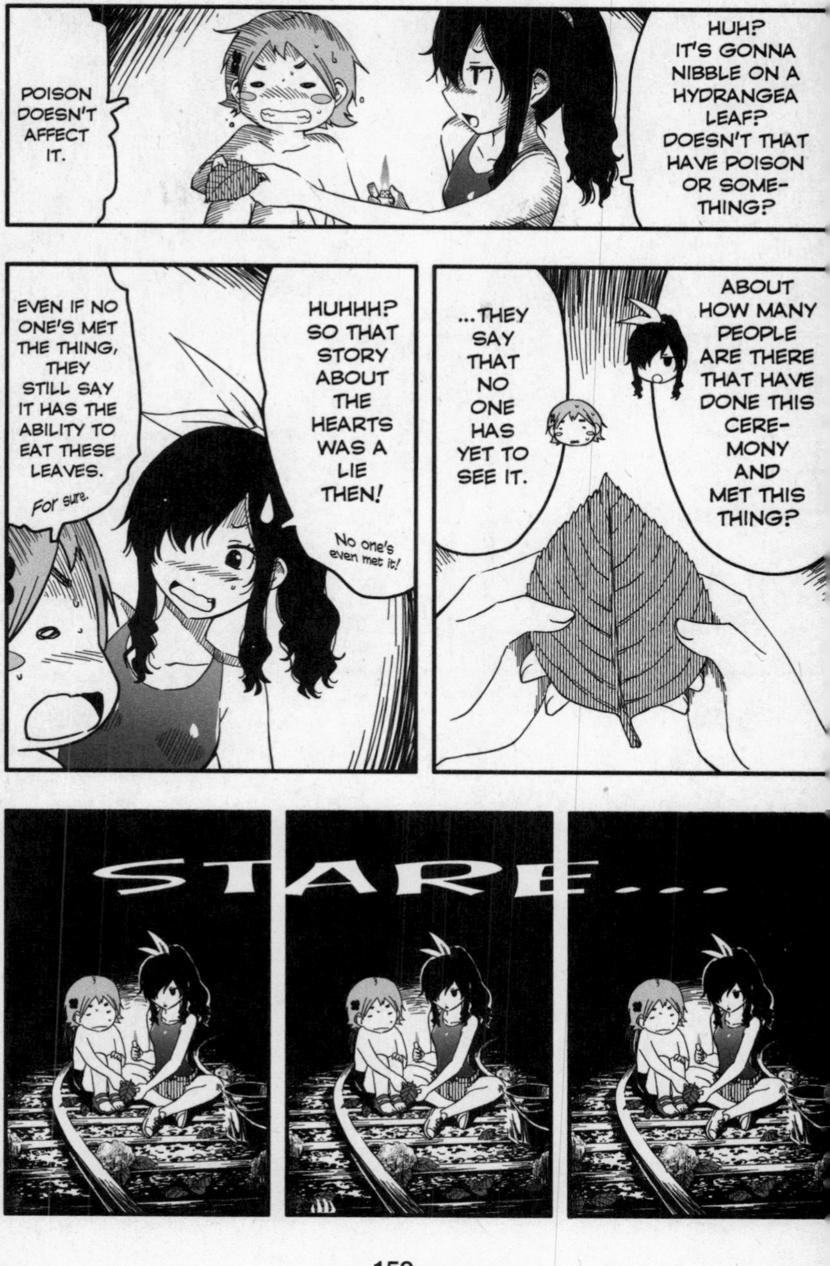
HUH? IT'S GONNA NIBBLE ON A HYDRANGEA LEAF? DOESN'T THAT HAVE POISON OR SOME-THING?
POISON DOESN'T AFFECT IT.
ABOUT HOW MANY PEOPLE ARE THERE THAT HAVE DONE THIS CERE-MONY AND MET THIS THING?
...THEY SAY THAT NO ONE HAS YET TO SEE IT.
HUHHH? SO THAT STORY ABOUT THE HEARTS WAS A LIE THEN!
No one's even met it!
EVEN IF NO ONE'S MET THE THING, THEY STILL SAY IT HAS THE ABILITY TO EAT THESE LEAVES.
For sure.
STARE...

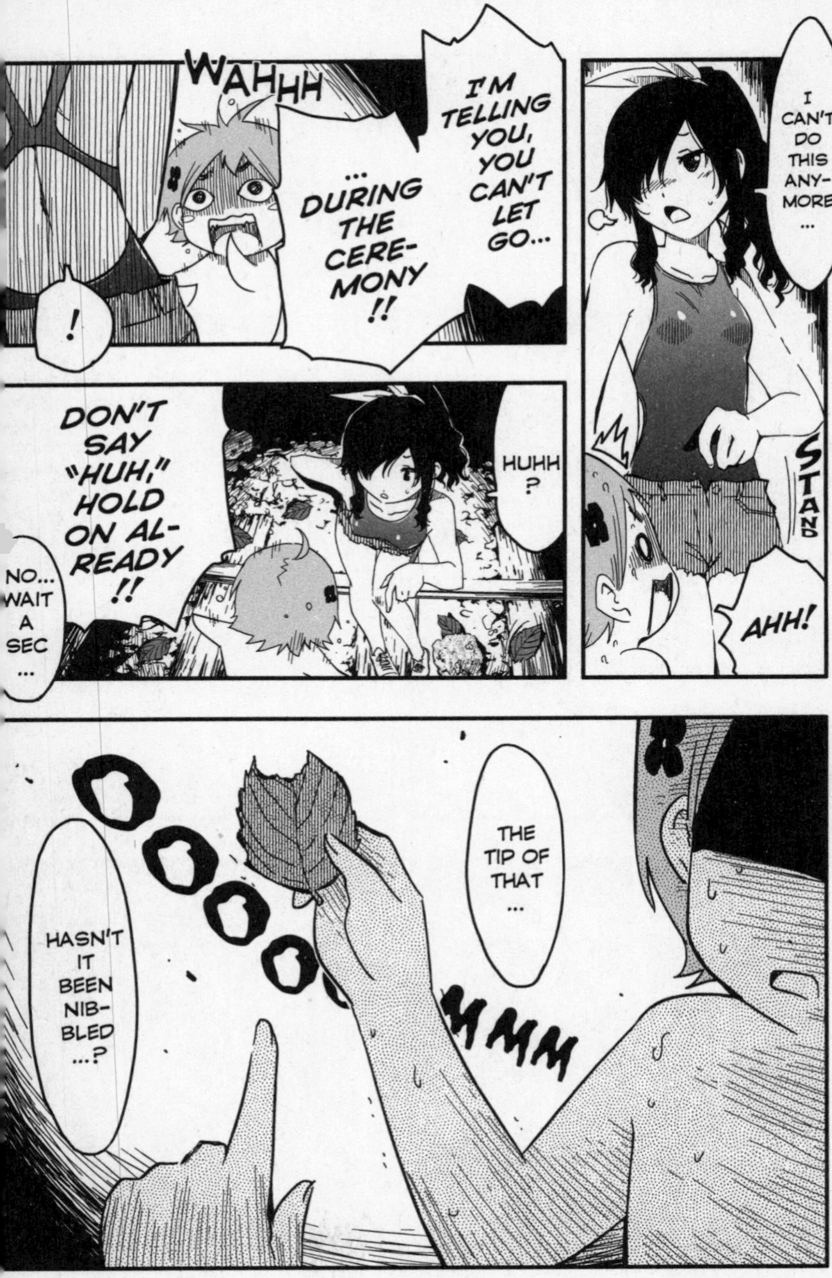
I CAN'T DO THIS ANYMORE...
STAND
AHH!
I'M TELLING YOU, YOU CAN'T LET GO...
...DURING THE CEREMONY!!
WAHHH
!
HUHH?
DON'T SAY "HUH," HOLD ON ALREADY!!
NO... WAIT A SEC...
THE TIP OF THAT...
OOOOOMMMM
HASN'T IT BEEN NIBBLED...?

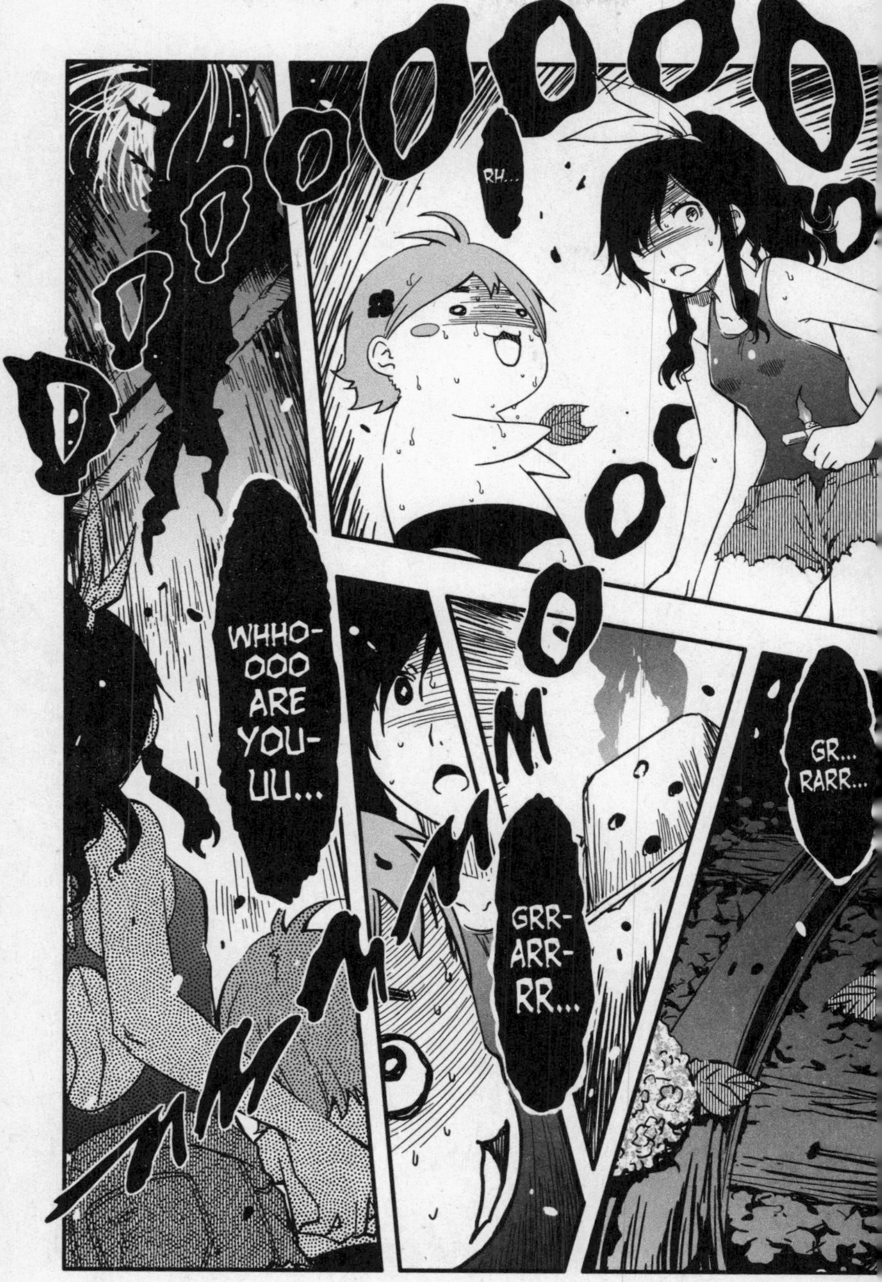
DOOOOOOOOOOOOOOOOOMMMMMM
RH...
GR... RARR...
GRR-ARR-RR...
WHHO-OOO ARE YOU-UU...

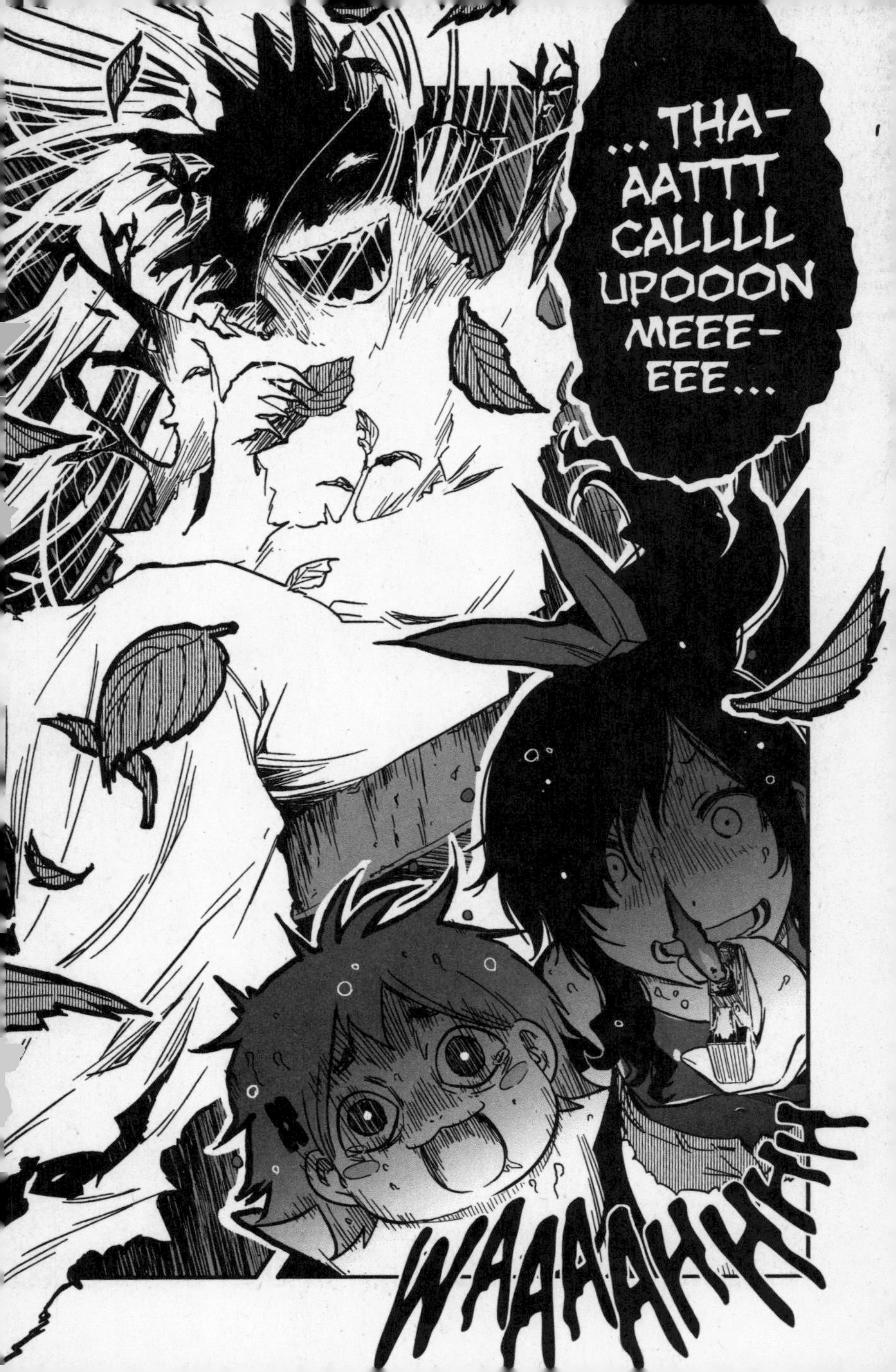
... THA-
AATTT
CALLLL
UPOOON
MEEE-
EEE...
WAAAAHHHH

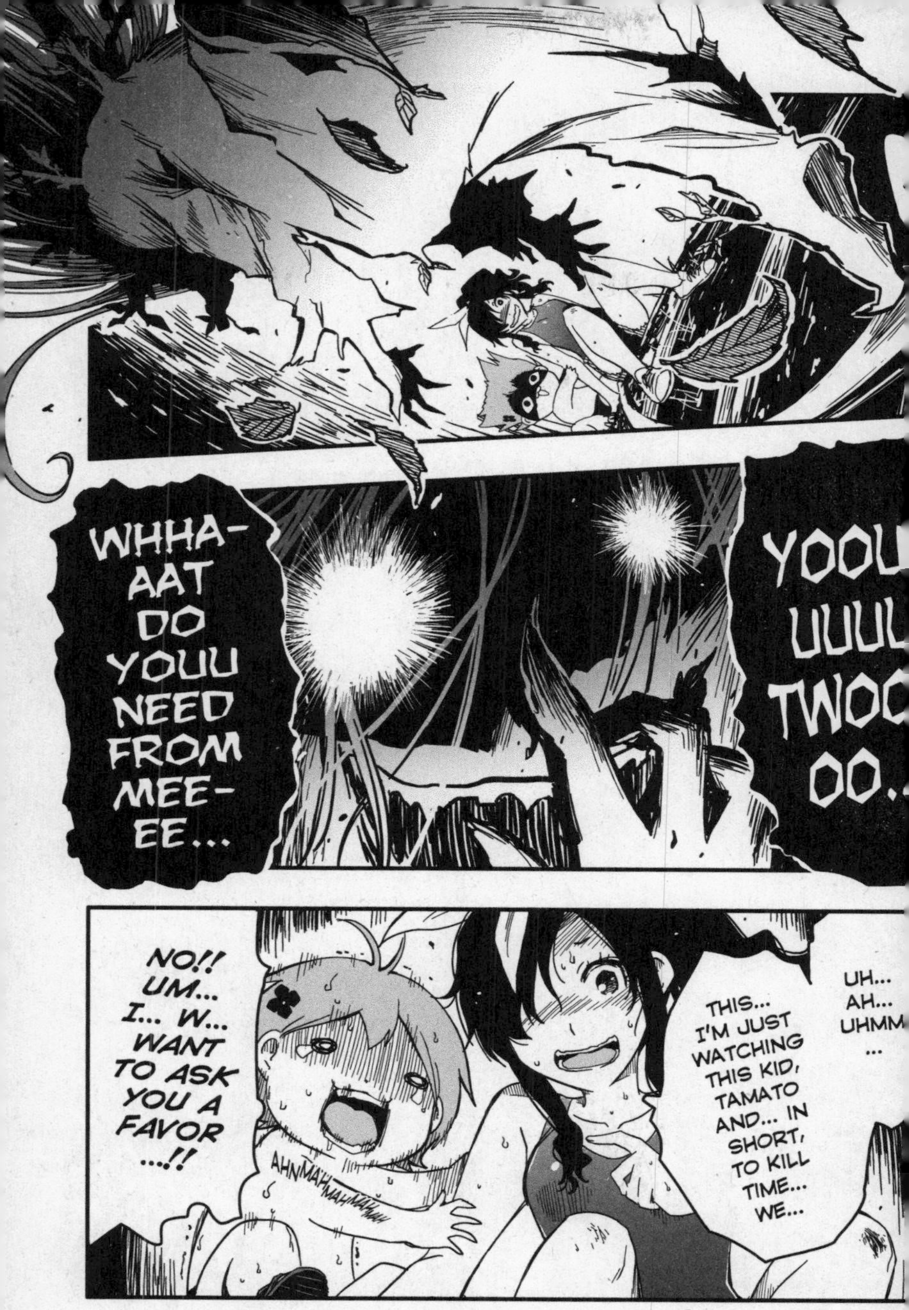
YOOU UUUU TWOO OO..
WHHA-AAT DO YOUU NEED FROM MEE-EE...
UH... AH... UHMM ...
THIS... I'M JUST WATCHING THIS KID, TAMATO AND... IN SHORT, TO KILL TIME... WE...
NO!! UM... I... W... WANT TO ASK YOU A FAVOR ...!!
AHNMAHMAHMAH

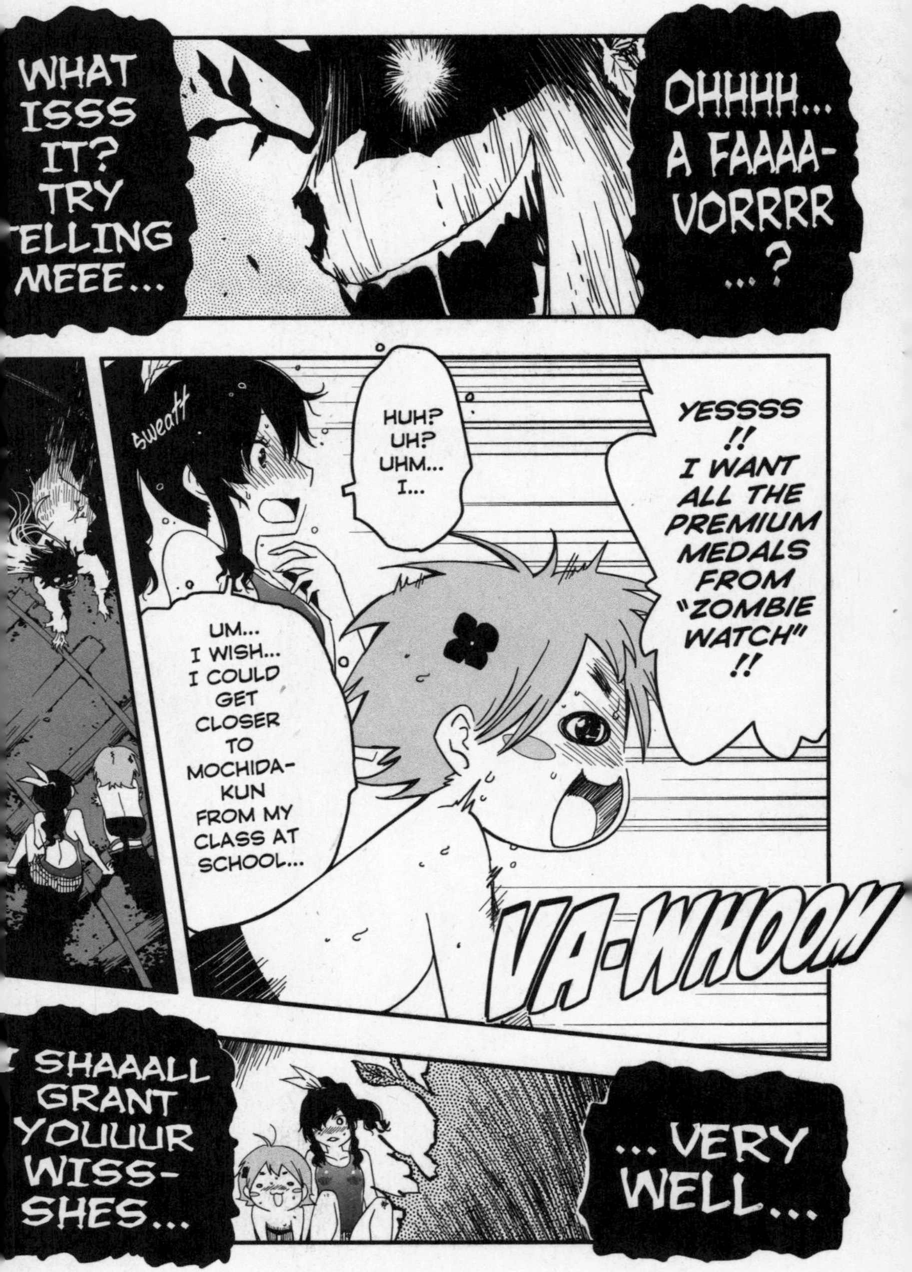
OHHHH... A FAAAA-VORRRR ...?
WHAT ISSS IT? TRY TELLING MEEE...
YESSSS!! I WANT ALL THE PREMIUM MEDALS FROM "ZOMBIE WATCH"!!
SWEAT
HUH? UH? UHM... I...
UM... I WISH... I COULD GET CLOSER TO MOCHIDA-KUN FROM MY CLASS AT SCHOOL...
VA-WHOOM
... VERY WELL...
I SHAAALL GRANT YOUUUR WISS-SHES...

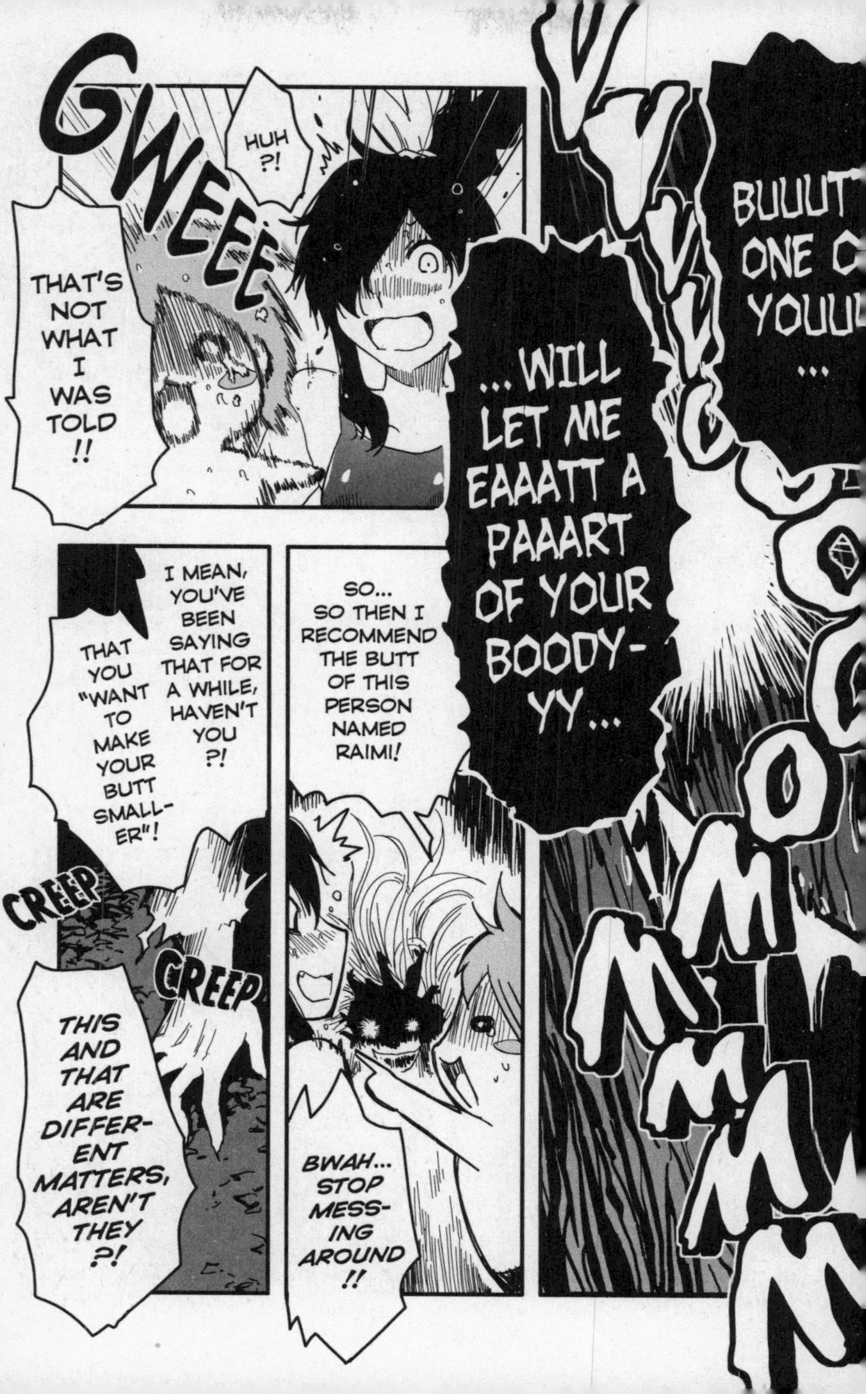
BUUUT ONE O YOUUU ...
... WILL LET ME EAAATT A PAAART OF YOUR BOODY-YY...
GWEEE
HUH ?!
THAT'S NOT WHAT I WAS TOLD !!
SO... SO THEN I RECOMMEND THE BUTT OF THIS PERSON NAMED RAIMI!
BWAH... STOP MESS-ING AROUND !!
I MEAN, YOU'VE BEEN SAYING THAT FOR A WHILE, HAVEN'T YOU ?!
THAT YOU "WANT TO MAKE YOUR BUTT SMALL-ER"!
CREEP
CREEP
THIS AND THAT ARE DIFFER-ENT MATTERS, AREN'T THEY ?!

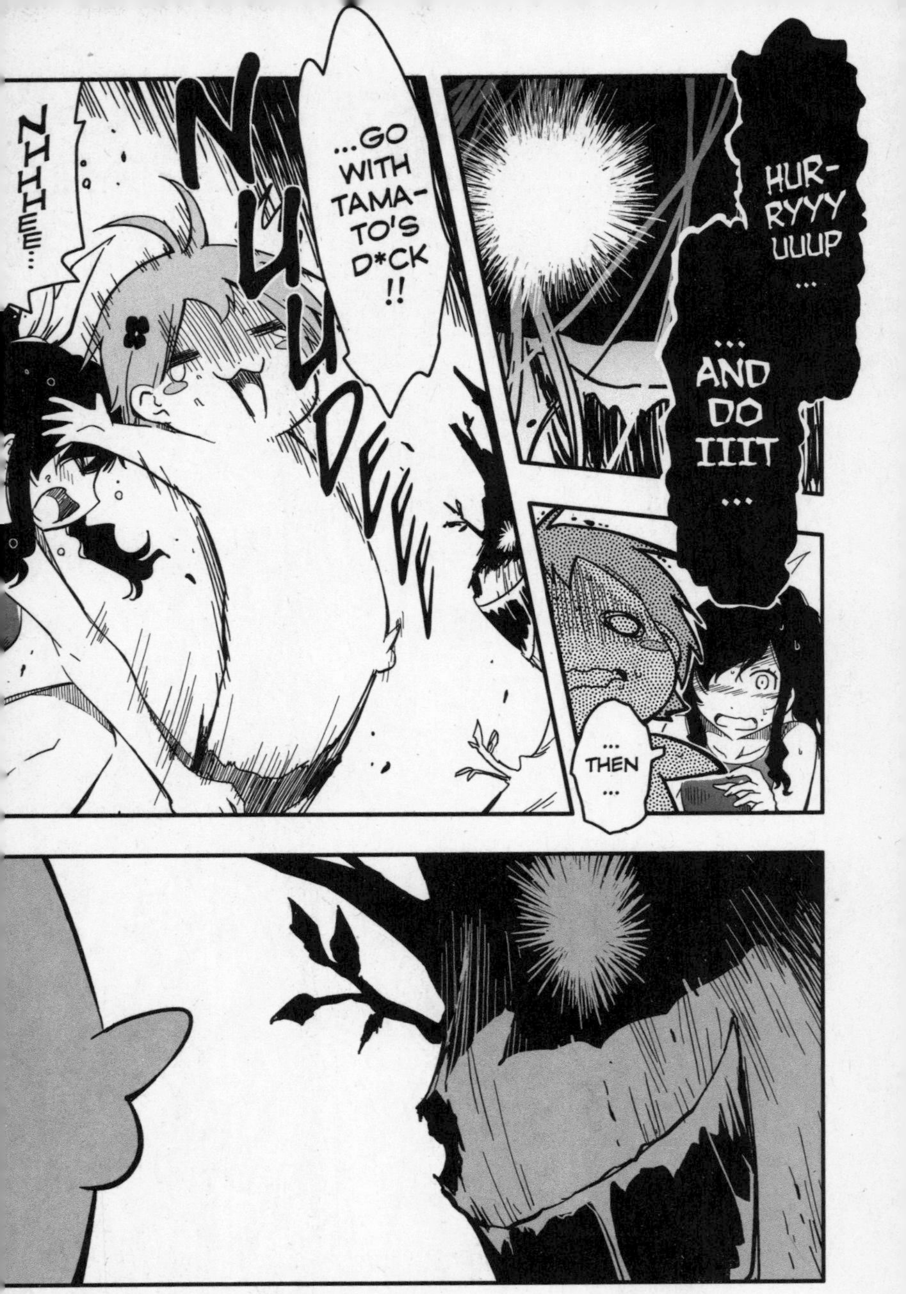
HURRYYY UUUP...
...AND DO IIIT...
...THEN...
...GO WITH TAMATO'S D*CK!!
NUUDE
NHHHEE...

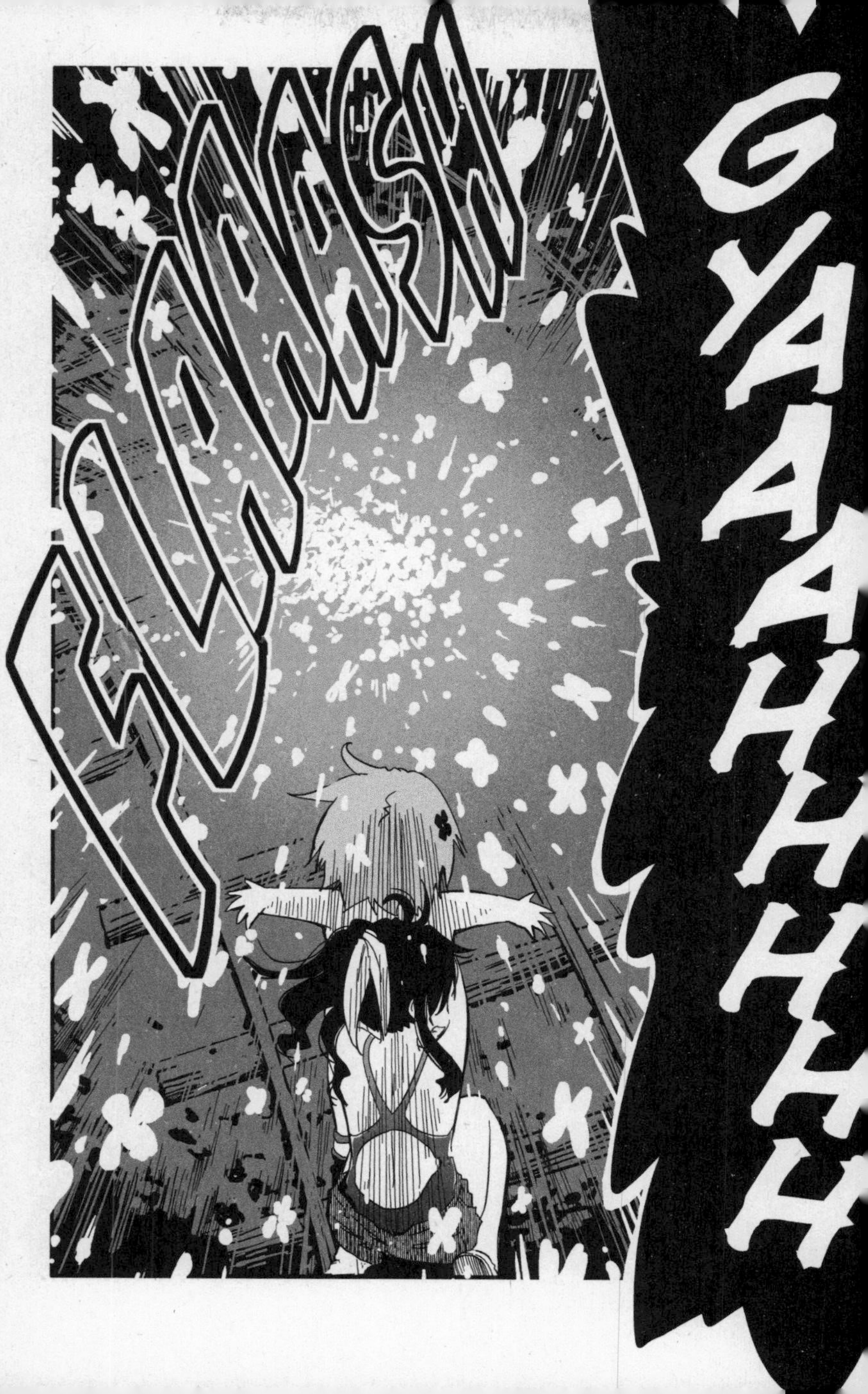
GYAAAHHHHH
FLASH

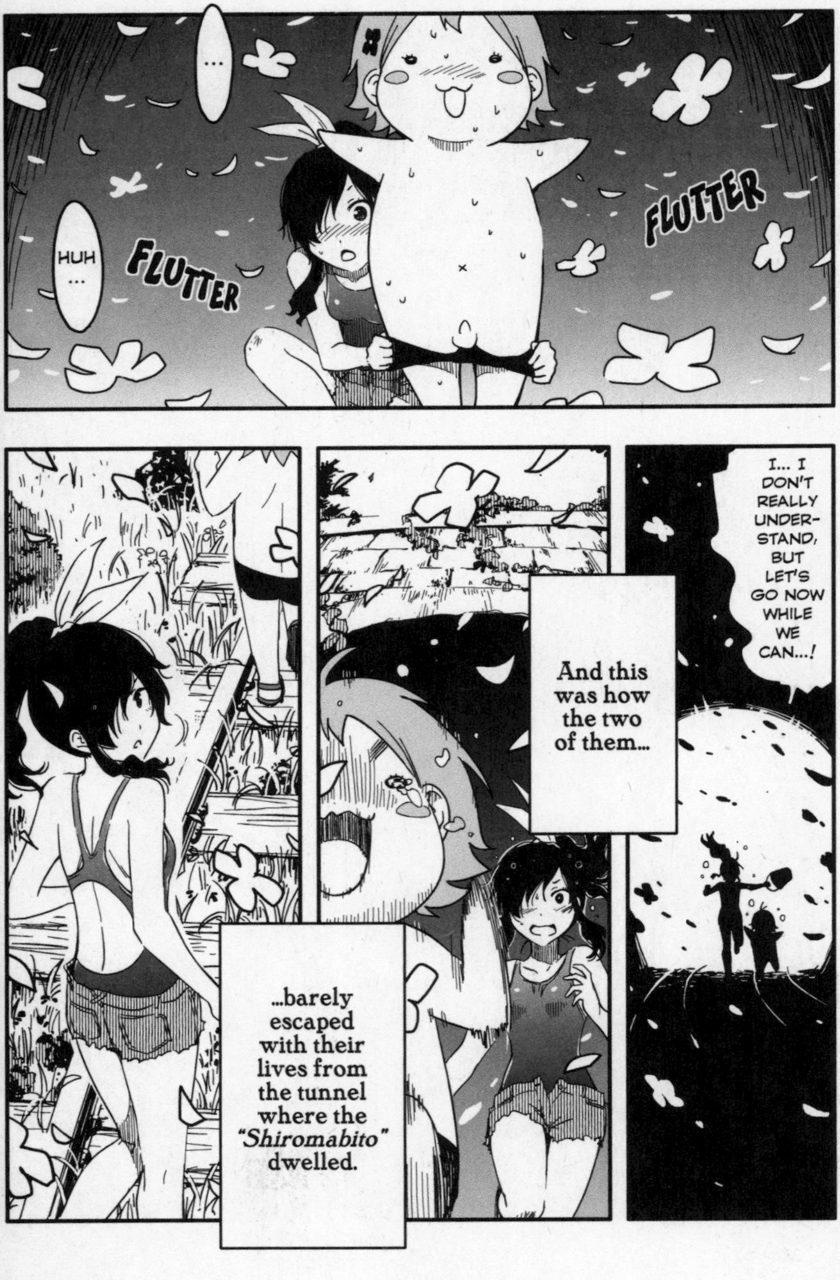
FLUTTER
...
FLUTTER
HUH ...
I... I DON'T REALLY UNDERSTAND, BUT LET'S GO NOW WHILE WE CAN...!
And this was how the two of them...
...barely escaped with their lives from the tunnel where the *"Shiromabito"* dwelled.

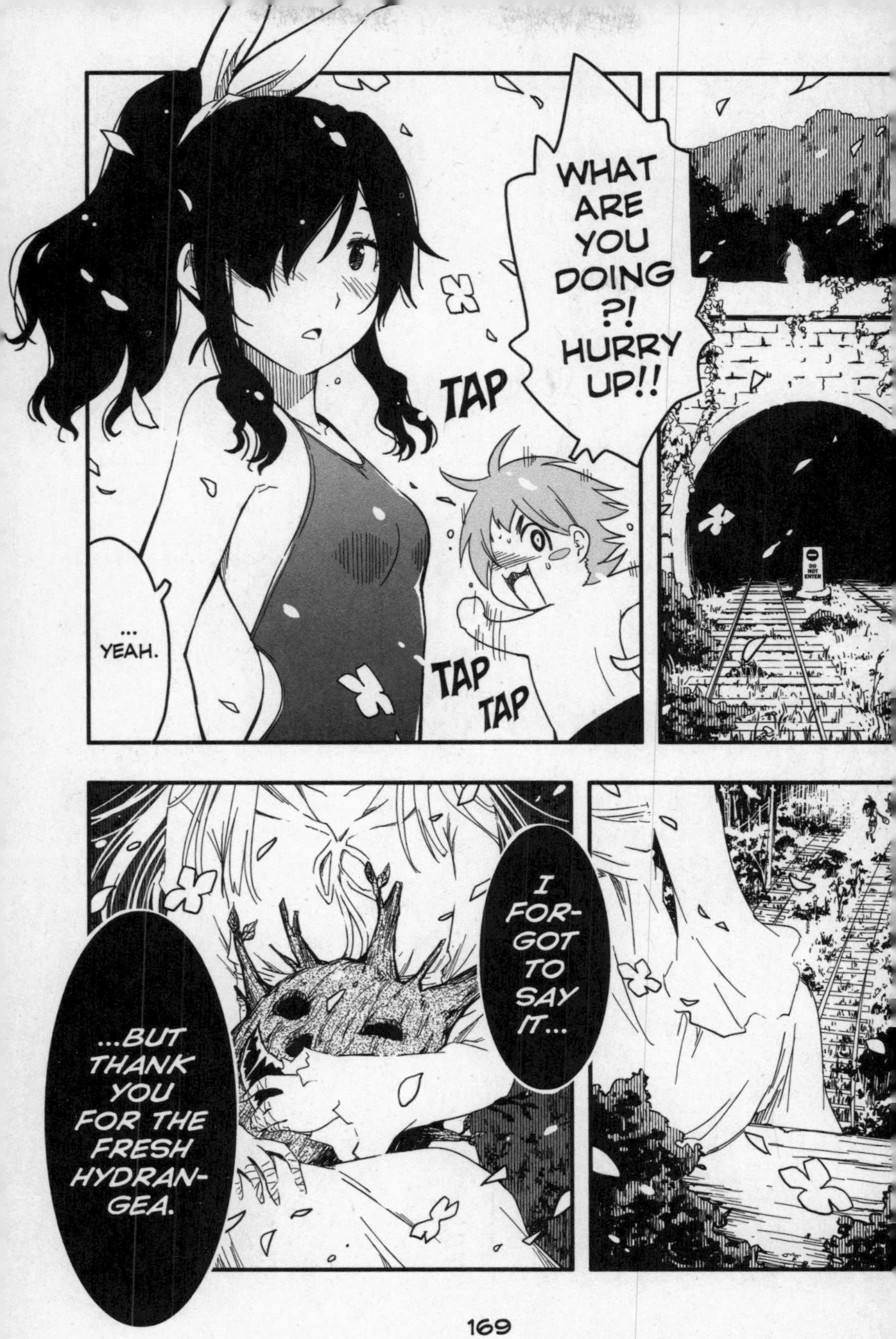
DO NOT ENTER
WHAT ARE YOU DOING ?! HURRY UP!!
TAP
TAP TAP
... YEAH.
I FORGOT TO SAY IT...
...BUT THANK YOU FOR THE FRESH HYDRANGEA.

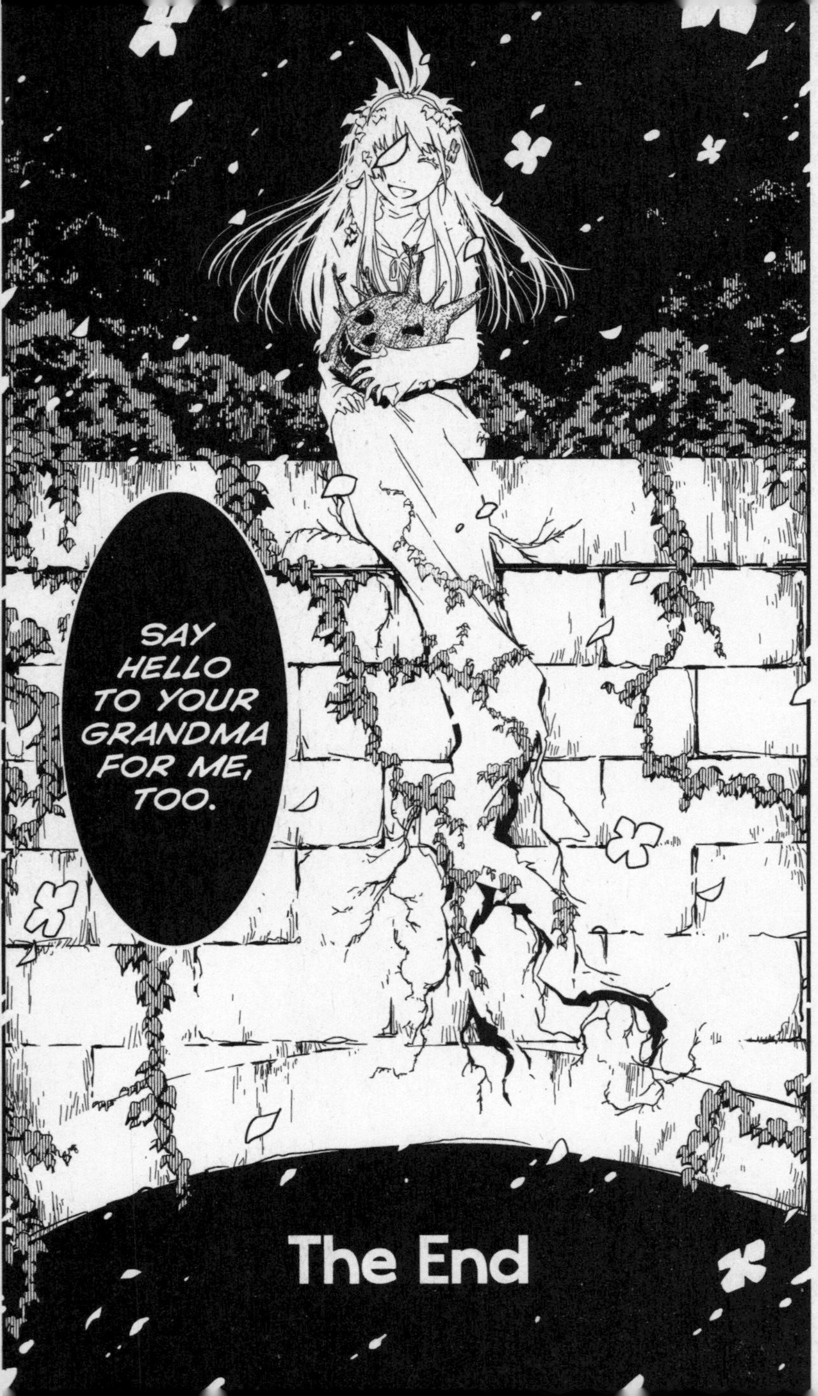
SAY HELLO TO YOUR GRANDMA FOR ME, TOO.
The End

~Bonus Gallery~

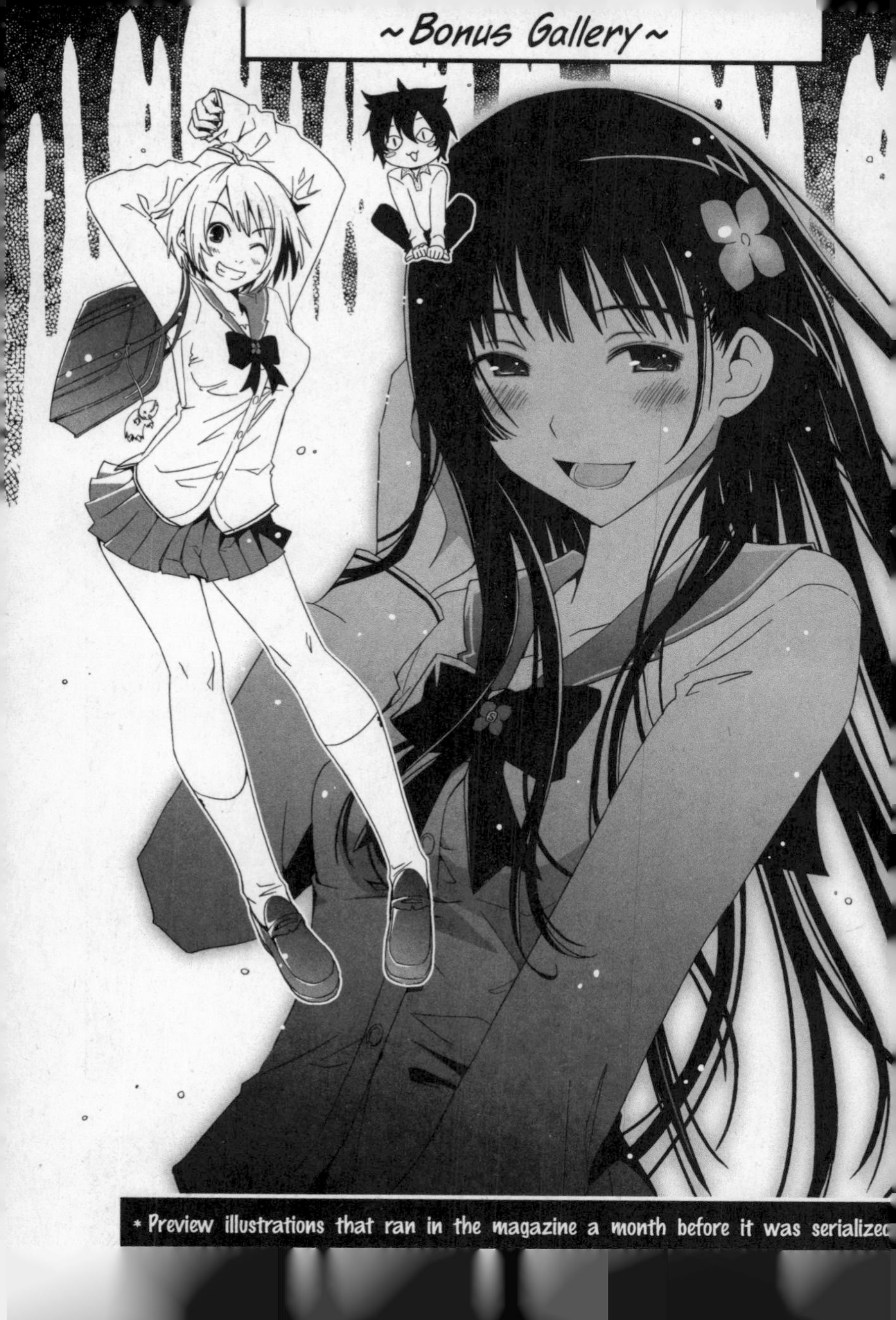

* Preview illustrations that ran in the magazine a month before it was serialized

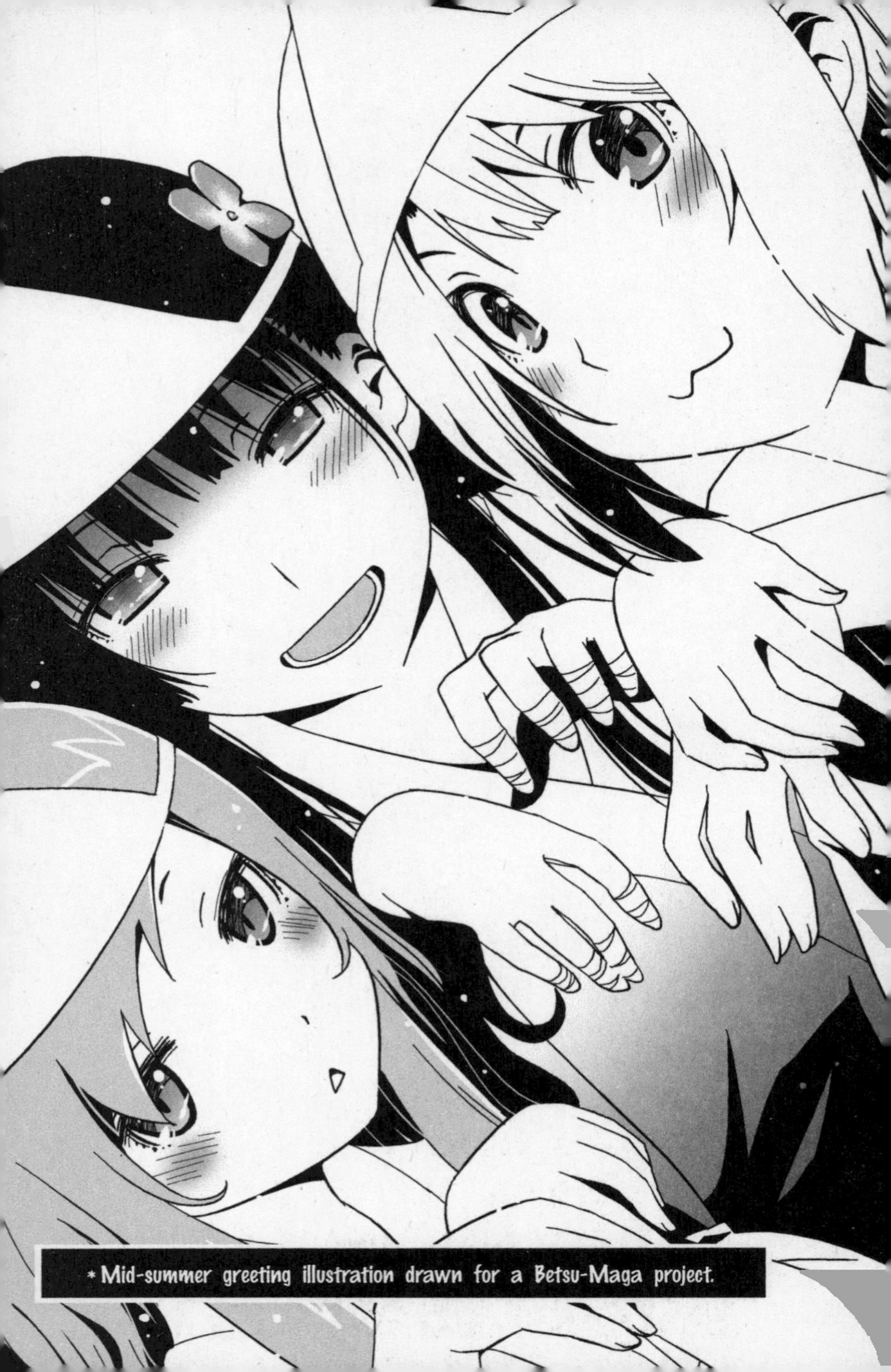

* Mid-summer greeting illustration drawn for a Betsu-Maga project.

"Only God Knows"

CLAP
CLAP
STARE...
...
GRIINNN
SO... REA-CHAN, WHAT HOPES AND DREAMS DID YOU WISH FOR JUST NOW?
UH... IT... IT'S A SECRET.
OH COME ONNN... TELL ME...
I... I CAN'T!
NO ONE BUT GOD CAN KNOW!
GOD
OH, REA-DONO.
I HAVE HEARD THEE.
SHIINE
buhh buu

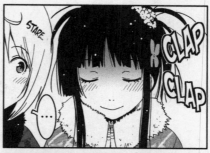

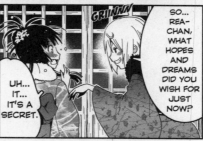

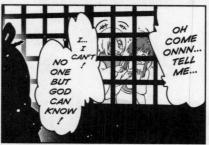

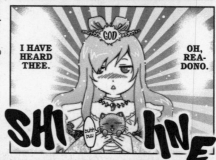

Printed in Issue 1 of "Magazine Special" for the year 2014

*A 4-panel comic drawn previously for Magazine Special.

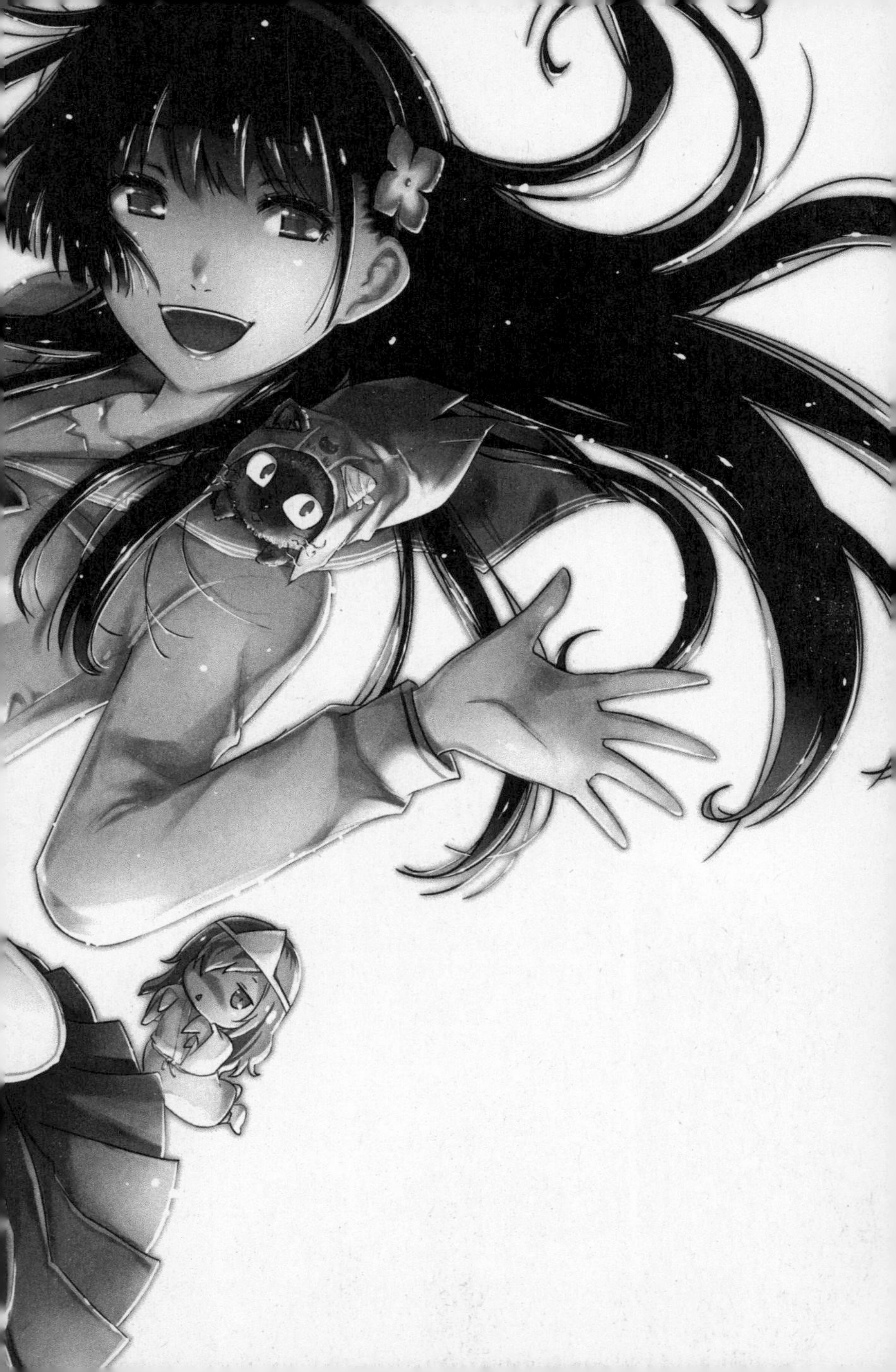

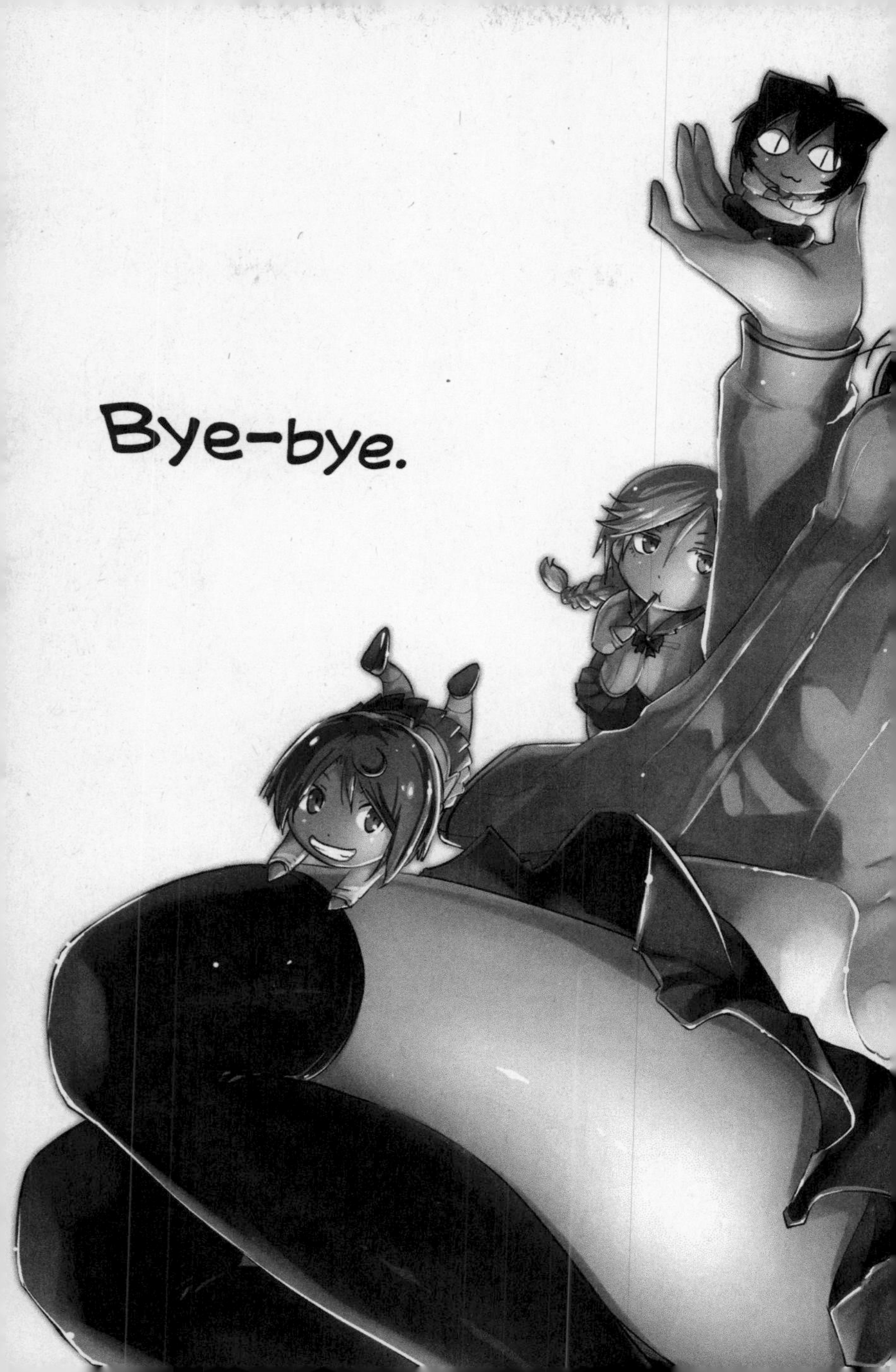
Bye-bye.

Kodansha Comics Trade Paperback Original.

nkarea volume 11 copyright © 2014 Mitsuru Hattori
glish translation copyright © 2015 Mitsuru Hattori

rights reserved.

blished in the United States by Kodansha Comics, an imprint of Kodansha
A Publishing, LLC, New York.

blication rights for this English edition arranged through Kodansha Ltd.,
kyo.

st published in Japan in 2014 by Kodansha Ltd., Tokyo, as *Sankarea*, volume 11.

anslation: Lindsey Akashi
ttering: Evan Hayden
iting: Ajani Oloye
dansha Comics edition cover design: Phil Balsman